To my grandchildren
Andrew and Eliyah

Other books by John Stevenson:

Ancient History: *A Framework for the Bible*

Doctrines of the Bible: *Outlines in Systematic Theology*

Facing the Flames: *A Fire Fighter's Meditations on the Spiritual Life*

First Corinthians: *Striving for Unity*

Facing the Flames: *A Fire Fighter's Meditations on the Spiritual Life*

Ecclesiastes: *A Spiritual Journey*

Ephesians: *The Wealth & Walk of the Christian*

Galatians: *Our Freedom in Christ*

Genesis: *The Book of Beginnings, Volume 1*

Hebrews: *The Supremacy of the Savior*

Historical Books of the Old Testament: *One God, One People, One Land*

James: *A Faith that Works*

Joshua, Judges, and Ruth: *Victory, Defeat, and Hope in an Age of Heroes*

Luke: *In the Footsteps of the Savior*

Mark: *The Servant Who Came to Save*

Messiah in a Manger: *Reflections on the Birth of Jesus*

Preaching from the Minor Prophets to a Postmodern Congregation

Prison Epistles: *Workbook and Mechanical Outline*

Romans: *The Radical Righteousness of God*

A Survey of the Old Testament: *The Bible Jesus Used*

Studies in the Book of

REVELATION

Theology in Pictures

John T. Stevenson

ISBN: 978-0-9822086-8-7

Redeemer Publishing
Hollywood, FL
www.RedeemerPublishing.com

228

Free Powerpoints and videos of related lectures
are available on
the John Stevenson Bible Study Page at
http://JohnStevenson.net

TABLE OF CONTENTS

Introduction to the Revelation of Jesus Christ: Revelation 1:1 1

The Prologue: Revelation 1:1-3 13

Opening Salutation: Revelation 1:4-8 17

In the Presence of Jesus: Revelation 1:9-20 28

An Overview of the Seven Letters: Revelation 2 - 3 40

Ephesus: Letter to the Loveless Church: Revelation 2:1-7 45

Smyrna: Letter to the Persecuted Church: Revelation 2:8-11 54

Pergamum: Holding Fast to Holiness: Revelation 2:12-17 64

Thyatira: Intolerable Toleration: Revelation 2:18-29 73

Sardis: Letter to a Dead Church: Revelation 3:1-6 81

Philadelphia: Letter to a Little Church: Revelation 3:7-13 92

Laodicea: Letter to the Lukewarm Church: Revelation 3:14-22 102

Before the Throne of God: Revelation 4:1-11 111

The Lion, the Lamb, and the Sealed Scroll: Revelation 5:1-14 122

The Four Horsemen & the Hoofbeats of History: Revelation 6:1-8 . . . 131

The Day of Wrath: Revelation 6:9-17 139

The Sealed Multitude: Revelation 7:1-17 151

Trumpets of Judgment: Revelation 8:1 - 9:21 162

The Angel and the Little Book: Revelation 10:1-11 179

Measuring the Temple: Revelation 11:1-2 185

The Two Witnesses: Revelation 11:3-14 194

Thy Kingdom Come: Revelation 11:15-19 205

The Cosmic Conflict: Revelation 12:1-17 213

The Beast: Revelation 13:1-10 226

The False Prophet: Revelation 13:11-18 235

The 144,000: Revelation 14:1-5 245

Judgment Day: Revelation 14:6-20 251

The Final Exodus: Revelation 15:1-8 262

The Seven Bowls: Revelation 16:1-21 267

The Vision of the Harlot: Revelation 17:1-18 283

The Judgment of the Harlot: Revelation 18:1-24 294

The Hallelujah Chorus: Revelation 19:1-10 306

The Rider on the White Horse: Revelation 19:11-21 315

The Thousand Year Reign: Revelation 20:1-15 325

A New Creation: Revelation 21:1-8 345

The City of God: Revelation 21:9 - 22:5 353

The Final Chapter: Revelation 22:6-21 367

Appendix 377

    The Problem with Preterism 378

    The Rapture Question 385

    Evidences for a Pretribulational Rapture 392

Bibliography 400

INTRODUCTION TO THE
REVELATION OF JESUS CHRIST

The Revelation of Jesus Christ, which God gave Him to show to His bond-servants, the things which must soon take place; and He sent and communicated it by His angel to His bond-servant John (Revelation 1:1).

Our title for this book, "Revelation," is taken from the opening verse of this book. It is the *Revelation of Jesus Christ*. Unfortunately, many people seem to think that the message of this book is hidden and mysterious. To be fair, there are some things in this book that fit such a description. But the main subject of this book is neither hidden nor mysterious. The main subject of this book is Jesus and He is revealed in this book with an amazing clarity. This is a revelation of Jesus.

A revelation is, by the very nature of the word, something that reveals. This is not a book that hides truth. To the contrary, this is a book that reveals truth. It reveals the truth that Jesus is going to be victorious. He is going to win. This message will come through clearly from beginning to end.

THE AUTHOR OF THE BOOK

The author of the book calls himself John in the first verse of the book. He gives his name again in verse 4 and two more times at the end of the book (21:2 and 22:8). Though it is a common name, it has traditionally been assumed that this is the same John who wrote the gospel account to whom church tradition has attributed. That same tradition accords him the authorship of the three short epistles that bear his name. Yet this is the only one of all those writings in which the author actually names himself.

What do we know about John? His home was in Bethsaida, a small fishing village on the northern shore of the Sea of Galilee (John 1:44). He and his brother James lived here and worked with their father, operating a prosperous fishing business. Then he met Jesus and that changed everything. James and John became followers of Jesus. They were nicknamed, "the sons of thunder" (Mark 3:17), probably because of their rowdy reputation or perhaps because of the time they asked Jesus about calling fire down from heaven onto certain unbelieving cities (Luke 9:54).

It was their mother who asked Jesus if her sons could be allowed to sit at His right and left hand in the kingdom (Matthew 20:20-23). One wonders if they had put her

1

up to the request. Yet in spite of their obvious overzealousness, Jesus loved these two brothers. They were a part of his inner circle. It was Peter and James and John who witnessed the glorified Christ on the Mount of Transfiguration. It was these three who saw Jesus raise the daughter of Jarius from the death. It was these three who accompanied Jesus into the Garden of Gethsemane on the night of His betrayal.

At the time of this writing, many years had now passed since Jesus had walked the earth with His disciples. The other apostles had all been killed, martyred for their faith. Only John still remained.

DATE OF WRITING

The question of the date of the book of Revelation is not new. This has been the subject of discussion among scholars for quite a number of years. The question has come under new scrutiny with the recent rise in popularity of Preterism, the view that teaches the Second Coming of Christ was fulfilled in the A.D. 70 fall of Jerusalem. However, it should be pointed out that an early date for the book of Revelation does not automatically mean an acceptance of the Preterist view.

There are two primary views as to the date of composition of the book of Revelation. The first view is to see it as having been written around 95 A.D.

| TRADITIONAL VIEW: 95 A.D. |

Church tradition has largely placed the writing of the book of Revelation near the close of the first century and during the reign of Domitian (81-96 A.D.). One of the apostolic fathers, Irenaeus, states that the Revelation of which John wrote had only recently been seen. While speculating on the identity of the Antichrist, he says:

> We will not, however, incur the risk of pronouncing positively as to the name of Antichrist; for if it were necessary that his name should be distinctly revealed in this present time, it would have been announced by him who beheld the apocalyptic vision. For that was seen not very long time since, but almost in our day, towards the end of Domitian's reign. (Against Heresies 5:30:3).

Irenaeus lived in the second century in Lyons in the province of Gaul where he served as the overseer of the church of that city. He is said to have been a disciple of Polycarp who had, as a young boy, had met the apostle John. Therefore, while his testimony is not that of an eye-witness, there is a certain strength to that testimony that we should not readily ignore without good cause. All of the early church fathers agree with this testimony.

On the other hand, the testimony of Irenaeus has been called into question on several counts. First of all, Irenaeus teaches that Jesus lived to be between 40 and 50 years old, a chronology that is rejected by nearly all scholars today. Secondly, the book from which we receive the testimony of Irenaeus is found only in the Latin translations and in a Greek quotation within Eusebius' Ecclesiastical History (3:18:3). Even if we accept the reading as it has come down to us, it is perhaps possible that Irenaeus was referencing Domitian's brief reign as praetor in A.D. 70 during which he had full consular authority while Vespasian was traveling to Rome (Tacitus, Histories 4:39).

Added to this is the testimony of one of the Syriac translations of the book of Revelation which contains in the preface a statement concerning the contents of the book:

> The Revelation, which was made by God to John the Evangelist, in the island of Patmos, to which he was banished by Nero the Emperor (2001:442).

The state of the churches in Revelation 2-3 suggest the churches had been in existence for some time rather than churches that had only just been established. We read of how the love of the church at Ephesus had grown cold and this is in contrast to the manner in which Paul describes that church in his epistle to the Ephesians.

There is no mention made of the church in Jerusalem. That church would have been scattered following the fall of Jerusalem and it would be many years before a church was recognized in that city.

THE EARLY DATE: PRIOR TO 70 A.D.

There are certain lines of evidence that have been used to point to an early (pre A.D. 70) date for the composition of the book.

1.   If we assume that the kings mentioned in Revelation 17:10 refer to Roman Emperors and then take the passage literally referring to five kings that have fallen while "one is," then we can simply count (1) Julius Caesar, (2) Octavius, (3) Tiberius, (4) Caligula and (5) Claudius to get to the "one who is" and see it as a reference to Nero.

      Under this scenario, the five emperors that have fallen would be the first five emperors of the Roman empire. The one that "now is" would be Nero. The one that would come for a little while would be fulfilled in the three men who tried to take the title for themselves following the death of Nero in A.D. 69. They were Galba, Otho, and Vitellius. Each reigned "for a

3

little while" and by the end of the year it was the Roman general Vespasian who was in control of the empire. The beast that is to come, described later in the book, could be a reference to Vespasian and/or Titus, the father-and-son team who invaded Palestine and eventually destroyed the temple.

2.   The letters in Nero's name can be shown to add up to both 666 (Hebrew) and 616 (Latin), both of which are found in Revelation manuscripts in those languages. We will look at this in further detail when we deal with Revelation 13.

3.   Revelation 2:9 and 3:9 speak of a continuing Jewish influence in the cities that confronted the churches; something that would be less likely after A.D. 70.

4.   The temple is said to be standing in Revelation 11. While it could be argued that this is a spiritual or symbolic vision, it is nevertheless significant that there is no mention of the temple having been destroyed. On the other hand, there is pictured at the end of Revelation 11 the ark of the covenant within the temple, something that had been missing since the destruction of the first temple, five hundred years earlier. This in itself suggests that we are not to take the temple vision too literally.

5.   The church is said to be suffering amidst a heavy persecution (6:9; 7:14; 12:11). The persecution under Nero was, by all accounts, much more severe than the one that took place under Domitian. It was this persecution that saw the martyrdom of both Peter and Paul.

6.   The continuing ministry of John following his exile and return from Patmos is still another possible evidence of an early date of the Revelation. Clement of Alexandria tells us of the ministry John continued to have after his return from Patmos:

> For when, on the tyrant's death, he returned to Ephesus from the isle of Patmos, he went away, being invited, to the contiguous territories of the nations, here to appoint bishops, there to set in order whole Churches, there to ordain such as were marked out by the Spirit (2008).

Clement goes on to tell us of an extensive ministry on the part of John. This would suggest one who has not yet reached the advanced age of 100 and the death of the tyrant would presumably refer to Nero rather than to Domitian.

7.   Clement of Alexandria also tells us of the completion of the canon of

Scripture as he deals with heretics who believed that revelation was a continuing phenomenon and that God was still in the process of writing books of the Bible:

> *For the teaching of our Lord at His advent, beginning with Augustus and Tiberius, was completed in the middle of the times of Tiberius. And that of the apostles, embracing the ministry of Paul, ends with Nero (The Stromata, or Miscellanies 7:17).*

John was one of the apostles. If we are to accept the testimony of Clement, then we must conclude that John received the book of Revelation prior to the close of the reign of Nero.

8.   The Roman world was in upheaval in the days just prior to the fall of Jerusalem. A.D. 69 is commonly called "the year of the four emperors." It dawned with the suicide of Nero at the outbreak of civil war as Galba from Spain declared himself to be the emperor and was accepted by the Praetorian Guard and the Senate. Within a few months, Galba was overthrown and replaced by Otho. Meanwhile, the armies of the Rhine proclaimed Vitellius as emperor and, still later, the eastern provinces threw their support behind Vespasian.

This upheaval would also have been evident in Palestine where the Jewish War of 66-73 A.D. witnessed the end of the Jewish state, the destruction of the Jewish temple, and the cessation of their entire sacrificial system. This had tremendous spiritual significance. Jesus Himself had foretold of the destruction of Jerusalem. For us to consider that God's written revelation continued for a period of twenty years beyond this period without a single mention of this event is difficult to fathom.

9.   From the very beginning, John says that this book concerns *the things which must soon take place* (Revelation 1:1). He repeats this in 22:6 and his readers have every right to expect an immediate significance to his words. In Revelation 22:10, the angel tells John not to seal up the words of the book because the time is near, a direct statement of the contemporary character of the book. This is in contrast to Daniel 12:4 where Daniel is told to seal up the book until the time of the end because the fulfillment would be long in coming.

On the other hand, we know from history that, within a generation of the death of Domitian, there was a significant event that took place in Jerusalem and in the land of Palestine. It was the Bar-Kochba revolt that was ignited when the Roman emperor Hadrian set out to build a pagan temple on the site of the original Jewish temple. The revolt was headed by

Simon Bar-Kochba ("son of the morning") who was attested to be the messiah by Rabbi Akiba. A false messiah being proclaimed by a false prophet is a scenario that is startlingly familiar to those who are acquainted with the book of Revelation.

At the same time, we must admit that the evidence of an early writing of the book of Revelation is compelling. In Philip Schaff's, *History of the Christian Church, Volume I*, Preface to the Revised Edition, he makes this statement: *"On two points I have changed my opinion – the second Roman captivity of Paul (which I am disposed to admit in the interest of the Pastoral Epistles), and the date of the Apocalypse (which I now assign, with the majority of modern critics, to the year 68 or 69 instead of 95, as before)."*

Does it really matter when the book of Revelation was written? I have to answer that, to some extent, it does. The book itself tells us that it contains events that are both past, present and future. John is told to write *the things which you have seen, and the things which are, and the things which will take place after these things* (Revelation 1:19).

It is correctly argued that many of the woes that are described in this book will take a special significance if viewed through the eyes of those who are going through the events of the Jewish revolt that led up to the destruction of Jerusalem in A.D. 70. On the other hand, this book is not addressed to the inhabitants of Jerusalem. It is addressed to seven churches in western Anatolia who are far removed from the revolt in Palestine and who are largely Gentile in their makeup. This suggests the Palestine revolt and the destruction of Jerusalem, at best, serve as a type and a pattern of other judgments to come.

Thus, whether the book was written prior to the fall of Jerusalem or even some twenty years after that event, it still uses imagery related to that event. It will be helpful that we not merely focus on the fall of Jerusalem, but that we also see a greater spiritual reality. It is for this reason that Christians of every age have been able to read this book, to see the spiritual struggles of their own age portrayed within its pages, and to gain comfort from its message. This is a book about spiritual conflict. It lets us know there is a spiritual war taking place. The conflict is between God and Satan. It is between the people of God and the people of Satan. Because we live on a battlefield, bad things happen. Tragedies and disease and disaster are all elements of this battle. But in the midst of the battle, there is good news. Jesus will win.

This will be a message of comfort to those churches in western Anatolia that are going through hard times. It will be a message proclaiming that the glorified Jesus is in control of history. This is the message that is given to the churches who are going through hard times. This is the message given to those who are being persecuted for their faith and who are being tempted to throw in the towel and to turn their back on the Christian faith. They need to know that there is an end in sight. There is going to be a winner in the cosmic conflict in which they find themselves. Jesus is going to win.

OVERVIEW OF THE BOOK OF REVELATION

The book of Revelation presents the most glorious picture of Jesus Christ in the entire Bible. At the same time, this is one of the most misunderstood books of the entire Bible. This is tragic. It is tragic because there is such a wonderful message presented throughout this book.

Revelation is the most "biblical" book of the Bible. That is to say, there are to be found in this book hundreds of quotes and allusions to the rest of the Bible. The author assumes that his readers know their Bible and especially the Old Testament, for the great majority of symbolism found here goes back to the Old Testament.

One example of this is seen in the Jesus/Joshua parallels pointed out by Warren Gage. The names Jesus and Joshua are the same. They are both seen as savior and deliverer. They are both pictured as destroying the evil city of the world. As one begins to look more closely at the details, one sees the following connections:

- There is a prostitute in the city identified by her scarlet cord.
- There is a Babylonian robe (the book of Joshua mentions that this is what tempted Achan).
- The city's fall is preceded by seven trumpets.
- The city falls and is burned by fire.
- One family is rescued from the destruction to become a bride in the royal family.
- Two spies/witnesses are sent prior to the destruction.
- There are a series of telescoping sevens.
  - Seven days the city is to be encircled.
  - Seventh day is to see the Israelites march around it seven times.
  - Seven priests are to carry seven trumpets around the city.
- Just as Joshua had twelve stones set up at nearby Gilgal, so also we read in Revelation of twelve foundation stones in the New Jerusalem.

Our problem is that most people today do not really know their Old Testament. They might have a passing familiarity with the old Bible stories, but fail to capture the subtle nuances that appear throughout the book of Revelation.

This book can be seen as chiastic in its outline. A chiasm is a type of parallelism that presents its corresponding segments up to a pivotal point and then echoes those same or similar points in the opposite order so that a symmetry is presented:

| Seven letters to seven churches (1-3) |
| Before the throne of God (4-5) |
| Seven seals: Judgments against nations (6) |
| 144,000 and seven trumpets (7-10) |
| Two witnesses (11) |
| Woman, dragon, male child (12) |
| Two beasts (13) |
| 144,000 and seven bowls (14-16) |
| Judgments against Babylon (17-18) |
| Christ rules and reigns from a throne (20) |
| New Jerusalem, the bride of Christ (19-22) |

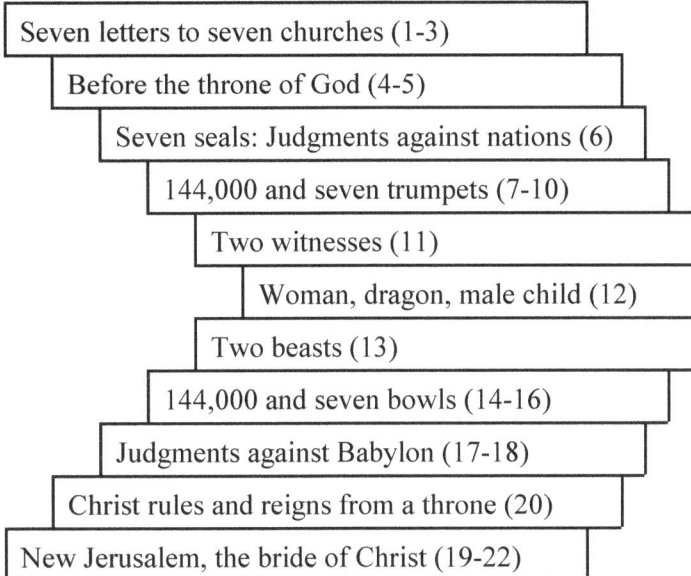

THE INTERPRETATION OF REVELATION

The main problem in interpreting Revelation is that it uses so much imagery and symbolism. Some of these symbols seem at first to be bizarre and confusing. We are confronted with beasts and scorpions and dragons and vials. There is a woman clothed with the sun and another woman clothed in purple and scarlet. There are seals and trumpets and bowls and plagues and visions. There are four living creatures and 24 elders and 144,000 people. There is a lamb with seven horns and a beast with seven heads. There have been many different approaches to interpreting all of this.

1.   Historical Approaches.

There are three different approaches that could be classified as historical in nature. That is, they see the visions and prophecies of Revelation as having been fulfilled throughout history.

• Preterism. This is the view that says the book of Revelation was fulfilled in the A.D. 70 fall of Jerusalem and that all of the seals and plagues and vials are pictures of God's judgment falling upon the people of that city. A full preterist is one who believes every part of this book had a first century fulfillment and that there is therefore no future return of Christ to be expected. Any of the visions or promises of Christ's return are made to refer to the Lord's judgment upon Jerusalem in A.D. 70. In contrast to such a position, a partial preterist

8

is one who sees the A.D. 70 event as a coming of Jesus which is subsequently to be followed by the final and ultimate return of Jesus in the future.

- Rome and the Early Christians: This view sees the entire book as a message of comfort to the early church that was going through persecution. The beast that battles against Christ is the Roman emperor and John promises that Rome will not succeed in its attempt to exterminate the followers of Christ.

- Ages of Church History: This view looks at the book of Revelation as portraying the entire age of church history from the date of writing to the present. The symbols used throughout the book are equated with various historical events during the last 2000 years. The beast is usually equated with the Roman Catholic Pope and the false prophet as the Roman church.

2.   The Symbolic Approach.

This view sees the entire book as a symbolic portrayal of the spiritual struggle taking place between God and Satan. The beast is said to represent evil in whatever form it takes as it battles the church.

3.   The Futurist Approach.

This view takes everything after the third chapter of Revelation and places it sometime into the future, not only into the future of the original readers, but also into our own future. The events represented in the seals and trumpets and vials are all to take place in the future during a period of great tribulation that will be followed by the Second Coming of Christ. Some have also taken the seven churches in chapters 2-3 to refer to seven periods of church history so that only the first chapter is seen to have direct application to the first century believers.

Which view is correct? Which approach should we take in studying the book of Revelation? I want to suggest that most of them have an element of truth. To a certain extent, several of these approaches can and should be used in conjunction when studying this book.

It cannot be denied that there is a Jewish flavor to this book. There are echoes throughout from the Old Testament and from the Jewish temple that call to mind the prophets and the people of the land of Israel. At the same time, this book is addressed within a specific historical framework and it contains specific messages to certain specific churches that are located, not in the land of Palestine, but in certain cities of Anatolia. The Christians in these churches are promised eventual victory in the midst of their problems. That means when we are seeing temple images, it will not be telling about the situation in Jerusalem as much as these images are being used to illustrate the churches. For example, we will seen the seven branched lampstand as a clear temple image, but we will be told that these seven lamps represent the seven churches that existed in John's day.

However, the message of this book goes far beyond the confines of the first century. Christians of every age have been comforted by the promises of this book. The source of this comfort is rooted in the symbolic portrayal of the spiritual struggle that is taking place between God and Satan and the promise of eventual victory for the people of God.

I believe it is also quite obvious that this book contains promises for the future. The culmination of that struggle between God and Satan and the eventual redemption of the earth is presented in this book. This means that we can see in the book of Revelation that which gives faith in the present as well as hope for the future, the symbolic as well as the specific, the personal as well as the prophetic.

Such an approach to the book of Revelation should not surprise anyone who is familiar with the Old Testament prophets. They often spoke in words that looked both to the present as well as to the future. There was very often a future message, but that future message always had an immediate application. For example, Amos could look at the impending threat of the armies of Assyria and regard that coming judgment as "the day of the Lord" (Amos 5:18). Likewise, Isaiah pictures the contemporary overthrow of Babylon in terms that imply the end of the world when God will *punish the world for its evil* (Isaiah 13:11). Joel describes an infestation of locusts as a judgment of God and then moves directly to speak of the judgments of the day of the Lord (Joel 1:15). In the same way, Jesus predicts the destruction of Jerusalem, something that was fulfilled in A.D. 70, and then goes on to describe His future coming and the judgments that would follow. The contemporary historical judgments are often seen as a type and a prelude and even the beginnings of the fulfillment of the future judgments that will follow. The two are regularly meshed together without regard for chronology.

How can this be? It is because the purpose of prophecy is never to give us a tidy chronology of the future. The purpose of prophecy is always to reveal that it is the same God at work, either in present history or in future prophecy, and that He is to be the object of our trust and our obedience. Its purpose is that we should recognize that God controls history and that we should obey Him and live so that our lives bring glory to His name.

How will this apply in our study of the book of Revelation? We will see the beast both as the early Roman Emperor as well as a possible future man of sin as well as anyone else who seeks to attack Christ and his church. We will look at the great tribulations that have taken place in the past and will be better prepared to face those that might still be in our future. Ultimately, this will be a message of hope and of looking for the return of Christ. It is this hope that binds us together.

GENESIS AND REVELATION

If Genesis is the book of beginnings, then Revelation is the book of culmination. Many of the things that are begun in Genesis are completed in Revelation. These two books are bookends. The themes that run through the Bible are bound between the covers of these two books.

Genesis	Revelation
The creation of the heavens and the earth.	A new heaven and a new earth.
The tree of life in the garden.	The tree of life in the new city.
A river runs through the garden of Eden.	A river runs through the New Jerusalem.
The first marriage: Adam and Eve.	The last marriage: The Last Adam to His church.
The beginning of the career of "that old serpent."	The end of Satan's career: The lake of fire.
Death enters.	Death is destroyed.
Man loses his life because of sin.	Man is given eternal life because of Jesus' payment for sin.
The beginning of sorrow.	Christ wipes away all tears.
The first sacrificial lamb.	The Lamb of God on His throne.
The first murder.	No more death.
The beginning of Babylon and its false religious systems.	The destruction of Babylon.

JOHN'S OTHER WRITINGS

The writings of the Apostle John can be grouped into three parts. First there is his gospel account covering the life and death and resurrection of Jesus. Second, there are three epistles that are written about the fellowship that we share as followers of Christ. Finally, there is the book of Revelation that has as its climax the return of Christ.

Gospel	Epistles	Revelation
Past	Present	Future
History	Doctrine	Prophecy
Begins in past eternity	Deals with life in the present	Takes us to future eternity
Jesus as the sacrificed lamb	Jesus as the reigning Lord	Jesus as the conquering Lion
Faith	Love	Hope

The book of Revelation has been the subject of considerable controversy. Whenever I teach on the subject of prophecy, I remind my students of one foundational premise. It is that prophecy is always easier to interpret after it has been fulfilled and, even then, it is not always so easy. This means that we ought to take case against overzealous dogmatism with regard to the various eschatological views.

THE PROLOGUE
Revelation 1:1-3

People tend to gravitate toward one of two attitudes regarding the book of Revelation. This first attitude is that they are afraid of it. They look at all of those terrible seals and trumpets and plagues and dragons and beasts, and they say to themselves, "Maybe if I ignore this book, it will go away." If you are reading this commentary, then this probably does not describe you.

The second attitude is the opposite extreme. This person can be stereotyped as the prophecy nut. He can be recognized by the maps and charts sticking out of his Bible that is underlined and color-coded and has all kinds of notes written in the margins. He has figured out each and every event of the future and can give an exact accounting of how each prophecy relates to every other prophecy and woe be to the hapless individual who might disagree. If I am being a little harsh on this individual, it is because I am describing the way I used to be as a young Christian.

Both of these attitudes are wrong because they each represent an extreme. On the one hand, we need never be afraid of the prophecies of this glorious book. On the other hand, they are not given in order to be a hammer that we use to go striking others over the head. Why is this book given? What is the purpose of the book of Revelation. I believe the answer is given in the opening verses of the book.

> *The Revelation of Jesus Christ, which God gave Him to show to His bond-servants, the things which must soon take place; and He sent and communicated it by His angel to His bond-servant John (Revelation 1:1-3).*

This is the revelation of Jesus Christ. If you approach this book as only a book that tells of future events, then you are going to miss the primary message of the book. The purpose of the book is to reveal Jesus Christ.

I love pictures. I am big on using visual aids in the classroom. There is something special about being able to see and to visualize and to understand. There is an old saying that goes, "A picture is worth a thousand words." I think that it is a true saying. Jesus seems to have thought so, too. He often preached in vivid, illustrative word pictures that we know as parables. As we come to the book of Revelation, we are coming to one of the art galleries of the Bible. We will be looking at theology in pictures. The book of Revelation is filled with pictures. But they are not an end unto themselves. They are designed to teach us about the Lord. They are theology in pictures.

Think about that title: "Revelation." What do you do with a revelation? You look at it. That is what we are going to do. The word "revelation is translated from a Greek word that means "to uncover." The Greek word is *apokalupsis* and, for this reason, the book is sometimes referred to as the Apocalypse. It simply means "the uncovering" This implies that the thing that is to be revealed was previously hidden. Jesus is uncovered in this book. At this point, you might object that Jesus had been revealed in the four gospel accounts. Matthew, Mark, Luke, and John all give vivid portraits of the earthly life of Jesus. If this is the case, then how can we say that Jesus was previously hidden and is now being revealed in this book of Revelation? It is very simple. In this book, Jesus will be revealed in all of His glory that was veiled throughout the gospel accounts.

Only once was the glory of Jesus outwardly manifested in the presence of the disciples while He was on earth. Peter, James, and John had accompanied Jesus up onto a mountain. While they were there, they witnessed the unveiled glory of Jesus.

> *Six days later Jesus took with Him Peter and James and John his brother, and led them up on a high mountain by themselves. 2 And He was transfigured before them; and His face shone like the sun, and His garments became as white as light. (Matthew 17:1-2).*

When this event takes place, Peter and James and John had already spent several years with Jesus. They had come to recognize that He was the Christ, the Son of God. But now they are confronted with that reality in a way they had never before experienced. They saw Jesus as more than just a Jewish rabbi. They saw Him in a way that no man had ever before been seen. Their reaction borders on the humorous.

> *And behold, Moses and Elijah appeared to them, talking with Him. 4 Peter said to Jesus, "Lord, it is good for us to be here; if You wish, I will make three tabernacles here, one for You, and one for Moses, and one for Elijah." (Matthew 17:3-4).*

I don't know how they recognized Moses and Elijah, but Peter is the first to speak up. He has an idea and he suggests that he builds three memorials. One will be to Jesus. One will be to Moses. One will be to Elijah. Do you see what Peter is thinking? He is placing Jesus up there on the same level as Moses and Elijah, the two great prophets of the Old Testament. But Jesus is not on the same level as Moses and Elijah. Jesus is much higher than Moses or Elijah. As if to point this out to Peter as well as to us, a voice comes down from heaven:

> *While he was still speaking, a bright cloud overshadowed them, and behold, a voice out of the cloud said, "This is My beloved Son, with whom I am well-pleased; listen to Him!" (Matthew 17:5).*

In essence, God says, "Peter, you shut up and listen to Jesus. He is my beloved Son, not Moses and Elijah." John never forgot that lesson. He was always to remember that Jesus was much greater than the prophets. He is the Son of God.

The experience that John had on the Mount of Transfiguration was now to be repeated. Once again before he died, John was to witness the glorified Christ. It will happen here in the book of Revelation. The glory of Jesus will once again be revealed. As we come to read John's account, we will be permitted to peak over his shoulder and to catch a glimpse of that same glory. It was given so that John could *show to His bond-servants, the things which must soon take place (1:1).*

Notice the future ramifications of this purpose. It is written to show believers *the things which must soon take place (1:1).* Not only does the book of Revelation begin with such a statement, it also will end with the same statement. In Revelation 22:6, we will again be told these exact words. It is at this point that you might object, "Revelation was written nearly two thousand years ago and many of its prophecies still have not come to pass. How can John say that they would soon take place?"

The answer is that there are elements of these prophecies that will soon be taking place from John's perspective. The prophecies of this book, as well as throughout the rest of the Bible, are often blended together without regard for chronological considerations. The distant is always viewed through the lens of the immediate and, in John's case, the immediate was very soon. Just as the first century believer was able to see the signs indicating the nearness of the fulfillment of these prophecies in his day, so also we can see similar signs indicating the nearness of the fulfillment of those same prophecies today. Does that discount the nearness? Not at all. It is here that we see the difference between the believer versus the skeptic. The skeptic says, "Where is the promise of His coming?" (2 Peter 3:4). The believer, on the other hand, determines to be on the alert, for he does not know on which day his Lord is coming (Matthew 24:42). This brings us to the blessing of this book.

> *Blessed is he who reads and those who hear the words of the prophecy, and heed the things which are written in it; for the time is near. (Revelation 1:3).*

There is a blessing that is given to the one who reads and hears and heeds the things that are written in this book. It is understood that not all are able to read. After all, this was a time of limited literacy. But there were also those who heard this book read. This is a beatitude. Do you remember the beatitudes? They were given by Jesus on the Sermon on the Mount. Each of them started with the phrase: "Blessed is the..." There will be seven beatitudes found in the book of Revelation running from the first chapter to the last.

15

Verse	Blessing
1:3	*Blessed is he who reads and those who hear the words of the prophecy, and heed the things which are written in it*
14:13	*Blessed are the dead who die in the Lord from now on*
16:15	*Blessed is the one who stays awake and keeps his clothes, so that he will not walk about naked and men will not see his shame*
19:9	*Blessed are those who are invited to the marriage supper of the Lamb*
20:6	*Blessed and holy is the one who has a part in the first resurrection*
22:7	*Blessed is he who heeds the words of the prophecy of this book*
22:14	*Blessed are those who wash their robes, so that they may have the right to the tree of life, and may enter by the gates into the city.*

This first beatitude is pronounced upon those who read this book and who hear and obey its teachings. Notice that it is never enough merely to hear the word of God. You must always obey. Knowledge of the word of God is never enough. God always demands that hearing be mixed with faith that leads to action.

This tells me something about this book. It will not merely be an academic exercise in future trivia. It will challenge you to change your life. It will challenge you to live differently. This is always the case with biblical prophecy. It always has this as its ultimate goal.

> *...instructing us to deny ungodliness and worldly desires and to live sensibly, righteously and godly in the present age, 13 looking for the blessed hope and the appearing of the glory of our great God and Savior, Christ Jesus (Titus 2:12-13).*

OPENING SALUTATION
Revelation 1:4-8

What kind of book is Revelation? It contains prophecy, but it also speaks to things that were taking place in John's day. It is apocalyptic in its outlook, describing the end of the world. It is also an epistle. As we come to this section, we see John utilizing the typical format of an epistle.

When you write a letter today, you typically follow a certain prescribed format. If it is a business letter, then you place your name and address at the top, followed by the name and address of the person to whom you are writing. Next follows a salutation that might read, "Dear Mr. So and so." Only then do you move into the body of the letter.

The customs of letter-writing in the ancient world were very similar. First would come the name of the author. Then would come the name of the person to whom the epistle was addressed. Finally would come a greeting.

John uses the same format here. He has already begun with an introduction to the book, but now he stops and addresses himself to "the seven churches that are in Asia." They will be listed by name when we come to verse 11.

> Ephesus
> Smyrna
> Pergamum
> Thyatira
> Sardis
> Philadelphia
> Laodicea

They are all located within about 150 miles of each other and they form a long, irregular oval across the landscape of western Turkey.

OPENING SALUTATION

1.	John's Greeting: *Grace to you and peace (1:4).*

	John's greeting is identical to the one commonly used by the Apostle Paul throughout his epistle. It was a greeting that combined the traditional Greek greeting with the traditional Hebrew greeting.

- "Grace to you" -- was used by the Greeks.
- "Peace," Shalom! -- is still used today in Israel.

John combines both of these into a singular greeting. At the same time, there is an order to this greeting. Both when John uses it here and when the Apostle Paul uses it elsewhere, grace always comes before peace. Perhaps there is a reason for that. You cannot have peace with God or the peace of God until you have first partaken of the grace of God. Without grace there can be no peace.

One of the problems with the world today is that people are trying to find peace apart from the grace of God. It will not work. We will not achieve lasting peace, either with God or with one another apart from the grace of God.

2.   The Source of Grace and Peace: *Grace to you and peace, from Him who is and who was and who is to come, and from the seven Spirits who are before His throne, [5] and from Jesus Christ (1:4-5).*

Here we have the source of grace and peace. It comes from a three-fold source. First it comes from the one *who is and who was and who is to come*. This is a reference to God. He is the God who is here. That sets Him apart from every other deity of paganism. None of the pagan gods were ever present. Their statues might be present, but they were always away on vacation. By contrast, the God whom we worship is ever-present. He is omnipresent. He is always here. But that is not all; He is also the God who was and who will be. He is ever present in time. He described Himself in Exodus 3:14 as, "I am that I am." He is the ever present One. He is the eternally existent One.

God gave this, not merely as one of His attributes, but as His very name. When Moses asked what is the name of God, the Lord answered, "I am that I am." This is significant. In the ancient world, a person's name described their fundamental identity. God is the self-existing One. It is from this phrase, "I am," that we derive the Hebrew name, "Yahweh." It is a name that transcends time. God is not bound by the restricting limits of time. He is the same yesterday, today, and forever (Hebrews 13:8). He is the only One who can say, "Before the world was created, I am. A billion years from now, I am." He is the eternal present tense.

This is a wonderful point of stability for us. We live in an age where everything is constantly changing, where nothing ever remains the same. Yet we have the God who is always the same and who never changes. He never gets older; He never goes out of date. He is not affected by the ravages of time because He transcends time.

18

Grace and peace also come from *the seven Spirits*. What are these spirits? They are a reference to the Holy Spirit. This description was first used by the prophet Isaiah.

> *Then a shoot will spring from the stem of Jesse, And a branch from his roots will bear fruit. 2 The Spirit of the LORD will rest on Him, The spirit of wisdom and understanding, The spirit of counsel and strength, The spirit of knowledge and the fear of the LORD. (Isaiah 11:1-2).*

This is a Messianic prophecy. It speaks of the coming of the One who will be a branch from the tree of Jesse. He will come on the scene and the Spirit of God will be upon Him. Notice the seven characteristics that are listed of the Spirit. He is the Spirit...

- Of the Lord.
- Of wisdom.
- Of understanding.
- Of counsel.
- Of strength.
- Of knowledge.
- Of the fear of the Lord.

We are going to see the number "seven" a lot throughout the book of Revelation. John already began His epistle by addressing the seven churches. Here are seven spirits. This is a number often associated with God. It is a number symbolizing completeness and perfection. The reference here to the seven Spirits of God is John's way of describing the Holy Spirit as perfect and complete.

Grace and peace also come from Jesus Christ. Grace and peace come from the Father, and from the Holy Spirit, and from the Son. What we have here is the doctrine known as the Trinity. There is only One God, but He exists as the Father, the Son, and the Holy Spirit.

Jesus is described in a number of ways in this passage. He is...

- The faithful witness. Jesus came to bear witness of the Father. One of His titles is the Word. A word communicates. It also bears witness.

> *No one has seen God at any time; the only begotten God who is in the bosom of the Father, He has explained Him. (John 1:18).*

We were able to know something about God from the creation. You can look up into the sky and you can say, "Whoever made this is really big and really strong." You can know more about God by reading the Scriptures. But the best way to know God is by getting to know Jesus.

- The firstborn of the dead.

When God says that Jesus is the firstborn from the dead, he does not mean that Jesus is the first person ever to come back from the dead. He isn't. There were a number of people who rose from the dead before Jesus rose from the dead.
- There was the son of the widow whom Elijah raised from the dead (1 Kings 17:22).
- There was the son of the Shunamite woman whom Elisha raised from the dead (2 Kings 4:32-36).
- Jesus raised the daughter of Jarius from the dead (Mark 5:38-42).
- Jesus raised Lazarus from the dead (John 11:43-44).

Jesus was not the first to rise from the dead. Why is He called the firstborn from the dead? It is because, of all the people who ever rose from the dead and of all the people who ever will rise from the dead, His resurrection is the most important.

That is what the idea of firstborn means. A firstborn in the ancient world held a position of preeminence. He had the lion's share of the inheritance. He was the leader of the family. He had the father's blessings. He was the first-place son. Because of this, the title of "firstborn" came to be used of anyone who held the position of preeminence, regardless of the chronology of their birthday. In the second century when a certain heretic would arise named Marcion, the bishop Polycarp would call Marcion the "firstborn of Satan."

Jesus holds the position of first place. His resurrection is the most important resurrection. Because He has risen from the dead, we shall also rise from the dead. His resurrection is the guarantee of our resurrection.

- The ruler of the kings of the earth.

Jesus is said to be the ruler of the kings of the earth. That is a striking claim and it was especially striking in that day. The Roman emperor claimed to be the ruler of the kings of the earth, but Jesus is the greater ruler. He has rule and authority over all emperors and kings and presidents. Do you remember what Jesus said when He stood before Pontius Pilate?

Jesus answered, "You would have no authority over Me, unless it had been given you from above" (John

19:11).

This is important to know. Governmental authorities have been given their authority from God. They exist because God has established them. They are answerable to a higher authority.

Jesus is the faithful witness. He is the firstborn from the dead. And He is the ruler of the kings of the earth. This would have been a great source of comfort to the believers who were living in the first century. They were being persecuted for the gospel they preached. Men hated them for their witness of Jesus. But He knows what it is like to be persecuted for being a faithful witness. He was a faithful witness who continued to be faithful, even as He went to the cross.

John writes these words to believers that are under the threat of death and they can take comfort in knowing that their Savior is the firstborn of the dead. He is the pattern that we shall all one day follow. Just as He rose from the dead, so we shall also rise from the dead.

As Christians are persecuted, there will be the temptation to lose heart. But they can be encouraged because Jesus is the ruler over kings and emperors and governors. No one will be able to do anything against His people without His knowledge and apart from His allowance.

OPENING BENEDICTION

> *To Him who loves us and released us from our sins by His blood (Revelation 1:5).*

John's words now take the form of a benediction. He points us to Jesus, the One who *loves us and released us from our sins by His blood*. Dr. Karl Barth, the famous theologian of the early 20th century, was once asked what is the most profound thought he ever had. He replied:

> Jesus loves me, this I know,
> For the Bible tells me so.

If you don't find that profound, it is because you have too small a view of who Jesus really is. He is the God-man. He is the One who was promised from all eternity. He is the faithful witness. He is the firstborn from the dead. He is the King of kings and Lord of lords. He is the Creator of the Cosmos and He loves us.

This is in the present tense. It describes a continuing action. He has loved us in the past and now He still loves us. His love is an unchanging love. It is also a powerful love. It is not passive. It has accomplished a great work. It has accomplished our redemption. It has released us from our sins.

There was a time when we were in bondage to sin and to its penalty. That has changed. We have been released. We have been set free from the bondage of sin. We no longer are bound to sin. We have also been freed from the penalty of sin. Jesus bore the penalty of our sins in His own body. As a result, God is free to bless us with every spiritual blessing.

> *...and He has made us to be a kingdom, priests to His God and Father (Revelation 1:6).*

This passage tells us two things. First it tells us that God has made us to be a Kingdom. God is building a kingdom. When Jesus first came to the earth, He proclaimed that He was come to bring a kingdom. He sent His disciples through the country proclaiming that the kingdom was at hand. After a while, people began to question and ask, "Okay, exactly where is your kingdom?"

> *Now having been questioned by the Pharisees as to when the kingdom of God was coming, He answered them and said, "The kingdom of God is not coming with signs to be observed; 21 nor will they say, 'Look, here it is!' or, 'There it is!' For behold, the kingdom of God is in your midst." (Luke 17:20-21).*

Do you hear what Jesus said? These men were looking for some great physical manifestation from heaven. They were looking for an earthly kingdom to be set up with palaces and royalty and soldiers and banners waving in the breeze. They were looking for God to send lightning from the sky and burn up the Romans and set up a physical kingdom.

Jesus said that this is not the way His kingdom is going to come. It will not come with signs to be observed. It will not be visually apparent so that man can point to it and say, "There it is!" The kingdom is not coming that way. Jesus says the kingdom was already in their midst.

How can this be? What kind of kingdom is this? It is the kingdom of God's people. Have you trusted in Jesus Christ as your Savior and Lord? If you have, then you are a member of God's kingdom. Indeed, you are an ambassador. You have been given a special commission by the king to represent Jesus Christ on earth.

He has made us a kingdom and He has also made us priests. What is a priest? The temple of Jerusalem had priests who were permitted to enter the temple and perform the services of worship. Ordinary people were not permitted to enter here. There were walls and barricades and warnings set up outside the temple to keep out people. Only the priests were allowed to enter inside the temple. Even the temple itself was partitioned off by a great veil so that there was a holy place where the priest could come and there was also the Holy of Holies where only the High Priest was permitted to enter and then only once a year.

The great veil separated the Holy Place from the Holy of Holies. On the outside of the veil, the priests were permitted to come and to offer incense. But no one was permitted beyond the veil into the inner sanctum of the Holy of Holies. Here had once stood the Ark of the Covenant. It had been a great chest overlaid with gold. Statues of two cherubim stood on either side of the lid, their gaze directed down to the surface of the Mercy Seat. This represented the throne of God upon earth.

Once a year, the high priest was permitted to enter into the Holy of Holies. This took place on Yom Kippur, the Day of Atonement. He would enter in and sprinkle blood of bulls and goats upon the Mercy Seat, atoning for the sins of the nation.

Do you remember what happened in the temple on the day Jesus died? The veil of the temple was torn in two from top to bottom. This was to symbolize that the way had been made open for all to come and to worship God. That temple was destroyed in A.D. 70. The sacrifices since that time have been halted and have never again been reinstated. But we still have a way into the most holy place. We enter, not through the blood of bulls and goats, but according to the blood of Christ that was shed for us. We are priests. We have been granted entrance into the presence of God. We can come with confidence to the throne of God.

A PROMISED RETURN

> *Behold, He is coming with the clouds, and every eye will see Him, even those who pierced Him; and all the tribes of the earth will mourn over Him. So it is to be. Amen (Revelation 1:7).*

We do not have to wait until the end of the Book of Revelation to see a promise of Christ's Second Coming. It is promised from one end of the book to the other. Such a promise is found here in verse 7. The details of this promise are striking:

1.   The Vehicle of His Coming: *He is Coming with the Clouds (1:7).*

The reference to Christ's coming with the clouds calls to mind the circumstances of His ascension. The scene was the Mount of Olives following the death, burial, and resurrection of Jesus.

> *And after He had said these things, He was lifted up while they were looking on, and a cloud received Him out of their sight. 10 And as they were gazing intently into*

the sky while He was going, behold, two men in white clothing stood beside them. 11 They also said, "Men of Galilee, why do you stand looking into the sky? This Jesus, who has been taken up from you into heaven, will come in just the same way as you have watched Him go into heaven." (Acts 1:9-11).

Luke's account in the book of Acts is quite matter-of-fact. Jesus and His disciples had walked up the Mount of Olives to the point that overlooked the city of Jerusalem. He gave some closing instructions to His disciples and then was "lifted up." The disciples were eye witnesses to this phenomenon. They continued to watch the ascending Jesus until *a cloud received Him out of their sight*. Suddenly, as they continued to look where Jesus had been, they became aware that their numbers had grown by two. Instead of eleven disciples, there were thirteen standing together on the Mountain.

Mount of Olive as seen from the Temple Mount

The promise of these two angels is that Jesus will come in just the same way as He had departed. How did He depart? He had gone up into the sky and had been visible until hidden by a cloud. In just the same way, He would return. John was there on that day and now, many years later, He relates that same promise. Jesus is going to come and, when He comes, He will come with the clouds.

This language calls to mind the reference to clouds in the Old Testament. The Lord is described in the Psalms:

> *He makes the clouds His chariot;*
> *He walks upon the wings of the wind (Psalm 104:3).*

24

It is obvious that we are not meant to take this literally. God does not need clouds to move about. It is because of this imagery that some have wondered whether the promise of Jesus returning in the clouds should also be understood only in a figurative sense. That might be the case were it not to the testimony of Luke in the book of Acts. There is very little in that passage to suggest a figurative understanding and every reason to believe that Christ was hidden by a literal cloud as He ascended into the sky.

At the same time, we must admit that the coming of Christ on the clouds does serve as a testimony to the fact that He is coming from heaven.

2.   The Visibility of His Coming: *Every eye will see Him, even those who pierced Him (1:7)*.

There is a false teaching making the rounds among Christian circles that says all of the prophecies of Christ's Second Coming were fulfilled in the A.D. 70 destruction of Jerusalem. This teaching is known as Preterism. There are a number of problems with such a teaching and one of them is found here in this verse.

Preterism says that the fall of Jerusalem was the fulfillment of the promise that Jesus would one day return, but this verse tells us that His return will be seen by everyone. Church history is uniform in its silence regarding the idea that anyone saw the returning Jesus at the fall of Jerusalem. It is not merely that the Jews in Jerusalem did not see him, and we have the eye witness testimony of Josephus who tells us a great deal about what took place at that time. The apostolic and church fathers are also universally ignorant of the idea that the fall of Jerusalem constituted the return of Christ.

This passage says that, when Jesus returns, every eye will see Him including those who pierced Him. How can this be? Those who pierced Him have long since died. But this same book of Revelation will teach of a general resurrection in chapter 20 when all will stand before the judgment of God (20:11-13). We can affirm that there is coming a day when every eye will see the returning Lord and every knee will bow and every tongue will confess that Jesus Christ is Lord (Philippians 2:10-11).

3.   The Victory of his Coming: *All the tribes of the earth will mourn over Him (1:7)*.

This phrase would have been familiar to anyone who knew their Old Testament. It is taken from a Messianic passage in the book of Zechariah:

I will pour out on the house of David and on the

25

inhabitants of Jerusalem, the Spirit of grace and of supplication, so that they will look on Me whom they have pierced; and they will mourn for Him, as one mourns for an only son, and they will weep bitterly over Him like the bitter weeping over a firstborn. 11 In that day there will be great mourning in Jerusalem, like the mourning of Hadadrimmon in the plain of Megiddo (Zechariah 12:10-11).

This is part of a larger passage that speaks of the Lord dealing with His people. He is the One speaking in this passage and He tells of a time when He will judge the world in righteousness.

- It looks to the time when His Spirit is poured out. This took place in Acts 2 at the Pentecost Event. But that was a pouring out on all flesh while this is said to be a pouring out "on the house of David." Are they two separate instances? Perhaps not. As a result of the grace of God being given through Christ, we can understand that all who come to Christ in faith are themselves joined to Christ and identified with Christ. Their very identity is now rooted in the person of Christ. If Christ is the rightful king of Israel, then we are co-heirs with Christ. If Christ is of the house of David, then there is a sense in which we share of that house, not in a physical sense, but in a spiritual sense.
  At the same time, we must remember that the church was initially a Jewish institution. The events of Acts 2 took place in an exclusively Jewish setting and it took place among the literal inhabitants of Jerusalem.

- It looks to a time of mourning. This is the mourning that takes place in the face of judgment. It is not necessarily a mourning over one's sins, but rather the mourning that takes place when one has been caught in sin and now has to face the results of that sin.

  This mourning is likened to *the mourning of Hadadrimmon in the plain of Megiddo.* We do not know the identity of Hadadrimmon, though we can suppose that it speaks of an ancient Canaanite personage who met his end in the Valley of Megiddo. This was the site of many ancient battles. Thutmoses III conducted a famous campaign here during which he captured the city of Megiddo. The city of Megiddo came to be associated with great military defeat. Josiah met his death here. It would be like calling a place today by the name of Waterloo because that also was the site of a famous battle.

There is coming a day when Jesus will return. It will be a time of rejoicing for those who love Him, but it will be a time of mourning for those who are not His followers. For them, it will be like a great military defeat. It will be a time of sorrow. Which is it for you? The answer to that question will be determined by what you do with Jesus. Have you trusted in Him as your Lord and Savior? Or have you chosen to follow a path of rebellion and independence?

IN THE PRESENCE OF JESUS
Revelation 1:9-20

We have already described the book of Revelation as "theology in pictures." The vivid images that will be presented throughout this book are meant, not only to teach, but to capture the imagination and excite the emotion.

RECIPIENT OF THE REVELATION

> *I, John, your brother and fellow partaker in the tribulation and kingdom and perseverance which are in Jesus, was on the island called Patmos because of the word of God and the testimony of Jesus. (Revelation 1:9).*

We are going to see some glorious things in this book. We are going to see visions of heaven and angels and all sorts of wondrous things. But the book does not begin so wondrously. It begins in a rather mundane fashion. It begins when John was going through some hard times.

Our first clue to those hard times is when he says that he is a *fellow partaker in the tribulation and kingdom and perseverance which are in Jesus.* John was going through some tribulation. That should not surprise us. Tribulation often comes with the package that is known as Christianity.

Our second clue that John is going through some difficult times is that he *was on the island called Patmos.* Now you might be thinking, "That doesn't sound so bad." A Mediterranean island. Sand and sea and sun. But that is because you have never been to Patmos. Imagine instead ten miles of rocky, barren desolation. It was a place to which political prisoners were exiled. Early church tradition has it that John had been sentenced here to do some hard time. Such banishment involved the loss of all civil rights. Any property he owned would have been confiscated by the Roman government. He was sent with only the clothes on his back to live on this island.

There were a lot of things that John could have said about himself. You ask some people to introduce themselves and out comes their resume. Men especially tend to be like that (not that you ladies are above that sort of thing). John could have said:

> "I am one of the apostles."
> "I'm not just an apostle, I'm one of the inner circle."
> "I was the apostle who was known as being the one that Jesus really loved."

But he said none of these things. Notice how John does describe himself.

> *Your brother.*
> *Your fellow partaker in the tribulation and kingdom and perseverance.*

John isn't out to elevate himself. To the contrary, he is out to show that you and he are united in a common bond. That bond is Jesus. There is a lesson here. It is that theology is not just for theologians. It is for all of God's people. It is for you, too.

REALITY OF THE REVELATION

> *I was in the Spirit on the Lord's day, and I heard behind*
> *me a loud voice like the sound of a trumpet, 11 saying, "Write in a*
> *book what you see, and send it to the seven churches: to Ephesus*
> *and to Smyrna and to Pergamum and to Thyatira and to Sardis and*
> *to Philadelphia and to Laodicea." (Revelation 1:10-11).*

The reference to "the Lord's day" is not the same thing as "the Day of the Lord." The Greek phrase that is used here is different from the way the Biblical writers typically described the Day of the Lord, both in the Septuagint as well as in the rest of the New Testament. By the second century, the phrase "the Lord's day" would be used by Christians to describe Sunday, the day on which the church traditionally met for worship. That seems to be the use here.

The revelation which was imparted to John took place in real-time history. This is not a "once upon a time" fairy tale. John was on a real island in the Mediterranean Sea and he was given a message which was to be delivered to real churches which were extant in that day.

> The voice that John heard is said to have been like the voice of a trumpet. This isn't speaking of its musical quality, but its volume. It was loud. The figure of speech is drawn from Isaiah 58:1 where God says to the prophet, "Raise your voice like a trumpet."

That tells me something about the book of Revelation. It is rooted in history. If I am to understand this book, then I must place it into the context of the world in which it was written. People run into all sorts of problems in understanding the book of Revelation when they take it out of the context in which it was given. They start to look for computers and missiles and thermonuclear warfare and the European Union and the book of Revelation is not about any of those things.

Like any other book of the Bible, indeed, like any other book, you can only understand it as you read it in order and in context, placing yourself into the sandals of those for whom it was originally written.

RESIDENCE OF THE REVELATION

Then I turned to see the voice that was speaking with me. And having turned I saw seven golden lampstands; 13 *and in the middle of the lampstands I saw one like a son of man... (Revelation 1:12-13a).*

John hears a voice like a trumpet. Apparently the voice was behind him. I don't know about you, but when a loud voice like a trumpet goes off behind me, I jump with a start. I have no doubt that John did the same.

He turns and he looks as he expects to see the speaker of the voice. But first, he sees *seven golden lampstands*. This is significant. You might be inclined to rush on past this phrase, but don't do it. It was significant to John, too, because he mentions these lampstands again in verse 13 and again in verse 20.

> This happens a lot in this book. John hears one thing and so he turns expecting to see that thing and instead he sees another thing that is somehow related to the first thing.
> - In Revelation 3:20, Jesus says that he stands at the door and knocks. But when John looks in Revelation 4:1 there is an open door in heaven.
> - In Revelation 5:8 John hears the new song of the 24 elders and the 4 living creatures, but when he looks in verse 11 there are countless thousands.
> - In Revelation 7, John hears the counting of 144,000, but when he turns and looks in verse 9, he sees a great multitude that no one can number.

What was the significance of the lampstands? It was associated with the Temple. In the original Tabernacle, there was a lampstand shaped like a living tree with one branch in the middle and three branches going to one side and three branches going to the other side (Exodus 25:31-37). This stylized tree was of solid gold and it had blossoms and bulbs and branches and it held seven oil lamps.

> A tree of light.
> A tree of life.

Light and life go together. John tells us that this is the case. In John 1:5 he tells us that in Jesus was life, *and the life was the light of the world.* Do you remember the first mention of a tree in the Bible? It was in the Garden of Eden. There were actually two trees in the garden.

- The tree of the knowledge of good and evil.
- The tree of life.

When Adam and Eve ate from the first tree, they were removed from the second tree. The first tree brought death; the second tree brought life. When the Lord gave instructions for the building of the Tabernacle and later for the Temple, it was not by chance that it included a lampstand in the shape of a tree. In this design was a promise of restored life, a tree that illuminated the way into the Holy Place.

This tells me something else about the book of Revelation. It is written on the foundation of the Old Testament. It is full of Temple Language. The symbols that we see throughout this book are not nearly so strange to us if we are familiar with our Old Testament.

At the same time, we will be reading new meaning into those Old Testament images. John sees the lampstand and it is described in such a way as to remind us of the temple in Jerusalem, but it has a significance that goes beyond that physical temple. In verse 20 we are told the meaning behind this symbol.

> *"...the seven lampstands are the seven churches."* *(Revelation 1:20).*

The lampstands refer to more than merely the ornamentation of the physical temple. They represent a spiritual reality. Who are the lampstands? You are! You have been called to be the light of the world.

> *"You are the light of the world. A city set on a hill cannot be hidden;* 15 *nor does anyone light a lamp and put it under a basket, but on the lampstand, and it gives light to all who are in the house.*
> *"Let your light shine before men in such a way that they may see your good works, and glorify your Father who is in heaven. (Matthew 5:14-16).*

You are the light of the world. You might be thinking, "Wait a minute, I thought that it is Jesus who is the light of the world." That is correct. Jesus is the light of the world. But you are called to do His work. You are called to shine with His flame. You will do so as long as you are connected to Him in the same way that a branch is connected to a tree.

You are the light of the world. That means you are not fulfilling God's purpose for you if you are not letting your light shine in a way that can be seen. How do you do that? How do you burn with the light of Christ? The answer is that you don't have to generate your own fire. A lampstand doesn't burn. It is only a container. The oil that it contains burns. If you are filled with the Holy Spirit of God, then He will burn in you.

Notice where Jesus is. He is in the midst of the lampstand. He is in the midst of the church. He is here. It is His presence that brings the burning. He is the vine to which all the branches must be connected to have life. He is the One who gives the life-giving Spirit. You trust in Him and love Him and be filled with Him and He

31

will do the rest.

The original lampstand from the Temple is portrayed on the Triumphal Arch of Titus commemorating the fall of Jerusalem in A.D. 70.

Do you remember the warning given to the church at Ephesus? That was the church which had lost its first love. It was a church of doctrinal strength; a church that had endured for the name of Christ and which had stood fast against wrong theology. They had only one problem. They had lost their first love. They exhibited...

- Right theology
- Growing church
- High level of purity
- A strong sense of tradition

All of these things were present in the church, but there was no love. As a result, they are given a very strong warning. It is a warning that is couched in the language of familiar symbolism.

> *"Remember therefore from where you have fallen, and repent and do the deeds you did at first, or else I am coming to you, and will remove your lampstand out of its place unless you repent." (Revelation 2:5).*

Do you see the warning? It is that if repentance does not take place, then there will be only six lampstands instead of seven.

John looks and he sees the lampstands and then he sees the one who is in the middle of the lampstands. He is described as being *one like a son of man*. This term had a particular significance to anyone who was familiar with the Hebrew Scriptures.

It is a term that was used in the book of Daniel.

John saw the fulfillment of that Old Testament prophecy. He saw Jesus, the one who became flesh and who became a Son of man. Before this book is over, we will be presented with this picture of the Son of Man being given all dominion and glory and a kingdom.

RAIMENT OF THE REVELATION

Now John focuses upon the figure who is standing in the middle of the lampstands. I'm not giving anything away by saying that this is Jesus. He is described as being *one like a son of man*. Notice that John could have called him a Son of Man - Jesus called Himself that often enough. But John does not do this. He describes the risen Lord as One who is *like* a son of man. This was a special title to the Jews. It had its origins in the Old Testament.

> *I kept looking in the night visions,*
> *And behold, with the clouds of heaven*
> *One like a Son of Man was coming,*
> *And He came up to the Ancient of Days*
> *And was presented before Him.*
> *14 And to Him was given dominion,*
> *Glory and a kingdom,*
> *That all the peoples, nations and men of every language*
> *Might serve Him. His dominion is an everlasting dominion*
> *Which will not pass away;*
> *And His kingdom is one*
> *Which will not be destroyed. (Daniel 7:13-14).*

John saw the fulfillment of that Old Testament prophecy. He saw Jesus, the One who became flesh and who became like a Son of Man. Now John focuses upon the raiment Jesus is wearing. It has special significance.

> *...clothed in a robe reaching to the feet, and girded across*
> *His chest with a golden sash. (Revelation 1:13).*

These garments are familiar to the reader of the Old Testament. They are the apparel of the high priest. Jesus is our high priest. You know the significance of the high priest. He was the only one permitted into the Holiest of Holies.

Only priests were permitted entry into the Temple. One would be selected by lots each morning and each evening to go into the Temple and offer incense upon the altar of incense while the people outside gathered to pray. On the right would be the altar of shewbread. On the left would be the golden lampstand of which we have spoken. In the middle would be the small altar of incense with its hot coals.

Past the altar of incense was a great curtain. It stood as a wall of separation from the innermost part of the Temple. No priest was ever permitted to go past this great veil. Except one - the High Priest. And he was only allowed to pass beyond the veil once a year. It would be on the Day of Atonement - Yom Kippur. He would pass beyond the veil to offer the blood of goats and calves as an atonement for the sins of the nation. This was all a picture of what Jesus did on our behalf.

Not...	But...
• Year after year	• Once for all
• With the blood of goats or calves	• By means of His own shed blood
• Into a Temple made with hands	• Into heaven itself.
• For the sins of the nation	• For the sins of the World

Do you remember what happened when Jesus died upon the cross? The veil of the Temple ripped in two. From top to bottom. The veil that separated men from God. The veil that kept men from entering into the presence of God. The death of Jesus changed that. It ripped the veil apart. He was the Great High Priest who put an end to that which separates us from God.

RADIANCE OF THE REVELATION

His head and His hair were white like white wool, like snow; and His eyes were like a flame of fire.

His feet were like burnished bronze, when it has been made to glow in a furnace, and His voice was like the sound of many waters.

In His right hand He held seven stars, and out of His mouth came a sharp two-edged sword; and His face was like the sun shining in its strength. (Revelation 1:14-16).

This must have been an amazing sight. And yet, as strange as it may have been, I believe that it was somewhat familiar to John. He had read of such a description before. It was seen in the book of Daniel:

I kept looking until thrones were set up, and the Ancient of Days took His seat; His vesture was like white snow and the hair of His head like pure wool. His throne was ablaze with flames, its

34

wheels were a burning fire. (Daniel 7:9).

The One that John sees now matches the Old Testament description of the "Ancient of Days." That is a title for God. Do you see the implications? It points to the deity of Christ. He is the "Ancient of Days." He is the One who lived from all eternity. He is the "I AM."

Verse 16 says that *in His right hand He held seven stars.* In verse 20 we shall see that these stars represent seven churches. But John hasn't read that yet. As he first sees this vision, he would tend to think of the Old Testament association of seven stars. On three different occasions, the Old Testament speaks of the Lord having power over a stellar constellation known as the Pleiades. This constellation is made up of a tightly knit group of seven stars. They are known as the Seven Sisters.

> *"Can you bind the cluster of the Pleiades, or loose the bands of Orion?" (Job 38:31).*

> *For those who turn justice into wormwood and cast righteousness down to the earth.*
> *He who made the Pleiades and Orion and changes deep darkness into morning, who also darkens day into night, who calls for the waters of the sea and pours them out on the surface of the earth, The Lord is His name. (Amos 5:7-8).*

The Old Testament taught that it was the Lord God who created the Pleiades and bound them. Now we see that it is Jesus who holds the seven stars in His hand. The implications of this shared identity are obvious. But that is not all. The coins displaying the Roman emperor often showed him with seven stars. This was a symbol of his supreme authority and lordship over the known world. By this symbol, Jesus is being depicted as King of kings and Lord of lords.

> *...and His feet were like burnished bronze, when it has been caused to glow in a furnace, and His voice was like the sound of many waters. (Revelation 1:15).*

What is the significance of the feet of Jesus being described as burnished bronze? There were two pillars that stood on either side of the doorway into Solomon's Temple. They were made of bronze. If heaven was God's throne and the earth was His footstool, then the Jews felt that these pillars represented the legs of God. This means Jesus is again being described in terms that represent His divinity.

Verse 16 says that *out of His mouth came a sharp two-edged sword.* This sounds rather gruesome at first reading. But remember that it is a symbol, a picture of a spiritual truth. It isn't as though Jesus is walking around somewhere with a literal sword hanging from His tonsils or a sharp case of halitosis. This is a living parable

35

of a spiritual reality. The sword represents the Word of God.

> *For the word of God is living and active and sharper than any two-edged sword, and piercing as far as the division of soul and spirit, of both joints and marrow, and able to judge the thoughts and intentions of the heart. (Hebrews 4:12).*

The sword is a picture of power and strength. It is sharp and it is able to cut deeply. The Word of God does that. The preaching of the Word is able to change men's lives.

The creation account in Genesis 1 is filled with references to God speaking forth by the word of His power. Throughout that chapter, we see the continued refrain, "And God said..." In each case, He spoke and it was done.

The gospel has that kind of power and not only when presented from a pulpit. You have that find of power when you share the gospel with a neighbor or a co-worker. The Lord promises that His word shall not return void; it will accomplish that for which it was intended.

> *So will My word be which goes forth from My mouth; it will not return to Me empty, without accomplishing what I desire, and without succeeding in the matter for which I sent it. (Isaiah 55:11).*

Satan likes to fool us into thinking that the Word has no power. He is a liar and a deceiver. It is like a robber being stopped by a police officer who points a gun at him. Imagine the robber trying to convince the police officer that the officer's gun has no bullets. Sounds silly? What would be even more silly is if the police officer believed the lie.

That is what we do when we fail to use the Word of God. It is powerful and it penetrates the hearts of men to change lives. It conquers men and women and kingdoms and worlds.

REACTION TO THE REVELATION

> *When I saw Him, I fell at His feet like a dead man. And He placed His right hand on me, saying, "Do not be afraid; I am the first and the last, 18 and the living One; and I was dead, and behold, I am alive forevermore, and I have the keys of death and of Hades. (Revelation 1:17-18).*

John's reaction to this revelation is striking. Literally. He falls to the ground as though shot with a 44 magnum. It sweeps him right off his feet.

I want you to notice something. John had lived with Jesus. He had eaten with Him and traveled with Him and talked with Him and slept with Him. He was familiar with the presence of Jesus. But now John sees the unveiled majesty of Christ and it is enough to sweep him off his feet. John will see a great many things in the book of Revelation.

- He will see the throne of God.
- He will see the lampstands.
- He will see the twenty four elders.
- He will see the lake of fire.
- He will see angels and demons and vials of wrath and trumpets of God.

But nothing will have such an effect on him as this vision of the glorified Christ. I think that we too often lose sight of the glory and the holiness and the majesty of God. It shows in our prayers and in our worship and in our lack thereof. Notice how the Lord identifies Himself. He does not call Himself "Jesus." Instead, He uses a title that echoes back to the Old Testament:

1.   *I am the first and the last (1:17).*

This self identification was especially significant to John because he would have been familiar with His Old Testament. It is an identification that is taken from the book of Isaiah.

> *Thus says the LORD, the King of Israel and his Redeemer,*
> *the LORD of hosts:*
> *I am the first and I am the last,*
> *And there is no God besides Me. (Isaiah 44:6).*

It is Yahweh who says, "I am the first and I am the last." Jesus echoes those words, but He says it of Himself. The emphasis here is on the eternal character of the Christ. Before anything existed, He was here. When the universe is a burnt-out cinder, He shall still be here.

2.   *The living One; and I was dead, and behold, I am alive forevermore (1:18).*

He is the Living One. Throughout the Old Testament, one of the regular titles for the Lord was *Elohim Hay'im*, the Living God. All of the other gods of the ancient world were dead. They were lifeless idols of wood and of stone. Likewise all of the gods of modern man are dead. Charles Darwin and Voltaire and Sigmund Freud and Carl Sagan are dead and buried. But God is the Living One.

3.   *I have the keys of death and of Hades (1:18).*

In the ancient world keys were a symbol of authority. Do you remember when Jesus gave authority to Peter? Jesus had asked the disciples who they thought He really was. Peter answered that He was the Christ, the Son of the Living God (Matthew 16:16). Because of His insight, Jesus gave authority to Peter over His kingdom.

> *"I will give you the keys of the kingdom of heaven; and whatever you bind on earth shall have been bound in heaven, and whatever you loose on earth shall have been loosed in heaven." (Matthew 16:19).*

Jesus holds the keys of the kingdom. He has authority over death. He conquered death when He rose from the dead. Death no longer has any power over Him. The gates of the grave have been unlocked so that He is able to grant eternal life to all who will come to Him.

RAMIFICATIONS OF THE REVELATION

> *"Therefore write the things which you have seen, and the things which are, and the things which will take place after these things.*
> *"As for the mystery of the seven stars which you saw in My right hand, and the seven golden lampstands: the seven stars are the angels of the seven churches, and the seven lampstands are the seven churches." (Revelation 1:19-20).*

Now we come to the meaning behind the symbols. Some of the symbols we have seen in this chapter have needed no explanation. The aspect of the One who is like a Son of Man speaks for itself. It is plain to see this is a description of the glorified Christ. But the stars in His hand and the golden lampstand are not so easy, and so, they are explained to us in the context of the passage.

The Seven Stars	⇨	The angels of the Seven Churches
The Seven Lampstands	⇨	The Seven Churches

To which Seven Churches does this refer? To the Seven Churches mentioned by name in verse 11. The following two chapters will contain personalized messages written to those churches.

Notice that each of those churches has an angel assigned to it. The word "angel" comes from the Greek word *aggelos*. It simply means "messenger." It is always the context that tells us whether it is a human messenger or a divine messenger. Throughout most of the book of Revelation when we see an *aggelos* it is a supernatural messenger – an angel. That might be the case here. Or this might refer to human messengers within the church, the preachers and teachers of those churches.

The point is that Jesus is in the midst of His churches. Those who minister within His churches are carried in the palm of His hand, a hand that still bears the marks of His love for you.

AN OVERVIEW OF THE SEVEN LETTERS
Revelation 2-3

We have been studying the vision that John had of the glorified Jesus. While on the island of Patmos, John had a vision of Jesus Christ in all of His splendor and majesty. But that is not all. Jesus gave a commission to John. He told John to write the things he saw and experienced into a book – this book of Revelation. We read in verse 19 that he was to *write therefore the things which you have seen, and the things which are, and the things which shall take place after these things*. This tells us in no uncertain terms that we should expect the message of this book to look both to the past, to the present, and to the future.

The Island of Patmos

It has been suggested by some that these letters to the seven churches of Revelation, in addition to being addressed to seven specific and historical churches in Asia Minor, also reflect seven periods of history in the life of the church.

- Ephesus is said to refer to the first century church that was in danger of losing its first love.
- Smyrna is said to represent the persecuted church of the second and third centuries.
- Pergamum is made to refer to the church that had aligned herself to the Roman Empire following the coming of Constantine.
- Thyatira is the medieval church that was tolerating false teaching.
- Sardis, the dead church that is called to wake up, is made to be the church either before or after the Reformation (depending upon your own doctrinal persuasion).
- The church at Philadelphia is said to be the church of the first and second Great Awakenings (and some include the Reformation). Dispensationalists like to identify their beginning with this era.
- The modern church is usually taken to be represented by Laodicea.

40

Others who hold to a similar view see Laodicea as the church of a future great tribulation, citing Revelation 3:10 as a promise of a pretribulational rapture, a hypothetical gathering of believers by Christ in a coming that precedes His actual Second Coming. The very fact that those who hold to this historical outline theory cannot easily agree on where the various eras are to fit into the prophecy tells us that the interpretation is not an obvious one. While I do agree that there are some interesting parallels, I don't believe there is enough to warrant an acceptance of this view.

Churches	John Gill	Hal Lindsey	Steve Singleton
Ephesus	33 - 100	33 - 100	33-100
Smyrna	100 - 312	100 - 312	100-312
Pergamum	312 - 590	312 - 590	300-600
Thyatira	590 - 1517	590 - 1517	600-1517
Sardis	1517 - 2nd Coming	1517 - 1750	1517-1750
Philadelphia	Millennial Reign	1750 - 1925	1750-Present
Laodicea	End of Millennium	1900 - Present	Tribulation

While the church at Ephesus is described as having lost its first love, there is little evidence that this was generally the case throughout the majority of churches in the first century. Likewise, to maintain that nothing bad could have been said of the church of the 16th to the 19th centuries is naive. Indeed, there are some who held to a similar historical parallel view in the 1800's who saw their day as the Laodecian era (note John Gill's view in the preceding chart). Alternately, there are those who place the Reformation either in the period of Thyatira, Sardis or even Philadelphia. It does not bode well for the interpretation when there is so little agreement as to what is being portrayed.

I feel that a better point can be made for the messages to these seven churches having certain chiastic elements, a pattern in which there is a corresponding parallel with the first and last segments of this section. We shall see a number of examples of this sort of pattern throughout the book of Revelation and it has been established that such an arrangement was very common in the Old Testament.

Thus, the first church, Ephesus, will be described as a church in which love has grown cold and that will be contrasted with the last church, Laodicea, which is neither hot nor cold, but lukewarm.

Ephesus: A love grown cold - warning of a removed lamp.

Smyrna: Poor, but nothing said bad of this church

Pergamum: Repent or I am coming quickly (2:16).

Thyatira: Hold fast until I come (2:25).

A mixture of good and bad in these churches

Sardis: Wake up or I will come like a thief (3:3).

Philadelphia: A little power, but nothing said bad of this church

Laodicea: Neither hot nor cold - warning of spewing out

Furthermore, an examination of a map will show that there is also a geographic formula and the letters begin with Ephesus and then work their way clockwise in a large oval to arrive finally at Laodicea. Thus, there is a geographic order and arrangement to these books.

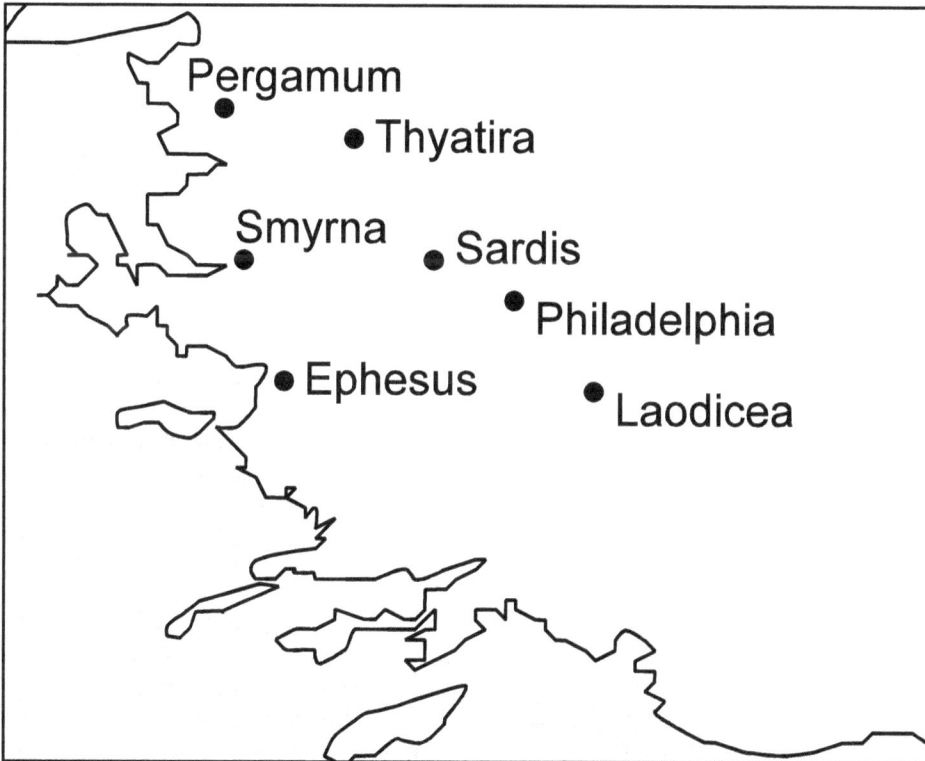

Finally, it should be noted that certain chiastic parallels can be drawn between the events and descriptions of Jesus in Revelation 1 with the message and description of Jesus as He is seen in chapters 2-3. The descriptions are repeated in a corresponding pattern that provides a distinct parallel.

From Jesus Christ, the **faithful witness**, the first-born of the dead (1:5).

...the ruler of the kings of the earth. To Him who loves us, and released us from our sins by His blood (1:5).

And having turned I saw seven golden lampstands; 13 and in the middle of the lampstands one like a son of man (1:12-13).

His **eyes** were **like a flame of fire**; 15 and His **feet** *were* like **burnished bronze** (1:14-15).

Out of His mouth came a **sharp two-edged sword** (1:16).

And He laid His right hand upon me, saying, "Do not be afraid; I am the **first and the last**, and the living One; and I **was dead**, and behold, I am alive forevermore, and I have the keys of death and of Hades." (1:17-18).

The seven stars are the angels of the seven churches, and the seven lampstands are the seven churches (1:20).

The One who holds the seven stars in His right hand, the One who walks among the seven golden lampstands(2:1).

The **first and the last**, who **was dead**, and has come to life (2:8).

The One who has the **sharp two-edged sword** (2:12).

The Son of God, who has **eyes like a flame of fire**, and His **feet** are like **burnished bronze** (2:18)

He who has the seven Spirits of God, and the seven stars (3:1).

He who is holy, who is true, who has the key of David, who opens and no one will shut, and who shuts and no one opens (3:7).

The Amen, the **faithful** and true **Witness**, the Beginning of the creation of God (3:14).

It can be seen from this chart that there is to be found a great deal of symbolism, both here as well as in the rest of the book of Revelation. It will be confusing until we realize there are four different ways in which such symbolism is presented.

- First, there is the symbolism that needs no interpretation because it is so obvious. This was the case in chapter 1 with the one who is like a Son of

43

man. It is obvious to the reader that he is none other than Jesus Christ.

- Second, there is the symbolism that is more difficult to understand and so the interpretation is given in the immediate context of the passage. That is the case in Revelation 1:20 where the stars and the lampstands are identified as the angels to the seven church and the seven churches themselves.

- A third group belong to those symbols that are taken from the other Scriptures. You will remember that John had been born and raised as a Jew. He had grown up knowing the Old Testament Scriptures. It is natural that he should recognize the symbolism that had been taken from the Old Testament and assume that his readers were also familiar with those same symbols. For example, when we arrive at Revelation 11:1-3, John will identify the two witnesses as "the two olive trees and the two lampstands that stand before the Lord of earth" (Revelation 11:3). He expects this reference to be enough to identify the two witnesses because he expects his readers to be familiar with the Old Testament prophecy of Zechariah 4:3-14.

- The final group of symbols are those that are not explained anywhere else in the Bible. Sometimes these can be understood if we can become familiar with the culture and the idioms of the first century.

There is one danger of which we must always be aware. We must always avoid the temptation of trying to read a meaning into every part and every portion of each symbol. For example, there was a song published by a Christian music group a number of years ago entitled, *The Champion*. It described a boxing match between Satan and Christ. In vivid detail, it described God as the referee, giving His instructions to the two antagonists and then beginning the conflict. Finally, Satan throws a devastating blow that hurls the Champion to the mat. The referee comes to count Him out, only to have Him rise in victory. The symbolism is obvious. Jesus is the Champion and His conflict with Satan is the spiritual battle between the forces of evil and the forces of righteousness. The knock down blow is the crucifixion and His rising is the resurrection.

Now, if you stopped the song and asked, "But what do the ring ropes represent?" you would be missing the main point of the analogy. The ring ropes do not represent anything. They are only there to support the main point of the analogy.

The book of Revelation is like that. Sometimes there will be things described that are meant only to support the main point of the symbolism. We do not need to pick apart every point. What we do need is to see the big idea. The big idea of the book of Revelation is Jesus and we need to see that He will ultimately win.

EPHESUS: LETTER TO THE LOVELESS CHURCH
Revelation 2:1-7

Ephesus was the most important seaport in all of Asia Minor. That has long since changed. I have had the opportunity to visit the site of Ephesus on several occasions. Where once there was a great, thriving harbor, today there are only deserted ruins and a swampy, mud-silted plain.

In the first century, the harbor at Ephesus made it a prime location for the prosperous seaport. The city was located on the banks of the Cayster River, three miles from the coast. A large harbor had been dredged from a wide bend in the river so that ships could sail up the river and right into the city to unload their load of cargo. Rich merchandise from all over the ancient world passed daily over the Ephesian docks.

Theater at Ephesus

Ephesus was at the hub of the major highway network of Asia Minor. As a result, the city was known as "the Market of Asia." The city sprawled across two hills that captured the sea breeze and created a wind tunnel effect that drove out the mosquitoes that would normally inhabit the plains around the area. Perhaps due to this feature and because of its central location in the province, they city had become one of the seats of political power and the Roman governor of the province resided here.

Ephesus was also a religious center. The city was considered to be the home of the mother goddess Diana, Artemis to the Greeks, the goddess of sex and fertility. A great temple to Diana was considered one of the wonders of the ancient world and was said to be four times the size of the Parthenon in Athens. Religion was big business in Ephesus.

> Nothing today remains of the once famous Temple to Artemis save a couple of isolated columns and some rubble.

Amulets, charms, and idols were sold in the agora and the city swarmed with fortune-tellers and soothsayers.

The message of the gospel was first preached in Ephesus by a Jewish convert named Apollos. His story is told in the book of Acts.

> *Now a certain Jew named Apollos, an Alexandrian by birth, an eloquent man, came to Ephesus; and he was mighty in the Scriptures.*
> *25 This man had been instructed in the way of the Lord; and being fervent in spirit, he was speaking and teaching accurately the things concerning Jesus, being acquainted only with the baptism of John; 26 and he began to speak out boldly in the synagogue. But when Priscilla and Aquila heard him, they took him aside and explained to him the way of God more accurately. (Acts 18:24-26).*

Statue of Artemis, Ephesus Museum

Apollos had heard the preaching of John the Baptist. He had heard the message that the Messiah was coming and would bring His kingdom. Apollos believed the message of John and he became a disciple of the Baptist. Now he was in Ephesus, preaching this message to the Jewish community which made up a considerable part of the city.

Also in the city were two other Jews named Priscilla and Aquila. They were associates of the Apostle Paul. They had met Paul in Corinth, but then they moved on to Ephesus. They heard Apollos preaching in the synagogue and they took him aside and shared with him how the One of whom John the Baptist proclaimed was Jesus of Nazareth who had died and had risen from the dead.

It was some time after this that Paul came to Ephesus and met several men who, like Apollos, had only heard of the preaching of John the Baptist. Indeed, these may have been some of the earlier converts of Apollos. Paul shared the gospel with them and they also believed.

46

For the next two years, Paul stayed at Ephesus, preaching and teaching daily in the philosophy school of Tyrannus. The effect of this ministry was dynamic. New converts had a great idol-burning party that threatened to overturn the economy of the metal workers guild (Acts 19:24-28).

As we come to the book of Revelation, many years have passed. Paul has written an epistle to the Ephesians, encouraging them to grow in their faith. The doctrinal foundation he laid is still to be seen in that church as a second epistle is now addressed to them. This one is addressed by Jesus.

OPENING SALUTATION

> *To the angel of the church in Ephesus write: The One who holds the seven stars in His right hand, the One who walks among the seven golden lampstands, says this (Revelation 2:1).*

The salutation contains a vivid description of Jesus. He is pictured in two ways. He is the one who...

> • *Holds the seven stars in His right hand.*
> • *Walks among the seven golden lampstands.*

What do these represent? What are the seven stars? What are these seven golden lampstands? The meaning has already been explained in the previous chapter.

> *As for the mystery of the seven stars which you saw in My right hand, and the seven golden lampstands: the seven stars are the angels of the seven churches, and the seven lampstands are the seven churches (Revelation 1:20).*

We do not have to guess at the meaning of these symbols. The meaning has already been given. They are explained in the context. This is frequently the case in the book of Revelation. This is a book that contains a great deal of symbolism, but more often than not, the symbolism is explained. We merely have to look for that explanation.

- The seven stars represent the angels of the seven churches.
- The seven lampstands stand for the seven churches to whom these messages are addressed.

There is a message here. Notice where Jesus is seen. He is standing among the lampstands. He has not gone off and forgotten about His churches. He is personally involved with all of their problems.

This is important for us to know. It is important because sometimes we forget that Jesus is in the midst of His churches. We get to thinking that Jesus was only interested in what happened a long time ago and that He has lost track of things. That is not the case. Jesus is still standing in the midst of the lampstands.

THE LORD KNOWS YOUR DEEDS

> *I know your deeds and your toil and perseverance, and that you cannot tolerate evil men, and you put to the test those who call themselves apostles, and they are not, and you found them to be false; 3 and you have perseverance and have endured for My name's sake, and have not grown weary. (Revelation 2:2-3).*

Jesus has some good things to say about this church. If we look at these qualities, we can agree that they are positive. This church had a good track record. There was a lot to commend this church.

- Their toil.
- Their perseverance.
- They did not endure evil men.
- They put false teachers to the test.
- They had endured testing.

There is much here to be commended. They are praised for their intolerance of evil living and evil teaching. This was a doctrinal church. It was a church that knew its doctrine. It was also an active church. They did not view Christianity as a spectator sport. Too many people think of Christianity in the same way they think of a football game — twenty two men who desperately need rest being watched by seventy thousand people who desperately need exercise. Ephesus was not like this. They were a church of workers. They were the kind of church in which most ministers would give their right arm to serve. But there was still a problem. It was a problem that struck at the very heart of the church. It was a problem of love.

AN ABANDONED LOVE

> *4 But I have this against you, that you have left your first love. 5 Therefore remember from where you have fallen, and repent and do the deeds you did at first; or else I am coming to you and will remove your lampstand out of its place unless you repent. (Revelation 2:4-5).*

48

This reference to an abandoned love is given as the very center point of the entire message to the Ephesian church. This is seen in its placement in the passage. The entire passage of Revelation 2:1-7 is given in the form of a chiasm. A chiasm is a form of parallelism that offers parallel thoughts and expressions. When there are a number of different points in a chiasm, our attention is intentionally directed toward the center. We can chart out the flow of thought as follows:

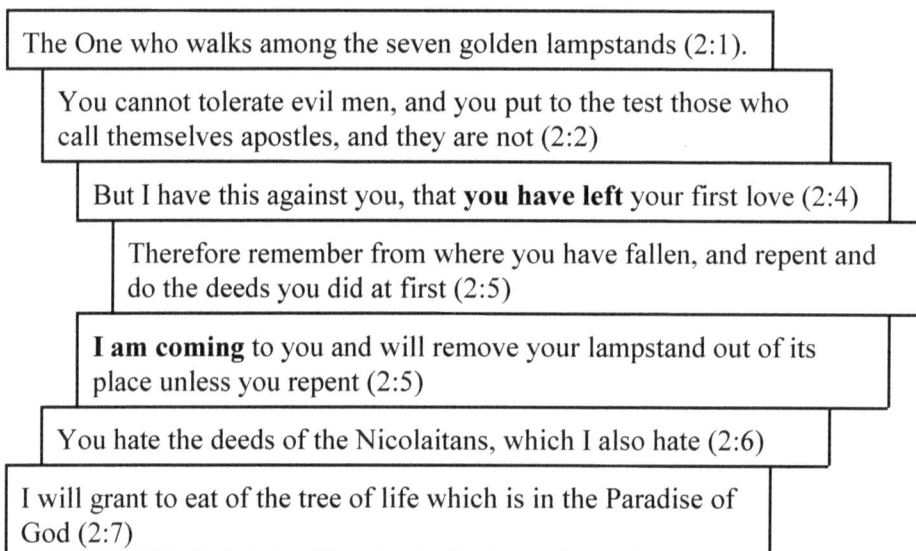

The One who walks among the seven golden lampstands (2:1).

You cannot tolerate evil men, and you put to the test those who call themselves apostles, and they are not (2:2)

But I have this against you, that **you have left** your first love (2:4)

Therefore remember from where you have fallen, and repent and do the deeds you did at first (2:5)

I am coming to you and will remove your lampstand out of its place unless you repent (2:5)

You hate the deeds of the Nicolaitans, which I also hate (2:6)

I will grant to eat of the tree of life which is in the Paradise of God (2:7)

Do you remember the first time you ever fell in love? It was a time of intensity. It was possibly a time of innocence. You wanted to spend every possible moment with that one who was the object of your love. Everything was fresh and exciting. But then time passed and perhaps that first love faded.

Why? What causes this problem? How do we get so wrapped up in the daily affairs of life that we lose our first love? It was not as if these believers had never loved Christ in the first place. A number of years earlier Paul had commended them for their reputation for love when he said that he had heard of their love for their love for all the saints (Ephesians 1:15).

I think that the problem at Ephesus was that the people began to focus on the teachings about Jesus rather than on the person of Jesus Himself. They began to focus on theology instead of the person behind the theology.

Love can grow cold if it is not carefully tended. Keeping your first love involves keeping your focus centered on the object of your love. How do you return to a love that has grown cold? Jesus gives the answer. This is the cure for a lost love. It is given in three parts.

1.   Remember where you were.

Remembering is important. The Sabbath day was given for this reason. It was to be a time of remembrance of the works of God and of the love of God. This is also the point of the Lord's Supper. It is to be a time of remembrance. If you are a Christian, then you need to remember where you used to be. Do you remember that time of love? Do you remember that intensity?

Repentance from past sins led you to a new joy of living to serve Christ and to know Him. You could not get enough of God's word. You wanted to be with other believers. You talked about the Lord all the time.

2.   Repent.

Remembrance of where you were will lead to a desire to turn around and to return to where you ought to be. This is called repentance. It is a change of mind and of heart and it leads to a change of actions. That brings us to our third point.

3.   Do the Deeds you did at first.

Notice this emphasis on your deeds. True love always brings with it a corresponding action. Love acts. At this point, you might be thinking to yourself, "But I don't feel the way I used to." That is okay. Jesus doesn't say to work up a feeling. He says to do the deeds that you once did. If your body gets involved, your feelings will eventually follow.

How do you regain lost love? You remember what it was like in the first place and then you go and you repent of the lost love and then you act as though that lost love was not lost. When you do that, the love starts. By the way, the same is true of faith. When you are having trouble believing, go to Him and repent of your lack of faith and then act as though that faith were there and then you will find that the faith starts.

At this point there is a warning. It is a warning of not returning to your first love. Failure to remember and repent and return to the former deeds will bring about a result.

> *Therefore remember from where you have fallen, and repent and do the deeds you did at first; or else I am coming to you and will remove your lampstand out of its place unless you repent. (Revelation 2:5).*

This is a warning of coming judgment. Jesus says, "Repent or else." Remember that there were seven lampstands in John's vision. Those seven lampstands represented seven churches. Jesus is saying, "Change your ways or else I might be left with six lampstands."

This brings us to a question. What is the nature of this threatened judgment? Jesus says that He will remove their lampstand out of its place. What does this mean? Does it mean that these people will lose their salvation? I don't believe so. Rather, let me suggest that this refers to a removal of the local church to whom this is addressed. If there is not a change, then before long this church will fall apart. It takes more than solid doctrine to keep a church together. It takes a living relationship with its Lord. There is no substitute for this.

My wife and I had the opportunity to visit the site of Ephesus on two separate occasions. There is no church there. The harbor has dried up and in its place is a swamp. The once crowded streets and marketplaces and theaters are only a remembrance of what they were. The city is in ruins. It stands as a mute testimony of the danger of a church that has lost its first love. The dried up harbor is a picture of the dried up love of the church. That which was once close and fresh and life-giving is now removed and absent.

THE NICOLAITANS

> *Yet this you do have, that you hate the deeds of the Nicolaitans, which I also hate. (Revelation 2:6).*

We are not told much about the Nicolaitans. They are not mentioned in any other book of the Bible. The two apostolic fathers, Irenaeus and Clement, each said that this group was originally made up of followers of Nicolaus, one of the first seven deacons of the church at Jerusalem (Acts 6:5). A number of his followers, misunderstanding his teachings, took the message of salvation by grace to mean that you can go and live as you please. They went and began to live a life of sin in the name of the grace of God.

That reminds me of a little girl who lived in our neighborhood many years ago. I was sharing the gospel with her and I tried to explain to her how our sin separates us from God and how Jesus came to die in our place and to take our sin away and to give us eternal life. I then asked her if she knew what she had to do to enter into that eternal life. She thought for a long moment and then replied, "Sin a lot!" She was wrong and the followers of Nicolaus were wrong. The Christian life is not to be a life that is filled with sin. That is a misuse of the doctrine of grace. Grace does not mean that we are now free to go out and sin a lot. It means that God has delivered us from sin so that we can be pure and holy and clean and set apart for His use.

51

THE PROMISE

> *He who has an ear, let him hear what the Spirit says to the*
> *churches. To him who overcomes, I will grant to eat of the tree of*
> *life which is in the Paradise of God. (Revelation 2:7).*

Jesus is going to end each message to each of these seven churches with a promise. In each case, it is a conditional promise. In each case, the promise is only offered to the one who overcomes. What does it mean to overcome? How can you overcome?

You first need to realize that Jesus is the overcomer. John pointed this out in his account of the life and ministry of Jesus. Jesus Himself taught that He had overcome the world.

> *"These things I have spoken to you, that in Me you may*
> *have peace. In the world you have tribulation, but take courage;*
> *I have overcome the world" (John 16:33).*

We are to find peace in the fact that Jesus has overcome the world. But that is not all. John also goes on to say that you can be an overcomer. He tells us this in his first epistle.

> *For whatever is born of God overcomes the world; and*
> *this is the victory that has overcome the world-- our faith. 5 And*
> *who is the one who overcomes the world, but he who believes that*
> *Jesus is the Son of God? (1 John 5:4-5).*

We can overcome the world when we come and place our faith in the One who has already overcome the world — Jesus Christ. This world is going to be difficult. There are rough times ahead. If you don't believe me, then look ahead a few chapters in the book of Revelation. You are going to experience problems. Some will be big and some will be little, although even these will seem big at the time. If you live on planet earth for any length of time, then something bad is going to come into your life.

Perhaps you've heard of Murphy's Law. It says that anything that can go wrong will go wrong. Then there is Petrov's Law. It says that Murphy was an optimist. While I do not endorse either of these two laws, I do have to point out that you will encounter various trials. That is the nature of life. Jesus promised that "in the world you have tribulation" (John 16:33).

How many times have you heard some well-meaning preacher say that once you become a Christian all of your troubles will end and life will become wonderful and peaceful? Our churches suffer from such a message. They are filled with people who are smiling on the outside, but who are hurting on the inside. Each one hides behind his own smiling mask, thinking that he is the only one who doesn't have it all together, each one afraid that the others might learn that he alone is not experiencing victory in Christ.

Let me dispel such ideas with an official announcement. You are in for hard times. You are going to encounter various trials. Bad times are coming. I haven't said this to discourage you. I am not trying to turn you into a pessimist or to fill your day with gloom and doom. The reason I want you too be aware that bad times are coming is so that you will get ready to meet them.

I spent nearly thirty years as a career fire fighter. It was a challenging career as I rose to the rank of Battalion Chief. In the fire service, we put together preplans of hazardous areas so that we would know how to handle any emergencies that might arise in those areas. In the same manner, God provides a preplan for Christians. It gives us instructions on how to get past the hazardous conditions ahead. It is called the Bible. What are you to do when hard times come? How do you meet problem situations? What do you do when disaster strikes? God has provided a means to deal with those coming difficulties.

Be an overcomer. Take the promises that God has given to you and apply them to your life. Begin depending upon Him for all things. Instead of being overcome by your problems, overcome those problems by trusting in the Lord.

Christ has already overcome the biggest problem. He has overcome death. If you come to Him in faith, then you will *eat of the tree of life which is in the Paradise of God*. Eternal life is a free gift for all who will trust in Him. Come to Him today. Be an overcomer.

SMYRNA: LETTER TO THE PERSECUTED CHURCH
Revelation 2:8-11

As you travel north from Ephesus, the first city to which you come is the modern city of Izmir. The pronunciation of that name was somewhat different in the first century. They called the city Smyrna. The meaning of the name continues to be debated even today, for its roots go back as far as the old Hittite language and perhaps even earlier. It may be related to the Greek word for "myrrh," the expensive ointment that was used in the burial of the wealthy. If so, then it is a fitting designation for the recipients of this short epistle.

The city of Smyrna was situated on the western coast of Asia Minor where the Hermus River flowed into the Aegean Sea. It had an inner harbor with a relatively narrow entrance that could be blocked off with a great chain. Rising over the city stood Mount Pagus, the traditional acropolis that was the spiritual center for every Greek city. The main street of the city was known as the "Street of Gold."

Like many of the cities in the area, this was a cosmopolitan smelting pot of different cultures. The city had roots in the ancient Hittite civilization of the past and legend had it that it was the birthplace of Homer. More recently, it had been rebuilt in the days of Alexander the Great and so had a heavy Greek influence. Rome had since

A street in modern Izmir

laid claim to the city and exerted a certain amount of influence so that, alongside the idols to Aphrodite and Zeus and Apollo, there were also idols to Roma and to Tiberius.

Smyrna had a long history of loyalty to Rome. The city had sided with Rome in the wars against the Seleucids and later against Mithradates. The citizens of the city had received permission in 26 A.D. to build a temple to the worship of Tiberius, the Roman emperor. The city would eventually become a center for the Caesar-cult. This would ultimately lead to a series of intense persecutions.

These persecutions would come from the Greeks and the Romans, but they would also come from another source. They would also come from the Jewish synagogue that was present in the city.

PERSECUTIONS ARE PROMISED

The Bible teaches that the Christian life will be one of general tribulation. Jesus told His disciples this on several occasions.

> *"Then they will deliver you to tribulation, and will kill you, and you will be hated by all nations on account of My name."* *(Matthew 24:9).*

> *"In the world you have tribulation, but take courage; I have overcome the world" (John 16:33).*

Neither was this message exclusive to Jesus. Paul and Barnabas related the same message to the early church.

> *There they strengthened the souls of the disciples and encouraged them to continue in the faith, saying, "It is through many persecutions that we must enter the kingdom of God." (Acts 14:22).*

> *You also became imitators of us and of the Lord, having received the word in much tribulation with the joy of the Holy Spirit (1 Thessalonians 1:6).*

The apostle John describes himself as a *"fellow partaker in the tribulation and kingdom and perseverance which are in Jesus" (Revelation 1:9).* That is not to say that you are not a Christian if you are not being persecuted or that you should go out and look for ways to be persecuted. These sorts of persecution come at various times and there are persecutions against Christianity going on even today.

Jesus writes a letter to those who are in the midst of persecution. To make matters worse, He is going to tell them that these persecutions are going to increase. They are going to get worse before they get better.

This message will be given in the form of a chiasm – an inverse parallel. This sort of parallelism was especially common among the writings of the Jews. As such, they are especially prominent throughout the Old Testament. Such stylistic parallelism was a sort of poetry. In this case, it is a parallelism of suffering. Notice the repeating refrain:

The first and the last, who was **dead**, and has come to life (2:8)

says this... (2:8)

I know your **tribulation** and your poverty (2:9)

Those who say they are Jews and are not, but are a synagogue of Satan (2:9)

Do not fear what you are about to **suffer** (2:10)

The devil is about to cast some of you into prison, so that you will be tested (2:10)

You will have **tribulation** for ten days (2:10)

He who has an ear, let him hear what the Spirit says to the churches (2:11)

He who overcomes will not be hurt by the second **death** (2:11)

What comes through loud and clear are these repeated references to suffering and tribulation. This was a church that was going to be suffering persecution and it is a reminder to us that persecution has been a regular part of the Christian church throughout its history.

PERSECUTIONS DON'T AFFECT THE DEAD

> *And to the angel of the church in Smyrna write: The first and the last, who was dead, and has come to life, says this (Revelation 2:8-11).*

Notice who is the author of this short epistle. It is not John. To be sure, John is writing the message, but he is only acting as the part of a secretary. He is writing what Jesus tells him to write. These seven messages to the seven churches are seven letters from Jesus to His churches.

Each one of these seven letters begins with a vivid picture. It is a picture of Jesus. It describes Him in such a way as to relate to the problems and the needs of that particular church. This picture is especially significant. He is described as *the first and the last, who was dead, and has come to life.*

I believe it is entirely possible that there is a play on words here with the name of the city. The Greek word σμυρνα (*smurna*) is the word for myrrh. It is also the name of this city.

- Myrrh was an expensive ointment that was used in the burial rituals of the wealthy.
- Myrrh was offered to Jesus as a narcotic while he was on the cross (Mark 15:23).
- After Jesus had died, His lifeless body was wrapped in myrrh and other spices as it was buried (John 19:39).

Do you see the point? This same Jesus who was given myrrh as a narcotic to a dying man, whose lifeless body was wrapped in myrrh, has risen from the grave and is writing to the residents of Smyrna (Σμυρνα). They are a people who once were spiritually dead and who have been made alive and have now entered a new realm of existence.

That is not all. These believers are being persecuted for their faith. They are losing their jobs because they refuse to participate in the pagan rituals that are associated with their trades. They are being arrested and they are under the threat of death. Polycarp, one of the elders of the church and a disciple of the Apostle John, will be burnt at the stake for being a Christian. They need to know that their Lord is the One who was dead and who is now alive and who has conquered death.

Are you going through hard times? Does it feel as though you have been forgotten? Do you wonder if your prayers are getting lost in the shuffle? Jesus has not forgotten you. He knows of your troubles.

This book of Revelation is going to present some great times of trouble and tribulation. Some of these tribulations took place in the past, but I believe there are similar trials going on even today. What you need to know is that Jesus wins. He is in control of the final outcome. He never makes a tunnel without a light at the end of it.

PERSECUTIONS HAVE THEIR OWN RICHES

> *I know your tribulation and your poverty (but you are rich)... (Revelation 2:9).*

When Jesus addresses himself to the church at Laodicea, He is going to point out that they think they are rich, but that they are really *wretched and miserable and poor and blind and naked* (3:17). The church at Smyrna had just the opposite situation. They were a church that, to the outward eye, appeared to be very poor, but in reality they had heavenly riches.

Who do you think of as the "power brokers" in the church and in Christianity today? I think that when the final judgment takes place, we might be very surprised to find who the Lord considers to be spiritually rich. It will likely be someone of whom we have never even heard.

PERSECUTORS ARE OFTEN RELIGIOUS

> *I know your tribulation and your poverty (but you are rich), and the blasphemy by those who say they are Jews and are not, but are a synagogue of Satan. (Revelation 2:9).*

Like many cities in that part of the world, the city of Smyrna had a sizeable Jewish population. These Jews took great pride in their Jewish heritage. They held to the Law and they got angry at anyone who took another view. They had rejected the teaching that Jesus was the Messiah and they instituted heavy persecutions against all those who preached the gospel. It is for this reason Jesus calls their meeting place "the synagogue of Satan." They were doing the work of Satan from the confines of their synagogue.

These Jews had come to terms with the idolatry that went on within their city. We do not read of them persecuting the Gentile pagans who indulged in idol worship and other pagan practices. They had, instead, a special hatred for those who had come to Christ.

Things have not changed much. You can tell the average Jewish person that you are an atheist and he will not be offended. He might even agree with you. But if you tell him that you are a Christian and that you have trusted in Jesus as the promised Messiah, then you will probably see the kind of reaction that is described here.

Notice that Jesus says these people *say they are Jews and are not, but are a synagogue of Satan*. This is not a denial of their race, but rather a denial of their spiritual heritage. They have rejected the Messiah of whom their prophets foretold and, in doing so, they have turned away from the God of Abraham to become a synagogue of Satan. They have lost the right to be known as Jews.

> *For he is not a Jew who is one outwardly; neither is circumcision that which is outward in the flesh. 29 But he is a Jew who is one inwardly; and circumcision is that which is of the heart, by the Spirit, not by the letter; and his praise is not from men, but from God. (Romans 2:28-29).*

Who possesses the promises of God today? Who are the spiritual seed of Abraham today? Who are the chosen people of God today? Who is God's holy nation today? Who is the royal priesthood of God today? The answer to all of these questions is the same – it is the church. God has set aside unfaithful Israel who rejected Him and has grafted in a new people made up of every nation and tribe and tongue.

> *But if some of the branches were broken off, and you, being a wild olive, were grafted in among them and became partaker with them of the rich root of the olive tree, 18 do not be arrogant toward the branches; but if you are arrogant, remember that it is not you who supports the root, but the root supports you. (Romans 11:17-18).*

Notice that there is a warning given here. The warning is that we should not become arrogant toward the Jewish people or take up a mantle of anti-Semitism. Rather, we ought to appreciate that cultural heritage that has brought the gospel to us. There is also a warning here that we do not become complacent in our attitude toward the truth.

> *Quite right, they were broken off for their unbelief, but you stand by your faith. Do not be conceited, but fear; 21 for if God did not spare the natural branches, neither will He spare you. 22 Behold then the kindness and severity of God; to those who fell, severity, but to you, God's kindness, if you continue in His kindness; otherwise you also will be cut off. (Romans 11:20-22).*

Do you see the warning? It is that you who have received the promises of God and who have become the spiritual seed of Abraham and God's chosen people and His holy nation and His royal priesthood can also be cut off and cast off if you do not approach God by faith. Being a member of a Christian church has no more power to save you than does being a physical descendant of Abraham.

This is important. We must teach our children that they do not become God's people just because they have been born into a Christian family. Our relationship with God is founded upon the same thing as was Israel's relationship with God – faith.

PERSECUTIONS ARE TEMPORARY

> *Do not fear what you are about to suffer. Behold, the devil is about to cast some of you into prison, so that you will be tested, and you will have tribulation for ten days... (Revelation 2:10).*

The believers at Smyrna were going through some hard times. It was not over yet. In fact, it had just begun. There were several reasons for this persecution.

- They were persecuted because their faith was militant. They were adamant about sharing their faith with others. They had a heart for mission. There is a lesson here. It is that Satan doesn't usually bother to persecute complacent Christians. They are already doing exactly what he wants them to do. Have you been persecuted lately? Has anyone mocked you because of your faith? If not, then perhaps it is because Satan does not see you as a threat.

- They were persecuted because they were absolutely and exclusively loyal to Jesus Christ. They would not share that level of loyalty with Caesar. This was especially striking in the city of Smyrna which was a host to the emperor-cult. There was a temple to Roma and another temple to Caesar. The Christians refused to be involved in this sort of worship. Because of this, they were considered to be unfaithful to Rome.

- They were persecuted because of their "atheism." Because they did not worship a visible image, it was thought that they did not worship any god at all and so they were termed "atheists" which means "no God."

- They were persecuted because they were thought to be cannibals. It was rumored that they ate the body and drank the blood of someone at their secret meetings. This misunderstanding of the Lord's supper led some to accuse them of cannibalism.

The bad news is that they would suffer persecution. The good news is that this persecution would only be temporary. It would be limited to "ten days" in duration. This reference to "ten days" is an example of a symbol that is not explained in the context. Does it refer to a literal ten days? Although this is possible, I do not think that it is the case. For one thing, we know from history that the persecutions at Smyrna lasted longer than ten days. One theory has been put forth that suggests these refer to ten different persecutions under ten of the Emperors of Rome.

- Nero (A.D. 64-68).
- Domitian (A.D. 90-95).
- Trajan (A.D. 104-117).
- Marcus Aurelius (A.D. 161-180).
- Serevus (A.D. 200-211).
- Maximus (A.D. 235-237).
- Decius (A.D. 250-253).
- Valerian (A.D. 257-260).
- Aurelian (A.D. 270-275).
- Diocletian (A.D. 303-312).

I think that a more likely interpretation is that these "ten days" describe a relatively short period of time during which the church at Smyrna would undergo persecution. They are like the ten plagues in the Old Testament except that these come against the people of God.

Is this kind of interpretation consistent with the Bible? I believe that it is. For example, in Psalm 50:10 we read that the Lord owns the cattle on a thousand hills. We cannot take this to mean that He does not own 1,001 cattle. Rather, we recognize this to be a figure of speech to describe a large number.

In the same way, this passage is letting the Christians of Smyrna know that, while tribulation is coming, it will not endure. This is a message of hope, telling them that they can weather the storm.

PERSECUTIONS CALL FOR FAITHFULNESS

> *Do not fear what you are about to suffer. Behold, the devil is about to cast some of you into prison, so that you will be tested, and you will have tribulation for ten days. Be faithful until death, and I will give you the crown of life. (Revelation 2:10).*

We have a letter that was written by believers at Smyrna in A.D. 156 that relates the account of the martyr of its elder and overseer, the aged Polycarp. The account tells of the arrest of the aged disciple and how he invited the arresting soldiers to sit and eat with him while he spent his last hour in prayer.

He was then taken into the stadium of Smyrna to stand before the proconsul. Although it was the Sabbath day, the Jewish community combined with the rest of the city, not only to view the spectacle, but even to do the work of dragging the wood into place so that he could be burned at the stake.

> *And at length, when he was brought up, there was a great tumult, for they heard that Polycarp had been apprehended.*
> *When then he was brought before him, the proconsul enquired whether he were the man. And on his confessing that he was, he tried to persuade him to a denial saying, "Have respect to thine age," and other things in accordance therewith, as it is their wont to say; "Swear by the genius of Caesar; repent and say, Away with the atheists." Then Polycarp with solemn countenance looked upon the whole multitude of lawless heathen that were in the stadium, and waved his hand to them; and groaning and looking up to heaven he said, "Away with the atheists." (Polycarp 9:1b-2).*

Polycarp refused to deny the faith and, when the proconsul offered to release him if he would only deny Christ, he replied...

> *"Fourscore and six years have I been His servant, and He*

hath done me no wrong. How then can I blaspheme my King who saved me?" (Polycarp 9:3).

When the crowd heard Polycarp's repeated and unrelenting confession of Jesus as the Christ, they were moved to anger.

> *When this was proclaimed by the herald, the whole multitude both of Gentiles and of Jews who dwelt in Smyrna cried out with ungovernable wrath and with a loud shout, "This is the teacher of Asia, the father of the Christians, the puller down of our gods, who teaches numbers not to sacrifice nor worship." (Polycarp 12:2).*

Polycarp was sentenced to be burned at the stake and was immediately led to a post around which heaps of wood and hay were quickly stacked. When the guards prepared to nail him to the stake, Polycarp replied:

> *"Leave me as I am; for He that hath granted me to endure the fire will grant me also to remain at the pile unmoved, even without the security which ye seek from the nails." (Polycarp 13:3).*

The elder of the church was tied to the stake and burned alive, becoming one of the many martyrs who died for the Christian faith. He showed by example what it means to be faithful unto death.

As John writes this message to the church of Smyrna, this persecution was already beginning to grow. It would soon burst forth in full flame.

PERSECUTED OVERCOMERS WILL ENDURE

> *He who has an ear, let him hear what the Spirit says to the churches. He who overcomes will not be hurt by the second death. (Revelation 2:11).*

I have an old friend named Bill Iverson who often tells people this simple riddle:

> Born once, die twice;
> Born twice, die once.

The riddle points to the fact that there are two deaths. There is the first death, that is, the one that is physical when your body is separated from your soul and spirit. But there is also a second death. This is the death that can really hurt you. This is the death that you need to fear.

The good news is that, if you have been born again through faith in Christ, then you will not be hurt by the second death. That is an enemy that has been defeated and you can experience the same conquest as you trust in Him.

PERGAMUM: HOLDING FAST TO HOLINESS
Revelation 2:12-17

I have already pointed out that there is a geographical order to the way in which these churches are presented. We can trace these on a map in the form of a wide oval as we began with Ephesus and then move north to Smyrna and then continue straight north to the capital city of Pergamum before turning inland to form the arc of this wide curving pattern.

On the wide, fertile valley through which the Caicus River flows on its way to the Mediterranean, there is a large, rocky hill that juts a thousand feet over the plain. In ancient times, this hill was chosen as the site for a military fort. It was given the name *Pergamos* which means "fort" (a *pergos* is a fort).

This city was now ancient and had become the official Roman capital of the province. Like Smyrna to the south, the emperor cult was practiced here. But it was not alone. Pergamum was also the center of a cult to Dionysus, the god of vegetation and fertility. He was also known by the name of Bacchus and, under that name, was the god of wine and drunkenness. The cultic practices of worship involved drunken orgies as the participant sought to become possessed by the god through wild dancing and the killing of animals and eating them. So decadent were these rites that Rome actually outlawed the Dionysus cult for a time, considering it to be too immoral even for their standards. Dionysus was thought to be the son of Zeus who died and rose again. There remains to this day a great altar to Zeus in modern Pergamum.

Ruins of Pergamos with the theater in the foreground and the temple to the emperor at the top of the acropolis

Another cult that was practiced in Pergamum was that of Asclepias, the servant god of healing. A medical university trained priests in the arts of healing. The symbol of the cult was a wooden staff with a snake coiled around it.

What does a Christian do who lives in a city like Pergamum? This is a city that was given over to pluralism, to false worship and to pleasure. How do you hold to Christianity in a city like that? Jesus gives the answer in verse 13: *I know where you dwell, where Satan's throne is; and **you hold fast** My name, and did not deny My faith, even in the days of Antipas, My witness, My faithful one, who was killed among you, where Satan dwells. (Revelation 2:13)*. That is your mission as a Christian. It is to hold fast...

- To God's name.
- To the faith.
- To holiness.

How do you do it? How do you hold fast to God in a city that is given over to the devil? I believe that Jesus gives the answer in these verses. The first point is that those who hold fast must have a knowledge of the Word.

A KNOWLEDGE OF THE WORD

> *And to the angel of the church in Pergamum write: The One who has the sharp two-edged sword says this (Revelation 2:12).*

This letter begins with a description of Jesus. It is a description that is taken from the glorious vision that John had in the first chapter of this book. He saw Jesus.

- Standing in the midst of golden lampstands.
- Clothed in a long robe.
- Wearing a golden breastplate
- His eyes flaming like fire
- And with a sharp two-edged sword.

As you first hear that description, you are inclined to imagine this holy warrior with a mighty sword in His right hand. But that isn't the way He is described. Revelation 1:16 doesn't say that the sword was in His hand. It is described instead as coming out of His mouth.

That gives us a clue as to the meaning of the symbol. This is a sword, and a sword is used to conquer, but it is not an excuse to go out and to beat people over the head. We are not talking about a visible, physical sword. This sword is symbolic. It represents the sword of the Gospel. It is a picture of the message of the cross. It is a picture of the message that tells you that God entered time and space to be born in a stable and to die on a cross. It represents the message that cuts through men's hearts and changes them from the inside out.

This is the sword of salvation. But it is still called a sword. Swords are cutting tools. They are designed to cut through things or through people. This reminds us of another sword that was seen at the very beginning of time. At the beginning of human history, the first man and the first woman were cast out of the Garden of Eden for eating of the forbidden fruit. They sinned and they were removed from the presence of God and from the tree of life. Something was placed in the Garden to keep them out. It was a mighty angel with a flaming sword. That was a sword to keep them out; this is a sword to bring them back in. This is a sword of salvation. It still cuts, but its cutting can be like the scalpel in the hand of the surgeon who cuts in order to bring life.

We are people of the word. The heavens were created by the word of the Lord. Throughout Genesis 1 we read the continuing refrain, *"And God said..."* followed by, *"And it was done."* There is power in the word. There is the power of judgment. There is also the power of salvation -- Romans 1:16 tells us the gospel *is the power of God for salvation to everyone who believes, to the Jew first and also to the Greek.* We are people of the word. We are people who believe in a propositional truth. We are people who have trusted in the sure and certain word of God.

Do you want to hold fast to Christ? If you do, then there are some things that you need to know about Christ.

- His death was sacrificial.
- His death was substitutionary.
- His death was triumphant.

When you believe the gospel, you come to the One who triumphantly gave Himself in your place as the final sacrifice for sins and you hold to Him in faith. If you have already believed in Him, then you stand fast in that faith. This brings us to our next point. Those who would hold fast need to make a life and death commitment.

A LIFE & DEATH COMMITMENT

> *I know where you dwell, where Satan's throne is; and you hold fast My name, and did not deny My faith, even in the days of Antipas, My witness, My faithful one, who was killed among you, where Satan dwells. (Revelation 2:13).*

Pergamum was not a nice place in which to live. The city was fulled with idolatry of every kind. Religious orgies and snake cults and emperor worship was found on every street corner. Jesus says that this was a place *where Satan's throne is.* In the midst of all of this stood the church. These were the people who had heard the gospel and who had repented and who had believed in Jesus Christ. They have been set apart by God. They have entered a new realm of living. They have been justified – declared righteous through the reckoning of Christ's righteousness. They have become citizens of heaven. There is only one problem. While they are citizens of heaven, they still have residency in Pergamum. They are holy people living in the midst of an unholy city.

Can you identify with this? If you are a Christian, then you are a holy person living in an unholy world. This speaks to where you are today. If you have a secular job, then you probably work with people who are unsaved. If you are a student in school, then you most likely sit in a classroom with people who do not believe in Jesus Christ. These people have a different outlook on life than you do. They view the world from a different perspective. They are not concerned with pleasing their Heavenly Father. They worship their own good. It is usually the deity of me. This false god goes under a variety of names. He is known as...

- "Me first"
- "My own way"
- "Looking out for number one"
- "What's in it for me?"

The world system sees nothing wrong with the worship of this kind of deity. In fact, they think you are just a little odd if your alliance is not directed in this way. The result is that the world seeks to persecute and destroy anyone who does not worship the way it does. That is what happened to Antipas. This is not the same Antipas described in the book of Acts. That Antipas was an enemy of Christians; this Antipas was a faithful witness of Christ.

Jesus calls Antipas, *"My witness, My faithful one, who was killed among you."* We do not know anything about this believer aside from what is given here. We are told only his name and that he was killed at Pergamum because of his faithful witness of Jesus Christ. Why was he killed? Because he was telling people about Christ in a world that is hostile to that message. You live in that same world. It may not be the city of Pergamum, but it is a part of that same world system. Does the world hate you? Do people hear your outlook on life and disagree" Are unbelievers antagonistic toward you because of the things you say about Jesus Christ? If they are not, then perhaps it is because you are not a faithful witness.

The Christian is involved in a spiritual war. The battle lines have been drawn and the conflict has begun. The forces of the enemy have made themselves known. Have you? Antipas was not afraid to choose sides. He did not try to straddle the fence. He committed himself and you are called to do the same. You will only be able to hold fast to the faith as you have made that sort of life commitment to Christ. For me to live is Christ; for me to die on His behalf is gain (Philippians 1:21).

Having such an attitude will help me to hold fast when I am tempted to compromise.

TEMPTATION TO COMPROMISE

> *But I have a few things against you, because you have there some who hold the teaching of Balaam, who kept teaching Balak to put a stumbling block before the sons of Israel, to eat things sacrificed to idols, and to commit acts of immorality. 15 Thus you also have some who in the same way hold the teaching of the Nicolaitans. (Revelation 2:14-15).*

This problem of compromise is exemplified in the reference to Balaam. You remember Balaam. He was a prophet who lived in the days of Moses. He was not a prophet of Israel. He was from Mesopotamia (modern Iraq). He was a traveling prophet for hire. He was in the profiteering business for the money he could make. He was called in by the foreign king Balak to pronounce a curse on the Israelites.

Balak was the king of Moab. He was sitting in his kingdom one day when he heard the news that a group of people had left Egypt and were now living in the Sinai Wilderness. Several neighboring kings had tried to wipe them out, but all had failed. It was rumored that these Israelites had a God that was stronger than any of the local deities. Balak called in professional help. The best prophet in the business was Balaam. Balaam was hired to come down and to place a curse on these Israelites.

Do you remember the movie, *Liar, Liar*? It is a cute story of a little boy who makes a birthday wish that his father, a lying lawyer, will always tell the truth. The wish comes true and the rest of the movie is an outrageous comedy in which, every time this lawyer opens his mouth, the truth comes out. Balaam must have felt the same way. He was hired by the king of Moab to come and to prophesy against Israel. But God met him on the way and gave him some instructions that could not be avoided. Balaam was forced to tell the truth. He was forced to pronounce the truth of God and a blessing upon God's people.

That is not the end of the Balaam story. Balaam came up with another way to attack the people of God. He advised the enemy king, "If you can't beat them, then join them." He instituted "operation compromise." He reasoned, if we cannot defeat the people of God because God is on their side, then we will defeat them by getting them to sin and by getting them to abandon God. He advised Balak to have his people mix socially with the Israelites and to get them to compromise their standards.

This is the teaching of Balaam. It is the attack of compromise. It is the mixing of the people of God with the people of the world so that the righteous standards of the people of God are lowered. This is one of the dangers of living in an immoral society. You begin to see the low moral standards of those around you and you gradually begin to lower your own standards to match.

This is what was happening in Pergamum. The Christians did not deny their faith, but they began to compromise some of their moral standards. They said to themselves, "We won't be as bad as the pagans, but we don't have to be fanatical about our Christianity." And so, they went to church on Sunday and they proclaimed the gospel, but their lives resembled that of their world throughout the rest of the week.

It is a danger that you face. You are in the midst of a spiritual battle. But most of you are not suffering outright persecution. There is no one who is trying to kill you for your faith. Instead, the attack you are facing is the same one that Balaam brought against the Israelites. It is the attack of compromise. What is the answer? How can a Christian live in a sinful world and not be affected by it? There are several principles that can help.

1.   The Principle of Prior Choice.

        Compromise is often the result of a lack of commitment. That is why we stressed that those who would hold fast to their faith must make a life and death commitment. If you do not have a plan of commitment to follow, then you will probably not be aware that you are off the right track.

2.   The Principle of Confidence.

        You don't need to apologize for being a Christian and for not adopting the world's standards. Stand tall! You are a member of a special people. You are a royal priest in the priesthood of the God of the universe. You are an heir to the kingdom. Now act like it.

3.   The Principle of Conviction.

        You cannot allow your standards to be based upon your feelings. Your feeling will change from day to day. Your feelings are subject to peer pressure. It is therefore important that you hold to a conviction that is stronger than your feelings.

        When she was a little girl, we used to hear upon occasion the words from our daughter that all parents hear from their children at one time or another: "But all the other kids are doing it!" My reply was to say, "I am not the father of all the other kids. I am your father and this household will live up to a certain standard of behavior." Our Heavenly Father says the same thing. He sets the standard and it is a standard that is worthy of our faith and our obedience. Does that mean that you never doubt or waver? Does it mean you never fear? No. But it does mean that you determine not to doubt in the darkness what you learned in the light.

4.   The Principle of Accommodation.

When you give into a little sin, it is easier the next time. Remember the lesson of Lot? Lot began by moving down into the plain of Sodom and Gomorrah. Soon he had moved into the city and his daughters had intermarried with the pagans. He lost his influence with his family and the result was disaster upon disaster.

The principle of accommodation says that each time you say, "Yes" to sin, it becomes easier the next time. You go to the Lord and ask Him to break those bonds of sin and then you determine not to make an accommodation for sin.

5.   The Principle of Accountability.

The people to whom you tie yourself in friendship will affect you. This is a principle of nature which means it is a principle that God has built into the very fabric of the universe. People will either pull you up or else they will drag you down. The most valuable possessions you can have are godly friends. Make yourself accountable to one or two or three other Christians who know of your weaknesses and who have permission to reprove you when you need it.

A CALL TO REPENT

> *Repent therefore; or else I am coming to you quickly, and I will make war against them with the sword of My mouth.(Revelation 2:16).*

We already talked about the sword going out of the mouth of Jesus and how it is a picture of the gospel. But there is a warning here that the word going out of His mouth is also a word of judgment. You will either embrace the sword of the gospel or else you will be judged by the sword of judgment. To what are you holding fast?

Because Pergamum was the seat of the local Proconsul, it was thereby the home of the one who "held the sword." That is, the governor here had the power of life and death over the people of the land. Jesus attributes this power to Himself. He is the One who truly "holds the sword." He has the power of real life -- eternal life.

70

Fire fighters are sometimes called in for the mundane and the ordinary. It was such a call that took them to a home where a little boy had his hand stuck in a narrow bronze vase. The little boy was in no pain and the vase was somewhat expensive, so they were reluctant to break it. They tried twisting it and turning it and lubricating it, all to no avail. Finally, the little boy asked, "Would it help if I dropped the penny which I am holding?

Our problem is that we hold fast to the wrong thing. Does that describe you? Is there a penny in your hand that is stopping you from holding fast to Jesus? I have a word for you from the Lord. Repent... or else.

RESULTS OF HOLDING FAST

> *He who has an ear, let him hear what the Spirit says to the churches. To him who overcomes, to him I will give some of the hidden manna, and I will give him a white stone, and a new name written on the stone which no one knows but he who receives it. (Revelation 2:17).*

Jesus ends this short letter to the church at Pergamum with a promise. In case you hadn't noticed, that is the way He closes each of these seven letters to the seven churches. In each case, it is a conditional promise. In each case, the promise is offered to *him who overcomes*. We have already noted the truth that Jesus is our overcomer and that we overcome by trusting in Him.

> *For whatever is born of God overcomes the world; and this is the victory that has overcome the world-- our faith. 5 And who is the one who overcomes the world, but he who believes that Jesus is the Son of God? (1 John 5:4-5).*

You can be an overcomer, not by anything you are able to do, but simply by coming to the cross in faith and entrusting yourself to the One who has overcome in your place. Notice what is the result of this overcoming.

1.   The Hidden Manna: *To him who overcomes, to him I will give some of the hidden manna (2:17).*

        Manna was the miraculous food that God gave to the Israelites while they were in the wilderness. Each morning, they would walk out of their tents and find this food laying on the ground. It was free to all who wished to pick it up and eat of it.

        Jesus said that He is the bread of life. The life that He offers is free to all who will come to Him and partake of Him. If you will believe in the One who overcame, then you will also be an overcomer and will have that bread of eternal life.

The Ark of the Covenant originally held inside it a pot of manna. The Jews had a tradition that said the Ark was taken by God into heaven and that it would one day be returned. They believed that when the Messiah came, He would bring that same pot of manna to feed His people.

That manna is a type of Jesus Christ. He is called "hidden manna." He is hidden right now. His presence is not obvious among us. He has ascended to heaven. But He is still with us. He is only hidden. He indwells each and every one of His believers. Just as the manna nourished the people in the wilderness, so also our hidden manna is a source of spiritual nourishment for us.

2.   A White Stone: *I will give him a white stone, and a new name written on the stone which no one knows but he who receives it (2:17)..*

A white stone was the symbol of innocence in the ancient court of law. On the basis of the death of Christ, we can be legally judged "not guilty" before the throne of God. If you have been identified with the Overcomer, then you share in His righteousness. Because He is righteous, you have been declared to be righteous.

A white stone was also used as an admission ticket to public festivals. We have an admission ticket into the Kingdom of God. Jesus is our stone of hope; the rock of our salvation. He is our entrance to God and on Him we stand. However, this white stone has something special about it. This white stone has your name on it. It is a new name and it is a name that no one else knows. I want to let you in on a family secret. I have a pet name for my daughter. It is a name that most of you do not know. You aren't going to know because I'm not going to tell you what it is. It isn't that big a secret, but I don't normally use it outside the confines of our family. It is special. It is only for her and I've been using it since she was a very little girl. When she hears it, she knows that it comes from her loving father. Jesus has a name like that for you. It is personal. It is special. It is a sign of His love and affection for you.

THYATIRA: INTOLERABLE TOLERATION
Revelation 2:18-29

If Jesus were to write seven letters to seven churches in America, we might be a little surprised at His choice of destinations. We might expect such letters to go to the churches at Fort Lauderdale and Los Angeles and New York. But we might be surprised to find that there was also a letter addressed to Flatbush, Indiana. Thyatira was that kind of town. It was the smallest of all of the seven cities mentioned in Revelation 2-3. It was a small place, off the beaten track. When Paula and I were taking a tour of the seven churches, this was the one that was skipped. It was out of the way. It would have meant a long and lonesome detour to go there.

Thyatira started out as a sentinel city. It has a small military outpost designed to slow down an invading army. Such an outpost was not designed to actually stop an invasion. It was designed only to slow down the enemy. Rome was now in power and there was peace throughout the land. There was no need for sentinel cities. There was now only a small garrison at Thyatira.

The fact that Jesus sends a message to the church of Thyatira is a reminder to us that God isn't interested only in the large and the powerful. He is also interested in the small and the weak and He writes to encourage those who are in small places.

This is the city from which Lydia came. You remember Lydia. She met Paul in Philippi. She was the first Christian convert in that city. She wasn't from Philippi. She was from Thyatira. What was she doing so far from home? She was a businesswoman. She was a seller of purple. There was a purple flower that grew in the area. This flower would be taken and crushed to produce a relatively inexpensive dye.

> There was a more expensive dye that was obtained from a rare shellfish, but Thyatira would have been known for the more common dye from the plant that grew in the area.

The city was located on a small hill in the inland plains of Asia Minor. Unlike Sardis and Pergamum, it had no high acropolis from which to defend its inhabitants. There was a trade route that ran though Thyatira on the way to Sardis and Pergamum. Because of this trade route, a number of trade guilds had opened up their shops here. These trade guilds lay at the root of the problem for the church at Thyatira. Membership in the guilds often involved attending guild dinners that were marked by pagan rituals and immoral conduct. To disassociate yourself from the guilds might mean losing your business, your job and your social standing in the community.

JESUS HAS A UNIQUE TITLE

> *And to the angel of the church in Thyatira write: The Son of God, who has eyes like a flame of fire, and His feet are like burnished bronze, says this (Revelation 2:18).*

The local god and religious guardian of the city of Thyatira was Tyrimnos, the son of Zeus. It is perhaps for this reason that Jesus is called the Son of God. This is the only place in all the book of Revelation where He is called this. He is the Son of God. Not Tyrimnos. Not Caesar. Jesus. Notice how he is described. There are two aspects to this description:

1.   He has eyes like a flame of fire.

        One of the relics of which Thyatira boasted was the all-seeing eye of Apollo. Here we see that it is Jesus who has the all-seeing eye. He was able to say to Nathanael, "I saw you under the fig tree." I don't know why that was significant, but Nathanael did. He sees you and knows what is significant in your life.

2.   His feet are like burnished bronze.

        What is the significance of the feet of Jesus being described as burnished bronze? There were two pillars which stood on either side of the doorway into Solomon's Temple. They were made of bronze. If heaven was God's throne and the earth was His footstool, then the Jews felt that these pillars represented the legs of God. This means Jesus is being described in terms that represent His divinity.

A PROGRESSIVE GROWTH

> *I know your deeds, and your love and faith and service and perseverance, and that your deeds of late are greater than at first. (Revelation 2:19).*

Jesus starts with words of commendation. He says, "I know you." He is the One who knows all things. He is the One with eyes of flames of fire. He sees everything. He knows your situation. He has not lost you in the shuffle.

74

There were some things about this church that were worthy of commendation. They had faith and love and service and perseverance. What is even more impressive is that their deeds were greater than when they had begun.

Jesus says they are better than they used to be. That is what sanctification is all about. You cannot rest on yesterday's victories and you cannot be content with yesterday's growth. Life involves movement and you are always moving either toward God or away from God.

A HOLY PEOPLE

> *But I have this against you, that you tolerate the woman Jezebel, who calls herself a prophetess, and she teaches and leads My bond-servants astray, so that they commit acts of immorality and eat things sacrificed to idols. 21 And I gave her time to repent; and she does not want to repent of her immorality. 22 Behold, I will cast her upon a bed of sickness, and those who commit adultery with her into great tribulation, unless they repent of her deeds. 23 And I will kill her children with pestilence; and all the churches will know that I am He who searches the minds and hearts; and I will give to each one of you according to your deeds. (Revelation 2:20-23).*

The problem at Thyatira was one of toleration. That is a buzzword today. Everyone calls for toleration in our society. The only socially intolerable sin today is the sin of intolerance. There were those within the church at Thyatira who would have fit right in. They were tolerant of false doctrine. Perhaps they did not want to go through the pain of confrontation. It is not a pleasant process. It is usually quite uncomfortable. There is always a temptation to overlook areas demanding confrontation. This leads to the toleration of false teaching.

Some of the Christians at Thyatira had been avoiding confrontation. They had fallen into a spiritual détente. They had called for a cease-fire in the midst of the spiritual battle. They had made peace with the enemy. That enemy is described as Jezebel.

Who is this woman? I do not know for certain, but it is entirely possible that she was a literal woman who was a member of the church at Thyatira. She might have set herself up as a prophetess. On the other hand, her name was probably not Jezebel. Instead, she is playing the part of Jezebel. Jezebel is a character from the Old Testament. She was a Phoenician princess who married Ahab, the king of Israel. Together they were the Bonnie and Clyde of the Old Testament. Jezebel decided that the religion of Israel needed to be updated, so she began to bring in all

75

of the false gods of the Phoenicians. This included the worship of Baal. The Israelites already had a problem with idolatry, but she made it much worse. She led Israel astray. She led the nation into sexual immorality.

There was a modern-day Jezebel in the church at Thyatira. She was playing the role of a prophetess. She was teaching that it was okay to participate in the guild dinners and with the accompanying pagan worship and the meats that were offered to idols and in the sexual customs of the day. She taught that, as long as you did not actually deny Christ, it was okay to be involved in all of these other functions.

There is a principle here for us today. I have not been invited to attend any dinners to honor a pagan deity, but a modern principle still applies. There are certain public functions I should not attend. When I am invited to a party that will involve drinking and intoxication and possible sexual misconduct, I should not attend. Sometimes such a function will be job-related. This was the case in Thyatira. That is no excuse to associate myself with influences that do not honor God.

In the case at Thyatira, Jesus says: *I gave her time to repent; and she does not want to repent of her immorality*. She has been warned. She has been given time to repent. But no repentance has been forthcoming. Therefore a series of escalating judgments are pronounced.

- Sickness
- Tribulation
- Death of children

This is a picture of church discipline. Before it gets to this point, the church is called to exercise a form of self-discipline to deal with sin within the church. Jesus gave some very specific instructions as to how it was to be carried out.

> *And if your brother sins, go and reprove him in private; if he listens to you, you have won your brother. 16 But if he does not listen to you, take one or two more with you, so that by the mouth of two or three witnesses every fact may be confirmed. 17 And if he refuses to listen to them, tell it to the church; and if he refuses to listen even to the church, let him be to you as a Gentile and a tax-gatherer. (Matthew 18:15-17)*.

This is the formula for discipline in the church. If you see that a believer is involved in a certain sin, you are to go to him and lovingly reprove him. If he listens to you and repents of that sin, then both of you are able to rejoice over that restoration.

If he does not listen, then take along one or two other Christians who can hear the matter and judge it. After all, it might be you who are mistaken and need to be corrected. If the sinning believer is still rebellious toward the reproof that has now been offered by these two or three Christians, then the matter is to be taken before the leadership of the church. If the sinning believer will not listen to the church, then it is to be assumed that he is really not a believer and he is to be treated as such. He no longer belongs to the body of Christ and he is to be delivered over to Satan.

That sounds very harsh, but in reality it is the grace of God at work. The sinning believer is given every chance to repent before he is finally removed from the church. It is only after warning after repeated warning that he is finally removed. Always in view is his desired restoration. The Lord does not wish to kick him out of the church. The Lord wants to restore him and to bring him back.

The church at Thyatira had not followed these principles of church discipline. They thought they could overlook sin in their midst. In this, they were the exact opposite of the church at Ephesus.

Ephesus	Thyatira
Lost your first love	I know your love
You cannot endure evil men	You tolerate Jezebel

Both of these are grievous errors. Both need to be resolved. Both can lead to the death of the church. Jesus promises a coming judgment against this church: *Behold, I will cast her upon a bed of sickness, and those who commit adultery with her into great tribulation, unless they repent of her deeds (2:22).* There is a play on words here. The church at Thyatira had been guilty of participating in spiritual fornication with Jezebel; now Jesus throws them all into a bed. It will be a bed of tribulation. This church is warned that it would suffer a period of "great tribulation." It would be a time of punishment for allowing false teachers to continue in the church. The result of this tribulation would be that the church would be purified and God would be glorified.

> *And all the churches will know that I am He who searches*
> *the minds and hearts; and I will give to each one of you according*
> *to your deeds. (Revelation 2:23).*

God knows your heart. If your heart is for God, then He knows it. You cannot hide anything from Him. If there is sin going on in the church, then He is able to remove some members so that the rest will remain pure. If the church will not keep itself pure through discipline, then Christ says that He will come and purify the church by removing those parts that are infected with sin.

Sin is very much like a cancer. Every body contains cancer cells. Usually your body's immune system will be enough to fight off the cancer cells in your body. Sometimes that immune system breaks down. Sometimes the only thing you can do with a cancer is to cut it out. Christ is the Great Physician. He warns the He might have to perform a spiritual surgery to cut out the cancer of sin that is eating away at His church.

A STEADFAST ENDURANCE

> *But I say to you, the rest who are in Thyatira, who do not hold this teaching, who have not known the deep things of Satan, as they call them-- I place no other burden on you. 25 Nevertheless what you have, hold fast until I come. (Revelation 2:24-25).*

There were those at Thyatira who had not fallen under the sway of the teachings of Jezebel. They had not been enticed by these teachings that were supposed to be the deep things of God but which were really the deep things of Satan.

To them, Jesus says, "Hold fast." They are the small stronghold within the church that is to hold fast against the incursion of apostasy. From all outward appearances, it looks as though they are going to be overwhelmed. Help is on the way. The cavalry is coming to the rescue. Jesus doesn't say, "Hold fast as long as you can and then get overwhelmed." He says, "Hold fast until I come." There is a promise here. It is that, no matter how hopeless things may seem, He is coming.

Just as Thyatira was a sentinel city, designed to hold for a time against an invading army, so the church is to be a sentinel, holding fast until reinforcements can be brought up. It reminds me of the old television westerns. The settlers would be surrounded by the Indians and were about to be overwhelmed when, in the very nick of time, the cavalry would arrive. The book of Revelation presents a glorious promise of the coming cavalry.

> *And I saw heaven opened; and behold, a white horse, and He who sat upon it is called Faithful and True; and in righteousness He judges and wages war. 12 And His eyes are a flame of fire, and upon His head are many diadems; and He has a name written upon Him which no one knows except Himself. 13 And He is clothed with a robe dipped in blood; and His name is called The Word of God. 14 And the armies which are in heaven, clothed in fine linen, white and clean, were following Him on white horses. (Revelation 19:11-14).*

This is the message of the book of Revelation. No matter how hopeless things seem to be, the heavenly cavalry is going to arrive in the nick of time. The enemy will finally and ultimately be overthrown and Jesus will win.

A GLORIOUS PROMISE

> *And he who overcomes, and he who keeps My deeds until the end, to him I will give authority over the nations; 27 and he shall rule them with a rod of iron, as the vessels of the potter are broken to pieces, as I also have received authority from My Father; 28 and I will give him the morning star. 29 He who has an ear, let him hear what the Spirit says to the churches. (Revelation 2:26-29).*

The promise that is given to those who overcome and who keep the Lord's deeds covers two areas:

1. A Promise of Authority: *To him I will give authority over the nations; 27 and he shall rule them with a rod of iron, as the vessels of the potter are broken to pieces, as I also have received authority from My Father (2:26-27).*

   Notice that there is a promise of a delegated authority. It flows from the Father to the Son to the church.

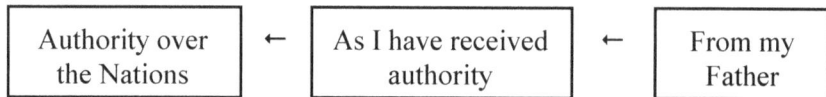

Authority over the Nations	←	As I have received authority	←	From my Father

   The church has no authority of its own. Its authority comes from the Son and is ultimately received from the Father. His authority has been delegated to us. We have been deputized to act in accordance with His commands. This reference to ruling over the nations with a rod of iron has echoes from the Old Testament. It is taken from one of the Messianic Psalms.

   > *I will surely tell of the decree of the LORD:*
   > *He said to Me, "Thou art My Son, Today I have begotten Thee.*
   > *8 Ask of Me, and I will surely give the nations as Thine inheritance, And the very ends of the earth as Thy possession.*
   > *9 Thou shalt break them with a rod of iron,*
   > *Thou shalt shatter them like earthenware." (Psalm 2:7-9).*

Notice that the church has entered into this promise. It is through the church that the nations are to be brought as a possession of the Son. Do you see it? This is the culmination of the great commission. Jesus told His disciples to go out and to make disciples of the nations. He told them to go out and to fulfill the Messianic promise that would make the earth the possession of the Son. As we are faithful to that commission, He promises that we shall rule and reign with Him.

2.   A Promise of "the Morning Star": *I will give him the morning star (2:28).*

When we hear of the morning star, we think of Venus. It is the brightest object in the sky after the sun and the moon. That is why it is so obvious in the morning, just before the rising of the sun. This is not the first mention in the Bible of the morning star. Peter also makes such a reference in his second epistle.

> *And so we have the prophetic word made more sure, to which you do well to pay attention as to a lamp shining in a dark place, until the day dawns and the **morning star** arises in your hearts. (2 Peter 1:19).*

Peter is speaking of the prophetic word that we have in the Scriptures. It acts like a lamp shining in a dark place. It brings illumination to where there was only darkness.

> Peter uses a different Greek word to speak of the "morning star." He speaks of the *phosphoros* while John refers to the *astera ton proinon*, the "early star."

A lamp in a dark place is a good thing. But how much better is it when the sun comes up and there are no dark places?

There is coming a new dawn. It will make the past age appear as though it were night and it will make the Scriptures appear as though they were merely a lamp in the night. We have a glimpse of that new dawn today. It is in Jesus. He is the morning star. He is the promise of the coming day. How do I know this is a reference to Jesus? Because the Bible tells me so.

> *I, Jesus, have sent My angel to testify to you these things for the churches. I am the root and the offspring of David, the bright **morning star**. (Revelation 22:16).*

The coming of Jesus was like the last star in the night sky. The other stars have faded and only one remains, announcing by its solitary light that the sun is about to rise. Jesus is the morning star and the fact of His coming is the announcement that the night is almost over. It will not be long now. Soon the day will dawn. The sun will rise. The Son will rise.

SARDIS: LETTER TO A DEAD CHURCH
Revelation 3:1-6

The original city of Sardis was built atop Mount Tomulus, a sharp peak that overlooks the joining of the Hermus and the Pactolus River. By the first century A.D., the city had grown down both sides of the mountain and had become a trading center. There was a large Jewish population in Sardis. This may have contributed to the early growth of the church since this would have provided a ready group who were already familiar with the Old Testament Scriptures.

There is a mall in the city. In the shops, there is evidence of both Jewish as well as Christian shops. One shop has a menorah on the inside of the shop while another has a cross on the outside of the shop. The shop owners made it clear that they stood for God. They announced it to the world. But that is not all. They also took pagan articles and scratched off the pagan markings and placed crosses over them. It is to this church that Jesus now turns His attention.

> *And to the angel of the church in Sardis write: He who has the seven Spirits of God, and the seven stars, says this (Revelation 3:1).*

Jesus describes Himself in a twofold way to this church. Both of these aspects are found back in Revelation 1 and they are both found in the Old Testament.

1. *He who has the seven Spirits of God... (Revelation 3:1).*

    This is mentioned back in Revelation 1:4, but long before then was an earlier reference dating back to the Old Testament. This title looks back to the words of Isaiah the prophet.

    > *Then a shoot will spring from the stem of Jesse, And a branch from his roots will bear fruit. 2 And the Spirit of the LORD will rest on Him, The spirit of wisdom and understanding, The spirit of counsel and strength, The spirit of knowledge and the fear of the LORD. (Isaiah 11:1-2).*

    This is a Messianic prophecy. It looks to the one who would come from the stem of Jesse, the father of King David. This second David would have resting upon him the seven-fold. He is the Spirit...

...of the Lord.
...of wisdom.
...of understanding.
...of counsel.
...of strength.
...of knowledge.
...of the fear of the Lord.

The number seven appears throughout the book of Revelation. It is a number that is often associated with God. It is a number symbolizing His completeness.

2.   *He who has... the seven stars... (Revelation 3:1).*

The first chapter of Revelation explains this symbol of the seven stars. They are a reference to the seven churches being addressed in this book.

> *As for the mystery of the seven stars which you saw in My right hand, and the seven golden lampstands: the seven stars are the angels of the seven churches, and the seven lampstands are the seven churches. (Revelation 1:20).*

The Old Testament makes no specific mention of seven stars. On the other hand, there are three different references to the constellation known to the Greeks as the Pleiades or "seven sisters" (Job 9:9; 38:31; Amos 5:8). Although we know today that there are up to 500 stars in this cluster, in that day there were only seven of these stars that were visible.

The idea of stars being representative of God's people goes back all the way to the dreams of Joseph. As a young man, Joseph had a dream that the sun and moon and eleven stars were bowing down to him. Both his brothers and his father recognized that this was a prophecy of how his brothers would one day bow before him.

If we understand this reference to the stars to be a picture of God's people, notice where they are located. They are in the hand of Jesus. They are in the place of safety.

A DEAD CHURCH & A LIVING REPUTATION

> *I know your deeds, that you have a name that you are alive, but you are dead (Revelation 3:1).*

The church at Sardis had a reputation. It had a reputation that it was alive. The problem with this reputation was that it was a wrong reputation. It had a reputation for being alive while it was really dead. The church looked alive. It did all of the things we normally associate with a living church. They had regular church meetings. They collected an offering. They sang hymns. They listened to the preaching of a sermon. They had a reputation for being alive. They did all of the outward things a church is thought to do. These things do not guarantee a living church. It is like a stuffed animal. It may look very nice, but it is dead. Sardis was a dead church. It was full of people who were spiritually dead. It was full of unbelievers.

Part of the problem at Sardis was not only that it was dead, but that it did not look dead. The members there had learned to "play the game" so that they could appear to be alive. Most of us take some concern over what others think of us. That isn't necessarily a good thing. When it takes place within the church, it can be tragic. It is like the fellow who goes to his doctor and his doctor asks, "How are you?" The patient replies, "I'm fine," even though he is in agonizing pain. Why does he do such a thing? Because he doesn't want his doctor to think badly of him.

It is interesting to note that Sardis is not said to be under any sort of attack or persecution. There is a reason for this. The world never persecutes a dead church. Satan doesn't mind having a church like this on every street corner. This kind of church poses no threat to Satan or to his world system. He likes to have people vaccinated with a little religion -- it keeps them from catching the real thing.

A DEAD CHURCH AWAKENED

Wake up, and strengthen the things that remain (Revelation 3:2).

When we see this injunction to "wake up," we should note that this same root word is used in a number of places to carry the idea of, "Be watching!" or "Be on the alert!" (See Matthew 25:13; Acts 20:31; 1 Peter 5:8). To fully appreciate this passage, you have to know something about the history of the city of Sardis. This city had once been the home of Croesus, the king of Lydia. You might know him as Midas. Later legend had it that everything Midas touched turned to gold. It was a byword in the ancient world to refer to someone as being "as rich as Croesus."

Herodotus tells the story of the Persian attack against the kingdom of Croesus. The attack came from Cyrus the Great, king of the Medes and the Persians. As the Persians invaded his land, Croesus set up his defenses atop the fortress at Sardis. The defensive walls atop the steep cliff were considered virtually impregnable. The Persians set up their siege, but could do nothing more and settled in for a long wait.

Ruins of Sardis with the ancient acropolis on which the fortress stood in the background

Then one day a Persian happened to notice that a Lydian soldier had dropped his helmet off the wall and it went bouncing down the mountain. Thinking that no one was looking, the Lydian soldier climbed down the wall and made his way down the steep cliff to retrieve his helmet and then went back up the same way. What had previously been invisible to the Persians now became apparent – there was a narrow and virtually unknown path leading up to the Lydian fortifications. On the following night, a squad of Persians took the same route up the mountain, climbing over the city walls to open the gates of the besieged city while the guards slept at their posts. In light of this story, the words of Jesus take on a new light. He tells the people of Sardis to wake up because He is going to come as a thief.

A DEAD CHURCH & REMAINING LIFE

Wake up, and strengthen the things that remain, which were about to die (Revelation 3:2).

Jesus does not give up hope on the church at Sardis. His exhortation is a message that it is still possible for this dead and dying church to be roused from its slumber to strengthen the things that remain. There still remained some flickering life in this church, the light of which was about to be extinguished.

What were these things that were about to die? I think it might be a reference to the influence of those few remaining believers within the church. In verse 4 we shall see that there were still a few believers left in Sardis. Their influence was greatly diminished. They were only hanging on by their fingernails, but they were hanging on. The lesson is that, as long as there is life, there continues to be hope.

84

A DEAD CHURCH CAN REMEMBER AND REPENT

Remember therefore what you have received and heard;
and keep it, and repent (Revelation 3:3).

Jesus calls for a threefold solution to the present predicament at Sardis. It is a call to remember, to keep it and to repent.

1.   Remember what you have received and heard: The people of Sardis had not so much turned their back upon the truth as much as they had merely forgotten. They had allowed other things to capture their attention until they had lost sight of the gospel. It was a case of the immediate capturing the attention of the important.

2.   Keep it: They are to guard and to keep the truth of the gospel. How do you do that? By going back day after day to sit in the shadow of the cross. By constantly remembering the sacrifice that was made on our behalf.

3.   Repent: What is repentance? It involves a change of mind (this is the strict definition of the word), but it is more than a mere mental assent. It also involves a change of attitude. It involves turning from your own agenda to turn toward God.

"Therefore bring forth fruit in keeping with repentance" (Matthew 3:8). This assumes that for repentance to be real and valid, there must be an accompanying result. Repentance is not the fruit. Repentance is inward; the fruit is outward. Repentance is an inner attitude; fruit is the outward result of that inner attitude. Repentance is not the fruit, but it is accompanied by real fruit if it is real repentance.

The message that Paul preached was that men *should repent and turn to God, performing deeds appropriate to repentance (Acts 26:20).* He called for men to perform deeds that were in keeping with their repentance. In Acts 20:21, Paul speaks of *"repentance toward God and faith in our Lord Jesus Christ."* Notice that repentance is directed toward God. We have sinned against Him and are to recognize our rebellious ways and turn to Him. The manner of that turning is seen in the second clause, it is *by faith in our Lord Jesus Christ.*

For the sorrow that is according to the will of God produces a repentance without regret, leading to salvation; but the sorrow of the world produces death (2 Corinthians 7:10). Notice that sorrow is not the same thing as repentance. There is such a thing as worldly sorrow that is not only distinct from repentance, but it leads to the very opposite of repentance. At the same time, we must point out that even Godly sorrow is not in itself repentance. It only leads to repentance but is not itself that repentance.

In 2 Timothy 2:25, Paul speaks of the importance of being patient and kind in the midst of opposition so that *God may grant them repentance leading to the knowledge of the truth*. Notice that it is repentance that leads to the knowledge of the truth and not the other way around. That is not to say that you have repentance without any knowledge of the truth, but repentance is not merely a matter of knowing or changing your mind, but it also involves a change of attitude. You repent and as a result you come to know the truth.

A DEAD CHURCH FACES JUDGMENT

> *Remember therefore what you have received and heard; and keep it, and repent. If therefore you will not wake up, I will come like a thief, and you will not know at what hour I will come upon you. (Revelation 3:3).*

Jesus warns that He will come like a thief against those who are not awaiting His return. What does this mean? What does it mean that He will "come like a thief?" Some have thought that it means He is coming to steal or to take something that does not belong to Him. But this is stretching the analogy to a place not permitted by the context. The context both of this passage and the rest of the Bible makes it very clear that the coming of Jesus will be unexpected.

> *But be sure of this, that if the head of the house had known at what time of the night the thief was coming, he would have been on the alert and would not have allowed his house to be broken into. 44 For this reason you be ready too; for the Son of Man is coming at an hour when you do not think He will. (Matthew 24:43-44).*

> *For you yourselves know full well that the day of the Lord will come just like a thief in the night. 3 While they are saying, "Peace and safety!" then destruction will come upon them suddenly like birth pangs upon a woman with child; and they shall not escape.*
> *4 But you, brethren, are not in darkness, that the day should overtake you like a thief; 5 for you are all sons of light and sons of day. We are not of night nor of darkness; 6 so then let us not sleep as others do, but let us be alert and sober.(1 Thessalonians 5:2-6).*

> *But the day of the Lord will come like a thief, in which the heavens will pass away with a roar and the elements will be destroyed with intense heat, and the earth and its works will be burned up. (2 Peter 3:10).*

All of these passages point to the same thing. They point to the Second Coming of Jesus Christ and the judgment He shall bring at that time. Notice this last passage also states that Jesus is coming as a thief. But this coming is certainly not going to be quiet or in secret. To the contrary, it arrives with a roar and with intense heat.

There is a reason I point this out. It is because of a popular teaching among many churches that says when Jesus returns, it will be to secretly snatch believers away. This reference to His "coming like a thief" has been taken to mean that His coming will go unnoticed. This is not the case. The fact that He is coming like a thief means that His coming will be unexpected in the world.

A DEAD CHURCH & A WORTHY FEW

> *But you have a few people in Sardis who have not soiled their garments; and they will walk with Me in white; for they are worthy. (Revelation 3:4).*

Sardis was known for its textile manufacturing. The name brand clothes came from Sardis. In the same way, there were some brand name Christians in Sardis. They were the remnant who were still spiritually awake, who had not forgotten or wandered from the faith and who were still faithful.

You might be inclined to ask, "Why didn't they change churches? Why didn't they leave and go to the Baptist church down the street?" The answer is that this was the only church in town. You could either meet with the church or else you could stay home. Jesus commends those who have remained. They had not soiled their garments -- that is, they had not allowed the sinful spirit of the church to affect their own character.

In addition to the textile manufacturing, there was a great gymnasium in the city of Sardis. The Greeks believed the ultimate beauty was the human body, so they practiced their exercises in the nude. This gymnasium was also the place of higher education. It was in the gymnasium that the Greeks passed to others their world view. The Greeks believed that man is the center of the universe. Christianity, by contrast, held that God is the center of the universe.

I have been to the gymnasium of Sardis. In a corner of that gymnasium has been found the remains of the largest synagogue ever to be found. The bema faces

Jerusalem and there are four stones that stand at the front and some chief seats. There is a table there with two eagles and a lion on either side. What are these symbols doing in a synagogue and what is a synagogue doing in a gymnasium? We do not know. It could be that the symbols that once stood for paganism were used by the Jews as symbols for God. If that is true, then it tells me that these Jews were seeking to redeem the city. Or were these Jewish people so comfortable with paganism that such proximity did not matter?

If you go along the bank of the Pactolus River, you find the most ancient ruins of Sardis. There is an open air shrine to Ashera. She brought fertility through sexual activities. The Greeks built a temple to Artemis here. The columns of this temple stand more than fifty five feet high. In the corner of this temple there is a little church. To get into the door of the church, you have to walk between the columns of the temple.

Ruins of the temple to Artemis outside of Sardis with the adjoining church on the lower left

The same question we have of the synagogue must also be asked of the church. Were they seeking to redeem their culture, or was it that they had become comfortable with the surrounding paganism? I do not know. But I do know that God has called us to be in the world yet not of the world. We ought to be placing our churches at the very center of the place that was previously given over to paganism. But in doing so, there is a warning. It is that we do not let that paganism affect our Christian life.

A DEAD CHURCH & A LIVING PROMISE

He who overcomes shall thus be clothed in white garments; and I will not erase his name from the book of life, and

88

I will confess his name before My Father, and before His angels.
6 He who has an ear, let him hear what the Spirit says to the
churches. (Revelation 3:1-6).

This passage has been addressed to a church that has been infected with a certain deadness. Nothing seems more hopeless than death. But we worship One who is able to raise the dead. He is able to raise those who are physically dead, He is able to raise those who are spiritually dead and He is able to raise dead churches. In light of such possibilities, a promise is given. It is a promise to the one who overcomes.

Each of the seven letters in Revelation 2-3 close with a promise to the one who overcomes. This is a promise given to the one who repents and who believes the gospel. John has said elsewhere that *whatever is born of God overcomes the world; and this is the victory that has overcome the world— our faith* (1 John 5:4). The one who overcomes in such a way is given three promises. There promises are arranged in a chiastic order:

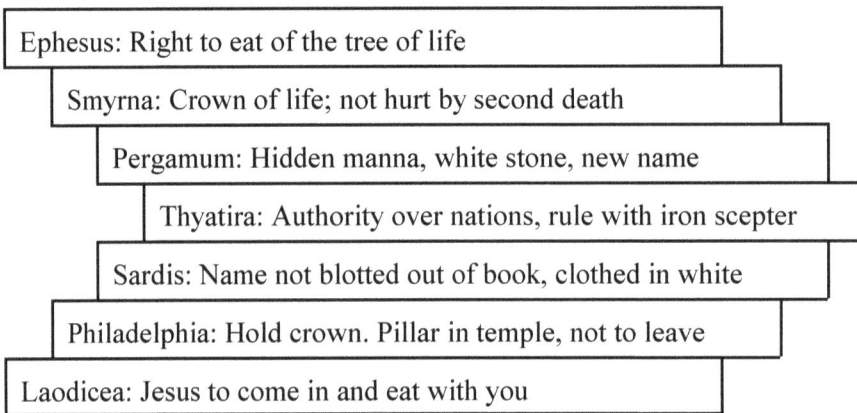

| Ephesus: Right to eat of the tree of life |
| Smyrna: Crown of life; not hurt by second death |
| Pergamum: Hidden manna, white stone, new name |
| Thyatira: Authority over nations, rule with iron scepter |
| Sardis: Name not blotted out of book, clothed in white |
| Philadelphia: Hold crown. Pillar in temple, not to leave |
| Laodicea: Jesus to come in and eat with you |

1.   A Promise of Purity: *He who overcomes shall thus be clothed in white garments (3:5).*

This is not speaking of physically white garments. This is merely a symbol of a spiritual reality. The white garments refer to a holy character. When we believe in Christ, we are identified with His holy character. We are clothed in His holiness. This is necessary because our own righteousness could never be good enough to satisfy God.

> *For all of us have become like one who is unclean,*
> *And all our righteous deeds are like a filthy garment; And*
> *all of us wither like a leaf, And our iniquities, like the*
> *wind, take us away. (Isaiah 64:6).*

89

Trying to stand before God on the basis of our righteous deeds is like trying to enter a fashion show dressed in dirty rags. We cannot please God on the basis of our good works because we don't have any good works. The good works that we have are not good works in His eyes. Therefore if we are to enter the kingdom of God, it must be on the basis of the good works of another. This is why Jesus died. He took our sins upon Himself and then He gave us the white robes of His own righteousness.

> *I will rejoice greatly in the LORD, My soul will exult in my God; For He has clothed me with garments of salvation, He has wrapped me with a robe of righteousness, As a bridegroom decks himself with a garland, And as a bride adorns herself with her jewels. (Isaiah 61:10).*

If you are a believer in Jesus Christ, then you have been justified, declared to be legally righteous in the eyes of the Lord.

2.   A Promise of Permanence: *I will not erase his name from the book of life (3:5).*

The idea of a book of life is an Old Testament concept. In one of the imprecatory Psalms, the psalmist asks that his enemies be blotted from the book of life.

> *Do Thou add iniquity to their iniquity,*
> *And may they not come into Thy righteousness.*
> *28 May they be blotted out of the book of life,*
> *And may they not be recorded with the righteous. (Psalm 69:27-28).*

Notice that having your name in the book of life is synonymous with having your name recorded with the righteous. It means that only the righteous have their names recorded in the book of life.

In ancient times, the king or governor of a land would keep a register of all the names of the people who lived in his kingdom. When a man committed a crime, his name would be removed from the register and he would no longer enjoy the privilege of citizenship. Such a practice serves as an illustration of God's actions against those who are false prophets:

> *So My hand will be against the prophets who see false visions and utter lying divinations. They will have no place in the council of My people, nor will they be written down in the register of the house of Israel, nor will they*

enter the land of Israel, that you may know that I am the
Lord God. (Ezekiel 13:9).

If a man moved away, his name was erased from the register and written into the register of the land into which he had moved. If a man died, his name was removed from the register. The king only kept the register of the living subjects of his kingdom who had not transgressed the laws of the kingdom.

How does this relate to what Jesus is saying to His church? Here is the meaning. Jesus says that some kings might erase your name from some of their books, but He will never erase your name from His book of life. Instead, He will confess your name before His Father and before His angels.

3.   A Promise of Recognition: *I will confess his name before My Father, and before His angels (3:5).*

The Father publicly acknowledged Jesus at His baptism. When Jesus came out of the water, a voice from heaven declared to all who were present, *"This is My beloved Son in whom I am well-pleased"* (Matthew 3:17).

God also acknowledged Jesus on the Mount of Transfiguration. The apostle John stood there with Peter and Andrew and heard the voice of God proclaim, *"This is My beloved Son in whom I am well-pleased; listen to Him!"* (Matthew 17:5). In the same way that the Father acknowledged the Son before the world, so also the Son will one day acknowledge us before the Father.

> *Everyone therefore who shall confess Me before*
> *men, I will also confess him before My Father who is in*
> *heaven. 33 But whoever shall deny Me before men, I will*
> *also deny him before My Father who is in heaven.*
> *(Matthew 10:32-33).*

This is a sobering passage. It helps us to understand what is a true Christian. A true Christian is one who confesses Jesus before men. If that doesn't describe you, then something is wrong. Perhaps you are like one of those dead church-goers of Sardis. Maybe you are going through all of the outward actions, but there is no indication of any spiritual life. You need to wake up and guard those first things and repent. If you are following Christ, then your life ought to reflect it. Is His character manifested in you? Are you confessing His name before the people around you? Then He will also confess your name before His Father in heaven.

PHILADELPHIA: LETTER TO A LITTLE CHURCH

Revelation 3:7-13

When you hear the name Philadelphia, you are inclined to think of Pennsylvania and the city of brotherly love. The name does carry that meaning, but it was in use long before Columbus discovered America. This original city stood in a wide valley on the road between Sardis and Laodicia in Asia Minor.

> The city of Philadelphia was named after its founder, Attalus II Philadelphius (159-138 B.C.). He was the king of Pergamum who was known for his loyalty to his brother in an age when brothers were usually rivals for a throne.

Philadelphia was located on a major fault line and in 17 A.D., the city suffered heavily from an earthquake. Writing three years later, the historian Strabo notes that there were still aftershocks and tremors to be felt. When a quake would hit, the only place of safety would be outside the city walls and away from the buildings. After the A.D. 17 quake, the city was rebuilt and renamed Neocarsarea ("new Caesar"), but the original name of Philadelphia still continued to be used.

We are not told how Christianity came to Philadelphia. There is not mention of the city in Paul's epistles or in the book of Acts. There is no record of the church plant that took place here. It was just a little church on the outskirts of big things.

A LITTLE CHURCH & A BIG KEY

> *And to the angel of the church in Philadelphia write: He who is holy, who is true, who has the key of David, who opens and no one will shut, and who shuts and no one opens, says this (Revelation 3:7).*

As this letter opens, it begins with a description of the one who is writing the letter. In this case, the writer of the letter is Jesus. This is important. John is writing the message, but he is only the secretary. He is writing what Jesus tells him to write.

This letter begins with a dramatic picture of Jesus. That is what the book of Revelation is all about. It is a book that reveals Jesus. You might have thought it was about gloom and doom and destruction and beasts and dragons and tribulation and wrath and many of those things can be found in the pages of this book. But it is ultimately a book about Jesus. If you have come to this book and haven't found

Jesus as the central theme, then you have missed what is the big idea of this book.

Notice how he is described.
- He who is holy
- He who is true
- He who has the key of David

We have already noted that keys were a symbol of authority. Do you remember when Jesus gave some special authority to Peter? Jesus gave a pop quiz and asked the disciples who they thought He was. Peter jumped up with the answer and proclaimed that Jesus was the Christ, the Son of God. Because of that insight, Jesus gave authority to Peter over His kingdom.

> *I will give you the keys of the kingdom of heaven; and whatever you shall bind on earth shall be bound in heaven, and whatever you shall loose on earth shall be loosed in heaven. (Matthew 16:19).*

Jesus gave to Peter the keys of the kingdom of heaven. Revelation 1:18 says that Jesus has the keys of hell and of death. Those aren't two separate sets of keys. They are one and the same. It speaks of authority over the kingdom and authority over hell and over death. But that is not all. In this passage, the key is described as the key of David. That takes us back to the Old Testament. It takes us back to the days of Isaiah and to the southern kingdom of Judah and to a time when the people had turned away from God to worship idols of their own making. The leaders of the nation were leading the people in this sort of wrongful worship and God promised that He would take the wicked leaders away and replace them with the one of His own choosing.

> *Then it will come about in that day,*
> *That I will summon My servant Eliakim the son of Hilkiah*
> *21 And I will clothe him with your tunic,*
> *And tie your sash securely about him,*
> *I will entrust him with your authority,*
> *And he will become a father to the inhabitants of Jerusalem and to the house of Judah.*
> *22 Then I will set the key of the house of David on his shoulder,*
> *When he opens no one will shut,*
> *When he shuts no one will open. (Isaiah 22:20-22).*

Eliakim was appointed to the position of royal custodian over the house of Hezekiah (Isaiah 36:3). He was given the authority to dispense the tax money in the royal treasury. He was also responsible for allowing people to come for an audience before the king. When he closed the door to the palace in your face, you would not be allowed to enter. When he opened a door for you, your way was secure. Jesus

Christ is the antitype of Eliakim. He has the key of David. No one can come to the God of Israel unless they come through Jesus.

This was significant to the church at Philadelphia because the city contained a large Jewish population. The Jews in that city were antagonistic to the church. They claimed that they were the recipients to the promises of God and they thought of the believers as renegades and heretics. They maintained that they were the only chosen people of God.

Jesus says that He has authority over the house of David and that includes having authority over the people of God. He is the rightful king of Israel and He is the heir to the throne of David. His people are those who are Jews on the inside – whose hearts have turned toward God.

A LITTLE CHURCH & AN OPEN DOOR

I know your deeds. Behold, I have put before you an open door which no one can shut, because you have a little power, and have kept My word, and have not denied My name. (Revelation 3:8).

We saw in the first point that we know the one who is the keeper of the keys. What does a key do? It unlocks that which has been previously locked so that the door can be opened. This brings us to the second point. It is that a little church only needs a little power to use an open door.

Notice how the door got open in the first place. The One who holds the keys opened the door. No one will be able to shut the door that He has opened.

- Not the pagan religious system
- Not the might of the Roman Empire
- Not the antagonistic Jews

The reason no one will be able to shut this door is because it was not opened by the believers at Philadelphia. It was opened by Christ Himself. When Christ opens a door, it stays open and it is not shut until He wants it shut.

Notice what Jesus says to the church at Philadelphia: *You have a little power, and have kept My word, and have not denied My name (3:8).* This church was not strong in itself. They were not rich. They did not have a great building. But what they did have was real. They had a purity of purpose and they had a little power with which they had been faithful. This metaphor of an open door is used throughout the Scriptures to describe an opportunity.

94

- In Colossians 4:3 Paul calls on the Colossians to pray that God might open up a door for the word to be proclaimed.
- In 1 Corinthians 16:9 he speaks of how *a wide door for effective service* has opened to him.
- 2 Corinthians 2:12 speaks of how he came preaching the gospel of Christ when a door was opened for him in the Lord.

Paul saw all sorts of opportunities – all sorts of open doors. And the notable thing about some of these open doors is that, to the casual observer, they might not have appeared to be open doors at all. You've heard the story of the two shoe salesmen who went to a third world country to sell shoes. The first one wrote back after a couple of weeks, "You might as well bring me back home. I can't sell shoes here because no one here wears shoes." The second one wrote back saying, "This place is a gold mine for business. No one here wears shoes and that means everyone is a potential customer. Send more shoes!!!" Are you facing an open door in your life? That door likely has several characteristics:

- It is a door of opportunity for some tremendous ministry.
- It is a door that might not be so obvious without the eyes of faith.
- It is a door that has been opened by Christ and no man is able to shut it.

Christ is not necessarily calling you to become a mega-minister or for your church to become a megachurch. But He is calling you to be faithful where you are and to use the little power that He has given to you and to keep His word.

A LITTLE CHURCH & A HOSTILE WORLD

> *Behold, I will cause those of the synagogue of Satan, who say that they are Jews, and are not, but lie– behold, I will make them to come and bow down at your feet, and to know that I have loved you. (Revelation 3:9).*

The church at Philadelphia was facing some stiff competition. It came from the local synagogue. The synagogue prided itself on being Jewish. They looked upon themselves as being God's chosen people and they looked with disdain on everyone else. In the process, they had somehow missed what it really means to be one of the chosen people of God.

We have already noted the words of Paul from Romans 2:28-29 where he speaks of the true Jew as *who is one inwardly*. He was saying that being Jewish is really about being a Christian; that Christianity is essentially Jewish and that if you have rejected Jesus, then you have actually rejected the Jewish Messiah, the One whose coming was promised by every one of the Hebrew prophets.

95

In case you haven't noticed, there has been some bad blood between the church and the synagogue over the past 2000 years. There have been times when the synagogue persecuted the church and there have been times when the church persecuted the synagogue and I'm here to tell you that none of that should ever have taken place.

Let me say it for the record so that there is no misunderstanding – there is no room in Christianity for anti-Semitism because our Lord and Savior was Jewish. For a Christian to display anti-Semitism is for him to rail against the very person of Christ.

On the other hand, when a synagogue or a temple or even a church sets itself up as the enemy of the gospel, that synagogue or temple or church has entered into partnership with Satan himself. That is why Jesus calls such a place the "synagogue of Satan."

You might be thinking to yourself, "We would never do anything like that! We are on God's side and we hold to the right theology and we belong to the right denomination." Let me remind you of what the Old Testament prophets had to say about that.

> *With what shall I come to the LORD*
> *And bow myself before the God on high?*
> *Shall I come to Him with burnt offerings,*
> *With yearling calves?*
> *7 Does the LORD take delight in thousands of rams,*
> *In ten thousand rivers of oil?*
> *Shall I present my first-born for my rebellious acts,*
> *The fruit of my body for the sin of my soul?*
> *8 He has told you, O man, what is good;*
> *And what does the LORD require of you*
> *But to do justice, to love kindness,*
> *And to walk humbly with your God? (Micah 6:6-8).*

Paul says something similar in the New Testament. He says...

> *If I speak with the tongues of men and of angels, but do not have love, I have become a noisy gong or a clanging cymbal. 2 And if I have the gift of prophecy, and know all mysteries and all knowledge; and if I have all faith, so as to remove mountains, but do not have love, I am nothing. 3 And if I give all my possessions to feed the poor, and if I deliver my body to be burned, but do not have love, it profits me nothing. (1 Corinthians 13:1-3).*

God isn't impressed with your theology and He isn't impressed with your church attendance and He isn't even impressed with your good works unless there is first a foundation of humility and faith and love. On the other hand, when you begin to show true humility and true faith and true love, then not only will God be pleased, but also those who were once at enmity with Christianity will themselves be changed. God says, "You show that humility and faith and love and *I will make them to come and bow down at your feet, and to know that I have loved you.*

A LITTLE CHURCH IN HARD TIMES

Because you have kept the word of My perseverance, I also will keep you from the hour of testing, that hour which is about to come upon the whole world, to test those who dwell upon the earth. 11 I am coming quickly; hold fast what you have, in order that no one take your crown. (Revelation 3:10-11).

Everyone who has lived in Florida for any length of time is familiar with storm warnings. This passage contains a storm warning. Such warnings have been given to God's people in the past.

*   Noah was warned of the coming flood.
*   Lot was told of the impending judgment of Sodom and Gomorrah.
*   Rahab was warned of the destruction of Jericho.

In the same way, this small church at Philadelphia is given a storm warning. She is told that there are bad times ahead. There is an hour of testing that *is about to come upon the whole world, to test those who dwell upon the earth.*

What is this "hour of testing" from which the church at Philadelphia was to be guarded? There is a very popular teaching today that says this refers to a future 7-year people of great tribulation that will come over the earth just prior to the Second Coming of Jesus Christ. It is said that, before this seven year tribulation can take place, there will be a "secret rapture" in which Christ will come silently and suddenly and take all of His believers away. The problem is that the Bible doesn't teach of such a secret coming of Christ. To the contrary, the Bible teaches that when Christ returns every eye shall see Him and it will be anything but secret.

What we have here in this promise to the church at Philadelphia is a temporal promise – a promise that was for a particular hour of testing and we are able to open our history books today and to see how wonderfully this promise was fulfilled.

Jesus was speaking to this little church in the latter half of the first century. It was a church that had been holding fast against persecutions and He tells them that these persecutions were going to get a lot worse before they got better. They did. Over the next 200 years there was wave after wave of persecution that swept over the entire known world. Christianity came under the attack of the greatest superpower the world had ever known. The emperors of Rome made it their mission to destroy the message of the crucified carpenter.

Though the hurricane of persecution savaged and all but obliterated the churches within the empire, there was one little church that continued to survive. It was the church at Philadelphia. Nor does the story end there. Islam swept over the Middle East in the seventh century and the churches in the Middle East were virtually destroyed. I don't know whether it is true, but I am told that a small church continued to exist throughout all of this period. Nor is that the end of the story. Although this promise was given to the church at Philadelphia, I believe that we are able to take that promise and find application for us today.

The storm warnings are still out. The persecutions that began in that first century so long ago have not ended. The church throughout much of the world is continuing to be persecuted, even as we speak. The earth is being tested by war and by famine and by disease and by various distresses and there were Christians today in certain parts of the world who are under the sentence of death for holding to the message of the cross.

I didn't say that to darken your day. I say it to tell you about the hope. For you who keep the word of His perseverance, He also promises to guard you through the hour of testing. There is a light at the end of your tunnel. You continue to trust in the Lord and you can weather whatever storm you are facing. You can hold out against the forces that threaten to bash your very world to pieces. Hold fast! Remain faithful!

In the summer of 2004, Paula and I had the opportunity to visit the city that was once Philadelphia (it is called by another name today). I was eager to see for myself the little church with the open door. Do you know what I found? I found it is no longer there. Why? I don't know. Perhaps the church died out. Perhaps the people moved away – there were a number of Greek and Turkish migrations that took place in the early part of the 20th century. Perhaps the Lord eventually closed the door that had been open for so many years. There is a principle here. It is that yesterday's faithfulness is not sufficient for the needs of today. You are called to hold fast and to remain faithful today.

A LITTLE CHURCH & A GREAT TEMPLE

He who overcomes, I will make him a pillar in the temple
of My God, and he will not go out from it anymore; and I will write
upon him the name of My God, and the name of the city of My God,
the new Jerusalem, which comes down out of heaven from My God,

and My new name (Revelation 3:12).

This letter to the little church at Philadelphia is one of seven such letters in the book of Revelation. Each of these letters is from Jesus and each letter ends with a promise.

This is a conditional promise. You know what it is to be given a conditional promise. It says, "If you do this, then I will do that." The condition for this promise and the condition for every promise given to every one of these seven churches is the condition of overcoming. Jesus says, "If you overcome, then there is a promise for you." How can I know whether or not I have overcome? What exactly do I have to do to overcome?" We have already noted that our overcoming is received through faith (1 John 5:4-5).

Have you come to Christ in faith, believing the message of the gospel? Have you come and trusted in the One who died in your place, relying upon Him and resting upon His finished work on your behalf? That is what it means to overcome. It means that you come and you trust in the One who overcame on your behalf. When you do that, there is a wonderful promise here for you. Notice the elements of this promise:

1.   The Promise of Permanence: *He who overcomes, I will make him a pillar in the temple of My God, and he will not go out from it anymore (3:12).*

This promise had a special significance to the people of Philadelphia. Remember that they lived in a heavy earthquake zone. Their city had been destroyed by an earthquake. Every time a tremor hit, the only thing to do was to get out of town before buildings started to collapse.

Jesus says there is coming a day when they will never have to worry about getting out of town. When they will not have to *go out from it anymore.* You come and trust in the One who overcame on your behalf and there is a promise of permanence. He says, "I will never lose you or forsake you."

2.   The Promise of Possession: *I will write upon him the name of My God, and the name of the city of My God, the new Jerusalem, which comes down out of heaven from My God, and My new name (3:12).*

It was customary in that day for a man to brand his property, whether material or animal or even human slaves. Jesus says that He is going to mark us as the personal property of God.

If you were to go through my house, there are a few things that you would find that have been marked as my personal possession. My personal Bible has such a mark on the inside cover. It is mine. We have the name of God written upon us. It is a mark of possession and a mark of protection.

Do you remember the mark of Cain? Cain was the first murderer in the Bible and God marked him so that no one would take vengeance upon him. That was a mark of protection. If God went through all that trouble to put a mark of protection upon a man who had murdered his own brother, how much more will He take care of you?

3.   The Promise of a Pillar: *He who overcomes, I will make him a pillar in the temple of My God (3:12).*

Don't miss the temple language. When you speak of the temple of God, you aren't using symbolism of the pagan temples throughout the ancient world, but rather this symbolism of the temple in Jerusalem. The main door in the temple in Jerusalem was flanked by two great pillars. These pillars were so significant that they had been given names: Jachin and Boaz. They were made of bronze. They were symbolic of something very special.

The Bible speaks of how heaven is God's throne and the earth is His footstool. While the Jews understood that God is a spirit and does not have a physical body, they nevertheless looked at the temple as the throne of God upon earth and, if the earth was His footstool, then the two pillars before the temple were representative of the legs of God as He was seated upon His throne.

Hold that thought for a moment because it has a direct impact of our understanding of this verse. When Jesus is described in the first chapter of Revelation, it is a description that is couched in temple language.

- He is presented among the seven golden lampstands (1:12-13)
- He is clothed in a floor-length robe and has a breastplate of gold (1:13). That is a description of the clothing of the High Priest.

The passage goes on to describe how His head and His hair were like white wool and how His eyes were like a flame of fire. And then in verse 15 we read of His legs and His feet. How are they described? They were like burnished bronze. Of what material were the columns in the Temple constructed? Those columns that represented the legs and the feet of God? They were made of bronze. This is pointing to the true identity of Jesus. You look at Him and you see the Temple. You look at Him and you see God.

That is not all. In our passage here in Revelation 3:12, Jesus says us that *He who overcomes, I will make him a pillar in the temple of My God.* How can this be? If the bronze pillars represent the very legs and feet of God and Jesus is described with those feet of bronze, then what we are promised is that we can become a functioning part of the very body of Christ.

Model of the temple in Jerusalem

You could go to the Temple in Jerusalem and you could look, but one thing you would never see was an image of God. There was an actual command against making such an image. God is invisible and you can't make an image of that which is invisible. The closest you ever got to such an image were in these two columns. The closest you ever got was to the feet of God.

The world comes today looking for an image of God and there is no image because God is the invisible God. He is "un-seeable." The closest they will ever get is to you. The church. The very feet of God. When you go to work tomorrow, you remember that you are the feet of God. You are to be walking in His ways and you are doing your work as a service to Him. When people ask about your walk – and they will eventually ask – you take that open door of opportunity and you tell them about the One who overcame on your behalf.

LAODICEA: LETTER TO THE LUKEWARM CHURCH
Revelation 3:14-22

And to the angel of the church in Laodicea write: The Amen, the faithful and true Witness, the Beginning of the creation of God, says this (Revelation 3:14).

The city of Laodicea lay at the hub of four important highways that came together in the fertile Lycos Valley. The road to Philadelphia and Sardis led to the north. A road leading to the coastal villages led to the south. The main road leading to Phrygia and Galatia led to the east and the main road to Ephesus led to the west.

Aqueduct at Laodicea

Laodicea sat on a wide plateau in the foothills of the Lycos Valley. From there, you can look to the northeast on the one side of the valley and see the small town of Colossae. Across the valley to the northwest you can see Hierapolis with its hot springs and bleached white cliffs looking like a shroud of freshly fallen snow.

The city of Laodicea had been founded by the Seleucid king Antiochus II (261-246 B.C.) and named after his wife Laodike. Under the Roman Empire it had risen to prominence as a center of trade and banking. The city was known for the fine wool of its black sheep that grazed in the hills nearby. The wealth of the city had attracted a school of medicine that produced an eye salve known as "Phrygian powder." There were several theaters in the city along with a hippodrome – a race track for horse racing. These entertainment centers gave Laodicea the reputation as the Las Vegas of the province of Asia.

This is the church to which Jesus now addresses Himself. It is the last of the seven churches, though its members might have considered themselves to be the first.

> And to the angel of the church in Laodicea write: The Amen, the faithful and true Witness, the Beginning of the creation of God, says this (Revelation 3:14).

This letter begins in the same way the previous six letters have begun, with a dramatic picture of Jesus.

1.   The Amen (3:14).

Our English word "amen" is a transliteration of a Hebrew word. The Hebrew word "amen" (אָמֵן) means "truth." This title has great significance. It is taken from the Old Testament where it was used by the prophet Isaiah to speak of God.

> Because he who is blessed in the earth
> Shall be blessed *by the God of truth* (בֵּאלֹהֵי אָמֵן);
> And he who swears in the earth
> Shall swear by the God of truth;
> Because the former troubles are forgotten,
> And because they are hidden from My sight! (Isaiah 65:16).

The "God of truth" is literally "the God of Amen." It is a title for God. The gods of the ancient world were known for their various attributes. There was a god of the sea and a god of war, a god of thunder and a god of grain. The God whom we worship is the God of truth. He has promised us certain things and we can be certain they will come to pass because He is the God of truth.

Jesus is the Amen. He is the God of truth. Because of this, He is known as the "faithful and true witness." What is a witness? A witness is one who has seen someone or something and who then tells others about it. When Jesus is called the "faithful and true witness," that presupposes not only that He is true and accurate about what He reports, but also that He has witnessed something that is worthy of reporting. He is the One who has borne witness of God. *No man has seen God at any time; the only begotten God, who is in the bosom of the Father, He has explained Him* (John 1:18).

2.   The Beginning of the creation of God (3:14).

Remember that Jesus is the One being described here. He is the source of everything that exists. He is the Master Architect. He is the Creator.

> *All things came into being by Him, and apart from Him nothing came into being that has come into being. (John 1:3).*

Jesus stands in the first place in all of creation. Look at everything that exists and realize that it all owes its existence to Jesus Christ. He was there at its beginning and He will be there at its end.

A CHURCH THAT MAKES GOD SICK

> *I know your deeds, that you are neither cold nor hot; I would that you were cold or hot. 16 So because you are lukewarm, and neither hot nor cold, I will spit you out of My mouth. (Revelation 3:15-16).*

Jesus is going to have nothing good to say about the church at Laodicea. He has addressed six other churches and, even though there have been problems, there was usually something good that could have been said about each one of them. That is not the case here. The problem was not one of false teaching. It was not a problem with gross immorality. It was that the church had grown lukewarm.

The Bible uses the idea of cold to refer both to things that are good as well as to things that are bad.
- Jesus spoke of how the love of many would grow cold (Matthew 24:12).
- Proverbs 25:25 says, *Like cold water to a weary soul, so is good news from a distant land.*

This description is served by a play on words with the physical site on which the city of Laodicea was situated. The city of Laodicea had a problem. It was in their water supply. The Lycos River ran down from the mountains and through the center of the valley, but it was subject to the flooding of spring thaws and so the cities of the valley were generally located some distance from the river.

The unexcavated site of Colossae

- The ancient site of Colossae which lies directly across the valley from Laodicea has not yet been excavated at this time of this writing, but when I visited the site in 2004, I noted a cold, bubbling stream that runs past the site of the town. When I reached down to place my hand into the waters, I found it to be ice-cold, even though this was in early June.
- Hierapolis was built atop some hot springs. The water there is full of minerals and is thought to be therapeutic.
- Laodicea had a water system that tapped into some similar mineral water, but it was not as close to the source, for the water had to be transported via a series of aqueducts and piping. At the center of the city was a large water distribution manifold that moved the water to various locations. By the time it got there, the water was no longer the cold mountain water like you would have at Colossae and it was no longer the hot mineral water you would have at Hierapolis. Instead it was lukewarm. Tepid.

The church at Laodicea was much the same way. Their Christianity had gone tepid and stale. They were not cold and refreshing. Neither were they hot and on-fire for the Lord. They were lukewarm.

There is a lesson here. There are few things worse than spiritual complacency. To be satisfied with where you are spiritually is to commit spiritual suicide. You are always moving in your spiritual life. You are either moving toward God or else you are moving away from God. The danger described here is the danger of moving away slowly.

We've all heard of the experiment with the frog and the frying pan. You can take a frog and sit him in a pan of water and begin gradually heating up the water over a long period of time and the frog will sit there and be boiled alive, even though he could easily jump to safety. The complacent Christian runs the same risk. He looks at his spiritual condition and he is

The author pointing out the water distribution manifold at Laodicea

satisfied, so he makes no move to change it. Jesus pronounces judgment against this church. He says, *"Because you are lukewarm, and neither hot nor cold, I will spit you out of My mouth."* It is a warning that the church will soon stop being the church.

A CHURCH BLINDED TO ITS NEEDS

> *Because you say, "I am rich, and have become wealthy, and have need of nothing," and you do not know that you are wretched and miserable and poor and blind and naked, 18 I advise you to buy from Me gold refined by fire, that you may become rich, and white garments, that you may clothe yourself, and that the shame of your nakedness may not be revealed; and eye salve to anoint your eyes, that you may see. (Revelation 3:17-18).*

The spiritual complacency of the church at Laodicea was accompanied by a corresponding spiritual pride. They did not think they had need of anything. They were proud of who and what they were. They were proud of their wealth. They were proud of their pseudo-spirituality. When Jesus spoke to the church at Smyrna, He described a poor church that was really rich. By contrast, he now describes a rich church that is really poor.

Smyrna	Laodicea
2:9. *I know your tribulation and your poverty (but you are rich)*	3:17. *You say, "I am rich, and have become wealthy, and have need of nothing," and you do not know that you are wretched and miserable and poor and blind and naked*

The church at Laodicea had fallen into a "prosperity theology." They thought that their material wealth as a measure of their spirituality. Laodicea was a wealthy city. One of the sources of their wealth came from the black sheep that were raised in the nearby hills. This wool was taken and spun into fine clothes. To have a black Laodicean sweater was considered to be the height of fashion.

Jesus says these well-dressed Laodicean Christians are spiritually naked. It makes you stop and think. Walk into most churches on a Sunday morning and you will see all of the latest fashion. If those people were suddenly transformed into their spiritual clothes, how many would find themselves wearing nothing? How many churches are full of spiritual nudists? Jesus calls them to come and to obtain for themselves that which they need:

1.   Spiritual Funding: *I advise you to buy from Me gold refined by fire (3:18).*

What does this mean? This is not speaking of literal gold. The gold refers to those things that are of spiritual value. They include the fruit of the spirit. They are love and joy and peace and patience and kindness and goodness and all of the other things that take place when one is filled with God's Holy Spirit.

These things must be refined by fire. Fire represents testing. Just as gold is purified when all of the impurities are burned out of it, so also the fruit of the Spirit in our lives becomes pure when all of the excess details of life are burned away. This can be done by the fires of persecution. It can also be done by the fire of a repentant heart. If these Laodiceans will repent and turn their hearts toward God, they can judge themselves and burn away their own complacency.

2.   Spiritual Clothing: *I advise you to buy from Me gold refined by fire, that you may become rich, and white garments, that you may clothe yourself (3:18).*

In contrast to the black sweaters of Laodicea, these Christians are advised to buy white garments. It is almost as though the black sweaters were a type of the spiritual condition of these Christians. They are to be traded in for the white clothes of righteousness. There will be a further mention of these white garments in the book of Revelation. It is seen at the coming of the bride.

> *And it was given to her to clothe herself in fine linen, bright and clean; for the fine linen is the righteous acts of the saints. (Revelation 19:8).*

In that passage, we are told the meaning of the white garments. They represent *the righteous acts of the saints.* If you are a Christian, you have been credited with the righteousness of Jesus Christ. But it does not stop there. You are now called to live a life that is consistent with that perfect righteousness that has been credited to you.

The Laodiceans are told to seek out those clothes – those works of righteousness that are the sign and evidence of their new position in Christ. Does that describe you? Are you a complacent Christian? A spiritual nudist? Is it time for a change of wardrobe?

3.   Spiritual Vision: *Eye salve to anoint your eyes, that you may see (3:18).*

The school of medicine at Laodicea manufactured an eye salve known as "Phrygian powder." Jesus tells these Christians that what they really need is spiritual eye salve. They need to have their eyes opened to their spiritual condition. When Paul wanted to pray for the church at Ephesus, his prayer was that they might see things as they really were.

> *I pray that the eyes of your heart may be enlightened, so that you may know what is the hope of His calling, what are the riches of the glory of His inheritance in the saints, 19 and what is the surpassing greatness of His power toward us who believe. (Ephesians 1:18-19).*

Do you remember Paul's conversion experience? He was made blind so that he could see. He desires that what happened to him might also happen to us. He wants our spiritual eyes to be opened. We are like the servant of Elisha who cannot see the heavenly reality that is in our midst.

A CHURCH IN NEED OF DISCIPLINE

> *Those whom I love, I reprove and discipline; be zealous therefore, and repent. (Revelation 3:19).*

I have a daughter. I love her very much and always have done so. But when she was growing up, I sometimes disciplined her. Did this mean I did not love her? Not at all. In fact, that discipline was a sign of my love and concern for her.

I have never disciplined the kid that lives down the street, even though he certainly needs it. I don't tell that child what to do. Why not? Because he is not my child. God's discipline of me is a sign of His love for me. It is one of the evidences that I am His child.

> *For those whom the Lord loves He disciplines, And He scourges every son whom He receives. 7 It is for discipline that you endure; God deals with you as with sons; for what son is there whom his father does not discipline? 8 But if you are without discipline, of which all have become partakers, then you are illegitimate children and not sons. (Hebrews 12:6-8).*

Jesus is not saying that He does not love the Laodicean believers. To the contrary, He is warning them that because He loves them, He is going to have to discipline them if they do not repent.

They are to move from complacency to repentance. Instead of concern, they have shown apathy. Instead of being zealous, they have been complacent. Instead of repenting, they have been satisfied to remain in the same rut. It reminds me of a little poem I heard many years ago:

108

Like a mighty turtle moves the church of God,
Brothers, we are treading where we've always trod.

That isn't very eloquent, but it gets across the idea. The problem with the church at Laodicea was that they were quite happy to go on doing the same things they had been doing. They were resistant to change and to repentance.

THERE IS A CHURCH WITH AN INVITATION

> *Behold, I stand at the door and knock; if anyone hears My voice and opens the door, I will come in to him, and will dine with him, and he with Me. (Revelation 3:20).*

Holeman Hunt produced a painting of Jesus that you may have seen. It portrays Jesus standing at a door and knocking. It is said that when he first painted it and put it on display, his friends came to look at it. One of them remarked, "There is no doorknob." Hunt replied, "The doorknob is on the inside." There is some truth to this. We are called to respond to the knocking of the Lord. The invitation here is the same one that is seen in the gospel of John.

> *All that the Father gives Me shall come to Me, and the one who comes to Me I will certainly not cast out. (John 6:37).*

There is a wonderful promise here. It is that if you come to Christ, you will not be cast out. If you open the door to Christ, he will enter. Have you opened the door? Have you come to Christ in faith and repentance, giving Him open access to your life? It is not enough to hear the gentle and persistent knocking. It is not enough to attend a church or to be a nice person or to listen to a sermon. It is not enough to feel the conviction of the Holy Spirit. You must still open the door.

A CHURCH ENTHRONED

> *He who overcomes, I will grant to him to sit down with Me on My throne, as I also overcame and sat down with My Father on His throne. 22 He who has an ear, let him hear what the Spirit says to the churches. (Revelation 3:21-22).*

Each of the seven letters to the seven churches has ended on the same note. Each has ended with a promise. It has been a conditional promise. It is a promise to the one who overcomes.

How do you overcome? By opening the door to the One who is knocking. By obtaining from Him those things that are necessary to your Christian life. By believing that Jesus is the Son of God and trusting in Him as your Lord and as your Savior. To the one who overcomes in this way is given the promise of a throne.

This promise of a throne came up one time when Jesus was on earth. The mother of James and John came to Him with a special request. It was to ask that her sons might sit with Jesus upon His throne in the kingdom.

What was requested by her on that day is now promised to those who overcome. It is a promise of heirship in the kingdom. But first there is a requirement. It is that we overcome as Jesus has overcome. Just as Christ defeated sin and death on the cross, I also must face sin and defeat it.

How can I possibly do this? How can I defeat sin and death? I defeat sin every time I depend on the finished work of Christ on my behalf. I defeat death every time I trust in the hope of the resurrection. One day, just as I have been identified with Christ in His battle against the world and the flesh and the devil, so also I will be identified with Christ as he sits on His glorious throne.

BEFORE THE THRONE OF GOD
Revelation 4:1-11

John was on the Isle of Patmos, and he wasn't there as a tourist. The island was more on the order of Alcatraz. It is a lonely, desolate, rocky place with sharp, rugged cliffs. You stand on one of the high points and you can see the entire island and you can see several other islands in the distance, but you cannot see the mainland. Yet John found himself the recipient of a vision that transported him not only off the island but off planet earth into heaven itself.

John is about to be given a glimpse of what is going on in heaven. He has been on Patmos. It has not been a comfortable place. It has been a place of hardship. But there is another reality that John is about to experience. This is important for you to hear. You need to hear this because you live in Patmos. You live in the nasty here and now. You are confronted by daily troubles. In the midst of those troubles, it is easy to forget that there is another reality.

In this chapter, we are going to move from earth to heaven. As we first read through the seven letters to the seven churches, we found ourselves identifying with their situations, their victories, and their defeats. But as we come to this chapter, we are going to enter a new realm. It will be a realm in which we are not used to walking. We are going to enter the very presence of God.

AN INVITATION TO HEAVEN

> *After these things I looked, and behold, a door standing open in heaven, and the first voice which I had heard, like the sound of a trumpet speaking with me, said, "Come up here, and I will show you what must take place after these things."*
> *Immediately I was in the Spirit; and behold, a throne was standing in heaven, and One sitting on the throne. (Revelation 4:1-2).*

The previous chapter, in the letter to the church at Laodicea, Jesus had said that He stand at the door and knocks. Now Jesus sees an open door in heaven. It is an open door that allows him entrance to see what otherwise could not be seen. He hears a voice. It is the same as the first voice that he had heard back in chapter one. It was described back there as the voice that sounded like a trumpet (Revelation 1:10).

This is not the first time that men had been given a glimpse of the heavenly throne. Growing up in a Jewish synagogue, John would have been very familiar with the Old Testament narratives that described the throne room of God.

Micaiah said, "Therefore, hear the word of the LORD. I saw the LORD sitting on His throne, and all the host of heaven standing by Him on His right and on His left." (1 Kings 22:19).

In the year of King Uzziah's death I saw the Lord sitting on a throne, lofty and exalted, with the train of His robe filling the temple. 2 Seraphim stood above Him, each having six wings: with two he covered his face, and with two he covered his feet, and with two he flew. 3 And one called out to another and said, "Holy, Holy, Holy, is the LORD of hosts, The whole earth is full of His glory." 4 And the foundations of the thresholds trembled at the voice of him who called out, while the temple was filling with smoke. (Isaiah 6:1-4).

I kept looking Until thrones were set up,
And the Ancient of Days took His seat;
His vesture was like white snow
And the hair of His head like pure wool.
His throne was ablaze with flames,
Its wheels were a burning fire.
10 A river of fire was flowing
And coming out from before Him;
Thousands upon thousands were attending Him,
And myriads upon myriads were standing before Him;
The court sat,
And the books were opened. (Daniel 7:9-10).

These are just a few of the passages that picture the throne of God in heaven (see also Job 1:6-12; 2:1-6; Ezekiel 1:4-28; 10:1-22; Hebrews 9:24). The point of picturing God's throne is to show God as the sovereign ruler of all creation. He is in control of the universe. He is reigning. Sometimes we get the idea that people are in control. We think that the President of the United States exerts a lot of power or we think that people who have a lot of money are in control. We tend to think that big business corporations and banking conglomerates are pulling the strings. It is all an illusion. The One who is really in charge is seated on the heavenly throne.

BEFORE THE THRONE

Immediately I was in the Spirit; and behold, a throne was standing in heaven, and One sitting on the throne.
And He who was sitting was like a jasper stone and a sardius in appearance; and there was a rainbow around the

throne, like an emerald in appearance. (Revelation 4:2-3).

Throughout the rest of the book of Revelation, it will be the throne of God that will be the central object of focus. Everything that follows will revolve around the throne. From it will come forth the judgments and from it will come forth the salvation of men.

1.   The Significance of the Throne: *A throne was standing in heaven, and One sitting on the throne (4:2).*

A throne was a place of control and sovereignty. It was the place of power. That is the point we are to understand. God is in control of creation. He is reigning. Sometimes we get the idea that people are in control. We start thinking that the president of the United States is in charge. That is merely an illusion. The One who is really in charge is seated on a throne in heaven.

2.   The Appearance of the One of the Throne: *And He who was sitting was like a jasper stone and a sardius in appearance (4:3).*

These were familiar stones to John. He is very specific to identify them with the appearance of the Lord. John was not a professional jeweler; he had no degrees in geology. He did not need one when it came to these stones. They were familiar to every Jewish schoolboy. They were associated with the high priest of Israel.

- The jasper was the last stone in the high priest's breastplate (Exodus 28:20).
- The sardius was the first stone in the high priest's breastplate (Exodus 28:17).

This is no coincidence. The high priest was God's personal representative on earth. His ministry was to serve the Lord. It is not surprising to find that two of the stones on his breastplate resembled the very presence of God in heaven.

3.   The Rainbow around the Throne: *There was a rainbow around the throne, like an emerald in appearance (4:3).*

The reference of the rainbow takes us back to Noah and the flood. This was the sign given to Noah and his family after they came off the ark. They had seen their entire world destroyed with the flood. God made a promise to Noah and his family. God promised He would not destroy the world again with a flood. He gave a sign to seal His covenant. The sign of His covenant was the rainbow.

We look at the rainbow when it rains and we remember God's covenant. But God also placed a reminder of His covenant in heaven. It is not there to remind Him of anything. He does not need reminders; He is not forgetful. It is there to remind us that we have a God who keeps His promises.

The rainbow usually comes only after the storm is over. There is something wonderfully significant about that. We are in the storm right now. Sometimes it feels as though we will be overwhelmed by the storms of life. But there is a place where the storm is over; it is the place of the rainbow. One day we shall arrive at that place.

THOSE AROUND THE THRONE

Have you ever been to Disney World? You take the monorail to the Magic Kingdom and you get off and walk through a hall and there before you at the end of the street is Cinderella's Castle. I don't care if you are six years old or sixty, you will find yourself standing there for a moment while you look at that Castle in all of its majesty. It is only after that moment has passed that you will be drawn to the other attractions and you will begin to enjoy all of the different details that make Disney World a children's paradise.

That is what happens here. As John is first caught up to heaven, he has eyes only for the throne of God. But as time goes on, he begins to notice other things and the goings on around the throne.

1.   The Twenty-four Elders.

> *Around the throne were twenty-four thrones; and upon the thrones I saw twenty-four elders sitting, clothed in white garments, and golden crowns on their heads. (Revelation 4:4).*

Someone has called this the presbytery of heaven. That is an appropriate title, for the Greek word that is translated "elder" in this passage is *presbyteros* and it is from this term that we get our word "Presbyterian."

Who are these 24 elders? What do they represent? The first thing that comes to mind it that they might be representatives from God's two economies, 12 from the Old Covenant and 12 from the New Covenant. How many tribes were there in the nation of Israel? How many portions of the inheritance were parceled out when the Israelites came into the land? How many disciples did Jesus choose?

114

The Bible is very clear in showing us that God has dealt with two groups of people, the descendants of Abraham under the Old Covenant and the spiritual descendants of Abraham under the New Covenant. But God has not left these two groups apart. He has taken them and He has made them into one.

> *Therefore remember that formerly you, the Gentiles in the flesh, who are called "Uncircumcision" by the so-called "Circumcision," which is performed in the flesh by human hands -- 12 remember that you were at that time separate from Christ, excluded from the commonwealth of Israel, and strangers to the covenants of promise, having no hope and without God in the world.*
>
> *But now in Christ Jesus you who formerly were far off have been brought near by the blood of Christ.*
>
> *For He Himself is our peace, who made both groups into one and broke down the barrier of the dividing wall, 15 by abolishing in His flesh the enmity, which is the Law of commandments contained in ordinances, so that in Himself He might make the two into one new man, thus establishing peace, 16 and might reconcile them both in one body to God through the cross, by it having put to death the enmity. (Ephesians 2:11-16).*

God does not have two churches. He does not have one assembly for Israel and another assembly for Gentiles. There is no segregation in heaven. He has one church. It is made up of all of His people. That means you belong to the same church to which Abraham belongs. You are a part of the same group of which David and Solomon are a part. If you have come to Christ in faith, then you are part of the family of God.

The presence of the 24 elders portray a united church. But that is not all they portray. They are also reminiscent of something else in the Old Testament. The Old Testament priesthood was organized into a series of different courses. They would rotate their priestly duties so that each course would serve twice a year. How many courses were there? There were 24 courses.

Each of these 24 courses would serve in the temple twice a year as a part of their regular duty. But there were also certain times when all 24 courses would come together at the Temple. These were for the special Feasts.

- The Passover and the Feast of Unleavened Bread
- The Feast of Trumpets and the Day of Atonement

As John sees this vision of heaven, it is expressed in the symbolism of the temple. The people of God are pictured as coming together to worship the Lord. This temple imagery continues as we see the Lamps and the Sea.

2.   Lamps and a Sea.

> *Out from the throne come flashes of lightning and sounds and peals of thunder. And there were seven lamps of fire burning before the throne, which are the seven Spirits of God; 6 and before the throne there was something like a sea of glass, like crystal... (Revelation 4:5-6a).*

There were seven lamps burning before the throne of God. This corresponds to the seven-branched lampstand which stood in the Temple. Revelation 1:19-20 tells us that these lamps represent the church. But what of the "sea"? The Jews were landlubbers. When they spoke of the ocean, they did so in fear. Think about it. Every time the Bible speaks of a Jew getting into a boat, he got into trouble.

- Noah's Ark — the whole world perished.
- Jonah — thrown overboard and served up as the main course.
- The disciples could barely cross the Sea of Galilee without sinking.
- Paul takes an ocean voyage to Italy and ends up being washed ashore.

This is not a stormy sea. This sea is like glass, like crystal. It is calm. It is peaceful. It has been calmed by the Lord. It reminds us of a time when Jesus spoke and the sea became calm.

In front of the Temple there was a great golden laver filled with water. This water was used for the purification rites. It was commonly known as the "Sea." John does not explain the meaning of this because no explanation is needed. This is Temple language and the reader is meant to understand that he has entered the realm of God's heavenly temple.

> Ezekiel 1 describes the same sea, but from a heavenly perspective: *Now over the heads of the living beings there was something like an expanse, like the awesome gleam of crystal, extended over their heads* (Ezekiel 1:22). *Now above the expanse that was over their heads there was something resembling a throne, like lapis lazuli in appearance* (Ezekiel 1:26a).

3.   The Four Living Ones.

> *...and in the center and around the throne, four living creatures full of eyes in front and behind.*

The first creature was like a lion, and the second creature like a calf, and the third creature had a face like that of a man, and the fourth creature was like a flying eagle. (Revelation 4:6b-7).

The next thing John notices is the presence of four living creatures standing around the throne. Commentators have come up with all sorts of ideas as who or what these living ones might be.

a.   The four gospel accounts.

- Matthew presents Jesus as the Lion of the tribe of Judah.
- Mark is said to present Jesus as a calf - a servant animal.
- Luke presents Jesus as the perfect man.
- John presents Jesus as the Son of God - pictured as an eagle.

b.   Four of the apostles

- Peter is said to be the lion.
- James, the brother of Jesus, is the calf.
- Matthew is the man.
- Paul is the eagle to takes the gospel to the world.

c.   The New Testament church.

d.   Four of the early churches (Jerusalem, Antioch, Alexandria and Constantinople).

e.   The four cardinal virtues.

f.   The four elements.

g.   Four motives of the human soul.

Which of those is correct? I don't think any of them are. I will suggest that the answer is found in the pages of the Old Testament. When John saw these four living creatures, he saw something of which he had read in the past. It is from the Old Testament book of Ezekiel.

As I looked, behold, a storm wind was coming from the north, a great cloud with fire flashing forth continually and a bright light around it, and in its midst something like glowing metal in the midst of the fire.
Within it there were figures resembling FOUR

LIVING BEINGS. And this was their appearance: they had human form,

> *Each of them had four faces and four wings.*
>
> *Their legs were straight and their feet were like a calf's hoof, and they gleamed like burnished bronze.*
>
> *Under their wings on their four sides were human hands. As for the faces and wings of the four of them,* 9 *their wings touched one another; their faces did not turn when they moved, each went straight forward.*
>
> *As for the form of their faces, each had the face of a MAN; all four had the face of a LION on the right and the face of a BULL on the left, and all four had the face of an EAGLE. (Ezekiel 1:4-10).*

Notice that the same creatures are here that are in John's vision. What are these "living beings"? They are angels. Ezekiel later has another vision where these four living creatures are explicitly identified.

> *And each one had four faces. The first face was the face of a cherub, the second face was the face of a man, the third the face of a lion, and the fourth the face of an eagle.*
>
> *Then the cherubim rose up. They are the living beings that I saw by the river Chebar. (Ezekiel 10:14-15).*

Notice that there has been a subtle change. Instead of the calf or the bull, now we see a cherub as one of the living creatures. Why? What is the point? The point is that these four living beings are merely representative of every type of life within the creation of God.

- The Lion represents the wild beasts.
- The calf represents the domesticated animals.
- Man represents all mankind.
- The eagle represents the kingdom of the air.

Because they are only representative of all living things, an angel could just as easily have been substituted for one of the animals. This explains how Ezekiel's vision could be different and yet still represent essentially the same thing. The emphasis is on the fact that they are alive. They are called the four living ones. They stand guard around the throne of God.

When a priest went into the Temple in Jerusalem in the days of the New Testament, he would see the lampstand on your left and the table of shewbread on the right and the altar of incense and beyond that, the veil. Once he passed through the veil, there was nothing. Just a bare rock. But in the days of the original Temple, this innermost chamber had been the resting place of the Ark of the Covenant. It was a wooden box overlaid with gold. The top of the box was of pure gold. It was called the mercy seat. It was considered to be the throne of God. It was here that the high priest would come once a year to sprinkle the blood of goats and calves.

Ark of the Covenant

On each side of the mercy seat was a golden figure. It was the figure of a cherub. Its wings were stretched out over the ark and its face looked down upon the mercy seat. But it was only a golden figure, a lifeless statue. The creatures that John sees around the throne of heaven are different. They are alive! They are not only alive, they are animated with life. They are speaking.

A SONG OF HOLINESS

> *And the four living creatures, each one of them having six wings, are full of eyes around and within; and day and night they do not cease to say, "Holy, Holy, Holy is the Lord God, the Almighty, who was and who is and who is to come." (Revelation 4:8).*

The four living creatures have a ministry. Their ministry is to worship the Lord. Their worship involves a proclamation of the holiness of God. It is the same proclamation that Isaiah saw in his vision of the holy temple.

> *Seraphim stood above Him, each having six wings: with two he covered his face, and with two he covered his feet, and with two he flew. 3 And one called out to another and said, "Holy, Holy, Holy, is the LORD of hosts, The whole earth is full of His glory." (Isaiah 6:2-3).*

Notice the threefold repetition of the holiness of God. This repetition is not without a purpose. It serves for emphasis. When you wanted to emphasize something in the Hebrew language, you would repeat it. This is why Jesus would say, "Truly, truly, I say to you..." You see this sort of parallel repetition often in the Bible. There is a holy of holies and a song of songs. But you hardly ever see something repeated three times.

Holy - Holy - HOLY!!!!

God is holy. He is not just the "man upstairs." He is not a nice old man with whiskers. He is not merely one of the boys. He is the holy God of the universe. And you had better recognize that when you come into His presence.

He is called *the Lord God, the Almighty, who was and who is and who is to come*. This is a graphic identification of the God who is. There are a lot of gods and goddesses who were worshiped in the ancient world. But the God of the Bible is distinctive. He is the God who was and who is and who is to come. He is the God who said to Moses on Mount Sinai, "I AM THAT I AM." He is the eternal God. He is the God of the ever present.

This is important for you to know. The God of the Bible is not merely a God of ancient history. He has not changed. The God who parted the Red Sea is still here. He is still able to answer your prayers.

WORTHY WORSHIP

> *And when the living creatures give glory and honor and thanks to Him who sits on the throne, to Him who lives forever and ever, 10 the twenty-four elders will fall down before Him who sits on the throne, and will worship Him who lives forever and ever, and will cast their crowns before the throne, saying, 11 "Worthy are You, our Lord and our God, to receive glory and honor and power; for You created all things, and because of Your will they existed, and were created." (Revelation 4:9-11).*

The declaration of holiness and the eternal nature of God brings about an immediate response on the part of the twenty four elders. Their worship is comprised of four actions:

- They fall down before the Lord.
- They worship Him.
- They cast their crowns before His throne.
- They sing a song of praise.

This is not the last time we shall see these twenty four elders fall down in worship before the throne. It will happen again in Revelation 5:14 and in 7:11.

The song the elders sing is a song describing the worthiness of worship. Have you ever sung this song? I don't mean you have necessarily repeated these exact words to a first century melody. I mean to ask, have you even come to the place of realizing God is truly worth giving all your glory and honor and power? Have you ever decided He was worthy of all your time and your money and your life? Have you ever taken your crown, those things you value most, and cast them at His feet? If you have, then I have good news for you. You have become a co-heir of Christ. You have entered into the family of God and someday you will see the vision John saw as you join in praise with the elders around the throne.

THE LION, THE LAMB, AND THE SEALED SCROLL
Revelation 5:1-14

On her thirteenth birthday, I took my daughter down to the seaport where I used to work and arranged a tour aboard a nuclear submarine. As a crew member guided us through the tight passageways, I was impressed by the quiet efficiency with which the entire vessel operated. We walked through the torpedo rooms, the galley and the dining areas. But the most impressive part of the ship was the control room. It was here that we saw the "brains" of the vessel. It was from here the captain would conduct maneuvers and it was from here the orders could be given to launch missiles.

There is a control room that directs the universe. Every drop of rain that falls, every bird that flies, and every decision we make is directed and overseen from this control room. Our problem is that we do not see what is going on in the control room. We look at everything going on around us and we think events are moving by mere chance. We can see no rhyme or reason. We have a limited perspective. But then we come to this chapter and we are given a glimpse of the workings of heaven.

THE SEVEN-SEALED BOOK

> *I saw in the right hand of Him who sat on the throne a book written inside and on the back, sealed up with seven seals.*
> *And I saw a strong angel proclaiming with a loud voice, "Who is worthy to open the book and to break its seals?"*
> *And no one in heaven or on the earth or under the earth was able to open the book or to look into it. (Revelation 5:1-4).*

As our chapter opens, we have been drawn into the control room of the universe. In the last chapter, we saw the beginning of John's vision and how he was struck by the scene of One who was sitting on the throne. It was described in language of the temple – there were the twenty four elders and a crystal sea and living creatures who represented all living creatures. They were all gathered around the throne of God.

John's attention is now drawn to the right hand of God. It holds something. Our translation calls it a "book." This is the Greek word *Biblon*. But the context seems to indicate that it is really a scroll. Verse 1 says that it contains writing on the inside as well as on the back. That seems to be describing a papyrus scroll. Scrolls were normally written only on one side, but this one contains so much material that it is written front and back.

You need to know that this is not the first scroll that the Bible speaks of that was written on the front and back. When the Lord first appeared to Ezekiel, He sent His message through a scroll that was written on the front and in the back.

> *Then I looked, and behold, a hand was extended to me; and lo, a scroll was in it.*
> *When He spread it out before me, it was written on the front and back, and written on it were lamentations, mourning and woe. (Ezekiel 2:9-10).*

God had a message of woe for the people of Israel. It was a message of warning. It was a message foretelling what was going to happen to the nation. It was a message that contained the plan of God for the people of God. I think the scroll that John sees here in Revelation is the same kind of scroll. It contains a message. It is a message containing the plan of God.[1]

Exodus 32:15 tells us that the tablets of the ten commandments were also *written on both sides*.

But that message is sealed. Its message is hidden from human eyes. We have no way of knowing what God's plan is for human history. We cannot guess what is in the mind of God. The only way that we can know His plan is for His sealed scroll to be unfolded for us. The call goes out for someone who will be found worthy to open the scroll and to break its seals. But no one is found to be qualified. Not the angels. Not Gabriel. Not any of the saints in heaven.

THE LION OF THE TRIBE OF JUDAH

> *Then I began to weep greatly because no one was found worthy to open the book or to look into it; 5 and one of the elders said to me, "Stop weeping; behold, the Lion that is from the tribe of Judah, the Root of David, has overcome so as to open the book and its seven seals." (Revelation 5:5).*

John weeps with frustration. Somehow he is aware of the awesome significance of the scroll. He is aware that it contains information relevant to the world in which

---

[1] It has been suggested by some that the fact that there are seven seals point to the fact that Roman law mandated there be at least seven witnesses to a legal will. However, the law did not specify that each of these witnesses place a separate seal upon the will.

he lives. Think about what would mean to a Christian who is going through hard times. Think about what it means to an old apostle who has been sentenced to live the rest of his life on a barren prison island. And so, he weeps. After all, he knows that it is a hard, cruel world. And unless the scroll is opened, it is going to go on being a hard, cruel world. But in the midst of his weeping good news comes.

The Lion of the tribe of Judah has overcome. This is a title for Jesus. It is a title that goes back to the Old Testament. Judah was called a lion's whelp in Genesis 49:9. It is in the same passage that we read of the promise that from Judah would come the future king. That prophecy was fulfilled when David became the king of Israel. He was from the tribe of Judah and

> Jesus is also called *the root of Jesse*. It is a title that goes back to Isaiah 11:10. That is interesting because in Jeremiah 23:5, He is called the branch of David. He is both the root and the branch. He is descended from Jesse, but Jesse is also descended from Him.

his sons became that royal line. Hundreds of years later, his descendants would be Joseph and Mary, the legal and natural parents of Jesus.

John hears the message that *the Lion of the tribe of Judah has overcome.* This is the message of the book of Revelation. It is the message we have already seen in this book and it is the overarching message we shall continue to see. It is the message that Jesus has won.

THE LAMB OF GOD

> *And I saw between the throne (with the four living creatures) and the elders a Lamb standing, as if slain, having seven horns and seven eyes, which are the seven Spirits of God, sent out into all the earth. (Revelation 5:6).*

John has just been told about the Lion of the tribe of Judah. He looks up and expects to see a lion, but he does not. Instead he sees a lamb. This was not any old lamb. It was a lamb which looked as though it had been slain. What does a lamb look like that has been slain? Its throat has been cut. It is a bloody sacrifice.

The principle of a sacrificed lamb goes back to the Old Testament. It goes back before the prophets and before the kings. It goes back before the Judges and before Moses and before Abraham. It goes all the way back to the Garden of Eden.

Do you remember what happened after Adam and Eve fell into sin? They recognized their nakedness and they found themselves ashamed. They tried to cover up with fig leaves. I'm not much into fashion design, but I don't think a fig leaf dress would be very durable; certainly not wash and wear. Prior to casting them out of the Garden, the Lord did something special for them.

> *The LORD God made garments of skin for Adam and his wife, and clothed them. (Genesis 3:21).*

Did you hear the story of when the chicken, the cow and the pig were having a discussion? The chicken said, "It is wonderful how we are able to serve the farmer at each morning's breakfast by providing him with bacon and eggs and milk." To which the pig replied, "For you this is merely the giving of a portion of your sustenance. For me it is a lifetime commitment."

That is what was involved in the making of these garments of skin. For Adam and Eve to wear such garments means that some animal had to be slain to provide the skins. That was a picture of Jesus. He is the ultimate sacrifice whose life was laid down to provide a covering from sin. It is through His death that we are clothed in a righteousness not our own.

This lamb looked as though it had been killed, yet it was standing. It was a lamb that had been sacrificed on the altar, but then had risen from the dead. Once again, this is a picture of Jesus in His death and in His resurrection. Do you remember when the disciples first saw the risen Jesus? One of the ways by which they recognized Him was when they saw the nail prints in His hands and His feet and when they saw the terrible scar in His side. These marks were still present in the body of the risen Jesus. I believe they are still present today. They are eternal reminders of what He has done for us. Thus, as John sees the lamb, he sees that it bears the marks of sacrifice. He looks at the lamb and recognizes that it has passed under the sacrificial knife.

As John continues to examine the lamb, he notices that it has some other characteristics that are not found on your everyday and average run-of-the-mill lamb.

1.   *Seven horns.*

>   Lambs do not have horns. That fact alone makes us take another look at the fact that this lamb not only has horns, it has seven of them. The horn was considered to be a symbol of strength in the ancient world. There are a number of Old Testament passages that illustrate this:

> > *And all the horns of the wicked He will cut off, but the horns of the righteous will be lifted up. (Psalm 75:10).*

> > *In fierce anger He has cut off all the strength (horn) of Israel; He has drawn back His right hand from before the enemy. And He has burned in Jacob like a fire*

125

consuming round about. (Lamentations 2:3).

> *On that day I shall make a horn sprout for the house of Israel, and I shall open your mouth in their midst. Then they will know that I am the Lord. (Ezekiel 29:21).*

In each of these passages, the horn can be seen to be a symbol of strength and of vitality. In a similar way, the apocalyptic literature of the Jewish apocrypha presented what is thought to be a vision of the Maccabees by a symbol of a lamb with horns (Enoch 90:9).

2.   *Seven eyes.*

We do not have to guess at the identity of the seven eyes. The passage tells us their meaning. They represent *the seven Spirits of God, sent out into all the earth.* They are pictured as seven eyes. These are the same seven spirits we saw back in Revelation 1:4 who were before the throne of God. They are described here as seven eyes. I think that there is a reason for this. It is because God wants us to know that He is watching. The Old Testament prophet Zechariah related the words of the Lord in describing seven eyes.

> *"For behold, the stone that I have set before Joshua; on one stone are seven eyes. Behold, I will engrave an inscription on it," declares the LORD of hosts, "and I will remove the iniquity of that land in one day." (Zechariah 3:9).*

The eyes of the Lord are pictured as traveling over the whole earth. There is no place you can go to escape their sight. Do you remember the story of Jonah? He thought that he could run to the Tarshish, but God was there. He told the sailors to cast him into the sea, but God was there. Even in the belly of the whale, God was still there. Go where he might, Jonah could not escape the presence of God. Neither can you.

Are you serving the Lord in some small way and wondering whether anyone notices your little work of service? Take comfort. God knows and will reward. Are you going through hard times? God knows. Are you only living in obedience to Him one or two days out of the week? His vision is not limited only to when you are in church. There is nothing that takes place that is outside of His knowledge. To the faithful, this is a vision of comfort. To those who are not faithful, this is a warning.

THE VICTORY OF THE LAMB

> *And He came and took the book out of the right hand of Him who sat on the throne.*
>
> *When He had taken the book, the four living creatures and the twenty-four elders fell down before the Lamb, each one holding a harp and golden bowls full of incense, which are the prayers of the saints.*
>
> *And they sang a new song, saying, "Worthy are You to take the book and to break its seals; for You were slain, and purchased for God with Your blood men from every tribe and tongue and people and nation.*
>
> *"You have made them to be a kingdom and priests to our God; and they will reign upon the earth." (Revelation 5:7-10).*

Notice that the elders sing a new song. I know some Christians that seem to think you should never sing anything new in church. But the Bible is always telling us to sing a new song.

> *Sing to Him a **new song**;*
> *Play skillfully with a shout of joy. (Psalm 33:3).*

> *And He put a **new song** in my mouth, a song of praise to our God;*
> *Many will see and fear,*
> *And will trust in the LORD. (Psalm 40:3).*

> *Sing to the LORD a **new song**;*
> *Sing to the LORD, all the earth. (Psalm 96:1).*

I don't know about you, but I tend to like the old songs. That is probably my conservative personality. I am the kind of person who likes to do things the way we've always done them, the kind of person who seems to think nothing ever ought to be done for the first time. But there is a time for a new song.

> *O Sing to the LORD a new song,*
> *For He has done wonderful things,*
> *His right hand and His holy arm have gained the victory for Him.*
> *(Psalm 98:1).*

We are called to sing a new song because we have entered into a new relationship. We have become a new people because of the new victory that has been won on our behalf. We have a new name. We have experienced a new birth and that calls for a new song.

In this new song, we learn something about the victory of the lamb. You don't normally think of lambs as being victorious. A lamb is an animal more designed to be a victim. We think of lambs being led off to the slaughter. Helpless. But in His very helplessness and in His very slaughter, this Lamb conquered. With His shed blood, He purchased *men from every tribe and tongue and people and nation.* But that is not all. What He has done with this diversified group from every tribe and tongue and people and nation is to accomplish in them that which He initially promised to Israel. He has *to be a kingdom and priests to our God.* Then the children of Israel first came to Mount Sinai, the Lord gave them a promise of a new relationship.

> *"Now then, if you will indeed obey My voice and keep My covenant, then you shall be My own possession among all the peoples, for all the earth is Mine; 6 and you shall be to Me a kingdom of priests and a holy nation." These are the words that you shall speak to the sons of Israel." (Exodus 19:5-6).*

This promise that was originally given to the nation of Israel has now been extended to *men from every tribe and tongue and people and nation.* All who have come to faith in the Messiah of Israel have entered into the promises of Israel. We have together been grafted into a single body where there is no longer Jew or Gentile, bond or free, male or female as regards to our status with the Lord.

THE SONG OF THE HEAVENLY HOSTS

> *And I looked, and I heard the voice of many angels around the throne and the living creatures and the elders; and the number of them was myriads of myriads, and thousands of thousands, 12 saying with a loud voice, "Worthy is the Lamb that was slain to receive power and riches and wisdom and might and honor and glory and blessing." (Revelation 5:11-12).*

The next song John hears comes from all the hosts of heaven. This includes the four living ones around the throne and it includes the twenty four elders. It also includes many more. It is a reminder that these living creatures and these elders represent a far greater number. They represent *myriads of myriads, and thousands of thousands.*

In one of the remakes of Alexander Dumas's *Man in the Iron Mask*, the Three Musketeers have come out of retirement to attempt to place the young rightful king upon the throne. The young king looks at Athos and asks, "Are you certain that you want to risk your life for me?" Athos replies, "All our lives, we have been awaiting a king who was worthy of our lives." In the same way, we worship a king who is worthy. That makes all the difference when we set out to serve Him This song focuses on the worthiness of the lamb. The lamb is said to be worthy to receive seven things:

- Power.
- Riches.
- Wisdom.
- Might.
- Honor.
- Glory.
- Blessing.

These seven things are rooted in Old Testament theology. They are ascriptions that are used of God. He is embodied in these seven characteristics. But in this passage, it is the Son who is given these descriptions.

THE SONG OF CREATION

> *And every created thing which is in heaven and on the earth and under the earth and on the sea, and all things in them, I heard saying, "To Him who sits on the throne, and to the Lamb, be blessing and honor and glory and dominion forever and ever." 14 And the four living creatures kept saying, "Amen." And the elders fell down and worshiped. (Revelation 5:13-14).*

The final song is sung by everyone. It includes the living ones and the elders and the angels and the animals and everything else in creation. This is striking because creation is not singing today. Creation is groaning today.

> *For we know that the whole creation groans and suffers the pains of childbirth together until now. 23 And not only this, but also we ourselves, having the first fruits of the Spirit, even we ourselves groan within ourselves, waiting eagerly for our adoption as sons, the redemption of our body. (Romans 8:22-23).*

Creation today is suffering the effects of the fall. If you don't believe this, I invite you to come and look at my lawn. I have to hire someone to make sure weeds do not take over the grass. The fact that we live in a fallen world means that weeds grow and that crops die and that floods and hurricanes hit. It means that roofs leak and that windows get dirty and that food spoils. It means that people sin and that some do not believe.

There is coming a day when everyone who lives will come to recognize that both the Father and the Son are worthy of our worship. Not everyone recognizes it now. But that does not make any difference because God is still in control. He continues to sit in the control room of the universe and He is in control of His domain.

Do you believe that? You may say you do, but is it reflected in your prayer life? Is it seen in your worship? Does your life demonstrate your belief that God is in control? There have been too many times when, because we have not seen a vision of God, we have acted flippantly toward Him and have not worshiped Him with the honor that is His due. Thus, we close this chapter with a call to worship. It is a call to join the hosts of heaven. Come to Him who is worthy! Come and worship the King!

THE FOUR HORSEMEN & THE HOOFBEATS OF HISTORY
Revelation 6:1-8

> *And I saw when the Lamb broke one of the seven seals, and I heard one of the four living creatures saying as with a voice of thunder, "Come." (Revelation 6:1).*

A lot of people read this passage and they are frightened. I can't really blame them. There are some frightening things in this passage. We are going to see four horsemen bringing war and famine and disease and depression and death. It would be enough to frighten any sane man. And yet, this passage is not written to frighten us. It is written to comfort us.

In the previous two chapters, John was given a magnificent vision. He was carried up into heaven. There he saw a throne and living creatures and elders. He also saw a book with seven seals. John wept when he thought that the seals might not be opened. He wept because he realized that these are God's seals and that they offer comfort to believers.

We are going to see some things in this chapter that may seem frightening. We will see four horsemen and the events that accompany them. If we are not discriminating in our reading, we will be frightened. We need to remember that the four horsemen are sent by God. They are like the cavalry coming to the rescue. They are a sign to believers that God's redemption is at hand.

THE RIDER OF THE WHITE HORSE

> *And I saw when the Lamb broke one of the seven seals, and I heard one of the four living creatures saying as with a voice of thunder, "Come."*
> *And I looked, and behold, a white horse, and he who sat on it had a bow; and a crown was given to him; and he went out conquering, and to conquer. (Revelation 6:1-2).*

John has been transported to heaven. There he has seen the throne of God and the four living ones and the 24 elders around the throne. He saw God holding the sealed scroll and he watched the call go out for one who was worthy to open the scroll. He wept when nobody could be found and then he rejoiced with the rest of heaven when the Lamb of God stepped forward to open the scroll.

Now, as the first seal is broken, John and the living ones and the elders all crowd around to read the page that has been revealed. However, this is no ordinary page. It is a living, breathing volume which leaps full-blown from the pages and thunders before John's vision.

I have heard a great deal of teaching on these four horsemen and what they represented. What most people seem to ignore is this is not the first time the Bible has described them. The Old Testament prophet Zechariah had a similar vision.

> *I saw at night, and behold, a man was riding on a red hose, and he was standing among the myrtle trees which were in the ravine, with red, sorrel, and white horses behind him.*
>
> *Then I said, "My lord, what are these?" And the angel who was speaking with me said to me, "I will show you what these are."*
>
> *And the man who was standing among the myrtle trees answered and said, "These are those whom the Lord has sent to patrol the earth."*
>
> *So they answered the angel of the Lord who was standing among the myrtle trees, and said, "We have patrolled the earth, and behold, all the earth is peaceful and quiet." (Zechariah 1:8-11).*

Zechariah describes four horsemen. They have been sent by God. They are servants of God. They have been sent to the earth. Their mission is to "patrol the earth." Apparently they are some sort of divine policemen, at work at keeping God's order upon the earth. Later on in Zechariah we see them once again, only this time there is a difference in the way they are described.

> *Now I lifted up my eyes again and looked, and behold, four chariots were coming forth from between the two mountains; and the mountains were bronze mountains.*
>
> *With the first chariot were red horses, with the second chariot black horses, 3 with the third chariot white horses, and with the fourth chariot strong dappled horses.*
>
> *Then I spoke and said to the angel who was speaking with me, "What are these, my lord?"*
>
> *And the angel answered and said to me, "These are the four spirits of heaven, going forth after standing before the Lord of all the earth." (Zechariah 6:1-5).*

Instead of describing four horsemen, this time Zechariah describes four chariots. Once again, their mission is described as "patrolling the earth." This time the color of the horses drawing these four chariots correspond more exactly to the four horses seen by John. The following chart gives a summary of the various horses, chariots,

132

and colors involved in these visions:

Zechariah 1:8-11	Zechariah 6:1-5	Revelation 6:1-8
Four horsemen	Four chariots	Four horsemen
Red Red Sorrel White	Red Black White Dappled	White Red Black Ashen

The four horsemen in Zechariah reported that "all the earth is peaceful and quiet" (Zechariah 1:11). But the four horsemen that John sees make no such proclamation. With their coming we see anything but peace and quiet.

1.   The Description of the White Rider: *And I looked, and behold, a white horse, and he who sat on it had a bow; and a crown was given to him (6:2).*

Who is the rider on the white horse? Bible scholars have argued over his identity for centuries. Some have thought that he represented this conqueror or that conqueror. Others have looked for a future conqueror, an Antichrist who is to come.

On the other hand, we have not been left in doubt about these horsemen. They are not the forces of Satan. They are the forces of God. It is for this reason that some have thought it to be Jesus Christ Himself. By the end of this book, we shall see Jesus riding on a white horse and wearing a crown and coming forth to conquer.

> *And I saw heaven opened; and behold, a white horse, and He who sat upon it is called Faithful and True; and in righteousness He judges and wages war.*
> *And His eyes are a flame of fire, and upon His head are many diadems; and He has a name written upon Him which no one knows except Himself. (Revelation 19:11-12).*

The similarities between these two horsemen are striking.

- Each rides a white horse.
- Each wears a crown.
- Each goes off to conquer.

It is for this reason that some have suggested that the rider of the white horse represents Jesus and His armies, the conquering King and His victorious church. There are two different words for "crown" used in these two passages. In Revelation 19:12 we see the rider with many "diadems" (διαδήματα) while here in Revelation 6:2 we see this rider with a "crown" (στέφανος). On the other hand, Revelation 14:14 describes *one like a son of man, having a golden crown* (στέφανον) *on His head,* a picture that nearly everyone agrees is a reference to Jesus.

Is this Jesus? I used to think it was, but I am not so sure anymore. The biggest problem is that this rider is one of four riders that go forth from the throne of God. He is not distinguished in any way above the other riders. That is not the way in which John presents Jesus within this book. When we see Jesus, there will be no doubt as to his identity. We will not possibly mistake Him for anyone else.

2.   The Weapon of the White Rider: *And I looked, and behold, a white horse, and he who sat on it had a bow (6:2).*

The rider of the white horse is given a bow. The bow was a sign of strength. This is reminiscent of the weapon mentioned by the Lord Himself following the Flood of Noah's day when He said that He would set His bow in the clouds (Genesis 9:13). The bow was used in that setting to describe the great strength of the Lord. It is used the same way here. This rider has a bow and he goes out to conquer.

3.   The Actions of the White Rider: *And he went out conquering, and to conquer (6:2).*

We are not told of the nature of this conquest. Is it a physical conquest or is it spiritual in nature? The description of the bow suggests the former is primarily in view. Even when the Lord spoke in Genesis of placing His bow in the heavens, this was given in the context of the physical destruction of the flood.

On the other hand, we saw in Revelation 2-3 a total of seven different references to the one who "overcomes." What is not so obvious from our English translation is that the Greek word translated "overcome" in those chapters is *nikao* (νικαω) and is the same word that is rendered here as "conquer."

This serves to remind us that we are involved in a great battle. It is a spiritual battle. The armies of the King of Light are pitted against the forces of the prince of darkness. Notice that we are not fighting a defensive war. We are not hiding behind the barred doors of the church, holding on by our fingernails against the siege of the enemy. We are on the offensive. We are attacking. We are the ones who are surrounding the enemy and battering against his defenses. This is what Jesus said to Peter.

"And I also say to you that you are Peter, and upon this rock I will build My church; and the gates of Hades shall not overpower it." (Matthew 16:18).

The picture is not of the church defending itself against the forces of hell, barely holding on in the face of repeated attacks. The picture is of the church smashing a great battering ram against the gates of hell and that those gates are weakening and they are about to spring asunder.

- When you are confronted with sin and turn away and do what is right, you have counter punched the forces of hell.
- When you take a little child and teach her the ways of truth, you are weakening the devil's tottering fortifications.
- When you share the gospel with your next door neighbor and he comes to believe in Jesus Christ as his Savior and Lord, you have just delivered another crushing blow to the enemy.

This is the message of Revelation. We are in a battle and Jesus is winning! Even when we see great conquests taking place on the political scene, even when nation rises against nation and kingdom rises against kingdom, the Lord is in control. In the midst of the smoke and heat of conflict, we cannot always tell from our perspective how the battle goes. It is easy to become disheartened as we hear the battle cries of the enemy. But we can take courage. We are winning the battle!

This is a great source of comfort to John. He has been banished to the island of Patmos. He has seen the persecution which is falling upon the church in the first century. He is witnessing the conflict between light and darkness. But he can be encouraged because Jesus is going to win. You can also take encouragement. Perhaps you have fallen upon hard times. Maybe you feel as though you have been defeated. It could be that circumstances have overwhelmed you. But there is good news. Jesus is going to win. And His people are going to win, too.

THE RIDER OF THE RED HORSE

And when He broke the second seal, I heard the second living creature saying, "Come."
And another, a red horse, went out; and to him who sat on

135

it, it was granted to take peace from the earth, and that men should slay one another; and a great sword was given to him. (Revelation 6:3-4).

The clattering hoofbeats of the first horse have no sooner faded away when the second seal is broken and a second horse gallops into view. Just as the first horse had a mission, this horse is also given a mission. Its mission is "to take peace from the earth."

John lived in the day of "Pax Romana." It was a day when many believed that warfare had been banished from the civilized world. But John is now made to realize that this is a false dream. As long as men rule the earth, there will be no peace. Indeed, peace has been described as that fleeting moment when everyone stops to reload. From John's day to today, there has not been peace upon the earth. There will not be peace upon the earth until the Prince of Peace comes and rules over all men.

Do you see the implications of this? It means that God is in control of war. He was not baffled by the armies of Napoleon. He did not start biting His nails with the advent of Hitler's Nazi Party. During the American War Between the States, the Union General Joseph Hooker prepared to meet the Confederate forces at Chancellorville. His forces vastly outnumbered that of the enemy and he held a superior position. On the morning of the battle, he called his generals to him and, at the end of the briefing, he proclaimed, "Not even God can take this victory from me." Whereupon he went out and suffered the most devastating defeat the Union Army was to experience.

The lesson is clear. It is that God is in control of history. We never need fear armies or powers or governments or men. The God of the universe is stronger than all powers on earth. And, if earthly have been allowed to rattle their sabers for a time, it is merely the sound of God's heavenly hoofbeats that you are hearing.

THE RIDER OF THE BLACK HORSE

And when He broke the third seal, I heard the third living creature saying, "Come." And I looked, and behold, a black horse; and he who sat on it had a pair of scales in his hand.
And I heard as it were a voice in the center of the four living creatures saying, "A quart of wheat for a denarius, and three quarts of barley for a denarius; and do not harm the oil and wine." (Revelation 6:5-6).

The third horse is a black horse. Just as the first two horses represented conditions upon the earth, so he also represents conditions upon the earth. This which he carries is symbolic for earthly situations.

1. A Symbol of Economy: *He who sat on it had a pair of scales in his hand (6:5).*

   Scales were to the ancient world what a cash register is to the modern world. Therefore, this third horseman is going to deal with the economic condition of the world.

2. A Symbol of Financial Difficulties: *"A quart of wheat for a denarius, and three quarts of barley for a denarius" (6:6).*

   A denarius was considered to be a fair day's wage for a Roman soldier. In the parable that Jesus told of the landowner who hired the workers, he paid them a denarius for their day of work (Matthew 20:2). A quart of wheat was considered to be food enough to last a man for that one day. In other words, this is describing a condition in which a man must work for an entire day just to feed himself. Such a man would not be able to adequately feed his family. However, the same voice declares that three quarts of barley can be had for a denarius. Barley was not as good as wheat. It was edible, but it was not as nutritious.

   This third horse describes a conditions of economic hardship created by inflationary prices. Now, maybe you are thinking to yourself, "Wait a minute. Things aren't as bad as all that. I am not suffering any real hardship." Maybe it is because you fall into the second category which is described here.

3. A Symbol of Prosperity: *"And do not harm the oil and wine" (6:6).*

   Oil and wine are the comforts of life. In the midst of economic hardships which most people experience, there are still a few who enjoy an abundance of food and the added luxuries of life, too. This was true in the first century. There were many people who were struggling merely to feed themselves and their families. Jesus said that we will always have the poor among us. But here is another truth. We will always have the rich among us.

   No matter how bad things get, there will still be those who are rich. No matter how good things get, there will still be those who are poor. Jesus said that you will always have the poor with you (Matthew 26:11). The question faced by every Christian is whether he will trust in physical riches that pass away on in spiritual riches that last for eternity.

THE RIDER OF THE ASHEN HORSE

And when He broke the fourth seal, I heard the voice of the fourth living creature saying, "Come."
 And I looked, and behold, an ashen horse; and he who sat on it had the name Death; and Hades was following with him. And authority was given to them over a fourth of the earth, to kill with sword and with famine and with pestilence and by wild beasts of the earth. (Revelation 6:7-8).

We are left in no doubt as to the identity of this last horseman. He is named for us. He is Death. He has a companion. His companion is Hades. Death statistics are astounding. One out of every one person dies. Death is no respecter of persons. And yet, this dark rider is not the normal death which eventually strikes down all men. His authority only reaches to a portion of mankind. His realm is death by disease and by violence.

Now we come to the final question. How are we to understand these four horsemen as a collective group? Are they some future apparition which awaits us? Are they reserved for some time of terrible tribulation which must befall us in the days and years to come? No. I don't think that they are only to be found in the future. I believe that they are a part of God's plan for this age in which we now live. From the vision of John to this day, we have witnessed the activity of these four horsemen. We have seen the preaching of the gospel and the conquest of Christianity. We have seen wars and rumors of wars. We have seen economic upheaval and the poor and the rich are still with us. We continue to see violent death in our society. These are not visions only of the future. They are also visions of the present. They are visions of God's program for history for yesterday and today and tomorrow.

This is a very bleak picture that John has painted for us. While we rejoice at the white horse of the gospel of Christ, we shudder as we hear the hoofbeats of warfare and of economic upheavals and of violent death. And yet, we should remember that it is God who sits on the throne and it is from His hand that the scroll of history has been taken and unraveled.

Do you tremble when you hear the hoofbeats? Take comfort, for the Lord of the horsemen watches over you and though they may appear frightful and uncontrolled, they are merely His servants. When you open tomorrow's newspaper and read of the things that are happening throughout the world, you are reading about the One who holds the reigns of human history - the God who sends the horsemen.

THE DAY OF WRATH
Revelation 6:9-17

The wrath of God isn't a subject about which we talk a lot. We would much rather talk about the love of God and the mercy of God. After all, who wants to hear about an angry God?

The subject of the wrath of God is one of the most neglected topics in churches today. Very few preachers speak on this subject. It has become something of a taboo to speak about God being angry toward sin. It is almost with embarrassment that some Christians admit that God is a God of wrath. And yet, this is the subject that we now approach as we come to the next two seals of the heavenly scroll.

THE FIFTH SEAL

> *And when He broke the fifth seal, I saw underneath the altar the souls of those who had been slain because of the word of God, and because of the testimony which they had maintained; 10 and they cried out with a loud voice, saying, "How long, O Lord, holy and true, wilt Thou refrain from judging and avenging our blood on those who dwell on the earth?"*
>
> *And there was given to each of them a white robe; and they were told that they should rest for a little while longer, until the number of their fellow servants and their brethren who were to be killed even as they had been, should be completed also. (Revelation 6:9-11).*

As we open to this passage, John witnesses the opening of the fifth seal. He has already seen the opening of the first four seals.

- The first seal pictured a conqueror going out to conquer. It reminds us of both the physical and spiritual conquests this world has seen.
- The second seal represented the results of the spiritual battle — the physical and social unrest that has plagued mankind since John's day.
- The third seal revealed economic upheaval. It pictured economic inflation and its results on the poor and the rich.
- And the fourth seal pictured the most terrible specter thus far — violent death.

Now, as we come to the fifth seal, it is introduced, not by a horseman, but by an altar.

1.   The Significance of the Altar: *I saw underneath the altar the souls of those who had been slain (6:9).*

This is the first mention that John has made of an altar. He has described other things that would have been present in the temple, but up to this point he has not mentioned an altar.

Isaiah's description of the throne room of heaven included an altar of incense. The sixth chapter of Isaiah tells of a wonderful vision which that prophet received of the throne room of God. As Isaiah saw the magnificent vision of the glory of the Lord in His temple, he realized his own unclean state.

> *Then I said, "Woe is me, for I am ruined! Because I am a man of unclean lips, and I live among a people of unclean lips; for my eyes have seen the King, the Lord of hosts."*
> *Then one of the seraphim flew to me, with a burning coal in his hand which he had taken from the **altar** with tongs.*
> *And he touched my mouth with it and said, "Behold, this has touched your lips; and your iniquity is taken away, and your sin is forgiven." (Isaiah 6:5-7).*

If you could have gone to the city of Jerusalem in the early part of the first century, you would have seen the temple of the Lord. Had you been permitted to enter into the temple, you would have seen on your left the golden lampstand. On your right would he the table of shewbread. And standing before you would be the altar of incense.

A priest would come here each morning and each evening to offer incense upon the altar. As he took the incense in a small bowl and sprinkled it upon the altar, the people would be gathered together outside the temple for the morning or evening prayers. As the incense fell upon the altar, it would touch the hot coals and produce a light sweet-smelling smoke which would fill the temple and rise up into the sky. This smoke represented the prayers of the people being offered up to God.

In Revelation 5:6 John described each of the 24 elders as holding a golden bowl full of incense, which are the prayers of the saints. However, there is no incense mentioned in connection with this altar. This altar has the souls of martyred believers gathered under it.

2.   The Souls and the Altar: *The souls of those who had been slain because of the word of God, and because of the testimony which they had main-*

tained (6:9).

These martyred believers had been put to death for the same reason that John had been sent to Patmos. It was because of their witness of Jesus.

3.   The Prayer from the Altar: *"How long, O Lord, holy and true, wilt Thou refrain from judging and avenging our blood on those who dwell on the earth?" (6:10).*

This is the prayer of the martyred believers that John sees under the altar. They are asking a question. Why does God allow sin to continue? Why does He allow a Hitler to live? Why doesn't He stop bad things from happening? The answer is found in the patience of God. God is patient. The same God who holds the universe together by His power daily holds together the life of the unbeliever who hates Him.

> *The Lord is not slow about His promise, as some count slowness, but is patient toward you, not wishing for any to perish but for all to come to repentance. (2 Peter 3:9).*

When you sin, God does not send down a great bolt of lightning and blast you into oblivion. He is patient. He is waiting for a time of future judgment. Why? It is because He does not want any of His people to perish. He is waiting for all those who will become His people to come to Him.

Let me ask you a question. What would have happened if God had grown impatient and decided to punish sin four days before you came to know Christ? You would have been judged and condemned and cast into hell! The reason that you are saved today is because God withheld His judgment against sin until you had come to Him in faith.

The reason you are saved today and not suffering the torment of hell is because God has been patient toward you. He was not willing that you should perish. He waited for you to come to repentance. He is still waiting. He is waiting for others to come to Him in faith, trusting in the provision that He has made for them. He is waiting for others to believe in .Jesus Christ and be saved. But He will not wait forever. There is coming a day when judgment will come. There is coming a day when the Lord will return to judge those who have rejected His salvation. There is coming a day when the heavens will pass away and the earth with all of its wickedness will be destroyed.

> *But the day of the Lord will come like a thief, in*

which the heavens will pass away with a roar and the elements will be destroyed with intense heat, and the earth and its works will be burned up. (2 Peter 3:10).

What is to be our response to this terrible vision? What effect does this teaching of the wrath of God have in our lives? This is an important question. This prophecy was not given to satisfy our curiosity about future events. Prophecy is never given for that reason. Why was this prophecy given? It was given to bring about a change in our lives. Peter is quick to point out the proper response.

> *Therefore, beloved, since you look for these things, be diligent to be found by Him in peace, spotless and blameless, 15 and regard the patience of our Lord to be salvation; just as also our beloved brother Paul, according to the wisdom given him, wrote to you." (2 Peter 3:14-15).*

The response to this teaching of the wrath of God is twofold. The first response is inward. It concerns our personal lives. Once we have seen what God's attitude is concerning sin, it should have an effect in our lives. We are to he at peace. We are to be spotless and blameless. We are to be free of sin. The wrath of God is a motivation to personal godliness.

The second response is upward. It concerns our view of the patience of God. When we see sin going unpunished and wrong and evil-doing flourishing, we should not be disheartened. Rather, we need to see this as a sign of the patience of God which has brought about our salvation.

Let me put this on a personal level. Have you suffered a wrong that has not been righted? Have you been stepped on so many times that you feel like a welcome mat? Do you always seem to get the short end of the stick? You are seeing the patience of God at work. That very same patience was necessary for your salvation. It is a sign of your salvation. This is reflected in the answer that is given to the souls under the altar.

4.   A Continuing Work: *They were told that they should rest for a little while longer, until the number of their fellow servants and their brethren who were to be killed even as they had been, should be completed also (6:11).*

This group of martyrs had asked for the judgment of God against those who had put them to death. In answer, God says, "I'm not finished yet." This is the answer of the patience of God. It is a lesson that we need to learn. We need to realize that bad things are going to continue to happen, but that it is okay because only after the storm has come and the rains have fallen can the fruit grow and be harvested.

5.   A Picture of Salvation: *And there was given to each of them a white robe (6:11).*

The image of the white robe is not a new one. It is found in a vivid prophecy of Zechariah.

> *Then he showed me Joshua the high priest standing before the angel of the Lord, and Satan standing at his right hand to accuse him.*
> *And the Lord said to Satan, "The Lord rebuke you, Satan. Indeed, the Lord who has chosen Jerusalem rebuke you! Is this not a brand plucked from the fire?"*
> *Now Joshua was clothed with filthy garments and standing before the angel.*
> *And he spoke and said to those who were standing before him saying, 'Remove the filthy garments from him." Again he said to him, See, I have taken you iniquity away from you and will clothe you with festal robes."* (Zechariah 3:1-4).

Joshua was the name of the high priest in Jerusalem in the days after the Babylonian Captivity. In this vision, Zechariah sees the high priest being accused by Satan. To make matters worse, Satan has a basis for this accusation. The purity of the high priest as represented by his clothing is filthy. This does not mean that Joshua was any worse than you or I. It simply means that all of us are impure when standing before a holy God. Even our good works are likened to filthy garments (Isaiah 64:6).

However, just as things are looking hopeless for Joshua, the angel announces that a change is to he made. The filthy garments that belong to Joshua are removed and a set of clean, unspotted clothes are given in their place. This is not merely a picture of the high priest of Jerusalem. He is representative of all men who come to God.

> *"Now listen, Joshua the high priest, you and your friends who are sitting in front of you —indeed they are men who are a symbol, for behold, I am going to bring in My servant the Branch.*
> *"For behold, the stone that I have set before Joshua; on one stone are seven eyes. Behold, I will engrave an inscription on it," declares the Lord of hosts, "and I will remove the iniquity of that land in one day."* (Zechariah 3:6-9).

Notice that Joshua is merely a symbol. When Zechariah sees Joshua standing before the angel of the Lord, he to understand that Joshua is a symbol of all men who must stand before God and give account. Like Joshua, we are all found to be lacking when we stand before God. We all wear the same filthy garments. We have all sinned and have fallen short of the glory of God. But there is also good news. The good news is that God has brought His Branch, the One who is from the root of Jesse and the royal tree of David. When He died upon the cross, He removed iniquity from the land.

However, there are also some who remain in their filthy garments. There are some who have rejected the Branch. They will also be judged. And on that day, they will face the wrath of the Lamb.

THE SIXTH SEAL

And I looked when He broke the sixth seal, and there was a great earthquake; and the sun became black as sackcloth made of hair, and the whole moon became like blood; 13 and the stars of the sky fell to the earth, as a fig tree casts its unripe figs when shaken by a great wind.

And the sky was split apart like a scroll when it is rolled up; and every mountain and island were moved out of their places.

And the kings of the earth and the great men and the commanders and the rich and the strong and every slave and free man, hid themselves in the caves and among the rocks of the mountains; 16 and they said to the mountains and to the rocks, "Fall on us, and hide us from the presence of Him who sits on the throne, and from the wrath of the Lamb; 17 for the great day of their wrath has come; and who is able to stand?" (Revelation 6: 12-17).

With the opening of the sixth seal, I believe that John moves from the realm of the present to the realm of the future.

- He has seen the conquest of the church.
- He has seen war and rumors of war.
- He has seen economic upheaval and violent death.
- He has seen the cry of martyrs.

All of these things were going on in John's day and some of them are still going on today. But with the opening of this sixth seal, we see something that has never been seen from John's day to the present. We see the wrath of God revealed.

144

As we read of the prophecies of this chapter, we should be aware that there is something of a parallel to be seen between the events of this chapter and the events described in the Olivet Discourse as described in Matthew's Gospel:

Matthew 24	Revelation 6
For many will come in My name, saying, "I am the Christ," and will mislead many (24:5).	And I looked, and behold, a white horse, and he who sat on it had a bow; and a crown was given to him; and he went out conquering, and to conquer (6:2).
And you will be hearing of wars and rumors of wars; see that you are not frightened, for those things must take place, but that is not yet the end. 7 For nation will rise against nation, and kingdom against kingdom... (24:6-7).	And another, a red horse, went out; and to him who sat on it, it was granted to take peace from the earth, and that men would slay one another; and a great sword was given to him (6:4).
...and in various places there will be famines and earthquakes (24:7).	And I looked, and behold, a black horse; and he who sat on it had a pair of scales in his hand. 6 And I heard as it were a voice in the center of the four living creatures saying, "A quart of wheat for a denarius, and three quarts of barley for a denarius; and do not harm the oil and the wine." (6:5-6).
	And I looked, and behold, an ashen horse; and he who sat on it had the name Death; and Hades was following with him. And authority was given to them over a fourth of the earth, to kill with sword and with famine and with pestilence and by the wild beasts of the earth (6:8).
Then they will deliver you to tribulation, and will kill you, and you will be hated by all nations on account of My name (24:8).	I saw underneath the altar the souls of those who had been slain because of the word of God, and because of the testimony which they had maintained (6:9).

But immediately after the tribulation of those days the sun will be darkened, and the moon will not give its light, and the stars will fall from the sky, and the powers of the heavens will be shaken, 30 and then the sign of the Son of Man will appear in the sky, and then all the tribes of the earth will mourn, and they will see the Son of Man coming on the clouds of the sky with power and great glory (24:29-30).	...and there was a great earthquake; and the sun became black as sackcloth made of hair, and the whole moon became like blood; 13 and the stars of the sky fell to the earth, as a fig tree casts its unripe figs when shaken by a great wind (6:12-13). "Fall on us and hide us from the presence of Him who sits on the throne, and from the wrath of the Lamb; 17 for the great day of their wrath has come; and who is able to stand?" (6:16-17).

In both cases, we have described throughout the first several parts of the passages those events that characterized both the first century as well as the entire scope of this present age. In both cases, the prophecy culminates with the return of Christ.

We should also notice the correlation between the prayers of believers and the power of God. The fifth seal depicts believers praying. For what were they praying? They were praying for God's judgment to come upon the unbelieving world. In the sixth seal this prayer is answered.

I think this is meant to teach us something about prayer. Prayer is not merely a spiritual exercise that we perform. Prayer changes things. The God who controls the universe acts in response to the prayer of His people. There is a direct correlation between the prayers of God's people and the patterns of history.

1.   Signs in the Heavens: *And there was a great earthquake; and the sun became black as sackcloth made of hair, and the whole moon became like blood (6:12).*

These things that John witnesses echo throughout the Old Testament Scriptures.

> *Behold, the day of the Lord is coming, cruel, with fury and burning anger, to make the land a desolation; and He will exterminate its sinners from it.*
> *For the stars of heaven and their constellations will not flash forth their light; then sun will be dark when it rises, and the moon will not shed its light.*
> *Thus I will punish the world for its evil, and the wicked for their iniquity; I will also put an end to the arrogance of the proud, and abase the haughtiness of the*

ruthless. (Isaiah 13:9-11).

What is this passage describing? Isaiah calls it an "oracle concerning Babylon" (Isaiah 13:1). He goes on to describe how the Medes would be stirred up against Babylon and would overthrow the city and that it would never be rebuilt. This is a prophecy that was fulfilled in history. Likewise, the Lord speaks through prophet Joel to foretell a destruction that is to come upon the earth. Once again, it is described as "the day of the Lord."

> *And I will display wonders in the sky and on the earth, blood, fire, and columns of smoke.*
> *The sun will be turned into darkness, and the moon into blood, before the great and awesome day of the Lord comes. (Joel 2:30-31).*

In the following chapter, Joel again mentions the day of the Lord and the effects that this day has upon the sun and the moon.

> *Multitudes, multitudes in the valley of decision.*
> *For the day of the Lord is near in the valley of decision.*
> *The sun and moon grow dark,*
> *And the stars loose their brightness. (Joel 3:14-15).*

Notice that this time the stars are also mentioned. We shall see this paralleled in the sixth seal of Revelation. Each of these passages have one thing in common. Each of them describes the judgment of God. Each of them describes the wrath of a righteous God upon unrighteous men.

Revelation 6:12	Isaiah 13:10	Joel 2-3
And there was a great earthquake; and the sun became black as sackcloth made of hair, and the whole moon became like blood	*For the stars of heaven and their constellations will not flash forth their light; the sun will be dark when it rises, and the moon will not shed its light*	*The sun will be turned into darkness, and the moon into blood (2:30-31).* *The sun and moon grow dark, and the stars loose their brightness (3:14-15)*

Now I want to ask you a question. When was the last time that these events took place? When was there a great earthquake and when did the sun grow dim and when did God pronounce judgment against sin?

It happened on a small hill outside the city of Jerusalem. The hill was named Golgotha. The place of the skull. It was here that the wrath of a holy God was poured out upon the Son of Man. It was here that the sins of the world were credited to the only Sinless One. It was here that we were redeemed. Do you remember the events that took place when Jesus died?

- There was darkness upon the whole land (Matthew 27:45).
- The great veil in the temple was torn from top to bottom (Matthew 27:51).
- There was a great earthquake as the ground shook and rocks were torn asunder and graves were opened and dead people were raised from the dead (Matthew 27:51-52).

Now we see a new truth. It is going to happen again. The same events which were seen at the death of Christ will be seen when He comes the second time.

- The sun an the moon will he darkened.
- There will be a great earthquake.
- And once again dead men will get up and walk.

Only, this time, there will be a difference. This time the kings of the earth will sit up and take notice. This time there will be no more unbelief. This time every man will realize that Jesus is King.

2.   The Reaction of Men: *And the kings of the earth and the great men and the commanders and the rich and the strong and every slave and free man, hid themselves (6:15).*

Do you remember the story of Joshua and the battle with the five Amorite kings? The battle took place before the walls of Gibeon. Five kings had gathered to do battle against the nomadic tribes of Israel. During the battle, great hailstones fell from the sky, devastating the Amorite armies. It was during that battle that Joshua called for the sun and the moon to stand still so that the enemy would not be able to escape under cover of darkness. The five kings were discovered hiding from the army of the Lord within a cave.

On the day that the Lord returns, the kings of the earth will once again wish to go into hiding within the bowels of the earth. But they will not be alone. John mentions seven different groups:

- The kings of the earth
- The great men.
- The commanders.
- The rich.

148

- The strong.
- Every slave.
- Every free man.

The first five groups describe people who consider themselves fearless. They are the self-sufficient. They are the powerful. But they are going to recognize their own inadequacy. The last two groups describe the two extremes in society. The rich and the poor, the slave and the free, the up and coming and the down and out will all face the coming of the Lord on an equal footing.

3.   A Hebraistic Appeal: *And they said to the mountains and to the rocks, "Fall on us, and hide us" (6:13).*

This is a Hebraism. It is a figure of speech. Similar figures of speech are found in Isaiah 2:19, Hosea 10:8 and in Luke 23:30. We use a similar figure of speech when we talk about someone who hides his head in a hole in the ground. It doesn't mean that people will literally be praying for landslides. But it does describe the appeal of one who has found that there is no escape from that final judgment.

I think that in a sense, we can view this as the prayer of the atheist, for he appeals to nature, the god of the atheist. There is coming a day when the atheist will look to the cosmos for help and he will find none.

4.   An Angry Lamb: *The wrath of the Lamb (6:17).*

This is a striking description. We would expect to read "the wrath of the Lion of the tribe of Judah. A lion would be a fitting personification of wrath. You would be afraid of an angry lion. But who has ever heard of an angry lamb?

Perhaps it is for this reason that this image is used. A lion is easy to provoke to wrath. But it takes an awful lot to provoke a lamb. And so, we see in this title a. reminder of the patience of God.

5.   The Day of Wrath: *For the great day of their wrath has come; and who is able to stand? (6:17).*

The answer to this question is going to be answered in the next chapter. Who will be able to stand before God in the day of judgment? Only those who have the seal of God upon themselves.

That day is coming. You must ask yourself the same question. Are you able to stand in that day? Are you ready to meet your God? That is the same question that the Old Testament prophet Nahum asked as he described the coming of the Lord.

> *Who can stand before His indignation? Who can endure the burning of His anger? His wrath is poured out like fire, and the rocks are broken up by Him.*
>
> *The Lord is good, a stronghold in the day of trouble, and He knows those who take refuge in Him.*
>
> *But with an overflowing flood He will make a complete end of its site, and will pursue His enemies into darkness. (Nahum 1:6-8).*

There are two kinds of people. There are those who have seen in the Lord a stronghold, who have come to Him in faith, and who have trusted in Him as Savior and Lord. There are also those who have rejected the Lord. Maybe you are in this latter category. Maybe you feel that you do not need the Lord. Perhaps you are one of the rich, or the powerful, or the strong. Maybe you feel that you are good enough. On that day, will you be able to stand?

THE SEALED MULTITUDE
Revelation 7:1-17

> *Do not harm the earth or the sea or the trees, until we have sealed the bondservants of our God on their foreheads. (Revelation 7:3).*

The previous chapter ended upon a solemn note. The kings of the earth and the rich and the powerful and everyone else are filled with terror as they witness the unveiled wrath of the Lamb. In the midst of their hopelessness, they cry out, "Who can stand before the wrath of the Lamb?" As we come to this chapter, we are given the answer. This is a chapter of comfort. It is here that we learn that the wrath of the Lamb is not directed against all men. Some are spared that wrath.

A SEAL OF PROTECTION

> *After this I saw four angels standing at the four corners of the earth, holding back the four winds of the earth, so that no wind should blow on the earth or on the sea or on any tree.*
>
> *And I saw another angel ascending from the rising of the sun, having the seal of the living God; and he cried out with a loud voice to the four angels to whom it was granted to harm the earth and the sea, 3 saying, "Do not harm the earth or the sea or the trees, until we have sealed the bondservants of our God on their foreheads." (Revelation 7:1-3).*

John has just witnessed the reaction of the kings and the generals and the rich and the powerful and the slaves and the free men at the unveiling of the wrath of the Lamb. Now he waits in anticipation of the judgment that is to follow. Four angels have gathered at the four corners of the earth. There will be none who will escape this judgment. All is in readiness. But suddenly, there is an interruption.

And I saw another angel ascending from the rising of the sun, having the seal of the living God (7:2). This angel comes up from the east. He is an angel with authority. He has the seal of the living God. This speaks of the authority that has been given to him. His mission is to bring life. *"Do not harm the earth or the sea or the trees, until we have sealed the bondservants of our God on their foreheads" (7:3).*

John had been watching the four angels in anticipation, waiting to see that wrath unleashed. But instead, he sees something else. Instead of seeing wrath, he sees a loving concern. Instead of seeing destruction, he sees a protection.

We learned about seals in chapter 5. A seal was a large metal stamp. It had a written signature engraved on one end. When you wished to put your seal on something, you would pour some clay or hot wax onto it and then you would press the seal into it. The result would be an engraved mark. This mark signified a number of things, but they all spelled authority.

- It signified authenticity. A message would be known to be true if it bore the seal of the writer.
- It signified ownership. Just as cattle are often branded to show that they belong to a particular rancher, so also items of value were marked with the seal to certify their legal ownership.
- The seal also signified protection. As such, it was used by Pontius Pilate to secure the tomb of Jesus. The seal of Rome was placed on the tomb and it could only be broken by someone who was higher in authority than the Roman governor.

Do you remember the mark of Cain? After Cain murdered his brother Abel, God set a mark upon Cain so that others would not seek to wreck vengeance upon him for his evil deed. This was a mark of protection. It signified that this man's life was under the protection of the Lord. If God was gracious enough to grant His protection to this rebellious murderer, do you not also think that He will grant protection to His people?

John's vision of the sealing of people prior to a coming judgment finds its roots in the Old Testament. The prophet Ezekiel had a vision of the destruction of Jerusalem. Before that destruction was allowed to fall, the Lord sent a man through the city to place a mark on the heads of His people.

> Then He cried out in my hearing with a loud voice saying, "Draw near, O executioners of the city, each with his destroying weapon in his hand."
> And behold, six men came from the direction of the upper gate which faces north, each with his shattering weapon in his hand; and among them was a certain man clothed in linen with a writing case at his loins. And they went in and stood beside the bronze alter. (Ezekiel 9:1-2).

These executioners are being called from the north. It was from the north that the invading armies of Nebuchadnezzar came down against Jerusalem in 586 B.C. Notice that it is God who is calling them against the city. But before they are permitted to attack, God sends the man with the writing case to place a mark on those who are remorseful over the wickedness of the city.

> Then the glory of the God of Israel went up from the cherub on which it had been, to the threshold of the temple. And

He called to the man clothed in linen at whose loins was the writing case.

And the Lord said to him, "Go through the midst of the city, even through the midst of Jerusalem, and put a mark on the foreheads of the men who sigh and groan over all the abominations which are being committed in its midst."

But to the others He said in my hearing, "Go through the city after him and strike; do not let your eye have pity, and do not spare. 6 Utterly slay old men, young maidens, little children, and women, but do not touch any man on whom is the mark; and you shall start from My sanctuary." So they started with the elders who were before the temple. (Ezekiel 9:3-6).

Notice that the mark is placed on the forehead of each man. It is the exact same location in which the 144,000 are sealed. It is also for the same purpose. It is so that the people of God will not fall under the judgment that is reserved for the rest of the world. There is a great truth here. It is that we have been sealed. God has set His stamp upon us.

Now He who establishes us with you in Christ and anointed us is God, 22 who also sealed us and gave us the Spirit in our hearts as a pledge. (2 Corinthians 1:21-22).

In Him, you also, after listening to the message of truth, the gospel of your salvation, having also believed, you were sealed in him with the Holy Spirit of promise, 14 who is given as a pledge of our inheritance, with a view to the redemption of God's own possession, to the praise of His glory. (Ephesians 1:13-14).

We have been sealed by God. The seal of God is His own Spirit. That Spirit is a mark of authenticity. It is also a mark which shows God's ownership of us. And it is also a seal of protection upon us. There are some bad things that happen in this world. However, I am protected. That doesn't

> When we come to Revelation 13, we shall see the mark of the beast. The servants of the beast will be sealed in the same way the servants of the Lord are sealed here in this chapter. The truth is that everyone is sealed. Everyone is marked. The only question is whose mark you bear.
>
> Similarly, we can point out that everyone comes under wrath. Those who receive the mark of the beast come under the wrath of God. Those who receive the seal of the spirit come under the wrath of the beast. The question is this: whose mark do you have and whose wrath do you want?

mean that bad things will never happen to me. But it does mean that they will always work together to produce good on my behalf.

153

THE 144,000

> *And I heard the number of those who were sealed, one hundred and forty four thousand sealed from every tribe of the sons of Israel:*
>
> *From the tribe of Judah, twelve thousand were sealed, from the tribe of Reuben, twelve thousand, from the tribe of Gad, twelve thousand, 6 from the tribe of Asher, twelve thousand, from the tribe of Naphtali, twelve thousand, from the tribe of Manasseh, twelve thousand, 7 from the tribe of Simeon, twelve thousand, from the tribe of Levi, twelve thousand, from the tribe of Issachar, twelve thousand, 8 from the tribe of Zebulun, twelve thousand, from the tribe of Joseph, twelve thousand, from the tribe of Benjamin, twelve thousand were sealed. (Revelation 7:4-8).*

John hears the roll call of those who are sealed. There are twelve tribes mentioned. But these are not the same 12 tribes that were always listed in the chronicles of the Jewish people. There are some differences.

The tribe of Judah is mentioned first. Judah was not the firstborn. Reuben was the firstborn. Reuben is always mentioned first in any list of the tribes of Israel. But this is different. Here it is Judah that is mentioned first. Judah was the royal tribe. It was the tribe of David and Solomon. It was the tribe of Jesus. Another difference between this list and others in the Bible is the omission of the tribe of Dan. It is excluded from this list.

Who are these 144,000? What do they represent? What is the significance of this number? The number is 12 x 12 x 1,000. We have already seen two groups of twelve in the 24 elders which are around the throne. They correspond to the 24 courses of the Old Testament priesthood and they also correspond to the combined peoples of the Old and New Covenants. But this time the two 12's are multiplied and then multiplied again by 1,000. The number 1,000 is used to describe a great number.

- Moses speaks of blessing the nation of Israel a thousand-fold (Deuteronomy 1:11).
- God is said to keep His covenant and His loving-kindness to a thousand generations (Deuteronomy 7:9).
- Joshua speaks about how a single Israelite can put a thousand enemy soldiers to flight (Joshua 23:10).
- The Lord owns the cattle on a thousand hills (Psalm 50:10).
- A thousand years are as a single day in the sight of the Lord (Psalm 90:4).
- God's covenant with Abraham was for a thousand generations (Psalm 105:8).

It is obvious that these numbers are not to be taken literally. When the Psalmist says that the Lord owns the cattle on a thousand hills, he does not mean that number 1,001 does not belong to Him. Likewise, when we see the number 1,000 here in Revelation, I do not think that it is limiting the number of God's sealed people to that amount.

Who are these 144,000? Are they some select group of Jewish people? I think that they are much more than that. Just as the 24 elders around the throne represented the 12 tribes and the 12 apostles of God's Old and New Covenants, so also I think that these 144,000 also represent the people of God's Old and New Covenants.

Now, if this is the case, that we are meant to understand these 144,000 as being representative of all of God's people, whether Jew or Gentile, then why are the specific tribes of Israel mentioned? I think that it is because the Lord did not want us to loose sight of our Jewish heritage. When you came to Christ in faith and believed in Him as your Savior and Lord, you entered into something that has a long tradition. You entered into the family of Abraham.

> *But it is not as though the word of God has failed. For they are not all Israel who are descended from Israel; 7 neither are they all children because they are Abraham's descendants, but: "Through Isaac your descendants will be named." 8 That is, it is not the children of the flesh who are children of God, but the children of the promise are regarded as descendants. (Romans 9:6-8).*

The church today is made up mostly of Gentiles. Does this mean that God's promise to Abraham has failed? Not at all. It simply means that it is being fulfilled in a different way. It is being fulfilled through the entire church made of both Jews and Gentiles. It is being fulfilled because we have all become the spiritual descendants of Abraham.

> *Therefore, be sure that it is those who are of faith who are sons of Abraham. (Galatians 3:7).*

> *And if you belong to Christ, then you are Abraham's offspring, heirs according to promise. (Galatians 3:29).*

If you came to Christ, you were grafted into a great tree. The root of the tree goes back to Jesse and to Judah and to Abraham. The branch of the tree is Jesus Christ. You have been grafted into that branch. This is important. God doesn't have two separate peoples. He doesn't have two churches. He has one church and one people.

> *For He Himself is our peace, who made both groups into*

> *one, and broke down the barrier of the dividing wall, 15 by abolishing in His flesh the enmity, which is the Law of commandments contained in ordinances, that in Himself He might make the two into one new man, thus establishing peace, 16 and might reconcile them both into one body to God through the cross, by it having put to death the enmity. (Ephesians 2:14-16).*

This means that for a Christian to be involved in anti-Semitism is to be like a dog that bites his own tail. We have roots and they are Jewish roots. We have traditions, and they go back thousands of years to a time when men met with God in a temple and a tabernacle, and even before that to when God spoke with Abraham face to face.

There is a teaching going around today called "Dispensationalism." It is a relatively new teaching. It has been around for less than 200 years. It was popularized in the last century by the Scofield Reference Bible. It teaches that God has two groups of people that He works with to two separate purposes.

> *A dispensationalist keeps Israel and the Church distinct* (Charles Ryrie, 1965:44).

> *The dispensationalist believes that throughout the ages God is pursuing two distinct purposes: one related to the earth with earthly people and earthly objectives involved which is Judaism; while the other is related to heaven with heavenly people and heavenly objectives involved, which is Christianity* (Lewis Sperry Chafer, 1936:107).

I would be forced to ask Mr. Chafer which purpose is God pursuing in the book of Revelation. Is it the earthly purpose or the heavenly purpose? Is it the work of Israel or the work of the church? The answer is that it is both. This book pictures God's people as one. There is a beautiful blending of the people of the Old Covenant with the people of the New Covenant so that there is one church and one family of God.

THE GREAT MULTITUDE

> *After these things I looked, and behold, a great multitude, which no one could count, from every nation and all tribes and peoples and tongues, standing before the throne and before the Lamb, clothed in white robes, and palm branches were in their hands; 10 and they cry out with a loud voice, saying, 'Salvation to our God who sits on the throne, and to the Lamb.*
> *And all the angels were standing around the throne and*

156

around the elders and the four living creatures; and they fell on their faces before the throne and worshiped God, 12 saying, "Amen, blessing and glory and wisdom and thanksgiving and honor and power and might, be to our God forever and ever. Amen." (Revelation 7:9-12).

John had just heard the numbering of the 144,000 from the tribes of Israel. As he looks up, what does he expect to see? He expects to see 144,000 people. But instead, he sees something else. This reminds me of what had happened in Revelation 5 when John was told of the Lion of the tribe of Judah. He looked up, expecting to see a lion, and instead he saw a lamb. The truth is that the lion is also a lamb.

Likewise, I do not think that John is seeing two different groups here, but only one. The 144,000 represent a great multitude, which no one can count. Instead of being from the physical descendants of the sons of Jacob, they are from every nation and all tribes and peoples and tongues.

The passage tells us that this was *a great multitude, which no one could count (7:9)*. This is a literal fulfillment of the Abrahamic Covenant; the promise which God gave to Abraham. On a dark, cloudless night the Lord came to Abraham in a vision, speaking to him and then leading him outside his tent to stand under the ancient sky.

> *Then He took him outside and said, "Now look toward the heavens, and count the stars, if you are able to count them." And He said to him, "So shall your seed be." (Genesis 15:5).*

It is true that many peoples descended from the physical seed of Abraham. But I think that this promise goes much deeper than that. It looks at all of God's people as the seed of Abraham. They are pictured as being *clothed in white robes (7:9)*. We saw in Revelation 6:11 the white robes of those who were martyred for their faith. We compared that passage with the vision of Zechariah 3. We saw the filthy garments of Joshua, the high priest of Jerusalem, being replaced with clean festal robes. We saw that Joshua was a symbol of all of God's people. All have sinned and fallen short of the glory of God. We all wear the same filthy garments. But Jesus died to take our sins away. When we came to Him, He took away our filthy garments and, in there place, He gave us fresh new robes of righteousness.

Palm branches were in their hands (Revelation 7:9). Just as the people of Jerusalem greeted Jesus with palm branches at His triumphal entry, so also we will one day greet Him. Palm branches were carried by the people during the celebration of the Feast of Tabernacles.

> *"On exactly the fifteenth day of the seventh month, when you have gathered in the crops of the land, you shall celebrate the*

feast of the Lord for seven days, with a rest on the first day and a rest on the eighth day.

*"Now on the first day you shall take for yourselves the foliage of beautiful trees, **palm branches** and boughs of leafy trees and willows of the brook; and you shall rejoice before the Lord your God for seven days." (Leviticus 23:39-40).*

The Feast of Tabernacles commemorated the entrance into Canaan after the wilderness wanderings. It looked at that time of rest after the hardships of the Sinai desert. This was the most festive time of the entire year. The harvest was over and all of the crops had been gathered. Now a harvest feast of thankfulness to the Lord was held. Jews from all over the land would travel to Jerusalem to attend this feast.

The feast lasted a week. On each day of the week, all of the people would gather to the temple. Each person would carry with him a palm branch to wave before the house of the Lord in a spirit of joyful worship. As the Temple music began, the worshipers would direct their palm branches toward the alter, praying that God would now send the salvation of the promised Son of David.

Now we see the fulfillment of the feast. The final harvest has taken place. God's people have been gathered to Himself. They have entered into the final rest of God and He has spread His tabernacle over them (7:15). John sees them gathered in joyful thanksgiving to worship the Lord who will tabernacle with them.

THE PEOPLE OF THE LAMB

And one of the elders answered, saying to me, "These who are clothed in the white robes, who are they, and from where have they come?"

And I said to him, "My lord, you know." And he said to me, "These are the ones who come out of the great tribulation, and they have washed their robes and made them white in the blood of the Lamb."

For this reason, they are before the throne of God; and they serve Him day and night in His temple; and He who sits on the throne shall spread His tabernacle over them.

They shall hunger no more, neither thirst anymore; neither shall the sun beat down on them, nor any heat; 17 for the Lamb in the center of the throne shall be their shepherd, and shall guide them to springs of the water of life; and God shall wipe every tear from their eyes." (Revelation 7:13-17).

John has heard the joyous pronouncements. Now he is questioned by one of the elders. This elder asks John the identity of the 144,000. It is not that the elder needed to know. The elder will answer his own question in just a moment. The reason he asks the question is so that John will ask the question. Sometimes our problem is not that we do not know the right answers, but rather that we don't know the right questions.

These are the ones who come out of the great tribulation (7:14). What is this "great tribulation?" A lot of people think that it refers to a seven year period in the future which will be followed by the second coming of Jesus Christ. Does the Bible teach this? I'm not so sure it does. Jesus taught His disciples that they would experience tribulation.

> *"These things I have spoken to you, that in Me you may have peace. In the world you have **tribulation**, but take courage; I have overcome the world." (John 16:33).*

If Jesus had wanted His disciples to think that the tribulation would not come for many hundreds of years, then He would not have said this. Paul told the church at Thessalonica that they were already suffering tribulation.

> *For indeed when we were with you, we kept telling you in advance that we were going to suffer **affliction**; and so it came to pass, as you know. (1 Thessalonians 3:4).*

This word which is translated "affliction" is the very same Greek word which is translated "tribulation" here in Revelation. Paul is not speaking of a tribulation that would come in the far future. He is describing something that these believers were going through right now.

Many people would object at this point, saying, "Wait a minute, John. I admit that there is tribulation today. But there is also a Great Tribulation which is to come. It is distinguished in the Bible as the Great Tribulation." To answer this objection, we can look at some passages which speak of "great tribulation." One place it is used is in Stephen's sermon before the Sanhedrin. Stephen had been speaking of the famine that took place in Egypt in the days of Joseph.

> *"Now a famine came over all Egypt and Canaan, and **great affliction** with it; and out fathers could find no food." (Acts 7:11).*

Once again the Greek term found in this verse is exactly the same as is used here in Revelation. Another example is seen in Paul's description of the gift which he received from the churches of Macedonia.

> *Now, brethren, we wish to make known to you the grace of*

> *God which has been given in the churches of Macedonia, 2 that in a **great ordeal of affliction** their abundance of joy and their deep poverty overflowed in the wealth of their liberality. (2 Corinthians 8:1-2).*

The same Greek word for "tribulation" is used here where it is translated "affliction." The truth is that the Bible teaches that there have been many times of "great tribulation."

This does not mean that there is not another such time coming in the future. Indeed, there are many parts of the world that are seeing "great tribulation" right now. The hoofbeats of the red horse and the black horse and the pale horse echo through our newspaper each day. But we have a promise. It is a promise of protection. It is a promise that, no matter how bad things get, God is with us and will treat us as His own prized possession. In the end, we shall stand before Him in white robes of righteousness.

They are before the throne of God (7:15). There is coming a day when we will see God face to face – when we shall stand before His throne and praise Him and serve Him. It is interesting to compare the description of the heavenly promises of this chapter with those given in Revelation 21-22.

Revelation 7	Revelation 21-22
"Do not harm the earth or the sea or the trees until we have sealed the bond-servants of our God on their foreheads." (7:3).	...and they shall see His face, and His name shall be on their foreheads (22:4).
They have washed their robes and made them white in the blood of the Lamb (7:14).	Blessed are those who wash their robes (22:14)
They are before the throne of God (7:15).	God Himself shall be among them (21:3).
They serve Him day and night in His temple (7:15).	I saw no temple in it, for the Lord God the Almighty, and the Lamb, are its temple (21:22). And His bondservants shall serve Him (22:3).
He who sits on the throne shall spread His tabernacle over them (7:15).	Behold, the tabernacle of God is among men (21:3).

Neither shall the sun beat down on them, nor any heat (7:16).	The city has no need of the sun or of the moon to shine upon it, for the glory of God has illumined it, and its lamp is the Lamb (21:23).
For the Lamb in the center of the throne shall be their shepherd, and shall guide them to springs of the water of life (7:17).	He showed me a river of the water of life, clear as crystal, coming from the throne of God and of the Lamb (22:1).
God shall wipe every tear from their eyes (7:17).	He shall wipe away every tear from their eyes (21:4).

For the Lamb in the center of the throne shall be their shepherd (7:17). Usually it is the shepherd who shepherds the lambs. But in that day, the Lamb of God will be our shepherd. In that day, we will be able to sing the Psalm of David:

> *The Lord is my shepherd,*
> *I shall not want*
> *He makes me to lie down in green pastures;*
> *He leads me beside the still waters.*
> *He restores my soul;*
> *He guides me in the paths of righteousness for His name's sake.*

In that day, there will be no need to walk any further through the valley of the shadow of death. There will be no evil to fear and we will be in a place of perfect peace.

> *Surely goodness and lovingkindness will follow me all the days of*
> *my life,*
> *And I will dwell in the house of the Lord forever.*

This is the message of the book of Revelation. It is that Jesus wins! Those who follow Him will win with Him.

THE TRUMPETS OF JUDGMENT
Revelation 8:1 - 9:21

The blowing of a trumpet signified many different things in the ancient world. It could be used as an alarm to announce the approach of an enemy. It could be a call to battle. Or it could be used to sound the ceasing of hostilities. It was used in the temple each morning as a call to worship and it was used at the coronation of the king. It was blown in time of rejoicing and it was used in time of judgment.

As we begin this next section in our study of Revelation, we will see seven trumpets. The will be primarily trumpets of judgment and of warning and of woe. This is striking in view of the fact that chapter 6 ended with the Second Coming of Christ and chapter 7 told us of those who came out of great tribulation. One would think that everything after this would be peace and blessedness. Instead, we are going to see another round of judgments.

This brings up an important point about the book of Revelation. It is not meant to supply us with a chronology of future events. Instead, we will be treated to a repeating series of visions and they will show us a number of the same themes again and again.

Chapters 4-7	Chapters 8	Chapters 16
Seven seals containing seven judgments	Seven trumpets announcing seven judgments	Seven bowls holding seven judgments
The Seventh seal introduces the seven trumpets	The Seventh trumpet introduces the seven bowls	The Seventh bowl introduces the fall of Babylon

When we read of these various groups of sevens that are nestled one inside the other, we cannot help but to be reminded of the instructions God gave to Israel on the taking of the city of Jericho. They were to march around the city for seven days. On each of these circuits, they were to follow seven priests who were carrying the ark of the covenant. On the seventh day, they were to march around the city seven times. Then the seven priests were to blow seven trumpets and the walls of the city would fall down.

We are going to see the same thing taking place here. There will be seven trumpets sounded. Then there will be an earthquake in which a tenth of the city will fall and the casualties will number seven thousand (Revelation 11:13). And then we will see a vision of the ark of the covenant (Revelation 11:19). Later in the book, we will read of seven bowls being poured out and they will culminate with the fall of the great city that is described as Babylon.

THE SILENCE OF HEAVEN

> *And when He broke the seventh seal, there was silence in heaven for about half an hour. 2 And I saw the seven angels who stand before God; and seven trumpets were given to them. (Revelation 8:1-2).*

John has witnessed the breaking of the six seals. With the breaking of each seal, there has been a vision. With the breaking of each seal, John has seen something take place. But now as we come to the breaking of the seventh seal, there is a change. This time there is a silence in heaven.

There is something special here. We can learn the value of silence. We don't usually like silence. When we are praying in a group and there is a period of long silence, everyone starts to get a little uncomfortable. We feel that someone ought to either pray or say, "Amen," so that everyone can talk. But there are times when we need to be silent. It is in the silence that sometimes we can hear the soft, gentle voice of the Lord.

Out of the silence comes action. It comes in the form of seven angels to whom are given seven trumpets. These are not seven new angels. They are described with the definite article – they are *the seven angels who stand before God*. This suggests we have already been introduced to these angels. They are likely to be understood as the same angels who were addressed in the seven letters to the seven churches of chapters 2-3.

THE POWER OF PRAYER

> *And another angel came and stood at the altar, holding a golden censer; and much incense was given to him, that he might add it to the prayers of all the saints upon the golden altar which was before the throne. 4 And the smoke of the incense, with the prayers of the saints, went up before God out of the angel's hand. 5 And the angel took the censer; and he filled it with the fire of the altar and threw it to the earth; and there followed peals of thunder and sounds and flashes of lightning and an earthquake. (Revelation 8:3-5).*

Back in the sixth chapter of Revelation, John had seen a vision of the souls of martyred Christians under the altar. They had been praying to the Lord for His judgment to fall and had been asking, "How long?" In response to that prayer, we saw the kings and the commanders and the rich and the mighty cry out in terror as they witnessed the coming of the wrath of the Lamb.

Now as we are in chapter 8, our attention once again is drawn to the altar. Once again, we see praying believers. Once again, the result of those prayers will be judgment upon the ungodly.

1.   An Addition to Prayer: *And another angel came and stood at the altar, holding a golden censer; and much incense was given to him, that he might add it to the prayers of all the saints upon the golden altar which was before the throne (8:3).*

Have you ever wondered whether your prayers were adequate? Think about this for a moment. When you are praying, you are addressing the God of the universe. You are conversing with the most sophisticated Being in the cosmos. Has it crossed your mind that your little, two-bit prayer might not be acceptable to the Lord of Creation?

This passage has both bad news and good news. The bad news is that your worst fears have been confirmed. Your prayers are not adequate. They are crude, rude, and indifferent. They tend to be shamefully selfish and sinful. But there is also some good news. It is that someone has been spicing up your prayers.

When our daughter first started cooking, the result was a bit bland. My wife and I would add some spice to the food as she was cooking it. God does the same thing to our prayers. He realizes that our prayers are not what they should be and so He makes provision on our behalf.

> *And in the same way the Spirit also helps our weakness; for we do not know how to pray as we should, but the Spirit Himself intercedes for us with groanings too deep for words; 27 and He who searches the hearts knows what the mind of the Spirit is, because He intercedes for the saints according to the will of God. (Romans 8:26-27).*

When you pray, you are not praying by yourself. The Holy Spirit is praying with you. You might not know how to pray, but the Spirit does. There is no communication gap between the Father and the Spirit.

2.   An Image of Prayer: *And the smoke of the incense, with the prayers of the saints, went up before God out of the angel's hand (8:4).*

The language here is reminiscent of the ceremonies within the temple. On each morning and each evening, one of the priests would enter into the temple. As he passed through the mighty cedar doors, he would see at his left the golden lampstand and on his right would be the table of shewbread. Standing before him would be the altar of incense.

It was to this altar that he would make his way, stopping before its softly glowing coals. Taking the incense from a small bowl, he would sprinkle it upon the altar. As the incense touched the hot coals, it would flare up in a sweet-smelling smoke that would fill the temple. Meanwhile, the people would be gathered outside the temple for prayer. As they saw the smoke of the incense swirl from the open door of the temple and rise into the sky, they would visualize their prayers rising up to heaven. In the same way, John now sees the prayers of believers mingling with the incense of the angel as they ascend to the Lord. He hears the prayers, he sees that which represents the prayers, and perhaps he even smells the sweet aroma of the prayers.

As we look at the imagery of the temple as described by John, we have seen the throne, the altar, and the lampstands. Yet there is one thing that has not been mentioned. There is one thing missing. It is the veil. What happened to it? It was torn in two when Jesus died on the cross and it has been taken down, never to be replaced. This is why we no longer come to the Lord through the ministry of an earthly temple or an earthly high priest. Jesus has become our high priest and He has removed the veil that once separated us from the presence of God. As a result, we know that we have an answer to our prayers.

3.   An Answer to Prayer: *And the angel took the censer; and he filled it with the fire of the altar and threw it to the earth; and there followed peals of thunder and sounds and flashes of lightning and an earthquake (8:5).*

The angel throws the contents of the censer down to the earth. This action brings about a result. The immediate result is seen in the peals of thunder and the sounds and the flashes of lightning and the earthquake. These are all signs of God's judgment.

There is a lesson here. It is that there is a direct correlation between your prayers directed toward heaven and God's actions upon the earth. Do you want to change the world? Start praying. I am convinced there is a power in prayer that we have not yet begun to tap. It will only be when we start seriously praying that we will change this world.

THE SEVEN TRUMPETS

*And the seven angels who had the seven trumpets prepared
themselves to sound them. (Revelation 8:6).*

We have already noted the similarity of this passage with the account of Joshua and
the Battle of Jericho. You remember the story. The children of Israel were coming
into the land of Canaan. The first city that stood in their way was the valley fortress
of Jericho. The Israelites had no siege engines. They had no battering rams. That
did not matter because God was on their side. He would accomplish the defeat of
Jericho. All the Israelites had to do was to obey the Lord's instructions.

God's instructions to Joshua were very specific. He was to take the entire army of
Israel and they were to march
around the city once each day.
The ark of the covenant was to
go before them and before the
ark was to go seven priests with
seven trumpets. Each day they
marched around the city. This
was to take place for six days.
On the seventh day, they
marched around the city seven
times. As they finished their
last circuit, the seven priests
blew the seven trumpets and the
walls of Jericho came tumbling
down. Now as John looks on,

> The Jericho account is not the only other time
> the Bible tells us of the sounding of seven
> trumpets. There are two other occasions, both
> of which come from the Old Testament.
>
> - When David had the ark of the covenant
>   brought into Jerusalem, seven priests
>   ushered it into the city with the blowing of
>   trumpets (1st Chronicles 15:24).
> - When the walls of Jerusalem were rebuilt
>   by Nehemiah, a dedication service was
>   held and seven attending priests were
>   described as having trumpets (Nehemiah
>   12:41).

he sees seven angels, each with a trumpet. They are about to sound the judgment
of God upon the earth.

Angel		Realm of Judgment
1	Judgment upon creation	A third of the earth, the trees, and all the green grass
2		A third of the sea and a third of the creatures and a third of the ships
3		A third of the rivers and springs of water
4		A third of the sun, the moon, and the stars and the night in the same way

5	Judgment upon men	Men who do not have the seal of God are tormented
6		A third of mankind is killed
7		The judgment of the dead

There are several observations we ought to make regarding these trumpets. First, notice that the first four of these trumpets announce judgment upon creation while the last two have their focus upon men. It is not that the earth has sinned, but the earth suffers for the sins of mankind because man has authority over the earth.

Second, observe that the judgments of the trumpets grow in intensity. The first four judgments hurt the dominion of men, the fifth brings pain to men, the sixth actually kills him, and the last brings eternal judgment upon him once he has died.

The third thing we should notice is that, while these judgments are from God, they are not His final and complete judgment. They only fall upon a portion of mankind, represented here by one-third. As such, they serve as a forerunner of the greater judgment to come.

Finally, we should remember that the temple ceremonies utilized seven trumpets in their ceremonies. 1 Chronicles 15:24 lists seven priests and tells us that they sounded trumpets before the ark of God (see also Nehemiah 12:41). We have seen temple language throughout the book of Revelation and this motif still continues here.

As we compare these seven trumpets with the seven seals of the previous chapter, we do not find an exact correlation, but there are some interesting similarities:

The Seven Seals	The Seven Trumpets
Begins with a group of four horsemen.	Begins with a group of four judgments against the creation.
The martyred saints under the altar cry out to the Lord in the fifth seal, asking when His judgment will come.	The fifth and sixth trumpets picture judgment upon mankind.
At the opening of the sixth seal, unbelievers seek to hide themselves from the wrath of the Lamb.	At the sounding of the seventh trumpet we see the final judgment of all men.

What are these trumpets? They are trumpets of warning. They announce the coming of various judgments that are themselves a prelude to the greater and final judgment. They are sounded to tell men to repent before the coming of that final judgment. They are also blown in order to encourage those who are downtrodden today and who are awaiting relief.

THE FIRST TRUMPET

> *And the first sounded, and there came hail and fire, mixed with blood, and they were thrown to the earth; and a third of the earth was burned up, and a third of the trees were burned up, and all the green grass was burned up. (Revelation 8:7).*

At the sounding of the first trumpet we see hail and fire falling upon the earth. We do not normally think of hail and fire taking place at the same time, but there was a time in history where it took place. It was during the plagues of Egypt. One of those plagues was a terrible fiery hail (Exodus 9:23-24).

What do you think was the reaction of the Israelites to that plague? Were they upset? Were they disheartened? I do not believe they were. I think they were encouraged. For one thing, the earth did not fall upon their land. It fell only upon the land of the Egyptians. Another reason for their encouragement was because the plagues were a sign to them of the strength of their God.

THE SECOND TRUMPET

> *And the second angel sounded, and something like a great mountain burning with fire was thrown into the sea; and a third of the sea became blood; 9 and a third of the creatures, which were in the sea and had life, died; and a third of the ships were destroyed. (Revelation 8:8-9).*

At the sounding of the second trumpet, John sees something that is like a great, burning mountain thrown into the sea. He does not say this is a mountain. He says it is like a mountain. The first judgment was upon the land. This judgment is upon the sea. A third of the waters of the sea become blood. This once again echoes of the judgments of the plague when the Nile River was turned to blood. This judgment affects, not merely a single river, but a third of all the oceans. It is a picture of the judgments that came against Egypt but now expanded to a worldwide level. At the same time, we must recognize that this is not designed to be a source of discouragement. We have a place of refuge. It is in the Lord.

> *God is our refuge and strength,*

A very present help in trouble.
2 Therefore we will not fear, though the earth should change,
And though the mountains slip into the heart of the sea;
3 Though its waters roar and foam,
Though the mountains quake at its swelling pride. Selah. (Psalm
46:1-3).

What is your natural reaction when you are confronted with life's natural disasters? It might be a big disaster like a hurricane or a tornado, or it might only feel like a big disaster like a flat tire on the highway. It is the thing that discourages you. It is one thing to one person and another thing to another person. It does not matter what it is; the cure is the same. It is to go to the place of refuge. That place of refuge is found in a person. It is found in the Lord.

THE THIRD TRUMPET

And the third angel sounded, and a great star fell from heaven, burning like a torch, and it fell on a third of the rivers and on the springs of waters; 11 and the name of the star is called Wormwood; and a third of the waters became wormwood; and many men died from the waters, because they were made bitter. (Revelation 8:10-11).

John's next vision is of a great, burning star that falls upon the rivers and waters of the earth. The picture of a star falling from heaven is an Old Testament theme. Isaiah uses similar words:

How you have fallen from heaven,
O star of the morning, son of the dawn!
You have been cut down to the earth,
You who have weakened the nations! (Isaiah 14:12).

Some have taken the words of Isaiah to refer to the fall of Satan, though he is not mentioned in the passage and the context points to the fall of the king of Babylon. This might be seen as significant when we remember that the book of Revelation will make further mention of Babylon.

The star has a name. It is called Wormwood. This is an unusual name. The Greek term is (*apsinthos*, ἀψινθος) and literally means "undrinkable" (from the Greek word *pino*, πινω, "to drink"). The idea of undrinkable water is a common Old Testament theme where water could mean the difference between life and death.

We see these two themes of poisoned waters and the king of Babylon come together in the book of Jeremiah. The prophet proclaimed the calamities that were falling upon the land were judgments against the sinning nation of Judah:

> *Who is the wise man that may understand this? And who is he to whom the mouth of the LORD has spoken, that he may declare it? Why is the land ruined, laid waste like a desert, so that no one passes through? 13 And the LORD said, "Because they have forsaken My law which I set before them, and have not obeyed My voice nor walked according to it, 14 but have walked after the stubbornness of their heart and after the Baals, as their fathers taught them," 15 therefore thus says the LORD of hosts, the God of Israel, "behold, I will feed them, this people, with wormwood and give them poisoned water to drink. 16 And I will scatter them among the nations, whom neither they nor their fathers have known; and I will send the sword after them until I have annihilated them." (Jeremiah 9:12-16).*

The picture here is of the bitterness of the water being a reflection of the bitter affliction the Lord was going to pour out upon the nation of Judah. In the same way, John sees a vivid picture of the affliction that descends upon men in this age.

THE FOURTH TRUMPET

> *And the fourth angel sounded, and a third of the sun and a third of the moon and a third of the stars were smitten, so that a third of them might be darkened and the day might not shine for a third of it, and the night in the same way. 13 And I looked, and I heard an eagle flying in midheaven, saying with a loud voice, "Woe, woe, woe, to those who dwell on the earth, because of the remaining blasts of the trumpet of the three angels who are about to sound!" (Revelation 8:12-13).*

The fourth trumpet of judgment affects the sun, the moon, and the stars. Just as the sun and the moon and the stars were said to have been brought about on the fourth day of creation, so here they are affected in this fourth trumpet.

Do you remember what was the ninth plague of Egypt? It was darkness. A veil of darkness covered the entire land of Egypt except for where the people of God lived. The result of the plagues was twofold. They accomplished the judgment of God upon Egypt. They also accomplished the deliverance of God's people from their bondage. These trumpets of judgment are seen to be accomplishing the same thing. They mark God's judgment upon the unbelieving world and they ultimately work together to bring about the deliverance of God's people.

The sun and the moon and the stars are examples of stability. You can count on them. You can set your watch by them. You may hear that the stock market has crashed or that the government has been overthrown or even that the Rock of Gibralter suffered an earthquake and sank into the sea, but if I tell you that the sun did not rise, that is earth-shattering. This reminds us that if your source of stability is rooted in anything but the Lord, then it is not enough. He is the only unchanging One.

As we come to verse 13 there is a pause. John sees *an eagle flying in midheaven, saying with a loud voice, "Woe, woe, woe, to those who dwell on the earth, because of the remaining blasts of the trumpet of the three angels who are about to sound!"* The first four trumpets are over. Three remain and these three are introduced by a message of woe. The message is very simple. To use the words of the old country farmer, it tells us, "Ya ain't seen nothin' yet!" Back in chapter 4 we saw the four living creatures singing, "Holy, holy, holy!" Now we see a different message: "Woe, woe, woe!"

THE FIFTH TRUMPET

> *And the fifth angel sounded, and I saw a star from heaven which had fallen to the earth; and the key of the bottomless pit was given to him. 2 And he opened the bottomless pit; and smoke went up out of the pit, like the smoke of a great furnace; and the sun and the air were darkened by the smoke of the pit. 3 And out of the smoke came forth locusts upon the earth; and power was given them, as the scorpions of the earth have power. (Revelation 9:1-3).*

As the fifth angel sounds, John again sees a star. This seems to be a reference to the same star that he had seen with the sounding of the third trumpet.

The Star in Revelation 8:10-11	The Star in Revelation 9:1
John saw the star fall from heaven.	John saw the star which had fallen from heaven.
Described in the aorist tense: John saw the star fall.	Described with the perfect participle: John saw the star having fallen.

What is the significance of this falling star? Is it a picture of Satan? When we come to Revelation 12, we shall see Satan being thrown down in a cosmic conflict and we will see him pictured as a great, red dragon whose tail brings down a third of the stars of heaven. It would seem from these pointers that Satan is in view here. When we come to verse 11 in this chapter, we will be introduced to "the angel of

171

the abyss" who is known alternately as Abaddon and Apollyon, two names that mean "destroyer."

Notice the reference to the key. The purpose of a key is to unlock things. This key is to the bottomless pit. It is used to unlock the pit. Who does the unlocking? It seems that the star is being personified to do this unlocking, though later in the book of Revelation we shall read of *an angel coming down from heaven, having the key of the abyss* (Revelation 20:1).

This is the first reference in the book of Revelation to the bottomless pit. We will see the beast coming out of this pit in Revelation 11:7 and 17:8. We see Satan bound and cast into this pit in Revelation 20:3. When Jesus cast the demons into the herd of pigs, they entreated Him not to send them into the abyss (Luke 8:31). On the other hand, Peter describes those angels who sinned and were cast into "pits of darkness, reserved for judgment (2 Peter 2:4) and Jude speaks of unfaithful angels who have been "kept in eternal bonds under darkness for the judgment of the great day" (Jude 1:6). These passages all seem to imply a realm to which fallen angels have been banished. Out of this realm comes smoke and out of the smoke comes locusts. Once again, this calls to mind one of the plagues of Egypt. However, these locusts are going to be described with some special and unique attributes.

- They sting like a scorpion
- They look like horses prepared for bottle
- They wear crowns of gold and have the faces of men and the hair of women
- They have teeth like a lion
- They have breastplates and wings

It seems obvious that these are not your normal, everyday locusts. Most Bible scholars agree that they represent something else. When the question of what else they represent, there is a great deal of diversity of opinion.

- Hal Lindsey suggested they may be either demon-possessed mutant insects or Cobra helicopters (1974:138-139).
- A. Plummer, scholar for the Pulpit Commentaries, states that these locusts symbolize unbelievers (Vol. 22, Pg 263).

Other interpretations include:

- The Romans in their invasion of Judea.
- The Gothic invasion of Rome.
- The Muslim followers of Mohammed.
- Killer bees.
- A future genetic bio-weapon.
- An invasion of warlike UFOS.

172

- The forces of decay.

I find all of these suggestions suspect, especially when we consider that none of them have Scriptural warrant and that all rely on speculation. On the other hand, we can make some very acute observations from the immediate text.

- They come from the bottomless pit (9:3).
- They have power only over unbelievers (9:4).
- They are able to torment men (9:5).
- Their king is the Destroyer – Satan himself (9:11).

This suggests a hoard of demons; we could call them spiritual locusts as they do not eat crops and grass, but they are nevertheless a plague on humanity. John tells us that power is given to them and this power is likened to the sting of a scorpion. I was once stung by a scorpion and I can tell you that, while it does not kill you, it is an agonizing pain. We should note there is an Old Testament reference that suggests an identification of the scorpion-like qualities of these locusts. It is found in the book of Isaiah in a context that speaks of the false teachers of Israel:

> *So the LORD cuts off head and tail from Israel,*
> *Both palm branch and bulrush in a single day.*
> *15 The head is the elder and honorable man,*
> *And the prophet who teaches falsehood is the tail.*
> *16 For those who guide this people are leading them astray;*
> *And those who are guided by them are brought to confusion.*
> *(Isaiah 9:14-16).*

The sting of a scorpion is in its tail. Notice how Isaiah describes the tail; it is the prophet who teaches falsehood. False teachers and their teachings are the spiritual poison. As we continue through Revelation 9, we are given further details about these locusts:

1. Instructions to the Locust Army: *And they were told that they should not hurt the grass of the earth, nor any green thing, nor any tree, but only the men who do not have the seal of God on their foreheads. 5 And they were not permitted to kill anyone, but to torment for five months; and their torment was like the torment of a scorpion when it stings a man. 6 And in those days men will seek death and will not find it; and they will long to die and death flees from them. (Revelation 9:4-6).*

   Normal locusts would come and consume every green thing; crops, leaves, grass, no vegetation was safe from their onslaught. These locusts are different. Their diet is different. They do not eat what locusts commonly eat. They are sent to harm those men *who do not have the seal of God on their foreheads.* And even then, their mission is not to kill but to torment.

The torment described is such that would cause the suffering one to long for death, yet death would not be easily attainable.

2. Appearance of the Locust Army: *And the appearance of the locusts was like horses prepared for battle; and on their heads, as it were, crowns like gold, and their faces were like the faces of men. 8 And they had hair like the hair of women, and their teeth were like the teeth of lions. 9 And they had breastplates like breastplates of iron; and the sound of their wings was like the sound of chariots, of many horses rushing to battle. 10 And they have tails like scorpions, and stings; and in their tails is their power to hurt men for five months. (Revelation 9:7-10).*

The description of the appearance of these locusts are meant to be symbolic. This means the individual details are significant and more than merely the sum of their parts.

Appearance like horses	Points to their rapid mode of travel. There is an old proverb that says a lie can travel around the world while truth is still getting dressed.
Faces like the faces of men	There is a face to false teaching and it is the face of men. False teachers can be hard to detect because they look so appealing and put a human face to their teachings.
Hair like the hair of women	While we are not told that these false teachers are women, they are said to have long hair like women.
The sound of their wings is like the sound of chariots and horses	This calls to mind those times in the Old Testament where the armies of heaven were heard rushing to battle (Ezekiel 1:24; 3:13).

3. The King of the Locust Army: *They have as king over them, the angel of the abyss; his name in Hebrew is Abaddon, and in the Greek he has the name Apollyon (Revelation 9:11).*

The king of the locust army is named in two different languages. This suggests him to be cross-cultural. He is an equal opportunity employer. His destructive work affects both Jews and Gentiles. Being Jewish does not save you and being Gentile does not save you.

THE SIXTH TRUMPET

> *The first woe is past; behold, two woes are still coming after these things. 13 And the sixth angel sounded, and I heard a voice from the four horns of the golden altar which is before God, 14 one saying to the sixth angel who had the trumpet, "Release the four angels who are bound at the great river Euphrates." 15 And the four angels, who had been prepared for the hour and day and month and year, were released, so that they might kill a third of mankind. 16 And the number of the armies of the horsemen was two hundred million; I heard the number of them. 17 And this is how I saw in the vision the horses and those who sat on them: the riders had breastplates the color of fire and of hyacinth and of brimstone; and the heads of the horses are like the heads of lions; and out of their mouths proceed fire and smoke and brimstone. 18 A third of mankind was killed by these three plagues, by the fire and the smoke and the brimstone, which proceeded out of their mouths. 19 For the power of the horses is in their mouths and in their tails; for their tails are like serpents and have heads; and with them they do harm. (Revelation 9:12-19).*

When the sixth trumpet sounds, John hears a voice. It is coming from the four horns of the altar of incense that stands before the throne of God. The pattern is taken from the temple; or perhaps we should say that the temple was designed after the heavenly pattern. This is what the writer to the Hebrews said when he described the earthly tabernacle, calling it "a copy and shadow of the heavenly things" (Hebrews 8:5). The tabernacle and later the temple were built to exact specifications. Each aspect of their construction was carefully prescribed. The tabernacle was a scale model of the heavenly reality.

The golden altar was the place of prayer. The aroma of incense rising from this altar pictured the prayers of God's people rising to heaven. As the prayers are being made from believers on earth, so the answers to those prayers go forth from the heavenly altar of incense. What was the content of those prayers back in Revelation 6? They were prayers for the judgment of God. Those prayers are about to be answered. The answer is announced by a voice coming from the altar.

1.   The Release of the Four Angels: *Release the four angels who are bound at the great river Euphrates (9:14).*

In the seventh chapter, we saw four angels at the four corners of the earth. They were about to bring judgment upon the earth but they were told to wait until the servants of God were safely sealed. Now we again see these four angels. This time, they are gathered at the Euphrates River.

The Euphrates River was the northern boundary for the realm of Israel during the days of David and Solomon. It was from here that invading armies had often come. The Assyrians, the Babylonians, and the Parthians had all come from across the Euphrates. In the same way, the Lord promises to release destruction upon those who continue to reject Him.

2.   The Number of the Horsemen: *And the number of the armies of the horsemen was two hundred million (9:16).*

The translation here is unfortunate. The Greek number is literally "double myriads of myriads." While it is true that a myriad was technically ten thousand and that we could multiply ten thousand times ten thousand and arrive at the number of two hundred million, that is not the point of the passage. John is not giving us a math lesson. This number stands as a parallel to an earlier number John has already given.

> *And I looked, and I heard the voice of many angels around the throne and the living creatures and the elders; and the number of them was myriads of myriads, and thousands of thousands (Revelation 5:11).*

Around the throne of God are seen "myriads of myriad," while the number of these horsemen are "double myriads of myriads." The point is that there is an army of heaven and there is also an army of hell and they both number in the myriads. The use of such numbers is taken from the Old Testament where we read from one of the Psalms of David:

> *The chariots of God are myriads, thousands upon thousands; The Lord is among them as at Sinai, in holiness. (Psalm 68:17).*

I have searched the commentaries and have yet to find a single one that will take this verse and say that the population of heaven is limited to one hundred million plus a few thousand or that the army of God numbers only twenty two thousand. And yet, a great many have taken the similar numbering found in Revelation 9:16 to be a specific numbering of some futuristic or even present day military force.

John is not taking a head count. This is figurative speech for describing a very large army. He views an invading horde of epic and overwhelming proportions. As he describes them, we cannot help but to be reminded of the previous plague of locusts:

Plague of Locusts	Invasion of Horsemen
They have breastplates of iron (9:9).	The riders have breastplates the color of fire and hyacinth and of brimstone (9:17).
The appearance of the locusts was like horses prepared for battle (9:7); and their teeth were like the teeth of lions (9:8).	The heads of the horses are like the heads of lions (9:17).
Smoke went out of the pit, like the smoke of a great furnace (9:2).	Out of their mouths proceed fire and smoke and brimstone (9:17).
They were not permitted to kill anyone, but to torment for five months (9:10).	A third of mankind was killed by these three plagues (9:18).
In their tails is their power to hurt men for five months (9:10).	The power of the horses is in their mouths and in their tails (9:19).
They have tails like scorpions, and stings (9:10).	Their tails are like serpents and have heads; and with them they do harm (9:19).

To be sure, there are also some differences. The Locusts are not permitted to kill anyone, but only to torment (9:5) while the horsemen are said to kill a third of men (9:18).

As we read this, we might be tempted to try to read into it some modern day fulfillment. If we are to understand this prophecy, we must look at it through the eyes of the first century believer to whom it was addressed. What did this mean to him? The figure of two hundred million men would be the entire population of the human race. Therefore, he sees all of mankind unleashed in this terrible warfare. Why does war exist? War is one of God's judgments upon unrepentant men. God has allowed its unleashing. One of its purposes is to drive men to repentance. We shall see this developed in the next paragraph.

THE CONTINUING REBELLION OF MEN

And the rest of mankind, who were not killed by these plagues, did not repent of the works of their hands, so as not to worship demons, and the idols of gold and of silver and of brass and of stone and of wood, which can neither see nor hear nor walk; 21 and they did not repent of their murders nor of their sorceries nor of their immorality nor of their thefts. (Revelation 9:20-21).

Now we are brought to the purpose of the trumpets. They are given to drive men toward repentance. Have you ever noticed that people generally do not turn to God when things are going good? They are too busy for God in times of prosperity. But let circumstances take a sudden negative turn and there is often a change. It is as General Douglas MacArthur once quipped: "There were no atheists in the foxholes of Bataan."

In the situation described here in the face of these plagues, this disaster is not enough to turn men to God. Like the pharaoh of old, they have hardened their hearts so as not to listen to the voice of reason. In spite of natural disasters, in spite of warfare, in spite of demonic activity, men continue to follow after idols of wood and of stone.

Many people hear the Christian message and their response is to say, "I don't want to commit my life to Christ today because I want to continue in my path of rebellion. I will wait until the end of my life and then I will come back to God." We see here the danger of such an approach. If you reject God today, there is no guarantee that you will accept Him tomorrow. If you do not repent today, you are introducing a hardening agent into your heart that will make tomorrow's resistance all the easier.

This brings us to one last question. What is to be the Christian's response to earthly tragedy? We are not like the Jewish rabbi who said that God would like to be able to stop earthly tragedy but is just not up to the task. On the contrary, we have seen that God is in complete control over His creation. When tragedy strikes, it is not only by God's permission, but ultimately from His hand. We do not deny the existence of tragedy. We understand that tragedy is very real and the hurt that accompanies it is also real. We recognize that, while God is able to stop tragedy, He has allowed it to come because of the eventual good that will result. This is seen in no place more vividly than in the cross.

> *For consider Him who has endured such hostility by sinners against Himself, so that you may not grow weary and lose heart. (Hebrews 12:3).*

We are to look at the example of Jesus who endured the cross because of the glory that would result and we are to emulate His example. When hard times come, we need not grow weary or lose heart. There is a joy that is set before us and a promise that we shall overcome.

THE ANGEL AND THE LITTLE BOOK
Revelation 10:1-11

Back when I was in high school, there was a short little rhyme about the creation that went like this:

> God created the world in six days flat.
> On the seventh day He said, "I'll rest."
> So He let the thing into orbit swing,
> To give it a dry run test.
>
> Six thousand years went right on by
> Before He took another look at the whirling blob.
> And with a shrug, He turned and said,
> "Oh well, it was only a six day job."

There are a lot of people who share this view of planet earth. They think that, if there is a God and if He did create the universe, then He must have gone on a long vacation and has not yet returned. Have you read a newspaper lately? It does not look as though there is a plan and purpose governing human history. However, the Bible teaches there is a goal and a plan to history. History is going toward a predetermined goal. It is moving in accordance with the plan of the Creator.

From our point of view, it is like looking at a beautiful tapestry through a microscope. We see only the jumbled threads. But God sees the complete panorama and He sees the entire design. To encourage us, He gives us a glimpse of that design here in the book of Revelation.

THE STRONG ANGEL

> *I saw another strong angel coming down out of heaven, clothed with a cloud; and the rainbow was upon his head, and his face was like the sun, and his feet like pillars of fire; 2 and he had in his hand a little book which was open. He placed his right foot on the sea and his left on the land (Revelation 10:1-2).*

John has just witnessed the plagues brought about by the first six trumpets. They represent all the bad things that take place throughout this age. They picture the war and the pestilences and the trials and the troubles. These trumpets are really judgments upon man. John has seen six of them. The seventh trumpet is about to be sounded. It will announce the return of Jesus Christ to earth. But first there is a pause.

We have already seen a similar pause in the seven seals. The first six seals followed one another in rapid succession. But before the seventh seal was broken, there was a pause. That pause was taken up with the sealing of God's people. This pause also involves God's people.

First six Seals	Sealing of God's People	Seventh Seal
First six Trumpets	Sealing of what the thunder speaks	Seventh Trumpet

1. The Coming of the Angel: *I saw another strong angel coming down out of heaven (10:1).*

   John has just seen six angels blow six trumpets. There is a seventh angel standing in the wings with his trumpet ready to sound. But first John sees another angel. He is identified as a "strong angel."

   - He is closed with a cloud.
   - The rainbow is upon his head.
   - His face is like the sun.
   - His feet like pillars of fire.

   These are familiar characteristics. These characteristics belong to the Lord. This means the angel depicted here is one of God's angels. He comes from the Lord and He comes bearing God's message.

2. The Little Book: *He had in his hand a little book which was open (10:2).*

   We have already seen the sealed scroll that was in the hand of the Lord in Revelation 6. Now we see an angel with a little book in his hand. There is a contrast to be seen between these two books.

Revelation 6	**Revelation 10**
It is called a book (*Biblion*) and is described as having writing on the front and back.	It is called a little book (*Biblarion*, the diminutive form of *Biblion*).
It is sealed with seven seals.	It is open.
It is in the right hand of the Father.	It is in the hand of the strong angel.

180

Only Jesus was worthy to open this book.	The little book will be given to John.

The sealed scroll of Revelation 6 contained the complete plan of God. It was a very extensive plan. For this reason, there was writing on the front and on the back of the scroll. It was a sealed scroll. It was not open for all to read. God's completed plan has not yet been revealed to men. We have the general outline of God's plan, but we have net been given every detail. There are many things about His plans that we do not know.

If the sealed scroll contains the complete plan of God, what is this little book? I think it might be a reference to the Bible – that portion of God's plan and purpose that has been revealed. It is an open book. It has been given to men. It contains the general outlines of God's plan, though it does not contain everything God knows about everything.

THE SEVEN PEALS OF THUNDER

> *And he cried out with a loud voice, as when a lion roars; and when he had cried out, the seven peals of thunder uttered their voices. 4 When the seven peals of thunder had spoken, I was about to write; and I heard a voice from heaven saying, "Seal up the things which the seven peals of thunder have spoken and do not write them." (Revelation 10:3-4).*

The strong angel cries out. In answer to his cry, the seven peals of thunder utter their voices. What are these seven peals of thunder? They are the seven peals of thunder that proceed from the throne of God in Revelation 4:5. They are another manifestation of the power and the strength of God. The Jews referred to thunder as the seven voices and regarded it as the voice of the Lord. This was taken from Psalm 29.

> *The voice of the LORD is upon the waters;*
> *The God of glory thunders,*
> *The LORD is over many waters.*
> *4 The voice of the LORD is powerful,*
> *The voice of the LORD is majestic.*
> *5 The voice of the LORD breaks the cedars;*
> *Yes, the LORD breaks in pieces the cedars of Lebanon.*
> *6 He makes Lebanon skip like a calf,*
> *And Sirion like a young wild ox.*
> *7 The voice of the LORD hews out flames of fire.*

8 The voice of the LORD shakes the wilderness;
The LORD shakes the wilderness of Kadesh.
9 The voice of the LORD makes the deer to calve
And strips the forests bare;
And in His temple everything says, "Glory!" (Psalm 29:3-9).

These thunders declare a solemn pronouncement. Their words are so important that John decides to take notes. He is going to write it down, but he is interrupted before he can do so. He is told to seal up the words and not to write them down.

What did the seven thunders declare? We are not told. We are not meant to know. There is an important truth here. It is that there are some aspects of God's plan that we do not know. This is important. It means I have to be careful to leave room for the unknown in my teaching about God. The one who leaves no room for the unknown leaves great room for error. I don't know all there is to know, but that is okay because I am told all I need to know.

THE ANNOUNCEMENT OF THE ANGEL

Then the angel whom I saw standing on the sea and on the land lifted up his right hand to heaven, 6 and swore by Him who lives forever and ever, Who created heaven and the things in it, and the earth and the things in it, and the sea and the things in it, that there will be delay no longer, 7 but in the days of the voice of the seventh angel, when he is about to sound, then the mystery of God is finished, as He preached to His servants the prophets. (Revelation 10:5-7).

John's attention now comes back to the strong angel. He is standing with one foot on the land and the other foot in the sea. He is going to make a pronouncement that will affect all the earth, and so he stands on both land and sea. What is this pronouncement? It is that there will be no more delay. The program of God will soon be completed. The goal of history is about to arrive, not in John's day, but *in the days of the voice of the seventh angel.* The seventh angel will be blowing the seventh trumpet. We have already seen six trumpets sound, but he is the last and he sounds the last trumpet. Paul tells us of a mystery that takes place at the last trumpet:

Behold, I tell you a mystery; we will not all sleep, but we will all be changed, 52 in a moment, in the twinkling of an eye, at the last trumpet; for the trumpet will sound, and the dead will be raised imperishable, and we will be changed. (1 Corinthians 15:51-52).

John also speaks of a mystery. He says that at the sounding of the last trumpet the mystery of God will be revealed. When we think of a mystery, we think of a murder mystery in which the truth is hidden and has to be searched out and discovered. The word "mystery" had a different connotation in the ancient world. There were certain mystery cults that were reputed to possess certain hidden truths. These truths were unknown to outsiders, but they were known to the initiates.

The mystery of God is like that. It includes those things that we, the initiated, have been taught, but which are not known or understood by the rest of the world. We know and believe that we have been declared righteous in the sight of God and that, as a result of this, we will be able to stand in the presence of the Lord. The world does not know this truth. It is a mystery to them but there is coming a day when it will cease to be a mystery because all will see that it is true.

We live in an age of mystery today. I look at my own life and I wonder if the sanctification process is really working. But there is coming a day when I will no longer wonder because I will see the completed work.

THE LITTLE BOOK

> *Then the voice which I heard from heaven, I heard again speaking with me, and saying, "Go, take the book which is open in the hand of the angel who stands on the sea and on the land." 9 So I went to the angel, telling him to give me the little book. And he said to me, "Take it and eat it; it will make your stomach bitter, but in your mouth it will be sweet as honey." 10 I took the little book out of the angel's hand and ate it, and in my mouth it was sweet as honey; and when I had eaten it, my stomach was made bitter. 11 And they said to me, "You must prophesy again concerning many peoples and nations and tongues and kings." (Revelation 10:8-11).*

John's attention is brought back to the little book the angel is holding. He is told to go and to take the little book from the angel. When he goes to do this, he receives some further instructions from the angel. He is told to eat the book. As we read this, it sounds very strange. Yet it would have had a familiar ring to John, for he had read of a similar event in the book of Ezekiel. The prophet Ezekiel witnessed a fantastic manifestation of the glory of the Lord. As the Lord spoke to him, he was given a scroll.

> *Then I looked, and behold, a hand was extended to me; and lo, a scroll was in it. 10 When He spread it out before me, it was written on the front and back, and written on it were*

lamentations, mourning and woe. (Ezekiel 2:9-10).

The scroll that was given to Ezekiel contained the plan of God for Israel. It was not a pleasant picture. It was made up of lamentations, mourning, and woe. Notice what Ezekiel was told to do with the scroll. He was not told to file it in his Bible study notebook. He was not told to place it on his bookshelf. He was told to eat it.

> *Then He said to me, "Son of man, eat what you find; eat this scroll, and go, speak to the house of Israel." 2 So I opened my mouth, and He fed me this scroll. 3 He said to me, "Son of man, feed your stomach and fill your body with this scroll which I am giving you." Then I ate it, and it was sweet as honey in my mouth. (Ezekiel 3:1-3).*

Ezekiel was to eat the scroll. He was to fill his body with its message. It was to become part of him. Then he was to go to the nation of Judah and give them the message. John is told the same thing. He is to take the scroll and eat it. It will become a part of him. It will affect his mouth and his stomach. Then he will be sent to speak the message of God to many peoples and nations and tongues and kings.

There is a lesson here. It is a lesson to pastors and to Bible teachers, to evangelists and missionaries and Sunday school teachers. It is a lesson to all who speak the message of God. Before you can effectively teach God's truth, that truth must become a part of your life. If your Christianity is to be contagious, you must first be infected with the real disease. Howard Hendricks used to say, "If your Christianity does not work at home, it does not work. Don't export it."

As I look at the life of Christ and see how He taught His disciples, I am struck by the fact that He taught as much by how He lived as by what He said. That is how we need to teach. This is why one of the requirements for an elder in the church is that his family be under control. I can fool a lot of people a lot of the time, but my family sees the real me. If you want to know what I am really like, go and ask my family. This is the reason John is told to take the little book and to eat it. It is to become a part of him. As a result, he will be able to speak its message to the world.

MEASURING THE TEMPLE
Revelation 11:1-2

At the close of the last chapter, we saw that mighty angel giving the little book to John. The apostle was told to take the book and eat it. The book was to become a part of him. As a result of eating the book, John would prophecy *concerning many peoples and nations and tongues and kings* (10:11). As we begin chapter 11, the same vision still continues. This is important because we can only understand chapter 11 in the light of the context of chapter 10. There will be in the beginning of this chapter a symbolic representation of John's preaching to peoples and nations and tongues and kings.

COMMAND TO MEASURE THE TEMPLE

> *Then there was given me a measuring rod like a staff; and someone said, "Get up and measure the temple of God and the altar, and those who worship in it." (Revelation 11:1).*

John has already been given a book to eat. We saw in the last chapter that symbolism came from the book of Ezekiel. Now he is given a rod with which he was so do a work of measuring. This symbolism also

> Both in John's eating of the book in the last chapter as well as in his measuring of the temple, he moves from being a passive observer to being an active participant in the vision.

comes from Ezekiel in which he is taken in a vision into the land of Israel, placed on a high mountain, and sees a structure like a city (40:2). He is confronted by a bronze-looking man with a line of flax and a measuring rod and together they go through the city, measuring each wall and gate. What is the purpose for this? Is it to give Ezekiel a lesson in ancient architecture? Is it to provide some interesting Bible trivia? No, it is to teach the people of Israel an important practical lesson. After the man has taken Ezekiel through the vision of the rebuilt temple, he hears a voice coming to him from the house of God.

> *Then I heard one speaking to me from the house, while a man was standing beside me. 7 He said to me, "Son of man, this is the place of My throne and the place of the soles of My feet, where I will dwell among the sons of Israel forever. And the house of Israel will not again defile My holy name, neither they nor their kings, by their harlotry and by the corpses of their kings when they die, 8 by setting their threshold by My threshold and their door*

*post beside My door post, with only the wall between Me and them.
And they have defiled My holy name by their abominations which
they have committed. So I have consumed them in My anger. 9
Now let them put away their harlotry and the corpses of their kings
far from Me; and I will dwell among them forever." (Ezekiel
43:6-9).*

Ezekiel is told the purpose of this vision of the temple. It is that the people of Israel
might be encouraged to put their sin away and walk in obedience to the Lord. Here
is the principle. If they will turn from their wickedness that led up to the
destruction of their city and their temple, then God will grant them a part in His new
temple.

The picture John sees is very similar. He is told to measure the temple, the altar,
and those who worship in it. Ever since John was confronted by the glorified Jesus
in chapter 1, his vision has been in the context of the temple. Jesus was standing
in the middle of the lampstands (1:12-13). There were twenty four elders seated
around the throne of God, reflecting the twenty four courses of priests who served
in the temple (4:4). The souls of the martyred believers were seen under the altar
(5:9). An angel stood before the altar of incense (8:3). Before we finish this
chapter, we shall see the ark of the covenant in the temple (11:19).

Which temple is this? Is it the temple of God in heaven? Or is it the temple in
Jerusalem? In a sense, it is both. The temple that had been in Jerusalem was
patterned after the true temple of God in heaven. The difference between the two
is that the earthly temple was destroyed by Titus in A.D. 70. It has never been
rebuilt. You can go to the site on which it once stood and you will find a Muslim
structure standing there.

It is for this reason that we can conclude the temple John is told to measure is the
one in heaven. This will be made clear in verse 19: *And the temple of God which
is in heaven was opened; and the ark of His covenant appeared in His temple*
(Revelation 11:19a). This temple is in heaven. It is the throne of God. It is a
spiritual temple, not one made of wood and stone. It is occupied by the people of
God.

In Old Testament times, the Lord decreed that His people should build a tabernacle,
a place where God would come to meet man. The tabernacle was the center of the
Jewish community. It was always located at the center of the camp of Israel. It had
a special priesthood who would serve as mediators between God and the people.
When they were in the wilderness, the presence of God was seen in the cloud by
day and in the pillar of fire by night. As long as the people saw the cloud and the
fire, they knew that God was with them.

Many years later, Solomon built a temple for the Lord in Jerusalem. Once again, the presence of God was signified by the coming of a cloud into the temple.

> *It happened that when the priests came from the holy place, the cloud filled the house of the LORD, 11 so that the priests could not stand to minister because of the cloud, for the glory of the LORD filled the house of the LORD. (1 Kings 8:10-11).*

The reason Jerusalem was blessed is because it was the place of the presence of God. It was here that God met man. The reason the destruction of the temple in the days of Nebuchadnezzar was such a tragedy to the Jews was because it meant there was no place on earth where God would meet with man. Even after the Jews returned to the land and rebuilt their temple, the manifestation of the presence of God never returned to the temple. They had a holy place and a holy of holies, but it was just an empty building. But then Jesus came on the scene. He is the One who could say, "Before Abraham was, I AM." He is the Word, the One who communicates God to men. He is the temple. He said that if you destroy this temple, He would raise it up in three days.

Where is Jesus today? He is in heaven. But He is also in men's hearts. He said, "I am with you always" (Matthew 28:20). God has a new temple. It is the church. We are the temple. *Do you not know that you are a temple of God and that the Spirit of God dwells in you?* (1 Corinthians 3:16). We are the temple and it is here that God meets men. This is where the Spirit of God resides today. This means that as John proceeds to measure the temple of God and the altar and those who worship in it, this is a picture of what God is doing with His people today. God has measured us out. He has set us apart. He has made us different. We are His selected group of people. We are His temple.

THE OUTER COURT

> *"Leave out the court which is outside the temple and do not measure it, for it has been given to the nations; and they will tread under foot the holy city for forty-two months." (Revelation 11:1-2).*

The temple and the altar made up only a portion of the entire temple compound in Jerusalem. A much greater area was taken up by the various outer courts. There was the Court of the Men and the Court of the Women and then you would go out beyond the dividing wall to find yourself in the much larger Court of the Gentiles. It was here that the moneychangers had set up their booths in the days of Jesus. Now John is told that this area has been given over to the nations. It is not reserved only for the Jewish people; everyone shall enter.

A model of Herod's Temple with the Court of the Gentiles in the foreground: Holyland Experience, Orlando, Florida

There have been some who wished to take this passage and to interpret it to refer to a literal temple in Jerusalem. But the problem is that it was not only the outer court that was trampled by the Gentiles, but the entire temple was trampled and even destroyed in A.D. 70. Others have sought to make this refer to a future temple, but John does not say this is a rebuilt temple. The following chart summarizes the various views of this temple:

Preterist View	Symbolic View	Futurist View
It refers to the literal first century temple that was destroyed by Titus.	It uses the symbol of the temple to refer to God's people, the church.	It refers to a literal future temple to be constructed before the Second Coming.
A literal temple	A symbolic temple	A literal temple
The 42 months refer to the time of the Roman War to the fall of Jerusalem.	The 42 months are symbolic of a time of testing.	The 42 months refer to the halfway mark in a future great tribulation.

Both the Preterist view as well as the Futurist view interprets this as a literal, physical temple standing in Jerusalem. The problem with both these views is that

188

every other reference to the temple by John in the book of Revelation has not been of a literal temple.

- John saw the lampstand, an article of temple furniture, and was told that it represented the seven churches.
- Jesus promised in Revelation 3:12 to make the overcomer a pillar in the temple of His God.
- The ones who come out of great tribulation are described as serving the Lord day and night in His heavenly temple (Revelation 7:15).
- At the end of this chapter, the ark of the covenant will be seen in the temple of God which is in heaven (Revelation 11:19). The same language is used in Revelation 14:17 and 15:5.
- When we see the vision of the New Jerusalem, we will read that there is no more temple because the Lord God and the Lamb are its temple (Revelation 21:22).

It can be stated in no uncertain terms that if this reference is to a literal, earthly temple, then it is the only such reference in all of John's book because every other reference to a temple in this book is to some other sort of temple beyond the physical temple in Jerusalem. Nor is such a usage unique to this particular book, for in his gospel account, John related the prophetic words of Jesus when He said, "Destroy this temple, and in three days I will raise it up" (John 2:19). John is quick to add, let we misunderstand, that He was speaking of the temple of His body (John 2:21).

This gives us the key to understanding the meaning of the symbolism. Jesus is the temple. It is within Him that the fulness of God dwells in bodily form. At the same time, the New Testament writers also described those who are in Christ as also being the temple (1 Corinthians 3:16; 6:19; Ephesians 2:21).

What does it meant by this measuring and what is meant by the giving of the outer court to the Gentiles? If we are indeed to see this vision as a measuring out of the people of God, when what we have in this passage is similar to that which took place with the sealing of God's people in Revelation 7. It is a sign of God's protection of his people.

Revelation 7	Revelation 11:1-2
144,000 sealed	Temple measured
The people of God protected	The people of God selected
This group envisioned as 144,000 from the tribes of Israel represented people of every tribe, tongue, and nation.	This group envisioned as the temple represents all of God's people.

At the same time, we are told that *they will tread under foot the holy city for forty-two months." (Revelation 11:2).* The reference to the holy city looks to Jerusalem and the fact that the Gentiles will have free reign over the city. Many year earlier, John would have heard Jesus stand in the Court of the Gentiles in Jerusalem and give a very similar prophecy.

> *Woe to those who are pregnant and to those who are nursing babies in those days; for there will be great distress upon the land and wrath to this people; 24 and they will fall by the edge of the sword, and will be led captive into all the nations; and Jerusalem will be trampled under foot by the Gentiles until the times of the Gentiles are fulfilled. (Luke 21:23-24).*

This prophecy was literally fulfilled in A.D. 70 when the Roman general Titus destroyed Jerusalem and carried the surviving Jews off into captivity. To this very day, Jerusalem is trampled underfoot by Gentiles. It has been argued by some that the Jews are today in possession of the city of Jerusalem, but Orthodox Jews are forbidden to walk upon the Temple Mount for fear they might inadvertently walk upon the site of the Holy of Holies. Who is it that has access to the Temple Mount today? Gentiles!

What is true physically of Jerusalem is also true spiritually of the church. We live in the age of the Gentiles. There was a time when the bulk of God's people were Jewish. That time is no longer. The church today is made up mostly of Gentiles.

> *For I do not want you, brethren, to be uninformed of this mystery-- so that you will not be wise in your own estimation-- that a partial hardening has happened to Israel until the fullness of the Gentiles has come in (Romans 11:25).*

The hearts of many of the Jewish people have been hardened to the gospel of Christ. However, it has only been a partial hardening; there are still many Jews who hear the message and believe. This hardening has taken place so that Gentiles might be saved.

Notice the reference in Revelation 11:2 to forty two months. It adds up to three and a half years. This is the first time we have seen a reference to this amount of time in John's writings, but it will not be the last. The number would have been familiar to John. It is from the Old Testament. Daniel made several references to such a number. In Daniel 7, we read of a vision in which four beasts come up from the sea. Each of these beasts represents an earthly kingdom.

- The first beast was like a lion; it represented the Babylonian empire.
- The second beast was like a bear; it represented the Persian empire.

- The third beast was like a leopard; it represented the Greek empire of Alexander the Great.

The fourth beast was like nothing that Daniel had ever seen. It was different than the first three. It had ten horns and from these ten horns sprung a small horn. Daniel's attention was drawn to this small horn.

> *As for the ten horns, out of this kingdom ten kings will arise; and another will arise after them, and he will be different from the previous ones and will subdue three kings. 25 He will speak out against the Most High and wear down the saints of the Highest One, and he will intend to make alterations in times and in law; and they will be given into his hand for a time, times, and half a time. (Daniel 7:24-25).*

This little horn is seen to arise again and again throughout the book of Daniel. He is described as coming to power on the heels of Alexander's kingdom and he is described as an enemy of the people of God. Notice the time of his power. It is *a time, times, and half a time*. Most scholars agree that this is merely another way of citing the period that John has described as 42 months. It is a period of three and a half years.

> *Out of one of them came forth a rather small horn which grew exceedingly great toward the south, toward the east, and toward the Beautiful Land. 10 It grew up to the host of heaven and caused some of the host and some of the stars to fall to the earth, and it trampled them down. 11 It even magnified itself to be equal with the Commander of the host; and it removed the regular sacrifice from Him, and the place of His sanctuary was thrown down. 12 And on account of transgression the host will be given over to the horn along with the regular sacrifice; and it will fling truth to the ground and perform its will and prosper. 13 Then I heard a holy ône speaking, and another holy one said to that particular one who was speaking, "How long will the vision about the regular sacrifice apply, while the transgression causes horror, so as to allow both the holy place and the host to be trampled?" 14 He said to me, "For 2,300 evenings and mornings; then the holy place will be properly restored." (Daniel 8:9-14).*

Who is this little horn? Is he someone who is yet to come? Is he the future anti-Christ? I do not think so. I would suggest that this prophecy in Daniel describes one who has already come. Notice the details that are given:

- He comes on the heels of Alexander's kingdom.

- He subdues three kings.
- He speaks out against the Most High.
- He wears down the saints of the Highest One.
- He attempts to make alterations in times and in law.
- He moves toward the south, toward the east, and toward the Beautiful Land.
- He magnifies himself to be equal with the Commander of the host.
- He removes the regular sacrifice.
- He tramples the holy place and the people of God for 2,300 evenings and mornings (a period of a bit less than three and a half years); but after that the holy place will be properly restored.

If you were familiar with Jewish history, you would realize this prophecy has already been fulfilled in a very literal manner. When Alexander the Great lay on his deathbed, his generals gathered around him and asked to whom he was leaving his kingdom. He replied, "To the strongest." By this answer, he ordained that his kingdom would be broken apart by warfare. Alexander's empire was initially divided up between eleven of his generals, but as they fell to fighting among themselves, two major powers ultimately emerged: Ptolemy and his descendants retained control of Egypt. Seleucus and his descendants took Mesopotamia and Syria.

Between these two rulers lay the tiny kingdom of Judah. For the next 150 years, the Jews found themselves first under one ruler and then under the next as the realm of power shifted from the Seleucids to the Ptolemies and then back again. Finally, a ruler came to the Seleucid throne known as Antiochus IV.

Antiochus IV was a dynamic ruler. He embarked on an aggressive Hellenistic campaign designed to unite all of his subjects. This involved leading them in the worship of the Greek gods. When the Jews revolted, he made it illegal to worship Yahweh or to own a copy of the Scriptures. He moved into the temple in Jerusalem and erected a statue of himself in the Holy of Holies. He stopped the temple sacrifices and he had unclean animals and even humans killed in the temple. He took for himself the title "Epiphanes" – "the manifested one," but the Jews referred to him as Antiochus Epimenes, "Antiochus the madman."

The Seleucids were driven out of Jerusalem by the revolt of the Jewish Maccabees. They succeeded in restoring and cleansing the temple and re-instituting the sacrifices after a period of a little over three years.

Do you see the pattern? The Jews recognized Antiochus as the little horn of Daniel. They referred to his pollution of the temple as the Abomination of Desolation. This is why Jesus surprised His disciples when He predicted an abomination of desolation yet to come. He said that Jerusalem would once again be taken by her enemies and once again a pagan would stand in the temple. History repeated itself in A.D. 70 when the Roman general Titus finally took Jerusalem after a campaign of nearly three and a half years.

All of this serves as a backdrop for John's vision. The truth is that we live in the times of the Gentiles. This world has been handed over to the nations. It is not being run by God's people. Bad things happen in the Court of the Gentiles. People get stepped on when Gentiles are treading underfoot the holy city. But that is okay because God has measured out His city.

Anyone was permitted to enter the Court of the Gentiles. The moneychangers were there. The sellers of the animals were there. Herod had built up the Court of the Gentiles with row upon row of tremendous colonnades. The Court of the Gentiles had all sorts of religious trappings. There was only one thing it lacked – the presence of God.

Only Jewish people were permitted to pass into the temple. There was a wall around the temple that kept out the Gentiles. It was called the dividing wall. It divided the Jews from the Gentiles. It divided the chosen people from the rest of the people. What this wall represents was broken down by the death of Christ.

> *But now in Christ Jesus you who formerly were far off have been brought near by the blood of Christ. 14 For He Himself is our peace, who made both groups into one and broke down the barrier of the dividing wall, 15 by abolishing in His flesh the enmity, which is the Law of commandments contained in ordinances, so that in Himself He might make the two into one new man, thus establishing peace (Ephesians 2:13-15).*

Christ has broken down the barrier of the dividing wall. There is no longer a division between Jews and Gentiles. God knows the people who are His. One day there will be a division again. One day He will return and He shall divide between those who are His people and those who are not His people; between the sheep and the goats, between the wheat and the tares, between the foolish virgins and the wise virgins, and between the tree that bears fruit and the tree that is barren.

In which group are you? Are you one of God's people? You can be. You can come to Jesus Christ in faith and be adopted into His forever family. You can become one of His chosen people as you enter into the presence of God.

THE TWO WITNESSES
Revelation 11:3-14

At the close of chapter 10, we were treated to the vision of a mighty angel giving a little book to John. The apostle was told to take the book and eat it. The book became a part of him. As a result of the eating of the book, John would prophesy concerning many peoples, nations, tongues, and kings (10:11). As we move through chapter 11, the same vision will continue. It is important to remember this because chapter 11 will only be understood in the light of the context of chapter 10.

Revelation 10	Revelation 11
John was told that he would be a witness concerning many peoples and nations and tongues and kings (10:11).	Two witnesses stand before the world and give their testimony; their witness.

THE IDENTITY OF THE TWO WITNESSES

> *And I will grant authority to my two witnesses, and they will prophesy for twelve hundred and sixty days, clothed in sackcloth. 4 These are the two olive trees and the two lampstands that stand before the Lord of the earth. (Revelation 11:3-4).*

Who are these two witnesses? What do they represent? Are they two people who lived in the past who are somehow reincarnated or resurrected? Are they two prophets who shall arise in the future? Or are they something else entirely? Bible scholars have hazarded all sorts of speculations as to their identity.

- Moses and Elijah.
- Enoch and Elijah.
- The Law and the Prophets.
- The Old and New Testaments.
- The church.

John seems to know exactly who they are. In other places in the book of Revelation, he has seen a symbol or a representation and he has been asked about its meaning and he has confessed his own ignorance, but not this time. He says that they *are the two olive trees and the two lampstands that stand before the Lord of the earth.*

You might be thinking, "That doesn't help my understanding at all." That is because you are not familiar with your Old Testament. But John was. And he recognized these two Old Testament symbols. They are found together in the vision of Zechariah.

> *Then the angel who was speaking with me returned, and roused me as a man who is awakened from his sleep.* 2 *And he said to me, "What do you see?" And I said, "I see, and behold, a lampstand all of gold with its bowl on the top of it, and its seven lamps on it with seven spouts belonging to each of the lamps which are on the top of it;* 3 *also two olive trees by it, one on the right side of the bowl and the other on its left side." (Zechariah 4:1-3).*

Zechariah was given a number of visions concerning the plans that God had for His people. I'm not sure that he understood all of them. He certainly didn't understand this one. He asked what it meant.

> *Then I answered and said to him, "What are these two olive trees on the right of the lampstand and on its left?"* 12 *And I answered the second time and said to him, "What are the two olive branches which are beside the two golden pipes, which empty the golden oil from themselves?"* 13 *So he answered me saying, "Do you not know what these are?" And I said, "No, my lord."* 14 *Then he said, "These are the two anointed ones, who are standing by the Lord of the whole earth." (Zechariah 4:11-14).*

Zechariah asks for the identity of the symbols of this vision. He is given an answer. He is told that they are the two anointed ones who are standing by the Lord. This reference to "two anointed ones" seems to be obscure, but it is not when we consider the context of the prophecy. In chapters 3 and 4 of Zechariah, the prophet makes mention of two particular leaders of Israel who had been anointed by God to positions of leadership.

- The first is Joshua the high priest (Chapter 3).
- The second is Zerubbabel the governor and descendant of King David (Chapter 4).

These two men were the representatives of the people of God. They served the temple of God. We read in Zechariah 4:9 that Zerubbabel laid the foundation of the temple of God and we can assume that, as that temple was completed, it would be Joshua the high priest who would bring acceptable offerings into that temple.

The fact that they are pictured in Revelation 11 brings us to a question. Are we meant to understand that two ancient Hebrew leaders are to be somehow reincarnated? Or is this to be two other people who are leaders of God's people in the same spirit and power of those original leaders? Or is this merely a matter of seeing two representative symbols of God's people in general?

It seems to be obviously significant that the olive tree was a picture of Israel. The olive tree was to Israel what the American Eagle is to the United States. It was used upon occasion by the prophets as upon their coins as a symbol for the nation. We have already seen here in Revelation where the lampstand is identified with the people of God. Back in chapter 1, we saw a vision of Jesus in the midst of the seven lampstands and we were told they represented the seven churches.

These two witnesses are described as anointed ones. I have to admit that the first time I read this passage, I though that it might be a messianic reference. After all, the Hebrew word "Messiah" means "anointed one." But when I looked this phrase up in the Hebrew, I found something different. The term here is *Bene Ha-Yetzher* – literally, "Sons of Oil." This is not a mistaken translation as the phrase "sons of oil" can indeed be seen as an idiom to refer to "anointed ones."

Oil played an important role in the ancient world. It was used for cooking, medicine and to give light. It was also used for religious purposes. The priests of God were set apart by a special anointing with oil. Likewise, the king of the nation was marked by an anointing with oil. In the book of Ezekiel, the Lord says that He has anointed the nation of Israel with oil (Ezekiel 16:9).

The concept of the anointing did not remain in the Old Testament. The New Testament also speaks of the anointing of God's people. John himself described that anointing.

> *But you all have an anointing from the Holy One, and you all know (1 John 2:20).*

> *And as for you, the anointing which you received from Him abides in you, and you have no need for anyone to teach you; but as His anointing teaches you about all things, and is true and is not a lie, and just as it has taught you, you abide in Him (1 John 2:27).*

Who are the witnesses? They are the sons of oil. They are the people of God who have been anointed with the oil of God, not some sort of physical oil, but with the Holy Spirit. They are those who believe in Jesus Christ.

- The anointing with oil in the Old Testament was given to the priest. We in the New Covenant have been made a kingdom of priests.
- Oil was used in the Old Testament to anoint the king. We are co-heirs with Christ, rulers of the world to come.
- Oil was placed into lamps to bring light at night. We have been called to be light to a world that dwells in darkness.

- Oil was used as a salve for healing. We have a ministry of healing to a world that is dead in its trespasses and sins.

Who are the two witnesses? You are! If you have come to Christ in faith, trusting in Him as your Lord and Savior, then you have been given the gift of His Holy Spirit. You have been commissioned as a witness and an ambassador for Christ and you have been called to represent Him here on earth..

1.   You have authority.

You have been delegated with authority from heaven. You are able to speak ex cathedra. Like Isaiah and Jeremiah and the other prophets of old, you can say, "Thus says the Lord!" To you have been entrusted the oracles of God.

2.   You are a witness.

What is a witness? It is one who has seen something or who has heard something or who has experienced something. We have called to be witnesses for Christ. That does not mean we must all be theologians. It only means we must speak what we have experienced.

3.   You have a ministry of prophecy.

I do not mean that you are able to predict what will happen next Tuesday, but I do mean that you are able to affirm that which is given to you in the Scriptures. You can announce that Jesus is coming and that His coming will mean judgment for some and salvation for others.

4,   Your ministry is based upon truth.

Why are there two witnesses? It is because, under Jewish law, evidence was legally established as being true only when it came from the mouth of two witnesses. That is why it was so significant when, at the transfiguration, Jesus was seen with Moses and Elijah. No two greater witnesses could be called. They represented the law and the prophets from the Old Testament and they appeared to bear witness of the person of Jesus. Christianity is based upon the evidence of witnesses. The message proclaimed by the apostles throughout the book of Acts was that they had seen with their own eyes the risen Christ.

We have also been called to be witnesses of Christ. That witness continues to be heard throughout the world. But there will come a time when the time of the witness will be at an end.

THE DURATION OF THEIR PROPHECY

> *And I will grant authority to my two witnesses, and they will prophesy for twelve hundred and sixty days, clothed in sackcloth. (Revelation 11:3).*

When we read of this period of time, we will immediately be struck with its similarity to the forty-two months that are mentioned in the previous verse. Chilton points out that the various statements of this length of time form a chiasm in Revelation 11-13 (1990:274). [2]

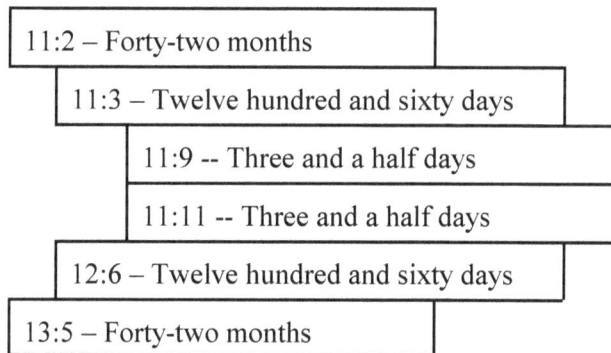

| 11:2 – Forty-two months |
| 11:3 – Twelve hundred and sixty days |
| 11:9 -- Three and a half days |
| 11:11 -- Three and a half days |
| 12:6 – Twelve hundred and sixty days |
| 13:5 – Forty-two months |

To what does this period of forty two months / twelve hundred and sixty days refer? It is a period of three and a half years. This was a particularly significant time to the Jews.

- When Elijah prayed that it would not rain, it did not rain in Israel for three and a half years.
- The Assyrians besieged Samaria for about three and a half years before its fall in 721 B.C.
- During the days of the Maccabees, Jerusalem was dominated by the forces of Antiochus for three and a half years.
- The ministry of Jesus is usually thought to have lasted for about three and a half years.
- Nero's persecution of the Christians lasted for three and a half years.
- From the time the Romans landed in Palestine to quell the Jewish revolt to the time when Jerusalem fell in A.D. 70 was a period of about

---

[2] Chilton goes on to point out how that "in each section of Revelation, St. John's figures harmonize with each other: The Seal-judgments are in fourths, the Trumpet-judgments are in thirds, and the numbers in chapters 11-13 correspond to three and a half (42 months and 1,260 days both equal three and a half years)" (1990:283).

three and a half years.

Can we see a pattern emerging? Each of these references to three and a half years seem to have one thing in common. Each reference deals with a time of difficulty, of testing, or of opposition.

We live in a time of opposition. Jesus said that in this world we will have tribulation. Bad things happen in times of opposition. People mock and do not want to listen. Christians are burned at the stake. Missionaries are murdered. Messiahs are crucified in times of opposition. And yet, we are not told to go into hiding. We are called to be witnesses of God. We are people with a message and we are to be proclaiming that message.

THE POWER OF THE TWO WITNESSES

> *And if anyone wants to harm them, fire flows out of their mouth and devours their enemies; so if anyone wants to harm them, he must be killed in this way. 6 These have the power to shut up the sky, so that rain will not fall during the days of their prophesying; and they have power over the waters to turn them into blood, and to strike the earth with every plague, as often as they desire. (Revelation 11:5-7).*

These two witnesses are given a great deal of power. It is a power that flows out of their mouth and it is a power over creation. We don't often talk about spiritual power and, when we do, we sometimes get the idea of people foaming at the mouth or working themselves up to some ecstatic experience. But the Bible talks about power. Jesus promised His disciples they would receive power from the Holy Spirit. As a result of receiving this power, they would be witnesses (Acts 1:8). That is what we see taking place here.

1.   The Power of their Mouth: *Fire flows out of their mouth and devours their enemies (11:5).*

We have already seen some similar imagery when Jesus was pictured with a sharp sword going out of His mouth. We are not to take this with rigid literalism. It is not a "fire breathing prophet." Instead, it is a picture of speaking forth the judgment of God. This is not a new image. It is taken from the pages of the Old Testament.

> *Therefore, thus says the LORD, the God of hosts,*
> *"Because you have spoken this word,*
> *Behold, I am making My words in your mouth fire*

And this people wood, and it will consume them. (Jeremiah 5:14).

> *"Is not My word like fire?" declares the LORD, "and like a hammer which shatters a rock?" (Jeremiah 23:29).*

The message that we preach will either burn in your heart and bring you to faith or else it will burn your soul in judgment. It will change you. It will either bring you to believe in Christ or it will harden you to the point where you will begin to hate Christ. The one thing it will not do is to leave you indifferent.

2.   The Power over Creation: *These have the power to shut up the sky, so that rain will not fall during the days of their prophesying; and they have power over the waters to turn them into blood, and to strike the earth with every plague, as often as they desire (11:6).*

The power given to these two witnesses takes us back to the great prophets of Israel. We are reminded of the two great prophets, Moses and Elijah.

- Elijah was able to pray that it might not rain and the rains ceased for the three and a half years of his prophesying.
- Moses stood before the Pharaoh of Egypt and turned the waters of the Nile into blood and smote the land with every manner of plague.

We look at those prophets and we are inclined to say, "But that was then and this is now. God does not do that any longer." Has God changed? Does He still answer the prayers of His people. The New Testament teaches that He does.

> *Is anyone among you sick? Then he must call for the elders of the church and they are to pray over him, anointing him with oil in the name of the Lord; 15 and the prayer offered in faith will restore the one who is sick, and the Lord will raise him up, and if he has committed sins, they will be forgiven him. 16 Therefore, confess your sins to one another, and pray for one another so that you may be healed. The effective prayer of a righteous man can accomplish much. 17 Elijah was a man with a nature like ours, and he prayed earnestly that it would not rain, and it did not rain on the earth for three years and six months. 18 Then he prayed again, and the sky poured rain and the earth produced its fruit. (James 5:14-18).*

What is the point of this passage? It is that we need to pray to partake of the same power for which Elijah prayed. He was a man with a nature like our own. He had the same kinds of problems we have. The only difference is that he prayed. Why don't you have that same kind of power? It is because you are not praying. When believers start praying, then the world will start to change in a mighty way.

THE MARTYRDOM OF THE WITNESSES

> *When they have finished their testimony, the beast that comes up out of the abyss will make war with them, and overcome them and kill them. 8 And their dead bodies will lie in the street of the great city which mystically is called Sodom and Egypt, where also their Lord was crucified. 9 Those from the peoples and tribes and tongues and nations will look at their dead bodies for three and a half days, and will not permit their dead bodies to be laid in a tomb. 10 And those who dwell on the earth will rejoice over them and celebrate; and they will send gifts to one another, because these two prophets tormented those who dwell on the earth. (Revelation 11:7-10).*

As John's vision continues to be unveiled, a new character enters upon the stage. He is called *the beast that comes up out of the abyss.* We saw the abyss back in Revelation 9. It was called the "bottomless pit." It signified the place of the forces of darkness. The lord of those forces was the angel of the abyss. Who is this beast? This is the first time John has mentioned the beast, but it is not the last time. He will be a dominant figure throughout the rest of the book of Revelation.

It seems that, for a figure of such importance, John would spend more time introducing him. Why does he not tell us exactly who is this beast? I believe it is because he assumes we are familiar with the Old Testament.

The seventh chapter of Daniel contains a prophecy that tells of the coming of an entire series of beasts. Each beast in that prophecy represents a great kingdom that would rise up to dominate the earth. The kingdoms of Babylon, Persia, and Greece are seen in quick succession. But it is the fourth beast that draws our particular attention.

> *Thus he said: "The fourth beast will be a fourth kingdom on the earth, which will be different from all the other kingdoms and will devour the whole earth and tread it down and crush it." (Daniel 7:23).*

The fourth beast was like nothing Daniel had ever seen. It was different from the first three beasts. It is further described as having ten horns. From these ten horns springs forth a small horn. It is this small horn that becomes the object of Daniel's attention:

> *As for the ten horns, out of this kingdom ten kings will arise; and another will arise after them, and he will be different from the previous ones and will subdue three kings. 25 He will speak out against the Most High and wear down the saints of the Highest One, and he will intend to make alterations in times and in law; and they will be given into his hand for a time, times, and half a time. (Daniel 7:24-25).*

In our last chapter, we saw how the little horn was fulfilled, at least in part, by the person of Antiochus Epiphanes, the Seleucid king who entered Jerusalem in 167 B.C. and who put a stop to the temple sacrifices. We saw how the same thing took place in A.D. 70 when the Roman general Titus took Jerusalem and entered into the temple and burned it to the ground. We saw how it is also fulfilled every time the forces of darkness move against the people of God.

Who is the beast? He is Satan's man of the hour. He might be a politician. Or he might be a preacher. He might be a lecturer or a false teacher or a well-known author. He might be a Nero or a Titus or a Napoleon or a Hitler. He might be a Darwin or a Richard Dawkins. He might be a Joseph Smith or a Charles Russell or a Mary Baker Eddy. Who is the beast? He is the one who stands in the place of God and seeks to draw glory from God by placing it upon himself.

1.   The Overcoming Conflict: *The beast that comes up out of the abyss will make war with them, and overcome them and kill them (11:7).*

   Throughout the book of Revelation, we have seen one central theme. It is that Jesus is going to win the great conflict between the forces of light and the forces of darkness. He is going to overcome. But now we see something different. Instead of Jesus overcoming, we see the beast overcoming. What has happened? Has God failed?

   That is the question we often are inclined to ask when we see God's people being defeated. There is a war going on and we are living in the midst of a spiritual battlefield. Battlefields are not pleasant places. Bad things can happen on a battlefield. It is easy to get depressed and shell shocked on a battlefield, especially when the enemy is winning.

   We learn here that there are times when Satan wins the skirmish. Christians are sometimes mocked and persecuted and even put to death. Atheists and agnostics rejoice when we are beaten. The citizens of Satan's city look out upon the church and it seems to have died. That is okay because there is coming a day when we shall rise. Here is the principle. No matter how bad things get, Jesus is going to have the final victory and His people will share in that victory.

2.   The Place of Conflict: *And their dead bodies will lie in the street of the great city which mystically is called Sodom and Egypt, where also their Lord was crucified (11:8).*

John sees the bodies of these two martyrs lying in the streets of the great city. To which great city does this refer? It *mystically is called Sodom and Egypt* because it shares certain spiritual qualities of Sodom and of Egypt. But it is the place where the Lord was crucified. It is a reference to Jerusalem.

Jerusalem will be seen in the book of Revelation as a type of that which has rejected Christ. It is likened here to Sodom and to Egypt. It will be likened in Revelation 17-18 to the city of Babylon. These are not new identifications. They go back to the Old Testament. Isaiah referred to Jerusalem and to Israel as Sodom and Gomorrah (Isaiah 1:9-10). The point is that, if God's people do not follow Him, then they are no longer God's people. They become instead the enemies of God.

THE RESURRECTION OF THE WITNESSES

> *But after the three and a half days, the breath of life from God came into them, and they stood on their feet; and great fear fell upon those who were watching them. 12 And they heard a loud voice from heaven saying to them, "Come up here." Then they went up into heaven in the cloud, and their enemies watched them. 13 And in that hour there was a great earthquake, and a tenth of the city fell; seven thousand people were killed in the earthquake, and the rest were terrified and gave glory to the God of heaven. (Revelation 11:11-13).*

By this time, we should be noticing that there is a direct correlation between the ministry of the two witnesses and the ministry of our Lord Jesus Christ. That same correlation extends to the church as seen in the following chart:

Two Witnesses	Jesus	The Church
Authority given to them.	Authority was given to Jesus.	Authority has been given to us.

They prophecy for 1260 days.	He ministered for about thee and a half years.	We are called to minister in this present time.
They are the two olive trees and the two lampstands.	He is the root of Jesse and the light of the world.	We are called to be sources of light and life.
They have power.	He demonstrated the power of God in His many miracles.	We have power in prayer.
The beast makes war with them and overcomes them and kills them.	He was arrested, tried, condemned, and crucified by His enemies.	We are at war with the forces of Satan.
After three and a half days, the breath of life from God came into them.	Jesus arose from the dead after three days and nights in the grave.	Though the world seems to win, the church will rise again.
They went up into heaven in the cloud.	Jesus ascended into heaven.	We shall be caught up to be with Him.

There is a tremendous truth here. It is that we have been identified with Jesus and we have become partakers in what He is and in what He does. He is the Son of God and we have become sons of God. He is the heir to the kingdom and we have become co-heirs with Christ. He has eternal life and we have been given eternal life. He is the light of the world and we are to be light to the world. He is righteous and we have been declared righteous as His perfect righteousness is credited to us. He is holy and we are called to be holy. He suffered, bled, and died and we are made partakers of His sufferings. He rose from the dead and we shall also rise from the dead to be like Him as we see Him as He is.

When people look at you, they ought to see Jesus. You are the only Jesus they will ever know. There is a sense in which you have been called to be Jesus to the world.

THY KINGDOM COME
Revelation 11:15-19

The year was 47 B.C. and the Roman world was in the turmoil of a civil war. Julius Caesar had just defeated the forces of Pompey at Pharsalus. In a whirlwind campaign, he sailed to Egypt and then marched north through Israel, Syria, and Anatolia where he met the forces of Pharnaces II, king of Pontus in a decisive confrontation. His message to the Roman Senate was short and powerful:

> Veni, vedi, vici.
> I came, I saw, I conquered.

This is the message of Revelation. It is a message of victory and of conquest. It is the message that Jesus is going to win and that we who believe in Him are going to win with Him.

THE SEVENTH ANGEL

> *Then the seventh angel sounded; and there were loud voices in heaven, saying, "The kingdom of the world has become the kingdom of our Lord and of His Christ; and He will reign forever and ever." (Revelation 11:15).*

In Revelation 8-9 we saw six angels blowing six trumpets. Each trumpet signified a judgment upon the unbelieving world. Now we come to the seventh trumpet. His is the last in the series; he is the last trumpet.

The trumpet is a common symbol in the Bible. Trumpets were used as a call to arms, they were used to call people to worship, they were used to mark the beginning of a celebration, and they were used in the coronation of kings. But there is only one place where a trumpet is called "the last trumpet."

> *...in a moment, in the twinkling of an eye, at the last trumpet; for the trumpet will sound, and the dead will be raised imperishable, and we will be changed (1 Corinthians 15:52).*

What is this event that is signified by the last trumpet? It is the day of resurrection. It is the day when Jesus returns to the earth. We read elsewhere that His coming is announced by the sounding of a trumpet.

> *For the Lord Himself will descend from heaven with a*

> *shout, with the voice of the archangel and with **the trumpet of*** ***God**, and the dead in Christ will rise first. 17 Then we who are* *alive and remain will be caught up together with them in the* *clouds to meet the Lord in the air, and so we shall always be with* *the Lord. (1 Thessalonians 4:16-17).*

Jesus Himself described His coming in the same manner when He spoke with His disciples on the Mount of Olives:

> *And then the sign of the Son of Man will appear in the sky,* *and then all the tribes of the earth will mourn, and they will see the* *Son of Man coming on the clouds of the sky with power and great* *glory. 31 And He will send forth His angels with a great **trumpet*** *and they will gather together His elect from the four winds, from* *one end of the sky to the other. (Matthew 24:30-31).*

There have been some who have tried to insist that the event described in Matthew 24:30-31 is separate and distinct from that which is seen in 1 Thessalonians 4:16-17; that the first describes the "rapture" of the church while the second describes the Second Coming of Christ. But the Bible seems to go out of its way to identify them as one and the same.

Matthew 24:30-31	1 Thessalonians 4:16-17
The Son of Man coming.	The coming of the Lord.
A great trumpet.	The trumpet of God.
The elect of God gathered.	Christ's people caught up.
Coming on the clouds of the sky.	...together with them in the clouds.

The Bible does not teach that there is a separate "rapture" that is followed by a later Second Coming of Christ. These are one and the same event. Jesus is going to come and He is going to gather His people and that event is signified here with the sounding of a trumpet.

There is coming a day when the trumpet of the Lord will sound. It shall be calling people to worship as every knee bows and every tongue confesses that Jesus is Lord. It shall mark the final judgment of the world and the beginning of an eternal celebration. It shall also mark the coronation of the King of kings.

At the opening of the seventh seal there was silence in heaven. Now at the opening of the seventh trumpet we hear loud voices in heaven. They announce that a dramatic change has come over the world. This change has to do with the kingdom.

The concept of the kingdom is rooted in the Old Testament. As far back as the days of Moses, God had promised to take the nation of Israel and make of them "a kingdom of priests."

> *"Now then, if you will indeed obey My voice and keep My covenant, then you shall be My own possession among all the peoples, for all the earth is Mine; 6 and you shall be to Me a kingdom of priests and a holy nation." These are the words that you shall speak to the sons of Israel. (Exodus 19:5-6).*

The main function of a priest was to mediate between God and man. While the prophet represented the message of God to the people, the priest came and represented the people to God. By the same token it was to be through the nation of Israel that the rest of the world was to be brought to God. The prophet Daniel had promised that this kingdom, once established, would never be destroyed.

> *In the days of those kings the God of heaven will set up a kingdom which will never be destroyed, and that kingdom will not be left for another people; it will crush and put an end to all these kingdoms, but it will itself endure forever. (Daniel 2:44).*

The prophets were very explicit in describing the boundaries, the signs, and the citizens of this kingdom. There was coming a day when the God of Israel would also be the God of Rome and of every other nation. On that day, God's chosen One would sit upon the throne of David and rule over the nations of the earth. The Jews understood that this kingdom would have its point of origin in Israel. From there, it would spread out to the whole earth. It was therefore to Israel that both John the Baptist and Jesus came proclaiming the kingdom of heaven was at hand.

What happened? Where is the kingdom today? Was it offered and then rejected and then taken away? Did we miss it? No. There is a sense in which the kingdom is still in our midst.

> *Now having been questioned by the Pharisees as to when the kingdom of God was coming, He answered them and said, "The kingdom of God is not coming with signs to be observed; 21 nor will they say, 'Look, here it is!' or, 'There it is!' For behold, the kingdom of God is in your midst." (Luke 17:20-21).*

The problem with the Pharisees was not that they did not see the kingdom. The problem with the Pharisees is that they did not recognize the kingdom when they saw it. What is the kingdom? It is the reign of God and it encompasses the people over whom God has rule. They make up a nation of every tribe and tongue and race. They are the chosen people of God. We call them today the church.

We see here in Revelation that the kingdoms of the world are going to become the kingdom of the Lord. What does this mean? It means that the church is going to be victorious. It means that the gospel will accomplish that for which it was intended, that it will spread to the ends of the earth and that men everywhere will come under the rule of God.

This is important. We Christians are often in danger of developing a fortress mentality. We have barricaded ourselves inside our churches and we envision ourselves as holding out against the attacks of the world. We have gone into a defensive mode. But you do not win wars by going on the defensive. You win by attacking and, when the church attacks the forces of Satan with the gospel, it will win. That is what Jesus told Peter when He first spoke about the building of His church.

> *I also say to you that you are Peter, and upon this rock I will build My church; and the gates of Hades will not overpower it. (Matthew 16:18).*

Jesus describes the church as taking an offensive posture against the forces of hell. The church is pictured as battering against the barricaded gates of hell and bursting through those gates and plundering its enemy. Every time an unbeliever repents and becomes a child of God, that is another crack in the gates of hell. Every time a decision is made to renounce sin and follow the Lord, Satan loses another battle.

That has tremendous practical implications in my own life. It means that my labor for the Lord is going to bear fruit. It means that when I share the gospel, the results are guaranteed. It means that when I teach the word, people will grow. It means my labors will not be in vain and that I am on the winning side.

It is nice to be on the winning side. I graduated from Southwest Miami High School. It was a tradition that each year on Thanksgiving Day our high school football team would play the team from Coral Gables High School. It was a tradition that each year our team would be beaten in that game. It had been happening for so many years that, by the time I came to that high school, I don't think our team expected to win.

I have a friend who attended the Coral Gables High School. He played on their football team and he told me their coach would call them in before the game and say, "Men, our team has never lost to Southwest High. Are you going to be the first?" Then they would go out and win another game.

I am certain there was a difference in the attitudes between the players of those two teams. These is something about being on a winning team that can motivate you to do better. That is why you need to know that Jesus is going to win.

THE SONG OF THE ELDERS

> *And the twenty-four elders, who sit on their thrones before God, fell on their faces and worshiped God, 17 saying, "We give You thanks, O Lord God, the Almighty, who are and who were, because You have taken Your great power and have begun to reign. 18 And the nations were enraged, and Your wrath came, and the time came for the dead to be judged, and the time to reward Your bond-servants the prophets and the saints and those who fear Your name, the small and the great, and to destroy those who destroy the earth." (Revelation 11:16-18).*

As the seventh angel sounds his trumpet and the proclamation of the fulfillment of God's kingdom is announced, the twenty-four elders break out in a song of worship. We first saw these elders in chapter 4. They were seated around the throne of God in heaven. They were dressed in white robes and wore golden crowns upon their heads. We pointed out that they are the heavenly counterpart to the twenty-four courses of the priesthood that served the earthly temple. They are seen thanking God that He has begun to reign.

1.   The God of Past and Present: *"We give You thanks, O Lord God, the Almighty, who are and who were (11:17).*

The translation is unfortunate when it makes it sound as though the Lord is being addressed as a plural. The translators of the NIV, the ESV, and the NKJV more correctly translated this to say "who is and who was." The wording in the Greek text is identical to that found in Revelation 1:4 where John pronounces grace and peace "from Him who is and who was and who is to come." The song of the elders does not describe God as the one who "is to come" because, as the song is sung, He has already returned. This is explained in the next phrase.

2.   The Present and Future Reign of Christ: *You have taken Your great power and have begun to reign (11:17).*

This brings us to a question. Is Jesus reigning today? There is a sense in which He is. Whether they realize it or not, He is reigning over the affairs of men. This is a regular theme within the Psalms.

> *God reigns over the nations,*
> *God sits on His holy throne {Psalm 47:8).*

> *The LORD reigns, let the peoples tremble;*
> *He is enthroned above the cherubim, let the earth shake!*

(Psalm 99:1).

At the same time, we must admit that the reign of God is not universally recognized. The kingdom is both now and not yet. It is both here today and also it is to come in the future. There is coming a day when the dominion of God will be recognized throughout the universe. On that day, every knee shall bow and every tongue shall confess that Jesus is Lord. On that day, He will judge the nations.

3.　　　The Day of Judgment: *Your wrath came, and the time came for the dead to be judged, and the time to reward Your bond-servants the prophets and the saints and those who fear Your name, the small and the great, and to destroy those who destroy the earth." (Revelation 11:18).*

There is coming in the future a day of judgment. For some, it will be a day of wrath as the condemnation of a righteous God calls upon unrighteous men. For others it will be a day of rewards as a loving God pours out His blessings upon His children.

You are going to be judged. The only question is which type of judgment it is going to be. Are you one who obeyed the voice of His prophets? Are you one of His saints, His holy people? Are you one who fears His name? If so, then you are promised a day of rewards.

This is important for you to know because it sometimes seems as though good goes unrewarded. You know what I am talking about. The time when you smiled at someone and only got a growl in return. The time you did something good and no one noticed. The time you overcame temptation and there was no one around to applaud your choice. For all those times, you need to know there was someone who noticed and there will be a reward.

THE OPEN TEMPLE

And the temple of God which is in heaven was opened; and the ark of His covenant appeared in His temple, and there were flashes of lightning and sounds and peals of thunder and an earthquake and a great hailstorm. (Revelation 11:19).

The context of this passage is the Second Coming. That is striking because the Second Coming has already been pictured at the end of Revelation 6. Now it is seen again. It will continue to be pictured on a number of different occasions throughout this book.

Throughout the book of Revelation, John's vision has contained "temple language." He saw Jesus by the lampstands and wearing clothing that was associated with the High Priests. He saw the Lord seated on his throne before the crystal sea (they called the laver of water before the Temple the sea). He sees the altar of incense and souls praying for retribution. Now he sees the ark of the covenant. The ark had been lost after the Babylonian Captivity. Jeremiah had prophesied that the ark would be no more and it had apparently met its end in the destruction of the temple by Nebuchadnezzar (Jeremiah 3:16). The ark had been missing for over five hundred years, but John sees it in his vision. It represents the very throne of God.

We have seen temple language throughout the book of Revelation. We saw the lampstand and we saw the crystal sea. We saw the altar of incense. Now we look past all of these to the innermost part of the temple. While the temple was standing in Jerusalem, the priests would enter each morning and each evening to offer incense upon the altar. But there was one part of the temple into which no priest was permitted to go. It was the room located beyond the veil. It was known as the holy of holies. It was separated from the rest of the temple by a great double veil. No man was permitted to pass through this veil except for the high priest, and then only once a year on Yom Kippur, the day of atonement.

In the days of Solomon, there had been only one article of furniture in this room. It was the ark of the covenant. It was a wooden box overlaid with gold. The box contained the tablets of stone on which the ten commandments had been written. It also contained Aaron's rod, the symbol of his priestly leadership, and it contained a pot of manna. The top of the ark was of pure gold. It was known as the mercy seat. It was recognized as the throne of God. On either side of the mercy seat were the images of cherubim, their heads bowed in reverence and their wings overspreading the mercy seat.

Once a year, on the day of atonement, the high priest would enter the holy of holies. In his hands would be a cup filled with the blood of bulls and goats. These animals had just been sacrificed on the front steps of the temple. He would now approach the ark of the covenant and he would sprinkle this blood upon the mercy seat.

Inside the ark were the tablets of the law. They symbolized the righteous standard of God. It is a standard that men have failed to obey. That failure demands death. But the blood of the sacrifice served to cover that failure. The offering of blood upon the mercy seat served to atone for the sins of the nation. It provided a substitutionary payment for sin as it demonstrated that a death had taken place.

The ark was no longer in Jerusalem in the days of the New Testament. It had been lost many hundreds of years earlier when Nebuchadnezzar plundered the temple and destroyed Jerusalem. When the high priest entered behind the veil in New Testament times, there was only a barren rock where the ark had once stood.

There was a Jewish legend, told in 2 Maccabees 2:4-8, of how Jeremiah had taken the ark and the other parts of the tabernacle and had hidden them in a cave on the mountain from which Moses had looked out over the Promised Land. It was said that the place would remain unknown until God gathered His people together and showed His mercy. What we see here is an unveiling of the ark of the covenant. It is done with the same sort of lightning and thunder and earthquake that had accompanied the original giving of the law. It is not unveiled in some cave in the Middle East. It is seen in heaven.

That is not all. In John's vision of the open temple and the ark of the covenant, there is something missing. The veil has been removed. It was torn asunder when Jesus died on the cross and it will never be replaced. This means the way has been opened for you to enter into the presence of God. It means you can come with confidence to the throne of grace. It means that, when you pray, you are entering into the presence of the God of the universe and He will answer.

THE COSMIC CONFLICT
Revelation 12:1-17

We live in a physical world. People often make the mistake of looking at the world they can experience with our five senses and think that is the extent of reality. If they cannot see it, touch it, taste it, smell it, hear it, or measure it with their instruments, then they assume it is not there. Far too often, the supernatural is equated with the irrational and the illogical.

The Bible teaches that the supernatural is just as real as those things that are seen. What would happen if the Lord enlarged our senses so that we could become aware of the spiritual world around us? This has happened many times, but none is so striking as in the days of Elisha. The prophet had warned the king of Israel on several different occasions of assassination attempts that were being planned by the neighboring king of Aram. Word got back to the king of Aram that his plans had been foiled again and again by Elisha and he sent an army out to capture the prophet. On the following morning, Elisha's servant came running in to wake his master with the news that the city was surrounded by hostile forces. Elisha's reply was striking.

> He replied, "Do not be afraid, for there are more with us than there are with them." 17 Then Elisha prayed: "O LORD, please open his eyes that he may see." So the LORD opened the eyes of the servant, and he saw; the mountain was full of horses and chariots of fire all around Elisha. (2 Kings 6:16-17).

Elisha was not afraid because he knew something his servant did not know. He knew that we live in a supernatural world and that it is real. This lesson will come to us again in this chapter of Revelation.

The cosmos is in conflict. You can see this taking place from the tiniest amoeba to the greatest galaxy. Nature portrays what Darwin called "the survival of the fittest" and it is a life and death struggle. That same sort of struggle is seen in the lives of mankind. There is a war going on and it serves as a backdrop for every other war and human conflict. It is not limited to planet earth. What we are going to see in this chapter is that the real war is a heavenly one.

THE WOMAN WITH CHILD

> And a great sign appeared in heaven: a woman clothed with the sun, and the moon under her feet, and on her head a crown of twelve stars; 2 and she was with child; and she cried out,

being in labor and in pain to give birth. (Revelation 12:1-2).

This vision appears as a great sign in heaven. It begins with a woman. She is clothed with the sun; she has the moon under her feet and on her head is a crown of twelve stars. Of what does this remind you?

Do you remember the dream of Joseph? Joseph dreamed that the sun and the moon and the stars were bowing down before him. Both his brothers as well as his father understood the meaning of the dream. It referred to his family. The sun was his father. The moon was his father's wife (or wives). The stars were his brothers, the sons of Israel.

The image that was introduced in the Old Testament has not changed here. It is still the people of God. It is still the nation of Israel. She is with child. She is not just pregnant; she is very pregnant. She is pictured in the midst of the labor pains of childbirth. The symbol of a woman in labor was familiar to the Jewish people.

> *As the pregnant woman approaches the time to give birth,*
> *She writhes and cries out in her labor pains,*
> *Thus were we before You, O LORD.*
> *18 We were pregnant, we writhed in labor,*
> *We gave birth, as it seems, only to wind.*
> *We could not accomplish deliverance for the earth,*
> *Nor were inhabitants of the world born. (Isaiah 26:17-18).*

Isaiah describes the difficult times of his people in terms of labor pains. The thing that made these labor pains so difficult to bear was that they did not seem to result in new life. Labor pains are a difficult thing, but they are made all the more difficult if they are not rewarded in the end by the birth of a baby. Jesus alluded to this same phenomenon:

> *Whenever a woman is in labor she has pain, because her*
> *hour has come; but when she gives birth to the child, she no longer*
> *remembers the anguish because of the joy that a child has been*
> *born into the world. 22 Therefore you too have grief now; but I will*
> *see you again, and your heart will rejoice, and no one will take*
> *your joy away from you. (John 16:21-22).*

Do you see what Jesus is saying? We are living in the times of travail. We are experiencing the pains of childbirth. Paul says that *the whole creation groans and suffers the pains of childbirth together until now* (Romans 8:22). But there is coming a day when we will see Him and then the anguish will be forgotten in the joy that sweeps over us.

ENTER THE DRAGON

> *And another sign appeared in heaven: and behold, a great red dragon having seven heads and ten horns, and on his heads were seven diadems. 4 And his tail swept away a third of the stars of heaven, and threw them to the earth. And the dragon stood before the woman who was about to give birth, so that when she gave birth he might devour her child. (Revelation 12:3-4).*

John's attention is directed now from the woman to heaven where there appears a great red dragon. His appearance is strange, yet familiar. The Greek word translated "dragon" is *drakon* (δρακων). It is the same word that is used in the Septuagint of Exodus 7:9-12 where Aaron and the Egyptian priests cast down their staffs and they become "serpents." At the same time, it is used elsewhere in the Old Testament to carry the idea of sea monsters and even the mysterious Leviathan. When we come to verse 9, the dragon will be identified as "the serpent of old who is called the devil and Satan."

He is pictured here as a dragon *having seven heads and ten horns*. This is meant to remind us of another vision that was seen by one of the prophets of God. Daniel describes a vision of a beast with ten horns. The vision begins with a series of succeeding beast, each rising up out of the sea. But it is when the fourth beast arises that we see one that is different from all those who came before.

> *After this I kept looking in the night visions, and behold, a fourth beast, dreadful and terrifying and extremely strong; and it had large iron teeth. It devoured and crushed, and trampled down the remainder with its feet; and it was different from all the beasts that were before it, and it had ten horns. 8 While I was contemplating the horns, behold, another horn, a little one, came up among them, and three of the first horns were pulled out by the roots before it; and behold, this horn possessed eyes like the eyes of a man, and a mouth uttering great boasts. (Daniel 7:7-8).*

Daniel did not understand the meaning of the vision, so he asked what was its significance. He was given this answer:

> *Thus he said: "The fourth beast will be a fourth kingdom on the earth, which will be different from all the other kingdoms and will devour the whole earth and tread it down and crush it" (Daniel 7:23).*

Daniel's vision had seen four beasts coming up from the sea. Each of those beasts represented an earthly kingdom that would arise and act in a "beastly" manner

215

toward mankind.

- The first beast was like a lion: It represented the Babylonian Empire of Nebuchadnezzar.
- The second beast was like a bear: It represented the Empire of the Medes and the Persians that was brought on by Cyrus the Great and which reigned from Egypt to the borders of India for the next two hundred years.
- The third beast was like a leopard: It represented the Greek Empire that was carved out by Alexander the Great with lightning rapidity, but which quickly splintered into several independent kingdoms, each ruled by his various generals.

The fourth beast was like nothing that Daniel had ever seen. It was different from the first three in that he could not liken it to any one particular animal with which he was familiar. It had ten horns. From these ten horns sprang forth a small horn. Daniel's attention was drawn to the small horn.

> *As for the ten horns, out of this kingdom ten kings will arise; and another will arise after them, and he will be different from the previous ones and will subdue three kings. 25 He will speak out against the Most High and wear down the saints of the Highest One, and he will intend to make alterations in times and in law; and they will be given into his hand for a time, times, and half a time. (Daniel 7:24-25).*

The prophecy of this little horn was dramatically fulfilled in the person of Antiochus Epiphanes, the Seleucid ruler who desecrated the temple in Jerusalem and who caused the sacrifices to cease for three and a half years. Such activities were echoed again in A.D. 70 when the Roman general Titus took the city of Jerusalem after a six month siege and burnt the temple to the ground, effectively putting an end to the sacrificial system.

The year previous to the fall of Jerusalem was known in Roman history as "the year of the four emperors." It could be said that three horns died that year, leaving Vespasian, the father of Titus, as the ruling emperor of Rome. It is noteworthy that Vespasian was the tenth of the caesars to claim power in Rome, although only seven of those ruled for any length of time.

(1)   Julius Caesar.
(2)   Octavius Augustus.
(3)   Tiberius.
(4)   Caligula.
(5)   Claudius.
(6)   Nero.

(7)   Galba.
(8)   Otho.
(9)   Vitellius.
(10)   Vespasian.

John does not give all of these details of the appearance of the dragon. He says only that it was big and red and that it had seven heads, ten horns, and seven crowns. That is meant as a hint to the meaning of the symbolism. Crowns are worn by kings. We have a picture of various rulers, yet they come from a single dragon.

All of this forms the backdrop of John's vision, but his attention is not drawn at this time to the horns or even to the small horn, but to the actions of the dragon. With his tail he *swept away a third of the stars of heaven, and threw them to the earth.* In verse 9, we will be told that he is thrown down, *and his angels were thrown down with him.* The Bible speaks elsewhere of fallen angels; those angels who sinned and who left their original estate (Jude 1:6). Daniel also has a vision of a being who *grew up to the host of heaven and caused some of the host and some of the stars to fall to the earth, and it trampled them down (Daniel 8:10).*

Throughout the trumpet judgments, we have seen the idea of a third repeated time and time again.

1st Trumpet	A third of the earth and the trees were burned up (8:7).
2nd Trumpet	A third of the sea became blood, a third of the sea creatures died, and a third of the ships were destroyed (8:8-9).
3rd Trumpet	A third of the waters were poisoned (8:10-11).
4th Trumpet	A third of the sun, moon, and stars were struck; no shining for a third of the day or night (8:12).
6th Trumpet	Third of mankind is killed by army from the Euphrates (9:15-19).

This is not the first time such language has been used in the Bible. When Ezekiel was describing the judgment of God that was to come against Jerusalem in the form of the Babylonian captivity, he said that a third would die by plague or be consumed by famine and a third would fall by the sword and a third would be scattered to the winds (Ezekiel 5:12). The point is not that the other two thirds are safe; the point is that everyone is ultimately judged.

Similarly, now we see Satan taking a third of the stars of heaven and causing their fall. This is a part of the growing intensity that we see as the movement of the book of Revelation. When we saw the four horsemen and one of them brought death upon a fourth of mankind. As we read of the trumpets, the destructive judgments are all described as wrecking havoc upon a third of the world. When we come to the seven bowls, we shall see that it impacts all of the world.

THE CHILD WHO IS TO RULE

> *And she gave birth to a son, a male child, who is to rule all the nations with a rod of iron; and her child was caught up to God and to His throne. (Revelation 12:5).*

Not everyone is in agreement as to the identity of this child. There are some who feel that, because the description of his birth takes place halfway through the book of Revelation, that it must be a reference to the early church. Who is this child?

- He is described both as a *son* and as a *male child*. The description seems redundant since all sons are necessarily male, but in this case, we have both together as the Greek literally reads, "She gave birth to a male son."

- He is to rule all the nations with a rod of iron. The idea of a rod of iron is first introduced in Psalm 2:9, a Messianic Psalm in which the Son is being told by His Father that he shall use such a rod to break the nations. This is repeated in Revelation 2:27 and in Revelation 19:15, each having obvious reference to Jesus.

- He is caught up to God and to His throne. It would be enough to describe His as having been caught up to God, but the author wants to go further than that and he also includes a reference to God's throne.

There can be little doubt that this is a reference to Jesus. He is the primary character within the book of Revelation as this book is about His revealing. John opened his book by calling it the Revelation of Jesus Christ (Revelation 1:1). Jesus is still being revealed in this passage.

In verse 4, we were told of how the dragon was lying in wait, seeking to devour this son. The Bible gives us all sorts of insights as to how Satan has worked in history, seeking to subvert the coming of the promised Messiah.

- No sooner had the promise of a seed been given to Adam and Eve then we read in Genesis 4 of the first murder where the offspring of Adam and Eve are being put to death.
- After Abraham is promised that the seed shall come through him, he finds his wife being taken by the Egyptian pharaoh. It is only through

the intervention of the Lord that she is restored to him.

- When the Israelites enter Egypt, the pharaoh of Egypt tries to have them destroyed, ordering that all newborn males be cast into the Nile River.
- In the days of the kings of Judah and Israel, the wicked queen Athaliah slays all of the descendants of David through whom is the promised seed. Only Joash survives.
- In the days of Esther, a genocidal plot is conceived to have all Jews put to death.
- Following the birth of Jesus, King Herod attempts to murder the child by having all newborn children in Bethlehem killed.

All of the plans of Satan were thwarted with the coming of Christ. Even the cross, which looked like a stunning victory on the part of the forces of Satan, turned into his defeat as Jesus rose from the dead and ascended into heaven.

THE WOMAN AND THE WILDERNESS

> *And the woman fled into the wilderness where she had a place prepared by God, so that there she might be nourished for one thousand two hundred and sixty days. (Revelation 12:6).*

We have already seen the woman as a symbol of Israel. She was introduced as having a crown of twelve stars (12:1), reminding us of the dream of Joseph who understood the twelve stars to be the twelve sons of Israel. Now we see her fleeing to the wilderness where she is protected by God and nourished for a period of *one thousand two hundred and sixty days.*

As we read of this period of time, some three and a half years in duration, we understand that we have already seen this same period of time attested in the book of Revelation. It has been mentioned on several occasions and will continue to be referenced:

Revelation 11:2	Revelation 11:3	Revelation 12:6	Revelation 13:5
42 Months	1260 Days	1260 Days	42 Months
Holy city to be trampled.	Authority given to two witnesses.	Woman protected in the wilderness.	Beast acts with authority.

In the same way that Elijah was protected in the wilderness during the time he was hiding from King Ahab, so also, we see the woman being both hidden and nourished in the wilderness. It is striking that these events can at least be seen in part in the Roman invasion of Israel in the events leading up to the fall of Jerusalem in A.D. 70. It was a time when the Holy City was trampled and when the Roman General Titus acted with authority over the land. On the other hand, it can hardly be described as a time when Israel was being protected in the wilderness. To the contrary, Israel was overrun first in Galilee and then in Judea in a series of battles that saw the complete conquest of the land.

Some have speculated that the Christians who were living in the land and who remembered the warnings of Jesus in His Olivet Discourse departed from the land and found refuge across the Jordan in the wilderness to the east. Eusebius, the early church historian, gives this account:

> But the people of the church in Jerusalem had been commanded by a revelation, vouchsafed to approved men there before the war, to leave the city and to dwell in a certain town of Perea called Pella. And when those that believed in Christ had come there from Jerusalem, then, as if the royal city of the Jews and the whole land of Judea were entirely destitute of holy men, the judgment of God at length overtook those who had committed such outrages against Christ and his apostles, and totally destroyed that generation of impious men (Church History 3:5:3).

This took place just prior to the Roman conquest of Jerusalem. As the Roman general Titus came against the city, the church at Jerusalem had fled the area, finding refuge in the area of Perea, located on the east side of the Jordan River.

THE DRAGON'S DEFEAT

> *And there was war in heaven, Michael and his angels waging war with the dragon. And the dragon and his angels waged war, 8 and they were not strong enough, and there was no longer a place found for them in heaven. 9 And the great dragon was thrown down, the serpent of old who is called the devil and Satan, who deceives the whole world; he was thrown down to the earth, and his angels were thrown down with him. (Revelation 12:7-9).*

In case we did not know it previously, the obvious is stated. There is a war taking place. It is a heavenly war, but its repercussions are felt upon the earth. On one side are the forces of the Son, led by the archangel Michael. He is mentioned twice in the Old Testament, both times in the book of Daniel. He is seen in a spiritual battle against the forces of darkness in Daniel 10:13 and 21. He is called *the great prince who stands guard over the sons of your people* in Daniel 12:1. He is also mentioned in Jude 1:9 confronting Satan over the body of Moses.

Opposed by Michael are the forces of Satan. He is described as a great dragon because of his strength. He is called the serpent of old because of his use of that animal at the fall in Eden. He is called the devil, a Greek word meaning "slanderer." He is also called Satan, a Hebrew word meaning "enemy."

The result of this conflict is that the dragon is defeated. The one who caused man to fall in the garden is now cast down. The power that sent John to Patmos has been dealt a defeat. When did this defeat take place? On the one hand, he was defeated at the cross. As He was about to go to the cross, Jesus spoke of how the ruler of this world was cast down (John 12:31). Paul speaks in Colossians 2:15 of how the Lord "disarmed the rulers and authorities." On the other hand, Paul could speak in Romans 16:20 of how "the God of peace will soon crush Satan under your feet," indicating the final defeat of Satan is still in the future.

THE SONG OF VICTORY

> And I heard a loud voice in heaven, saying, "Now the salvation, and the power, and the kingdom of our God and the authority of His Christ have come, for the accuser of our brethren has been thrown down, who accuses them before our God day and night. 11 And they overcame him because of the blood of the Lamb and because of the word of their testimony, and they did not love their life even to death. 12 For this reason, rejoice, O heavens and you who dwell in them. Woe to the earth and the sea, because the devil has come down to you, having great wrath, knowing that he has only a short time." (Revelation 12:10-12).

John now hears a joyful proclamation. It is a proclamation of victory. It is given in the form of a song with three stanzas.

First Stanza (12:10)	Centers on the heavenly victory and the establishment of the kingdom of God in the face of Satan's defeat.
Second Stanza (12:11)	Looks at the earthly victory of the people of God as it focuses on the way in which Satan was cast down.
Third Stanza (12:12)	Calls heaven to rejoice and earth to tremble.

1. Satan as the Accuser: *The accuser of our brethren has been thrown down (12:10).*

   Satan is an accuser. That is the role that defines him in the book of Job. A graphic picture is seen there of the accusation he brought against Job, even when Job had done nothing wrong. If he could not accuse Job of wrongdoing, he would accuse him of wrong motivations. We have an accuser who is in the accusation business. He is described as accusing believers "night and day." He is incessant in his accusations. But the good news is that we have an Advocate – One who speaks on our behalf. 1 John 2:1 says that "if anyone sins, we have an Advocate with the Father, Jesus Christ the righteous." Our advocate is righteous. That is a good thing because our defense lies within the realm of His righteousness. We have been credited with His righteousness so that the accusation against us has been overturned.

2. Believers as Overcomers: *They overcame him because of the blood of the Lamb and because of the word of their testimony (12:11).*

   The accusation from the accuser was overcome in two ways. It is really one way, but that way has a result and both are mentioned here.

   - The first way is because of the blood of the Lamb. This speaks of what Christ accomplished on our behalf on the cross. He was our sacrifice. His death served to pay the price demanded of our sinfulness. Romans 6:23 says that "the wages of sin is death, but the gift of God is eternal life in Christ Jesus our Lord."

   - The second area of overcoming is the word of their testimony. The point is that real faith in Christ will have real results in a person's life. Faith that is internal will make itself known by external words and deeds.

3. Joy to Heaven and Woe to Earth: *Rejoice, O heavens and you who dwell in them. Woe to the earth and the sea (12:12).*

   The casting down of Satan brings corresponding rejoicing and warnings of woe. Heaven is able to rejoice because Satan has been cast down. His power is broken. No more can he accuse the brethren. No more can he lay a charge against God's elect (Romans 8:33). He is powerless to make the martyrs deny their faith. And yet, the martyrs are still martyred and he is still able to attack the church on earth. The battle in heaven may be over, but the battle on earth still rages.

222

THE EARTHLY BATTLE

> *And when the dragon saw that he was thrown down to the earth, he persecuted the woman who gave birth to the male child. 14 And the two wings of the great eagle were given to the woman, in order that she might fly into the wilderness to her place, where she was nourished for a time and times and half a time, from the presence of the serpent.*
>
> *15 And the serpent poured water like a river out of his mouth after the woman, so that he might cause her to be swept away with the flood. 16 And the earth helped the woman, and the earth opened its mouth and drank up the river which the dragon poured out of his mouth. 17 And the dragon was enraged with the woman, and went off to make war with the rest of her offspring, who keep the commandments of God and hold to the testimony of Jesus. (Revelation 12:13-17).*

Unable to fight any longer against the forces of heaven, the dragon now turns his attention to the people of God who are on earth. Powerless to attack the Son, the serpent now turns against the mother who bore Him.

There is a principle here. It is that the world will try to do to you what it can no longer do to Jesus. You are Jesus to the world. When the world wants to see Jesus, they will look at the church. And when the world wants to persecute Jesus, they will persecute the church. That means you should not be surprised when you do what is right and people still do not like you. You are in good company as they did not like Jesus, either.

The battle goes on. The dragon has been defeated and cast down, but his tail still swishes. Because he cannot get at Jesus, he takes out his wrath against us. But in the midst of this battle drama, there is a source of comfort.

1. A Way of Escape: *And the two wings of the great eagle were given to the woman, in order that she might fly into the wilderness to her place (12:14).*

    The drama with the woman continues. We described her in the beginning of this chapter as Israel. That identification has not changed. And yet, her offspring are described in verse 17 as those *who keep the commandments of God and hold to the testimony of Jesus.* This is striking, for it suggests to us that the woman is not merely Israel, but specifically that portion of Israel that has accepted Jesus as the true Messiah.

    This image of Israel being given the wings of an eagle is taken from the Old Testament. The Lord says in Exodus 19:4 when he is speaking to Israel,

223

"You yourselves have seen what I did to the Egyptians, and how I bore you on eagles' wings, and brought you to Myself."

What God did for the nation of Israel, He continues to do for His church. He appoints for His people a "safe place." It is not a place in heaven, for we are still here on earth. It is a place in the wilderness.

2.   A Provision of Perseverance: *She was nourished for a time and times and half a time, from the presence of the serpent. (12:14).*

This is the same period of time that we have seen alluded throughout chapters 11 and 12. It is the same time where the Holy City was given to the Gentiles and where the two witnesses were given a ministry to speak the word of God. It is the same period that we shall see in the next chapter wherein authority and power will be given to the beast. It was echoed in the past when the pagan king Antiochus desecrated the temple and it was again echoed when the Romans conquered the land of Israel.

There is a sense in which we are still in those wilderness times. We are still under the threatened attack of Satan, yet we find ourselves nourished and protected in the wilderness.

3.   A Diverted Attack: *And the serpent poured water like a river out of his mouth after the woman, so that he might cause her to be swept away with the flood. 16 And the earth helped the woman, and the earth opened its mouth and drank up the river which the dragon poured out of his mouth (12:15-16).*

The imagery calls to mind such Old Testament narratives as the flood, the parting of the Red Sea, and the opening of the earth to swallow up Korah and his followers who rebelled against the leadership of the Lord. The attacks of the dragon come to naught as the earth itself is bent to overcome such attacks. The description calls to mind one of the Psalms of deliverance:

> *Therefore, let everyone who is godly pray to You in a time when You may be found;*
> *Surely in a flood of great waters they will not reach him.*
>
> *7 You are my hiding place;*
> *You preserve me from trouble;*
> *You surround me with songs of deliverance. Selah. (Psalm 32:6-7).*

At the same time, there is an eschatological echo to this promise of the deliverance from a flood. The book of Daniel in describing the coming of the Messiah and the events that would follow made mention of a flood:

> *Then after the sixty-two weeks the Messiah will be cut off and have nothing, and the people of the prince who is to come will destroy the city and the sanctuary. And its end will come with a flood; even to the end there will be war; desolations are determined. (Daniel 9:26).*

Attempts have been made to see at least a measure of fulfillment of such a flood in the events of the Roman invasion of Israel when the spring flooding of the Jordan threatened to prevent Jewish refugees from escaping into the wilderness to the east.

Others have sought a more symbolic interpretation and have suggested that we are to see it as a "river of lies" sent forth by the serpent. William Hendriksen points out how "the evil one tries to engulf the Church in a stream of lies, delusions, religious '-isms', philosophical falsehoods, political utopias, quasi-scientific dogmas, but the true Church is not fooled. Worldly people, on the other hand, are ready to swallow the entire river!" (2001:142). Such a view sees the opening of the earth as a symbol of God's protection, similar to when Korah and his followers were swallowed up by the earth in the days of Moses. It is along these lines that Mounce points out that "the flood is a common metaphor in the OT for overwhelming evil" (1997:241).

What we can see, no matter which interpretation is adopted, is that this river from the mouth of the dragon can be seen in contrast to the river of the water of life that shall be seen in Revelation 22:1-2 that is given for the healing of the nations. Here is the point. Satan is the destroyer. He wishes to bring people down. By contrast, the water that comes from the Lord is for healing and it is offered today to the nations.

4.   A Powerless Rage: *The dragon was enraged with the woman, and went off to make war with the rest of her offspring (12:17).*

As our chapter closes, the war still continues. The rage of the dragon is still directed against the offspring of the woman. This rage has been seen both in the way the world has persecuted the Jews and it is also seen in the way the world has persecuted the church. The war continues, but its outcome is certain. Jesus is going to win.

> The offspring of the woman is defined in verse 17 as "those who keep God's commandments and have the testimony about Jesus."

THE BEAST
Revelation 13:1-10

Revelation is a prophetic book. It speaks of things that were and that are and that are to come. It is relevant to the past, the present, and the future. Yet like the prophets of the Old Testament, its message can only be understood in the light of the situation in which it was given.

John was living in the midst of some difficult times. The church was going through persecution. He himself had been banished to the rocky island of Patmos. This is the background against which this prophecy is given. This means that the book of Revelation is not merely an exercise in prophetic trivia. It is not given merely so that we can formulate our eschatological time lines with which we can impress other people. These prophecies are not trying to give a detailed chronology of future events. They are given to encourage people who are going through hard times.

Every portion of the Bible is written for a specific purpose. It always has one goal ultimately in mind. It is given to make you live differently. Our Bible teaching needs to be founded on that principle. At the end of each sermon we hear, we ought to ask the same question: How should my life now be different?

John is writing with that kind of purpose in mind. He wants Christians to be different. He wants them to be encouraged and strengthened and faithful. How will he accomplish this? He tells of the heavenly vision that has been given to him. Its purpose is that people might believe and that they might continue in their faith in the midst of difficult times.

This chapter opens with John standing on the sand of the seashore. Remember that this vision is one that he received while on the Island of Patmos. Perhaps we are to envision this location for the vision.

THE COMING OF THE BEAST

> *And he stood on the sand of the seashore. And I saw a beast coming up out of the sea, having ten horns and seven heads, and on his horns were ten diadems, and on his heads were blasphemous names. 2 And the beast which I saw was like a leopard, and his feet were like those of a bear, and his mouth like the mouth of a lion. And the dragon gave him his power and his throne and great authority. (Revelation 13:1-2).*

226

Chapter 13 continues the narrative begun in the previous chapter. John has seen a woman give birth to a son. Confronting her was a dragon who sought to destroy her son as He was born. He eluded the dragon's attack and was caught up to heaven. Thwarted in his attempt, the dragon now seeks to vent his anger upon the woman. She also escapes his clutches, being carried off to a place of safety on the wings of an eagle.

The Woman	The Dragon	The Son
Israel	Satan	Jesus Christ
Escapes into the wilderness	Tries to destroy woman and child and fails	Caught up to heaven

Chapter 12 closes with the dragon who has been identified in that chapter as Satan making war on the people of God. Chapter 13 opens, not with a dragon, but with a beast coming out of the sea.

The opening description of the beast is all too familiar. The beast is described in exactly the same terms in which the dragon of the previous chapter was described. He was a dragon having seven heads and ten horns (Revelation 12:3).

The images that John sees are not new. They are lifted from the pages of the Old Testament. Daniel tells of a series of beasts, each one representing the coming world empires.

- The first beast was like a lion: it represented the Babylonian Empire.
- The second beast was like a bear: it represented the Empire of the Medes and the Persians.
- The third beast was like a leopard: it represented Alexander's Macedonian Empire that swept across the entire known world with lightning rapidity.
- The fourth beast was unlike anything that had come before. It is described as having seven heads and ten horns.

All of the beasts in Daniel's earlier vision are back, but this time they are all combined into a single beast. Notice the detailed comparison of these two visions:

Daniel's Fourth Beast	Revelation's Beast
Comes up out of the Sea (7:3).	Comes up out of the Sea (13:1).
Ten horns are ten kings (7:7, 24).	Ten horns are ten kings (13:1; 17:12).

227

Another horn becomes the dominant ruler (7:24-26).	Beast as a person (19:20) becomes a dominant ruler (17:12-13).
Stamped with the feet (7:7)	Feet of a bear (13:2)
Great iron teeth (7:7)	Mouth of a lion (13:2).
Blasphemous (7:25).	Blasphemous (13:5).
Persecutes saints (7:21).	Persecutes saints (13:7).
Power for a time, times, and a dividing of a time (7:25).	Power for 42 months (13:5).
Defeated by God who then sets up the Kingdom (7:21-27).	Defeated by God who then sets up the Kingdom (19:11 - 20:6)

Adapted from Gary Cohen (2001:40).

John's vision is not merely a single kingdom. It is a combination of all the world's kingdoms. It is the world system that includes the Pharaoh of Egypt who confronted Moses at the Exodus, yet which also includes Herod who tried to have Jesus put to death. It includes the Romans with their emperor worship and it includes every government that has set itself against God. Chilton makes the following observations about the formulation of the idea of the "beast":

> In the beginning we are told of how Adam and Eve refused to become "gods" through submission to God, and sought autonomous and ultimate godhood instead. By submitting to a beast (the Serpent) they themselves became "beasts" instead of gods, with the Beast's mark of rebellion displayed on their foreheads (Gen. 3:19); even in redemption they remained clothed with the skins of beasts (Gen. 3:21). (1990:278-79).

The Bible tells us that governments have been ordained and established by God (Romans 13:1). Yet those same governments that are designed to help people live more humanely often end up taking upon themselves the qualities of beasts.

THE CAREER OF THE BEAST

> *I saw one of his heads as if it had been slain, and his fatal wound was healed. And the whole earth was amazed and followed after the beast;* 4 *they worshiped the dragon because he gave his authority to the beast; and they worshiped the beast, saying, "Who is like the beast, and who is able to wage war with him?"* 5 *There*

was given to him a mouth speaking arrogant words and blasphemies, and authority to act for forty-two months was given to him. (Revelation 13:3-5).

As John continues to watch, he sees that this seven-headed beast has been injured. It looks *as if it had been slain.* This language is strikingly similar to the vision John has already described of a lamb standing as is slain (Revelation 5:6). This is not mere happenstance; we are supposed to see these two images in parallel as they contrast with one another.

The Lamb	The Beast
Standing as if slain – a picture of the death and resurrection of Christ.	One of his heads was "as if it had been slain," but is then healed.
Seven heads and seven eyes representing the seven spirits of God.	Seven heads and ten horns representing a challenge to God's authority.
The elders worship the Lord upon His throne who gave authority to the Son.	The world worships the dragon because he gave his authority to the beast.

The beast is presented in contrast to the lamb. The beast is opposed to Christ and is that which seeks to supplant Christ. As Christ went to the cross and rose from the dead, so also one of the heads of this beast appears to be slain. This brings to mind the promise of God to Adam and Eve in the Garden of Eden. It was there God promised that the serpent would receive a wound to his head.

> *And I will put enmity*
> *Between you and the woman,*
> *And between your seed and her seed;*
> *He shall bruise you on the head,*
> *And you shall bruise him on the heel. (Genesis 3:15).*

The seed of the woman is Jesus. Because we have been joined to Him in faith, we have a promise that we will partake in this victory. The seed of the serpent refers to Satan and all those who follow him. Jesus was bruised on the cross, but it was not a bruise of defeat. When Jesus died, He won a great victory over Satan. When he rose from the dead, Satan was dealt a mortal blow. We saw this in the last chapter where the great red dragon was cast down to the earth. He was overcome by the blood of the lamb.

This brings us to a question. If Satan has been conquered, why does he still cause so many problems? It is because he has been cast down to the earth. He is no longer free. He is under condemnation and he knows that his time is short. He was defeated on the cross, but it appears as though he has come to life and is stronger than ever.

This was seen in the early days of the church. People were coming to Christ life and right. Peter would preach in the temple and thousands would come to repentance. It seemed in those early days as though nothing could slow down the explosive growth of the church. But then the opposition began to harden and that period of early growth seemed to slow.

We can see that same process throughout the history of the church. There have been times of great spiritual revival. There have been great awakenings to the presence of God. Great colleges of the past such as Princeton and Yale were formed for the training of pastors and missionaries. But then the period of growth began to slow and the love of Christians began to cool and it appeared that Satan began to grow stronger.

John describes the beast as being given *a mouth speaking arrogant words and blasphemies, and authority to act for forty-two months (13:5).* The authority of the beast is a derived authority. He is given authority. Who has given him authority? It is the dragon. Satan claims to have authority. That is what he said to Jesus at the temptation.

> *And he led Him up and showed Him all the kingdoms of the world in a moment of time. 6 And the devil said to Him, "I will give You all this domain and its glory; for it has been handed over to me, and I give it to whomever I wish. 7 Therefore if You worship before me, it shall all be Yours." 8 Jesus answered him, "It is written, 'You shall worship the Lord your God and serve Him only.'" (Luke 4:5-8).*

Do you see Satan's claim? He said that the world had been handed over to him and that he could give it to whomever he desired. Jesus did not dispute this claim. Instead, John tells us that the whole world lies in the power of the evil one (1 John 5:19). What Jesus would not do in bowing down to Satan, the beast seeks to accomplish in the rest of the world. The beast seeks to be worshiped. This is striking when we remember that it was in the first century that the Romans began to seek to impose emperor-worship upon its subjects.

To what does this period of forty-two months refer? This is the same period of time described in Revelation 11:2 where John was told that the nations would *tread under foot the holy city for forty-two months."* In our treatment of that passage, we noted that this number has come up again and again, both in the Bible as well as in history.

- It is the same duration as when Elijah prayed that it would not rain and there were no rains in Israel for a period of three and a half years (James 5:17).
- It is the same amount of time in which the temple was overrun by the Seleucid forces in the days of the Maccabees prior to their expulsion and the subsequent cleansing of the temple.
- This was roughly the same amount of time from the Roman invasion of Israel to the fall of Jerusalem to Titus in A.D. 70.

This is the period of what appears to be Satan's victory. It was seen when Antiochus desecrated the temple. It was seen again when the Roman army destroyed the temple in A.D. 70. It is seen whenever the forces of Satan persecute the church and seek to destroy its people. The people who worship the beast are always turning against the people who do not. From our point of view, it often looks as though they are winning.

THE CONQUEST OF THE BEAST

> *And he opened his mouth in blasphemies against God, to blaspheme His name and His tabernacle, that is, those who dwell in heaven. 7 It was also given to him to make war with the saints and to overcome them, and authority over every tribe and people and tongue and nation was given to him. 8 All who dwell on the earth will worship him, everyone whose name has not been written from the foundation of the world in the book of life of the Lamb who has been slain. (Revelation 13:6-8).*

As John continues to unfold this vision before our eyes, we see the beast go on the offensive, both in what he says and in what he does. His attack is threefold:

- He blasphemes against God.
- He speaks against those who dwell in heaven.
- He makes war with the saints.

Satan has no power against the first two of these groups. He speaks against them, but his words are empty of power. It is different with the third group. He not only makes war with the saints, he also overcomes them.

We have seen this concept of an overcomer a number of times in Revelation. But the term has always been used of Jesus and His followers overcoming the forces of darkness. Now there is a difference. The beast is seen as the overcomer. He is overcoming the people of God. There are times when Satan wins. There are times when people hear the gospel and they have the opportunity to choose between God and Satan and they choose Satan. There are times when people look at good and look at evil and they choose to do evil.

We live in troubled times. Bad things happen in times of trouble. Christians are persecuted and burned at the stake and fed to the lions. Messiahs are crucified in times of trouble. There is a movement going around today in Christian circles that says you can name it and claim it and frame it. They picture the Christian life as being all sweetness and light. They say if you come to Christ all of your problems will be solved and, if you still have problems, then you just are not believing hard enough. It is a lie. Don't get me wrong. I believe in Christian victory. I believe that we have to claim the victory that we have in Jesus, but we also have to recognize that we live in troubled times.

John says of this beast that *all who dwell on the earth will worship him (13:8)*. You will always worship something. Either you will worship the Lord or else you will worship the beast. What are you worshiping? If it is not Jesus, then it won't be long until you are worshiping something else.

Translators are divided as to how we should understand the latter part of verse 8. This is reflected in a comparison of the New American Standard translation with that of the New International Version:

New American Standard	New International Version
...everyone whose name has not been written from the foundation of the world in the book of life of the Lamb who has been slain	*...all whose names have not been written in the book of life belonging to the Lamb that was slain from the creation of the world*
The names of persevering saints have been written in the book of life since the foundation of the world.	The plan for Jesus to go to the cross was established in the book of life at the creation of the world.

Technically, the Greek text can be used to support either reading, though it is the NIV that follows the word order found in the original. However, the same phrase is used with a similar word order in Revelation 17:8 where both translations speak of those *whose names have not been written in the book of life from the creation of the world* (NIV).

The point of the passage seems to be that God knows what He is doing and He has known about it for a very long time. The events that shake us up do not shake Him as His plan stands firm, having been established from the foundation of the world. This results in a word of comfort to His people.

THE COMFORT OF THE SAINTS

> *If anyone has an ear, let him hear.* 10 *If anyone is destined for captivity, to captivity he goes; if anyone kills with the sword, with the sword he must be killed. Here is the perseverance and the faith of the saints. (Revelation 13:9-10).*

At this point we are given a promise. That is a good thing because, by the time we reach this point, we are in need of a promise. What we have just seen is not very pleasant. We have been reading of Satan overcoming the saints. That is a sobering picture that affects how we live and what we believe.

John is going to give a promise, but first he gives a call to listen. Why does he do this? Because far too often we hear and do not really listen. Sometimes we hear but it has no effect. As a parent and a grandparent, I can identify with this. A child is told to do something and the sound waves travel through the air and echo in the child's ears. There is hearing, but it produces no reaction on the part of the child. So it is with us. How many times do we hear the word of God and then go away unchanged? This is a call to listen and to apply the truth of God's word to your life.

1.   A Promise of Retribution: *If anyone is destined for captivity, to captivity he goes; if anyone kills with the sword, with the sword he must be killed (13:10).*

      This is an unfortunate translation. If you look at the phrase "is destined" in most translations, you will see it is italicized. This is done to let you know that the phrase was added by the translators in an attempt to clarify what they felt was the meaning of the passage. I believe this was a failure and I want to suggest that we are to understand the first phrase in the same way we are to understand the second phrase.

      If anyone is involved in taking God's people into captivity, he will eventually suffer that same captivity. If anyone kills God's people with the sword, he will be killed in the same manner. This is one time where the King James Version has done a better job than most of the newer translations:

> *He that leadeth into captivity shall go into captivity: he that killeth with the sword must be killed with the sword. Here is the patience and the faith of the saints* (KJV).

      This is a promise of judgment upon the enemies of Christ. Have you suffered a wrong for the cause of Christ? Don't worry, God knows and He is going to balance the books. Knowing that can make all the difference in enduring the present time of trouble.

2.   A Basis for Perseverance and Faith: *Here is the perseverance and the faith of the saints (13:10).*

John's words give us one of the reasons why Christians persevere. It is found in the belief in the coming judgment. We continue to live faithfully today because we believe it will matter tomorrow. We are people who believe something, but our distinction does not stop with belief. Because we have come to believe differently, we have also come to live differently. Belief cannot be divorced from life and any attempt to do so will result in a lifeless faith.

When I was a very young Christian, I heard some teaching that said one can come to faith in Christ, trusting in Him as a personal Savior without any recognition that He is also Lord. Such a hypothetical "Christian" might go all his life without seeing any obedience to God or without manifesting any fruit in his life. This sort of "easy believism" teaching comes from the beast.

By contrast, the Bible gives us a number of descriptions of what a Christian is and only a few of them deal with what he believes. I am not saying that belief isn't important. You cannot be a Christian if there is no belief. But if belief is real, then it will manifest itself in outward action.

Such a realization will lead us to some serious self examination. Such self examination is good once in a while. The Bible exhorts us to examine ourselves to see whether we are truly in the faith (2 Corinthians 13:5). Has Jesus made a difference in your life? What is there about you that can only be explained in terms of the supernatural? I don't mean that you are perfect or that you have arrived at a place where no further growth in possible or even necessary. But are you growing in Christ? Are you becoming more like Him? Are you living in the perseverance and the faith of the saints? If you are not, the answer is not to go back and do more works. The answer is to go back to the cross and believe the gospel so that it might change your life.

THE FALSE PROPHET
Revelation 13:11-18

The prophets of the Old Testament were the spokesmen of God. They represented themselves to Israel as bringing the message of God to the nation. But from the very beginning, there was a warning against those who were mere pretenders; those who said they were from God, but who were merely seeking to advance their own agenda. In the second half of Revelation 13, we are introduced to such a figure.

THE COMING OF THE SECOND BEAST

> *Then I saw another beast coming up out of the earth; and he had two horns like a lamb and he spoke as a dragon. (Revelation 13:11).*

We have already seen a first beast in the earlier part of this chapter. We saw that it was an image taken from the Old Testament book of Daniel in which he saw a successive series of beasts, each representing a kingdom that would arise and exercise authority. The characteristics of those various beasts were brought together by John as he described the ultimate beast as one arising to stand against the people of God.

In John's day, this ultimate beast would have been best characterized by the Roman empire and its emperors. They exercised an iron rule over the known world. When that rule seemed to be shaken by the death of the Emperor Nero and the rebellion of the Jews, this was only a temporary setback as the Roman Emperor Vespasian rose to become the new emperor and his son, Titus, completed the subjugation of the Jews and the conquest and destruction of Jerusalem. When we look at this father/son team and their victorious Roman legions, we can hear the echo of those who give the beast worship, saying, "Who is like the beast, and who is able to wage war with him?" (Revelation 13:4).

Now we are introduced to a second beast. He is a caricature of the lamb. Just as the lamb was seen with two horns, so also this beast has two horns. They are even described to us as *two horns like a lamb* in case we should happen to miss the similarity. But the similarity does not extend to his voice. He speaks as a dragon. Because of this, we will eventually learn that he is a false prophet and will be described by that term in Revelation 16:13 (see also 19:20).

There is an important lesson here. If you want to determine the validity of someone's ministry, one of the things you have to do is to listen to what he says. Deuteronomy 13:1-3 says that even if a prophet or a dreamer has given signs or wonders that have come true, if he calls you to worship and serve other gods, you are not to listen to him. The point is that it is possible for a prophet to say and to do things that have all the appearances of supernatural authority and still speak falsely. One is to be judged, not merely on the basis of what he is able to do, but also on the basis of what he says about God.

THE WORK OF THE PROPHET

> *He exercises all the authority of the first beast in his presence. And he makes the earth and those who dwell in it to worship the first beast, whose fatal wound was healed. 13 He performs great signs, so that he even makes fire come down out of heaven to the earth in the presence of men. 14 And he deceives those who dwell on the earth because of the signs which it was given him to perform in the presence of the beast, telling those who dwell on the earth to make an image to the beast who had the wound of the sword and has come to life. (Revelation 13:12-14).*

The first beast and the second beast are seen in contrast with one another. That is not to suggest that they are working at cross purposes. Instead we see a deliberate collusion. The goal of the second beast is to bring men to worship the first beast. Perhaps this is one of the reasons the second beast will become known as the false prophet. The true prophets of Israel made it their business to try to bring men to worship the Lord. This false prophet seeks to have men worship a false lord.

The First Beast	The Second Beast
Rises from the sea (13:1).	Rises from the earth (13:11).
Has the characteristics of a leopard, a bear, and a lion.	Speaks with the voice of a dragon
Ten horns like the beasts of Daniel's vision.	Two horns like a lamb.
Given authority to act.	Given same authority.
He makes war against the saints.	He makes people worship the first beast.

If the first beast exercises military might, the second beast seems to call for a type of philosophical, spiritual, and supernatural power, performing great signs and even calling fire down from heaven. When we hear of signs and fire being called from heaven, we think of Elijah and other prophets of God. The point about this second beast is that, at first glance, he looks like one of the prophets of God. But if we listen to his agenda, we find that it is completely opposite that of the prophets. They warned against idolatry; he solicits people into idolatry. They give the true teaching of God, he gives false teachings that blind people to the truth.

As we read of the goal of this second beast, to make people worship the first beast, we can hardly help but to be reminded of the emperor worship that had taken root in the first century. A temple had been constructed in Pergamum in honor of Octavius Augustus around 28 B.C. This led to flurry of Caesar worship, especially in Anatolia and the lands to the east. The point has been made that these temples were designed to worship the genius of the emperor instead of worshiping the man himself, but this distinction was likely lost on the common population. The emperors who followed adopted the same practice, though at first the emperor was not given the status of deity until after he had died, causing the Emperor Vespasian to quip with dry humor as he lay on his deathbed, "I think I am becoming a god."

THE WORSHIP OF THE BEAST

> And it was given to him to give breath to the image of the beast, so that the image of the beast would even speak and cause as many as do not worship the image of the beast to be killed. (Revelation 13:15).

When the Roman Emperor Nero committed suicide in A.D. 69, he was only 31 years old. Suetonius tells us that people *"continued to circulate his edicts, pretending that he was still alive and would soon return to confound his enemies."* Later that same year, there was a report in Anatolia that Nero had come back to life again. Tacitus makes mention of this report:

> About this time Achaia and Asia Minor were terrified by a false report that Nero was at hand. Various rumors were current about his death; and so there were many who pretended and believed that he was still alive (Histories, Book 2).

These reports and others like them continued to be circulated. Suetonius goes on to say that *"twenty years later, when I was a young man, a mysterious individual came forward claiming to be Nero; and so magical was the sound of his name in the Parthians' ears that they supported him to the best of their ability, and only handed him over with great reluctance"* (1979:246).

In a similar manner, the false prophet is described as being given the ability to give breath to the image of the beast so that it acts as though it were a living being. To what does this refer? Scholars have come up with all sorts of speculation, but it might be helpful to remember some of the ideas in the first century that served as a historical backdrop to this vision. Josephus reports how, prior to Nero, the Emperor Caligula ordered that a statue of himself be placed for public worship in the temple of the Jews in Jerusalem.

> Accordingly, he sent Petronius with an army to Jerusalem, to place his statues in the temple, and commanded him that, in case the Jews would not admit of them, he should slay those that opposed it, and carry all the rest of the nation into captivity (Wars 2:10:1).

As Petronius, the legate of Syria, marched south with three legions, the Jews came to him to plead their case and the action was postponed. Before it could be carried out by force of arms, Caligula was assassinated and the order was rescinded. Nor was this the first time such a thing had been attempted. Long before the birth of Jesus, a Greek monarch known as Antiochus Epiphanes had erected a statue of Zeus in the temple in order to forcibly convert Jews to paganism. War had ensued and the Jews had successfully resisted. The point therefore is that the idea of a pagan ruler setting up an image in the Jewish place of worship had unfortunately become something of an ongoing motif at the time of the writing of the book of Revelation. It had happened before and it would happen again.

THE MARK OF THE BEAST

> *And he causes all, the small and the great, and the rich and the poor, and the free men and the slaves, to be given a mark on their right hand or on their forehead, 17 and he provides that no one will be able to buy or to sell, except the one who has the mark, either the name of the beast or the number of his name. (Revelation 13:16-17).*

Joseph Mangina points out that "under the beasts' reign, human beings themselves become commodities. No one can be a stakeholder in the system who does not bear the mark of the beast, written on hand or forehead" (2010:165).

Some have thought that John is speaking of a literal tattoo that would be placed upon the hand or forehead while others have gone so far as to read into the text some sort of 21st century computer chip imbedded under the skin. But we did not treat Revelation 7 in such a manner when we read of believers receiving the seal of God upon their foreheads and I don't believe we ought to take such a literalist view here.

> *"And it shall be when your son asks you in time to come,*

238

saying, 'What is this?' then you shall say to him, 'With a powerful hand the LORD brought us out of Egypt, from the house of slavery. 15 And it came about, when Pharaoh was stubborn about letting us go, that the LORD killed every first-born in the land of Egypt, both the first-born of man and the first-born of beast. Therefore, I sacrifice to the LORD the males, the first offspring of every womb, but every first-born of my sons I redeem.' 16 So it shall serve as a SIGN ON YOUR HAND, and as phylacteries ON YOUR FOREHEAD, for with a powerful hand the LORD brought us out of Egypt." (Exodus 13:14-16).

The scene was the Passover in Egypt. The Lord is establishing a memorial for His people whom He is about to deliver. This memorial will become so ingrained upon the Israelites that it will become a fundamental part of everything that they do and everything that they think – a sign on their hands and bound to their heads.

Forty years later when the Israelites were preparing to go into the promised land, they were to take with them all of the teachings of the Lord and were told, *You shall bind them as a sign on your hand and they shall be as frontals on your forehead* (Deuteronomy 6:8). This was the same command repeated for a different generation. It meant only that in everything they did and in everything they thought they were to remember the Lord.

In Ezekiel 9:4, the Lord instructs His servant to go through the city of Jerusalem *"and put a mark on the foreheads of the men who sigh and groan over all the abominations which are being committed in its midst."* This is a mark of protection. It signifies those people who look at the sin taking place within their own city and who wish it were otherwise. It is not a literal mark. This is symbolic language. It is the same idea that we saw in Revelation 7 when we saw the 144,000 being sealed on their foreheads. The Bible tells us that we have all been sealed with the Spirit of promise (Ephesians 1:13). We don't go around with the letters J-E-S-U-S tattooed to our forehead. This is a spiritual seal. I believe that the mark described in Revelation 13 is of a similar nature. It is a spiritual mark. It portrays the manner in which Satan's people follow him both in what they do and in what they think.

The mark upon the hand and upon the forehead calls to mind the words of the Lord in Deuteronomy 5 where His people were to bind the law upon their hands and upon their foreheads, indicating that the law was to be reflected in their thoughts and in their deeds. But now John describes a Satanic counterfeit in which, not the law of God, but the number of the beast is to be placed upon the hand and foreheads of his people. James Papandrea points out one manner in which this scenario came to be manifested during the early days of the church:

In late 249 C.E., the Emperor Decius issued a decree that required all inhabitants of the empire to show their loyalty by making a sacrifice to the Roman gods and to the emperor. Those who refused were accused of treason, a crime punishable by death. Those who complied were given a certificate, called a libellus, which would prove that they had made the required sacrifice and would attest to their loyalty to the emperor. This libellus would include the emperor's name, with his imperial titles, and would be signed by witnesses. One could be required to produce the document at any time. When enforced, one could not participate in commerce without it (2011:157).

The world no longer calls for us to produce a document showing our loyalty to its worldly system. But it nevertheless has its mark that it places on its people and it is ultimately intolerant of anyone who does not conform.

THE NUMBER OF THE BEAST

Here is wisdom. Let him who has understanding calculate the number of the beast, for the number is that of a man; and his number is six hundred and sixty-six. (Revelation 13:18).

John introduces this verse with a short statement that lets us know we are facing a riddle that takes a certain degree of wisdom to unravel. He uses the same reference to the need for wisdom when he speaks in Revelation 17:9 of the meaning of the seven headed dragon and how the seven heads represent seven mountains upon which the woman sits. It is a clue there of a specific place and it seems to be a clue here of a specific person.

The early church father, Irenaeus, writing in the second century, speaks of the different theories and propositions that had been put forward by Christians to solve this puzzle. This was usually accomplished by looking at a person or people's name and then calculating what was the numerical equivalent of the sum of the letters that made up their name. This process, known as gematria, was commonly known throughout the ancient world and would have been more natural to a people who did not utilize our modern day Arabic numbering system (1, 2, 3, 4...) but regularly used letters as numerical equivalents. An example of this is seen in the ruins of Pompeii where a bit of graffiti proclaims, "I love her whose number is 545."

This would seem fairly straightforward, but John has already given us a hint that this puzzle will not be so easy to decipher. He has introduced it with the preface that we will need wisdom. John writes his message in Greek, but his native language was Hebrew. As in Greek, so also in Hebrew, letters were used with numerical equivalents.

א	ב	ג	ד	ה	ו	ז	ח	ט	י	כ	ל	מ	נ
1	2	3	4	5	6	7	8	9	10	20	30	40	50

ס	ע	פ	צ	ק	ר	שׁ	ת
60	70	80	90	100	200	300	400

When we utilize this table and then examine some of the names of antiquity, one that fits this puzzle is that of *Neron Kesar* – the emperor we know as Nero Caesar. Nor are we the only ones who have come to this conclusion. We cannot help but to note the similarity of this passage to the so-called Sibylline Oracles of the first century. Their name is taken from a series of Roman oracles of much greater antiquity with which they bear no relation. These later oracles were penned in the second century and seem to reflect a copying of the book of Revelation. What is significant for our study is the interpretation suggested by these oracles as they link the various persons of the prophecy to rulers of the first century.

In wars exceeding powerful shall he be; *And he shall have the initial sign of ten;* *And in like manner after him to reign* *Is one who has the alphabet's first letter;* *Before him Thrace and Sicily shall crouch,* *Then Memphis, Memphis cast headlong to earth*	This suggests Augustus who extended his sway over Greece and Egypt with the fall of Antony and Cleopatra
By reason of the cowardice of rulers and of a woman unenslaved who falls upon the wave. And laws will he ordain for peoples and put all things under him;	The woman mentioned here is Cleopatra who lost to Augustus in the naval battle at Actium.
But after a long time shall he transmit His power unto another, who shall have three hundred for his first initial sign, *And of a river the beloved name,* *And the Persians he shall rule and Babylon;* *And then shall he smite Medians with his spear.*	This refers to Tiberius (his name reflects the Tiber River), the emperor who ruled after Augustus.
Then shall one rule who has the initial sign of the number three.	Gaius Caesar, known commonly as Caligula.

And then shall be a lord *Who shall for first initial have twice ten;* *And he shall come to Ocean's utmost water* *And by Ausonia cleave the refluent tide.*	This is a reference to Klaudios (we know him as Claudius).

Throughout this section of the Sibylline Oracle (Book 5), the name of each emperor is signified by a numerical reference that is taken of the first letter of his name. This pattern continues as we are now introduced to Nero.

> *And one whose mark is fifty shall be lord,*
> *A dreadful serpent breathing grievous war,*
> *Who sometime stretching forth his hands shall make*
> *An end of his own race and stir all things,*
> *Acting the athlete, driving chariots,*
> *Putting to death and daring countless things;*
> *And he shall cleave the mountain of two seas*
> *And sprinkle it with gore; but out of sight*
> *Shall also vanish the destructive man;*
> *Then, making himself equal unto God,*
> *Shall he return; but God will prove him naught.*

Nero here is described as a "dreadful serpent" and mention is made of his athletic prowess in chariot racing. Nero fancied himself as a charioteer and competed in the Greek games. One of the construction projects attempted during his reign was the digging of a canal through the Isthmus of Corinth. At the end, Nero set himself up against the Christians, instituting a persecution against them. Yet when the tide of public opinion turned against him, he committed suicide.

> *And after him shall three kings be destroyed*
> *By one another. Then a great destroyer*
> *Of pious men shall come, whom seven times ten*
> *Shall point out clearly.*

When Nero killed himself, he had no heir to the empire. Three different rulers rose and fell in rapid succession before General Vespasian assumed the purple. The reference to "seven times ten" points to the Greek spelling of Vespasian's name: *Ou espasionos*. The prophecy goes on to reference Titus, Domitian, Nerva, and Hadrian.

Whether one assumes that the Sibylline Oracle was derived from the book of Revelation (I think this likely) or whether there is some other relationship between these two books, it is at least evident that the Sibylline Oracle gives us an ancient interpretation of some of the symbolism of the book of Revelation in general and specifically of this passage.

The immediate problem presented in seeing the number of the beast as a reference to Nero is that, a hundred years later, the early church father Irenaeus placed the writing of the book of Revelation several decades after the death of Nero: *For that was seen not very long time since, but almost in our day, towards the end of Domitian's reign* (Against Heresies 5:30:3). There are one of two possible solutions to this problem. First, we must admit that it is possible that Irenaeus was mistaken. It would not be the only time he has made a historical error. The other possibility is that John is using Nero as a type of either some future enemy of Christianity or that he is using Nero as a type of all such enemies. We have already noted that there is a similar pattern found in the reference to 42 months / 3 and a half years which is the same length of time that Jerusalem was under the oppression of Antiochus Epiphanes in the time between the Old and New Testaments.

Perhaps another solution might present itself if we were to look for the significance of the number 666 within the pages of the Scriptures. This number appears in 1 Kings 10:14 and its parallel passage of 2 Chronicles

> Lupieri points out that "the connection between 6 and Satan is very strong, however: the golden statue of Nebuchadnezzar, which is connected to Babylon, is said to be 60 cubits high and 6 cubits wide" (2006:218).

9:13 where we read that the weight of gold which came to Solomon in a single year was 666 talents. It could be that there is a mere coincidence, but it could be that we are to read of this one who sets himself up as a great ruler to be worshiped and we are to be reminded of a great king of the past who, though he began well, turned from the Lord to worship money and idols.

If this is the case, it means we do not need to relegate this passage to only a historical footnote of the past with no present or future application. What was true in the first century is still true today. The minions of Satan are still at work in the world today and they are still ready to bring false accusations against the people of God. The beast that comes today is often seen in the guise of patriotism or of tolerance. It is not limited to any particular nation or political party, but is multifaceted in its demand for allegiance. By contrast, Christians have a higher citizenship. Our allegiance is to the God of creation and our citizenship is of a heavenly nature.

It may even be that the beast we face seems to have had a heritage of good beginnings and the desire to raise up "one nation under God." We should not be overly surprised when we see the winds of culture begin to blow in a different direction and a government and a people who once seemed to espouse a measure of faith in God now turns their backs on Him.

Does this mean that Christians are to be seen as subversive to local governments? Not at all. We are instructed in the Scriptures to pay taxes where demanded and to give honor to whom it is due, whether king, president, or politician. Governments and those who lead them are established by God. We can and should pray for our leaders and seek the peace of our nation, living in peace with all men as we are able. But we should never forget that our primary allegiance is to the Lord.

THE 144,000
Revelation 14:1-5

The central chapters of Revelation form a unit that looks, from John's perspective, to the past, the present, and the future, though we should admit that there is considerable overlap between these designations.

Chapter 12	Chapter 13	Chapter 14
The dragon is cast down while the Son is born who shall rule the nations	Two beasts rise up from the sea and fight against the people of God, leading many astray	The people of the Lamb are sealed while judgments come against the earth
Past	Present	Future

The last chapter ended with a vision of the two beasts joining together to overcome the saints of God. It was a dark picture. The Christians appeared to be losing. As we come to this chapter, we move from the two beasts to the Lamb on Mount Zion. It is a movement from those who have the mark of the beast on their forehead and hand to those who have the name of the Lamb written on their foreheads. It is a movement from those who are preoccupied with buying and selling to those who are preoccupied with the Lord.

THE VICTORIOUS LAMB

> *Then I looked, and behold, the Lamb was standing on Mount Zion (Revelation 14:1a).*

The previous chapter treated us to a sobering vision of two beasts. One was seen to be a false prophet while the other had characteristics of a political leader, but they were both working to the same purpose, to set themselves up against the Lord and His people and to force the nations to worship after their own desires. As chapter 14 opens, the scene has changed substantially. Instead of the two beasts, we see the Lamb.

We were first introduced to the Lamb back in Revelation 5:6 where we saw him "standing, as if slain." Now we see the same Lamb and He is still standing. This serves to remind us that we serve the Living Lord. He is the One who died and who rose from the dead and who lives today.

He is described as standing on Mount Zion. This is the only reference to Zion in the book of Revelation, though it is not the only reference in the writings of John. John 12:15 quotes the Old Testament prophet Zechariah when he tells Jerusalem, the "daughter of Zion," that her King is coming, seated on a donkey's colt (Zechariah 9:9). Zion was the name of the mountain on which the old city of Jerusalem stood. It came to be used of the city itself. The name Zion literally means a "dry place," but the name usually looks more to the fact that this was the place on which the temple stood and from where God's presence was manifested. As such, the writer of the epistle to the Hebrews could speak of Mount Zion as "the heavenly Jerusalem (Hebrews 12:22). It is in such a way that we are to understand the reference to Zion in this passage.

THE SEALED CONGREGATION

Then I looked, and behold, the Lamb was standing on Mount Zion, and with Him one hundred and forty-four thousand, having His name and the name of His Father written on their foreheads.(Revelation 14:1).

We saw the numbering of the people of God back in Revelation 7. Their number was given as 12 x 12 x 1,000. In that chapter, John heard the number of those who were sealed and then he looked and saw *a great multitude, which no man could number, of all nations, and kindreds, and people, and tongues, stood before the throne, and before the Lamb* (7:9). We suggested that the group of which John heard and the group we saw were the same people. They are the people of God who have been sealed with the name of the Lord.

Revelation 13	Revelation 14
The Beast orders his people to receive a mark on their hand or forehead with either the name of the beast or the number of his name	The followers of the Lamb have his name and the name of His Father on their foreheads
The mark signifies possession	The seal signifies both possession and protection
All who receive the mark are destroyed	All who are sealed are preserved.

All of mankind is divided into one of these two groups. You have one of these two marks upon you. Either you have the mark of the beast or else you have the mark of the Lamb. You need to ask yourself a question. What characterizes your life? Is your life marked by the Lamb?

As we see this full number of 144,000 we note that none have been lost; that all have come to Mount Zion. When we come to Revelation 22:4 it will be confirmed that all the servants of God have His name on their foreheads. This is the seal which was described as being on the foreheads of his people in Revelation 7:3. It is here in Revelation 14:1 that we first learn this seal consists of the name of the Lamb and the name of His Father.

Do you remember what was on the forehead of the high priest in the Old Testament? He was required to wear a turban with a golden plate affixed to his forehead on which would be the engraving: "Holy to Yahweh." We have the same calling to be a nation of priests who are holy to the Lord.

THE SPECIAL SONG

> *And I heard a voice from heaven, like the sound of many waters and like the sound of loud thunder, and the voice which I heard was like the sound of harpists playing on their harps. 3 And they sang a new song before the throne and before the four living creatures and the elders; and no one could learn the song except the one hundred and forty-four thousand who had been purchased from the earth. (Revelation 14:2-3).*

When you wished to describe a great and mighty sound in the ancient world, you could describe it as either the sound of thunder or as the sound of many waters. Both of those images are brought to bear in this passage. Yet there is something more that is added – it is *the sound of harpists playing on their harps*. Notice that John does not actually see these harpists just as he does not see the thunder or the many waters. He is describing the song that comes from those who are before the throne. It is loud but it is also melodious.

Just as we saw the twenty four elders singing a new song before the Lord in Revelation 5:9, so here also we find that a new song is being sung before the Lord. There is nothing wrong with old songs, but on five different occasions the Scriptures call us to sing to the Lord a new song (Psalm 33:3; 96:1; 98:1; 149:1; Isaiah 42:10; see also Psalm 40:3 and 144:9). Why is there such an emphasis on the singing of a new song? It is because our worship ought to reflect the newness of the redemption to which we have been called. We are destined to a new life and a new way of living that coincides with the new song that we sing. In the chapters to come, we will read of a new heaven, a new earth, and a new Jerusalem. We will read how God is making all things new (Revelation 21:5). Such a new creation calls for a new song.

If you have been careful in your reading of the book of Revelation up to this point,

247

this passage will seem familiar, but we have already heard elements of this passage earlier in the book.

Revelation 5:6-11	Revelation 14:1-4
And I saw between the throne (with the four living creatures) and the elders a **Lamb** standing, as if slain (5:6)	Then I looked, and behold, the **Lamb** was standing on Mount Zion (14:1)
	And they sang a new song before the throne and before the four living creatures and the elders (14:3)
...the four living creatures and the twenty-four elders fell down before the Lamb, each one holding a **harp** (5:8)	...and the voice which I heard was like the sound of harpists playing on their **harps** (14:2)
And they sang a new song (5:9)	And they sang a new song (14:3)
You were slain, and **purchased** for God with Your blood men from every tribe and tongue and people and nation (Rev 5:9)	These have been **purchased** from among men as first fruits to God and to the Lamb (14:4)

We have come full circle to see heaven, earth, mankind, the salvation that God has provided, and how His people are brought into His presence.

THE SANCTIFIED PEOPLE

These are the ones who have not been defiled with women, for they have kept themselves chaste. These are the ones who follow the Lamb wherever He goes. These have been purchased from among men as first fruits to God and to the Lamb. 5 And no lie was found in their mouth; they are blameless. (Revelation 14:1-5).

This group of 144,000 are said to have been undefiled with women by virtue of their being chaste. The term translated "chaste" is *parthenos* (παρθενος), correctly rendered as "virgin" in the KJV. The imagery of this language is drawn from the Old Testament where we regularly read of the "virgin daughter of Zion" or "the virgin of Israel" as a way of speaking of the redeemed of Israel (Isaiah 23:12; 37:22; Jeremiah 14:17; 18:13; 31:4, 21; Lamentations 1:15; 2:13; Amos 5:2). Alternatively, the prophets used the image of marital unfaithfulness to depict the spiritual unfaithfulness of the nation of Israel.

248

It is in the same way that Paul speaks in 2 Corinthians 11:2 of how he sought to present the church as a "pure virgin" to Christ. Similarly, when we come to the final chapters of Revelation, we will see the church likened to a bride adorned for her husband (Revelation 21:2). We are described as undefiled and chaste, not because we are so pure, but because we have been cleansed by the blood of the Lamb and have been purified through the work of the cross. Paul speaks in Colossians 1:21-22 of how we who were once hostile to God through our evil behavior have now been reconciled through the death of Christ so that we might be found *holy and blameless and beyond reproach*.

Verse 4 says that *these are the ones who follow the Lamb wherever He goes*. What does it mean to follow Jesus? It means to walk as He walked. We don't have to ask ourselves how God would have us live, because He has given us a living example. Jesus was a teacher who taught by example. He lived the life that we are supposed to live. Do you want to know how you ought to treat your neighbor? Look at Jesus. Do you want to know how to deal with people who don't like you? Look at how Jesus dealt with people who did not like Him.

Verse 4 also says that *these have been purchased from among men as first fruits to God and to the Lamb*. To understand the concept of the first fruits, we must go back to the Israelite festival of the first fruits. In the first month of the Jewish religious year, the Jews observed three different feasts (Leviticus 23:4-14).

- Passover took place on the 14th day of the month. It was designed to be a reminder of how God had delivered the Israelites from the plague of the firstborn and had brought them out of their slavery in Egypt.

- Unleavened bread was a week-long observance that lasted from the 15th through the 22nd day of the month. During this entire week, the Jews removed all of the leaven from the bread they ate. This was a remembrance of their separation from the culture of Egypt. God had taken them and made them a people who were to be set apart from the rest of the world.

- Firstfruits took place on the day after the Sabbath following the Passover. Thus it always took place on the first day of the week. On this day, each Israelite was to bring the first sheaf of grain that he had harvested. It should be remembered that in Canaan, the harvest took place in the spring at the end of the rainy season. Bringing his sheaf of grain before the Lord, he was to have the priest wave it before the entrance of the tabernacle.

All three of these ceremonies have a special significance to the Christian. The Passover looks to the manner in which the wrath of God has passed over us. Just as the lamb's blood on the doorposts caused the angel of death to pass over that household, so our identification with the death of Christ causes God's wrath to be removed from us. Jesus is our Passover Lamb.

The feast of unleavened bread looks to the sanctification process that God works in the life of the believer as He sets us apart to Himself. We have been called to remove from our lives the influence of the world and to be holy, pure, and devoted to the Lord.

The feast of firstfruits looks at Jesus who rose from the dead on the first day of the week and whose resurrection promises that we will also one day rise from the dead. In the same way the sheaf was waved before the Lord, so also there is coming a day of harvest when the wheat will be divided from the tares and the sheaf that God has chosen will be brought to His house and pledged to His service.

You have been bought with a price. The price tag reads, "The life of the Son of God." You were not cheap. You have been purchased and you no longer belong to you. You belong to the Lord and now you need to start living accordingly.

JUDGMENT DAY
Revelation 14:6-20

One of my favorite classes in high school was creative writing. The teacher was a little old Jewish woman who had an editor's eye combined with a grandmother's smile. On the first day of class, she went to the chalk board and wrote down the sentence:

"The dog bit the man."

Her instructions to us were very simple. We were to take this sentence and make a story out of it. We came back to class the next day and shared our stories with the rest of the class. It was fascinating. One student had turned it into an allegory. Another presented it as a comical situation. A third portrayed a vision of dejection. Some students wrote from the dog's point of view, others from the point of view of the man, and still others from that of a third party.

The book of Revelation is like that. It has a series of central themes that run through its pages, yet it is really a series of portraits. Each portrait is different, yet each works together to bring a wonderful panorama of the plan and purpose of God.

THE ANGEL AND THE GOSPEL

> *And I saw another angel flying in midheaven, having an eternal gospel to preach to those who live on the earth, and to every nation and tribe and tongue and people; 7 and he said with a loud voice, "Fear God, and give Him glory, because the hour of His judgment has come; worship Him who made the heaven and the earth and sea and springs of waters." (Revelation 14:6-7).*

The last time angels were mentioned in John's revelation was the seven angels with the seven trumpets in chapters 8-11. Now we see another angel. He is flying in midheaven, that is, the sky. When we come to Revelation 19:17, we will see a reference to the birds that fly in midheaven. The reason this angel flies in midheaven is because his mission has to do with things on earth. His mission involves the preaching of good news *to every nation and tribe and tongue and people*. It is a call to repentance, to fear God and give him glory and to worship Him.

His message is described as *an eternal gospel*. Does this mean it is a different message than the gospel that we proclaim of the death, burial,

> This is the only place in any of John's writings in which he uses the term "gospel."

and resurrection of Jesus? That is certainly part of the message, but the message is bigger than that. It is described as an eternal gospel because it is a message that was planned before the foundation of the world and which shall endure forever. At the same time, the specific thing that is mentioned here about this message of good news is that God is sovereign and that the hour of His judgment has come. Such a message is not inconsistent with the gospel of the death, burial, and resurrection of Jesus. It s a fundamental part of that message. It is because Jesus died and rose again that God's sovereignty and coming judgment can be described as a message of good news.

THE ANGEL AND BABYLON

> *And another angel, a second one, followed, saying, "Fallen, fallen is Babylon the great, she who has made all the nations drink of the wine of the passion of her immorality." (Revelation 14:8).*

This is the first time Babylon has been mentioned in the book of Revelation. It will not be the last. When we come to Revelation 17-18 we will see two chapters devoted to the fall of this city. Each time, it will be called "the great." To what does this refer? Is this describing a return to the fallen city on the Euphrates or are we to understand it as something else?

The symbolism of Babylon takes us all the way back to the book of Genesis where we find the account of the Tower of Babel. Our English translations have done us a disservice by distinguishing between the two different names of Babel versus Babylon. The Hebrew text of the Old Testament contains no such distinction; they are identical. Yet this passage does not merely mention Babylon; it addresses "Babylon the great." Those words are an echo of the prideful reflection of King Nebuchadnezzar in Daniel 4:30 when he said, "Is this not Babylon the great, which I myself have built as a royal residence by the might of my power and for the glory of my majesty?" In that instance, the Lord brought the prideful king low, causing him to act the part of a wild beast. In the previous chapter we noted certain religious and political rulers who were characterized as beasts and now we hear a proclamation of judgment against Babylon the great.

In John's day, the city of Babylon was long past its prime. It is for this reason that most scholars feel that John is not speaking of the literal city of Babylon, but of the city which holds the spiritual heritage of that ancient city. He has already utilized such symbolic language in Revelation 11:8 when he spoke of Jerusalem at *the great city which mystically is called Sodom and Egypt*. The further description of Babylon as the city *who has made all the nations drink of the wine of the passion of her immorality* is taken from the prophet Jeremiah.

252

Babylon has been a golden cup in the hand of the LORD,
Intoxicating all the earth.
The nations have drunk of her wine;
Therefore the nations are going mad. (Jeremiah 51:7).

Jeremiah makes the point that the sins of Babylon did not remain in Babylon. They had an intoxicating effect on the surrounding nations. Sin has a way of doing that. It spreads and it permeates and it influences others. By contrast, we cannot help but to be reminded of a different cup that comes from the hand of the Lord. He calls us to come and to drink, not to be intoxicated, but to receive His Holy Spirit. His cup does not drive the nations mad; it brings a gentle sanity. The world says, "Drink and forget your troubles." Jesus says, "Drink and remember."

The spirit of Babylon can still be seen today. It can be seen when prayer in public schools is outlawed. It can be seen when the killing of babies through abortion is made legal. It can be seen when marriage becomes an abomination and when those who hold to a biblical view of marriage are persecuted by the state. Just as Babylon fell in her day, so all who take up the spirit of Babylon will eventually fall.

Babylon is described as having *made all the nations drink of the wine of the passion of her immorality (14:8)*. In Revelation 14:4 we saw the 144,000 represented as those who "have not been defiled with women, for they have kept themselves chaste." We suggested that this was referring to a spiritual purity. In the same way, the immorality which is seen in Babylon is primarily a spiritual unfaithfulness.

What is spiritual unfaithfulness? It is giving glory or love or honor or attention to another which is due to God. Paula and I were watching a television game show one day in which a hundred people were asked, "What is first place in your life?" The answers ranged from family to job, spouse, sports, and even one man who said that his car was the most important thing in his life. Out of the hundred people who were interviewed, not one placed the Lord as first place. Not one of them gave God the pre-eminence.

THE ANGEL AND JUDGMENT

> *Then another angel, a third one, followed them, saying with a loud voice, "If anyone worships the beast and his image, and receives a mark on his forehead or on his hand, 10 he also will drink of the wine of the wrath of God, which is mixed in full strength in the cup of His anger; and he will be tormented with fire and brimstone in the presence of the holy angels and in the presence of the Lamb. 11 And the smoke of their torment goes up forever and ever; they have no rest day and night, those who*

*worship the beast and his image, and whoever receives the mark
of his name." 12 Here is the perseverance of the saints who keep
the commandments of God and their faith in Jesus. (Revelation
14:9-12).*

Whereas we saw the previous angel proclaiming the eternal gospel, we now see that
those who reject that gospel message and who instead worship the beast and his
image are condemned to an eternal punishment that is described in the most graphic
terms.

1. Judgment of Wrath: *He also will drink of the wine of the wrath of God,
    which is mixed in full strength in the cup of His anger (14:10).*

    The symbolism of God's anger being seen as a cup of wine is taken from
    the Old Testament prophet Jeremiah where the Lord proclaims through the
    prophet, *"Take this cup of the wine of wrath from My hand and cause all
    the nations to whom I send you to drink it. 16 They will drink and stagger
    and go mad because of the sword that I will send among them"* (Jeremiah
    25:15-16).

    There is a reminder here of how Jesus spoke of drinking the cup that God
    had given to Him. When the soldiers came to arrest Him, He told Peter to
    sheath his sword because it was time for Him to drink of that cup (John
    18:11). Because Jesus drank of the cup of the righteous anger of God, we
    do not have to drink of that cup. Instead, we are invited to a table where we
    drink the cup of His blood. We benefit from His death on our behalf
    because He died on our behalf.

2. Judgment of Fire: *He will be tormented with fire and brimstone in the
    presence of the holy angels and in the presence of the Lamb (14:10).*

    The Scriptures consistently utilize the description of fiery burning to
    describe the final judgment. There are some scholars who, while affirming
    the Bible's teaching of an eternal hell, question the literalness with which
    we are to hold to such descriptions as a burning fire, an undying worm or
    darkness. Charles Hodge in his *Systematic Theology* writes of the fire in
    hell: "There seems to be no more reason for supposing that the fire spoken
    of in Scripture is to be literal fire, than that the worm that never dies is
    literally a worm. The devil and his angels who are to suffer the vengeance
    of eternal fire, and whose doom the finally impenitent are to share, have no
    material bodies to be acted upon by elemental fire. As there are to be
    degrees in the glory and blessedness of heaven, as our Lord teaches us in
    the parable of the ten talents, so there will be differences as to degree in the
    sufferings of the lost: some will be beaten with few stripes, some with
    many" (2005:617).

3.   Judgment of Eternal Duration: *And the smoke of their torment goes up forever and ever; they have no rest day and night (14:11).*

There have been many attempts to read the future judgment of God as either being one of limited duration or of consisting merely of an annihilation of body and soul. There are some who are quick to point out that the phrase translated "forever and ever" is a double use of the Greek word *aion* (αἰων) that can describe merely "an age." However, this same term is also used to describe the eternality of eternal life (John 3:16 and everywhere else in John) as well as the eternality of God Himself (Romans 16:26 speaks of τοῦ αἰωνίου θεοῦ – the everlasting God). John could not be any clearer. He uses the same terms that describe God Himself being eternal and eternal life being eternal to also speak of the eternal duration of the punishment of the wicked.

This is a promise of eternal judgment. It is not a new promise. It is a theme that runs all the way back to the Old Testament. It is taken from the imagery of the destruction of the enemies of Israel.

> *For the LORD has a day of vengeance,*
> *A year of recompense for the cause of Zion.*
> *9 Its streams will be turned into pitch,*
> *And its loose earth into brimstone,*
> *And its land will become burning pitch.*
> *10 It will not be quenched night or day;*
> *Its smoke will go up forever.*
> *From generation to generation it will be desolate;*
> *None will pass through it forever and ever. (Isaiah 34:8-10).*

Isaiah speaks of a day of judgment coming upon the nations. There are times when we see this taking place in history, but there is also coming a day of final judgment when all will stand before the Lord to give an accounting. The good news for the Christian is that he has One who has taken that judgment upon Himself.

4.   Hope in the Face of Judgment: *Here is the perseverance of the saints who keep the commandments of God and their faith in Jesus (14:12).*

Do you ever get tired of doing what is right? Do you ever feel discouragement? Do you ever feel like walking away and leaving your Christian life behind you? There is source of strength here for you. It is a motivation to endure.

255

There is coming a day of judgment. The books are going to be balanced. Notice that the two concepts of "the commandments of the Lord" and that of "faith in Jesus" are described in tandem. John sees them as synonymous.

> *By this we know that we have come to know Him, if we keep His commandments. 4 The one who says, "I have come to know Him," and does not keep His commandments, is a liar, and the truth is not in him; 5 but whoever keeps His word, in him the love of God has truly been perfected. By this we know that we are in Him: 6 the one who says he abides in Him ought himself to walk in the same manner as He walked. (1 John 2:3-6).*

> *This is His commandment, that we believe in the name of His Son Jesus Christ, and love one another, just as He commanded us. 24 The one who keeps His commandments abides in Him, and He in him. We know by this that He abides in us, by the Spirit whom He has given us. (1 John 3:23-24).*

How can you tell if a person has believed in Jesus? Look at his life and see if he is keeping the commandments of Jesus. How can you tell if a person is keeping the commandments of Jesus? Talk to him and see if he is trusting Jesus.

A BLESSING TO THOSE WHO DIE

> *And I heard a voice from heaven, saying, "Write, 'Blessed are the dead who die in the Lord from now on!'" "Yes," says the Spirit, "so that they may rest from their labors, for their deeds follow with them." (Revelation 14:13).*

Paul says in Philippians 1:21 that "for me, to live is Christ and to die is gain." Here in this passage, that same sentiment is expressed as a beatitude. You remember the beatitudes – they were sayings of Jesus that described one as "blessed."

"Blessed are the poor in spirit"
"Blessed are those who mourn"
"Blessed are the gentle"
"Blessed are those who hunger and thirst for righteousness"

In each of these cases, the object for which a person is blessed goes contrary to popular thinking. We are tempted to say, "Blessed are the rich in spirit; blessed are

256

those who have nothing about which to mourn; blessed are those who are satisfied with their righteousness." This beatitude is no different. We might like to say, "Blessed are those who go on living and who don't have to die because the Lord will return to rapture them away." But it is the believer who dies who is to be considered as blessed. Why is this? It is because he has arrived at the goal for which he is laboring. He has become like Christ. Instead of struggling with the Christian life, this person's struggles are now over. Death brings the rewards for his labors.

There are going to be seven beatitudes in the book of Revelation.

- Blessed is he who reads and those who hear the words of the prophecy (1:3).
- Blessed are the dead who die in the Lord from now on! (14:13).
- Blessed is the one who stays awake and keeps his clothes (16:15).
- Blessed are those who are invited to the marriage supper of the Lamb (19:9).
- Blessed and holy is the one who has a part in the first resurrection (20:6).
- Blessed is he who heeds the words of the prophecy of this book (22:7).
- Blessed are those who wash their robes (22:14).

This is a special blessing that is given "from now on." Death throughout the Scriptures is seen as an enemy. Paul says in 1 Corinthians 15:26 that the last enemy that will be abolished is death. But there is a sense in which death has already been defeated. The sting of death was removed upon the cross when Christ made the supreme sacrifice for sins. As a result, we can look at death, not as something final, but as a temporary rest. Death is not the end for the Christian; it is his birthday into eternal life.

THE SON WITH THE SICKLE

Then I looked, and behold, a white cloud, and sitting on the cloud was one like a son of man, having a golden crown on His head and a sharp sickle in His hand. 15 And another angel came out of the temple, crying out with a loud voice to Him who sat on the cloud, "Put in your sickle and reap, for the hour to reap has come, because the harvest of the earth is ripe." 16 Then He who sat on the cloud swung His sickle over the earth, and the earth was reaped. 17 And another angel came out of the temple which is in heaven, and he also had a sharp sickle. 18 Then another angel, the one who has power over fire, came out from the altar; and he called with a loud voice to him who had the sharp sickle, saying,

"Put in your sharp sickle and gather the clusters from the vine of the earth, because her grapes are ripe." 19 So the angel swung his sickle to the earth and gathered the clusters from the vine of the earth, and threw them into the great wine press of the wrath of God. 20 And the wine press was trodden outside the city, and blood came out from the wine press, up to the horses' bridles, for a distance of two hundred miles. (Revelation 14:14-20).

This section begins with the phrase, "I looked, and behold." That was the phrase used to introduce the transition in Revelation 4:1 when we moved from the messages of the seven churches to John's vision of the heavenly throne. It was also used to introduce the varied-colored horses and their riders in 6:2, 6:5, and 6:8. It was used in Revelation 7:9 when John heard the numbering of the 144,000 and then looked to see the great multitude from every nation. It was used in Revelation 14:1 to transition from the vision of the beasts to the Lamb standing on Mount Zion.

Now we see it again and it also marks a transition. We have just heard a blessing pronounced upon those who die in the Lord and now John looks and, instead of seeing those who die in the Lord, He sees a vision of one sitting on a white cloud. How does this relate to what John has just heard? It seems to me that the reason the dead are blessed is because they get to see the very thing that John now describes. They get to see Jesus.

1.   The One on the Cloud: *Then I looked, and behold, a white cloud, and sitting on the cloud was one like a son of man, having a golden crown on His head and a sharp sickle in His hand (14:14).*

This is the only reference in the entire Bible to a white cloud. When the Israelites came to Mount Sinai, there was a thick cloud upon the mountain and the words used to describe it indicate a deep darkness. When Ezekiel has his vision, he sees "a great cloud with fire flashing forth continually and a bright light around it" (1:4). This cloud is seen as a throne for the returning Messiah. John's description of "one like a son of man" takes us back to the book of Daniel.

> *I kept looking in the night visions,*
> *And behold, with the clouds of heaven*
> *One like a Son of Man was coming,*
> *And He came up to the Ancient of Days*
> *And was presented before Him (Daniel 7:13).*

The Son of Man was the title by which Jesus most often referred to Himself. It points to the fact of His humanity, but it also points to the fact of His exaltation. He is the Son of Man who comes into the very presence of God. John says elsewhere that *no one has ascended into heaven, but He who descended from heaven: the Son of Man* (John 3:13).

Jesus is described *having a golden crown on His head.* The head which once bore a crown of thorns now boasts the crown of victory. But our attention is directed to the sickle in His hand. A sickle is an instrument utilized for the cutting of crops at the harvest. Its long curved blade would be used in a wide swinging motion to cut the stem of either a stalk of wheat or, in this case, a vine of grapes. As John watches, he sees the earth being reaped by the one with the sickle.

2.   The Time of the Harvest: *"Put in your sickle and reap, for the hour to reap has come, because the harvest of the earth is ripe" (14:15).*

These words are an echo of the prophetic instructions given by the prophet Joel when he spoke of a final judgment in the Valley of Jehoshaphat. The judgment is of the nations and the prophet calls for them to be gathered together.

> *Let the nations be aroused*
> *And come up to the valley of Jehoshaphat,*
> *For there I will sit to judge*
> *All the surrounding nations.*
> *13 Put in the sickle, for the harvest is ripe.*
> *Come, tread, for the wine press is full;*
> *The vats overflow, for their wickedness is great (Joel 3:12-13).*

Joel's prophecy places this in the Valley of Jehoshaphat. The problem is that the Bible never speaks of such a place. Instead we are told in 2nd Chronicles 1 of an epic battle that took place in the days of Jehoshaphat when a multitude of nations gathered against the people of God. Instead of trusting in his own military strength or prowess, Jehoshaphat trusted in the Lord and marched out with temple musicians and singers at the head of his army. When they came to the place of the battle, they found that it had already begun without them.

> *For the sons of Ammon and Moab rose up against the inhabitants of Mount Seir destroying them completely, and when they had finished with the inhabitants of Seir, they helped to destroy one another. 24 When Judah came to the lookout of the wilderness, they looked toward the multitude; and behold, they were corpses lying on the ground, and no one had escaped. (2 Chronicles 20:23-24).*

The Lord had caused the enemies of Judah to begin fighting among themselves so that they destroyed one another. When Jehoshaphat and his army arrived on the scene, it was to look out over a valley of corpses. Thus the name Jehoshaphat came to take on a special significance, for it means "Yahweh who judges." The story became a symbolic meta-narrative for describing the future judgment of God. The point is that God will protect His people and He will judge the nations.

3.   The Winepress of God: *So the angel swung his sickle to the earth and gathered the clusters from the vine of the earth, and threw them into the great wine press of the wrath of God (14:19).*

A wine press in the ancient world normally consisted of a large stone vat into which grapes would be placed and then workers would step on the grapes, mashing them beneath their feet so that its juice could flow down a trough to be collected in a wineskin. There was an old Hebrew expression that referred to wine as "the blood of grapes" (Genesis 49:11; Deuteronomy 31:14). This image is brought to bear in John's vision as the wine press flows, not with wine, but with blood.

4.   A Vision of Blood: *Blood came out from the wine press, up to the horses' bridles, for a distance of two hundred miles (14:20).*

Two hundred miles (the Greek text reads 600 stadia) is roughly the distance from Dan, the northernmost point of Israel's territory in the days of the Old Testament, to Elath on the shores of the Gulf of Aqaba, where Solomon once built his fleet of ships. The point is that the entire land of Israel would be covered in blood. This very graphic language is echoed in the Jerusalem Talmud where it relates the story of the Bar Kochba revolt in the second century A.D. and how the Romans "went on killing until their horses were submerged in blood to their nostrils" (Taanis 4:5).

Once again, the A.D. 70 fall of Jerusalem becomes the backdrop against which we are meant to view this vision of judgment. What happened to Israel in that day is only a foretaste of what shall happen to the nations on the last day. This idea of seeing Israel as a microcosm of the world is not a new one. It goes all the way back to the days of Moses. In the table of nations in Genesis 10 there are 70 nations mentioned. This coincides with Exodus 1:5 where the number of Israelites who entered Egypt in the days of Jacob is said to be 70. Nor is this a coincidence, for we read in Deuteronomy how there is a deliberate correlation between the nations and the number of the sons of Israel:

> *When the Most High gave the nations their inheritance,*
> *When He separated the sons of man,*
> *He set the boundaries of the peoples*
> *According to the number of the sons of Israel.*

(Deuteronomy 32:8).

There is a sense in which Israel was called to be the representative for all the nations of the world. This tiny country was to be a kingdom of priests, a nation of representatives. As such, what is true of Israel becomes true of the rest of the world. It is for this reason that we see here in Revelation the judgements against the world pictured in terms that will remind us of Israel.

THE FINAL EXODUS
Revelation 15:1-8

The exodus event was the supreme redemptive event of the Old Testament. It was this event that gave freedom to God's people and birth to the nation of Israel. This event serves in the New Testament as a forerunner to a greater exodus. The New Testament counterpart to the Old Testament exodus was the cross.

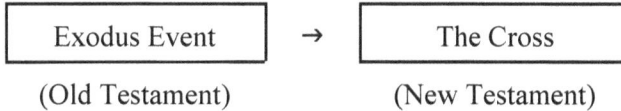

Exodus Event	→	The Cross
(Old Testament)		(New Testament)

On the Mount of Transfiguration when Moses and Elijah appeared with Jesus who was manifesting his glory, Luke's account tells us that they were speaking of His exodus which He was about to accomplish in Jerusalem (see the Greek text of Luke 9:31). In a very real sense, the cross is to the New Testament what the Exodus was to the Old Testament. As we come to this chapter, we will see overt references to Moses and to plagues and it will bring to mind the events of the Exodus, not merely to recapitulate those events, but as a way of looking at a future deliverance of God's people.

THE SEVEN ANGELS

> *Then I saw another sign in heaven, great and marvelous, seven angels who had seven plagues, which are the last, because in them the wrath of God is finished. (Revelation 15:1).*

This chapter begins with *another sign in heaven*. This is the third and final time that John sees a sign in heaven. The first two instances were in chapter 12.

- The sign of a woman arrayed with the sun representing Israel.
- The sign of a great red dragon representing Satan and his kingdom.

This final sign begins with a vision of seven angels with seven plagues. As soon as we hear of plagues, we are reminded of the plagues that came upon Egypt in the days of Moses. It was a time when the hand of the Lord was against that land in order to deliver His people, but it also served as a judgment against Egypt.

Rather than ten plagues as took place in the days of Moses, we are introduced here to seven angels with seven plagues. We have seen groupings of seven throughout the book of Revelation. There have been seven churches and seven seals and seven trumpets. This is the last grouping of seven. From henceforth, each time we see the

262

number seven it will be describing someone or something that has already been introduced.

These seven plagues are said to be *the last, because in them the wrath of God is finished.* Some have taken this to mean that all of the seals and trumpets and plagues are describing a long, twenty one part sequence of the future. But such a view is neither necessary nor preferred. When we came to the sixth seal, we saw the kings of the earth expressing their fear of the arrival of the day of the wrath of the Lamb. It was a picture of the return of the Lord. Then the seventh seal introduced the seven trumpets. As had been the case with the seals, so also the trumpets depicted visions of God's escalating judgment upon the earth. When we came to the seventh trumpet, we were told that *the kingdom of the world has become the kingdom of our Lord and of His Christ* (Revelation 11:15). It was still another indication of the return of the Lord. In chapter 12, the visions began anew and took us back to the birth of Christ and the cosmic conflict with the dragon. Now as we come to the last set of seven, we are told that it will be within the sequence of seven bowels that the wrath of God will be finished. We can chart the action as follows:

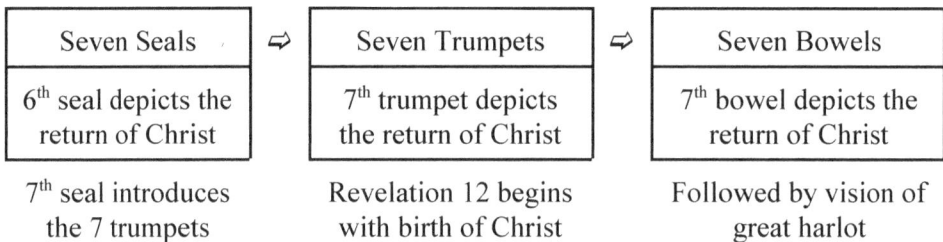

Seven Seals	⇨	Seven Trumpets	⇨	Seven Bowels
6th seal depicts the return of Christ		7th trumpet depicts the return of Christ		7th bowel depicts the return of Christ

7th seal introduces the 7 trumpets	Revelation 12 begins with birth of Christ	Followed by vision of great harlot

Thus what we have is not a chronological sequence of twenty one consecutive events that will take place one after the other in the future, but rather three sets of symbolic representations of spiritual realities of both past, present, and future, each culminating with the same future coming of Christ. It is like going to an art exhibit in which there are a variety of paintings all following a central theme. The theme is of Jesus. We know this because the entire book of Revelation opened with the statement that this is the revelation of Jesus Christ (1:1).

A HOLY CONVOCATION

And I saw something like a sea of glass mixed with fire, and those who had been victorious over the beast and his image and the number of his name, standing on the sea of glass, holding harps of God. (Revelation 15:2).

We last saw something like a sea of glass in the vision of Revelation 4. It was the vision of the throne of God and before that throne was described that which was *like a sea of glass, like crystal* (Revelation 4:6). In the context of the lampstand with the seven lamps, we noted that this was imagery derived from the temple and that the laver of water that stood before the temple was known as "the sea."

Now we see once again the sea of glass, but this time it is mixed with fire. Those who stand upon it have come through the fire and have been *victorious over the beast and his image and the number of his name*. The battle is over and the victory has been won. Instead of weapons of warfare, the forces of this host hold in their hands the harps of God.

THE SONG OF MOSES

> *And they sang the song of Moses, the bond-servant of God, and the song of the Lamb, saying, "Great and marvelous are Your works, O Lord God, the Almighty; Righteous and true are Your ways, King of the nations! 4 Who will not fear, O Lord, and glorify Your name? For You alone are holy; For all the nations will come and worship before You, for Your righteous acts have been revealed." (Revelation 15:3-4).*

This reference to the "song of Moses" is meant to remind us of something that took place back in the Old Testament. It was after the Israelites passed through the Red Sea and when the armies of the pharaoh were swallowed up that Moses led the Israelites in a song of victory. The song is found in Exodus 15. It is a song that praises the Lord as our strength, our song, and our salvation.

That song is sung again here in Revelation 15. This time, it is not to focus upon the deliverance of Israel from Egypt, but to show us the greater deliverance of which the first was only a type. But notice that the song does not reference the destruction of the nations or the judgment of the nations, but instead gives a promise that the nations will come and worship the Lord. This song calls to mind the promise that God made to Abraham how through him all the world would be blessed (Genesis 12:3).

You will remember that when the Israelites entered the promised land, forty years after the exodus from Egypt, they encountered Rahab and her family who had heard of the events of the exodus and had come to believe in the God whose mighty hand was revealed in those events. She says to the spies:

> *"For we have heard how the LORD dried up the water of the Red Sea before you when you came out of Egypt, and what you did to the two kings of the Amorites who were beyond the Jordan,*

*to Sihon and Og, whom you utterly destroyed. 11 When we heard it,
our hearts melted and no courage remained in any man any longer
because of you; for the LORD your God, He is God in heaven
above and on earth beneath. (Joshua 2:10-11).*

Rahab had heard the events of the exodus and the subsequent events of God's
leadership of the Israelites to the very borders of Canaan and she and her family had
recognized the reality of the God of Israel. Now as we come to Revelation 15, we
find that Rahab was merely a precursor for all the nations who have come to see the
marvelous works of the Lord and have come to worship Him.

SEVEN BOWLS AND SEVEN PLAGUES

*After these things I looked, and the temple of the
tabernacle of testimony in heaven was opened, 6 and the seven
angels who had the seven plagues came out of the temple, clothed
in linen, clean and bright, and girded around their chests with
golden sashes. 7 Then one of the four living creatures gave to the
seven angels seven golden bowls full of the wrath of God, who lives
forever and ever. 8 And the temple was filled with smoke from the
glory of God and from His power; and no one was able to enter the
temple until the seven plagues of the seven angels were finished.
(Revelation 15:5-8).*

Now the scene changes once again. This time John is given a view into *the temple
of the tabernacle of testimony*. Notice that it is both the temple and the tabernacle
which are in view. The tabernacle hearkened back to the days of Moses. It was the
portable tent that stood at the center of the camp of Israel. It was here that God
made His presence known. It was not until the days of Solomon that the tabernacle
was replaced by the temple. The temple was built to same dimensions as the
tabernacle except that the temple was twice as large as the tabernacle. In John's
vision, the imagery of the tabernacle and the temple are combined.

Instead of a priesthood within this temple-tabernacle, John sees seven angels. They
are the same seven angels who were introduced at the beginning of this chapter with
seven plagues. They are clothed in clean linen and girded with golden sashes. They
are dressed in the same way that the Son of man was described back in Revelation
1:13. This description echoes back to the Old Testament where the garments of the
high priest were overlaid with sashes (Exodus 28:40).

These angels are given *seven golden bowls full of the wrath of God*. These will be
poured out upon the earth in the next chapter, but for now, our attention is directed
to the temple as it fills with smoke from the glory of God. Once again, the

265

description takes us back to the book of Exodus where the climactic event of that book concludes with the presence of the Lord entering the newly constructed tabernacle and filling the holy of holies with the smoke of His presence.

> *Then the cloud covered the tent of meeting, and the glory of the LORD filled the tabernacle. 35 Moses was not able to enter the tent of meeting because the cloud had settled on it, and the glory of the LORD filled the tabernacle. (Exodus 40:34-35).*

Do you remember what happened when Jesus died upon the cross? All three of the synoptic gospels tell how the veil of the temple was torn in two from top to bottom (Matthew 27:51; Mark 15:38; Luke 23:45). The death of Christ provided for the way of entry into the presence of God. But here we see that no one is able to enter the temple until the seven plagues held by the seven angels are completed. While the death of Christ satisfied the just demands of God upon sin, those who have rejected the Son will find that they face the full measure of that wrath.

This brings us to a question. What is to be the Christian's response when he sees the wrath of God directed against the world? This passage points to two responses. First, there is a warning. It is a warning against those who would think lightly of God. He is not to be trifled with. As C. S. Lewis used to say, He is not a tame lion. He is big and He is powerful and He acts according to His own will. Secondly, there is a source of comfort here. When bad things happen in the word, it is a sign of God's judgment for the way unbelievers treated Jesus and it is also a sign of God's judgment for the way they treat His people.

Have you ever seen a mother grizzly bear when someone threatens her cubs? I have not seen it and I don't want to see it. A large, sedate, slow-moving animal is transformed into a thundering engine of destruction that moves against the offender with the speed of an express train. Don't mess with her kids! That is the way the Lord is with His children.

THE SEVEN BOWLS
Revelation 16:1-21

One of the most dramatic narratives of the Bible is the confrontation between Moses and the pharaoh of Egypt. On one side stood the prophet of God, dressed in the simple robes of a shepherd of Midian. On the other side sat the pharaoh of the most powerful kingdom on the face of the earth, surrounded by all the pomp and riches of his court. The man of God spoke forth the message of the Almighty, "Let my people go!" The pharaoh refused and, in response to his refusal, the man of God brought a terrible plague against the land. The Egyptians cried out and the pharaoh relented, only to harden his heart once the plague had been lifted. Again and again the nation was stricken, but the result was that the pharaoh's heart became harder and harder.

The same process can be seen taking place in the world today. It is seen in the unbeliever who ignores God all this life, living as though God does not exist. He then suffers a tragedy. What is his reaction? He shakes his fist at God and says, "This is your fault." It is this same process that we shall see on a world-wide scale in this chapter.

The last chapter ended with a vision of seven angels holding seven plagues. When we heard of the plagues, we were reminded of the ten plagues that had been brought against Egypt in the Old Testament, and to make sure of that connection, we saw the people of God singing the Song of Moses, the victory song of those who had come out of Egypt. As this chapter opens, the command is now given for those plagues to be poured out upon the earth.

BOWLS OF WRATH

> Then I heard a loud voice from the temple, saying to the seven angels, "Go and pour out on the earth the seven bowls of the wrath of God." (Revelation 16:1).

We have already seen seven churches represented by seven lampstands, seven stars representing seven angels, and then seven seals and seven trumpets. This is the final series of sevens that will be shown. Yet as we come to this series of seven, it will seem surprisingly familiar. There is a striking resemblance seen when we compare the seven trumpets seen in Revelation 8-11 with the seven bowls that are seen in this chapter:

Seven Trumpets		Seven Bowls
Revelation 8-11		Revelation 16
Third of earth burned (8:7)	1	Poured on the earth (16:1)
Third of sea to blood (8:8)	2	Poured on the sea (16:3)
Third of waters & springs (8:10)	3	Rivers & springs (16:4)
Third of sun darkened (8:12)	4	Poured on sun (16:8)
Bottomless pit (9:1-2)	5	Throne of beast (16:10)
Euphrates (9:13-14)	6	Euphrates (16:12)
Voices from heaven with lightning, thunder and earthquake (11:15-19)	7	Great voice from the throne with lightning, thunder, and earthquake (16:17-18)

The structure of the vision of the bowls is almost identical with that of the vision of the trumpets, yet there is a difference. The trumpets announce the coming of calamity while the bowls actually bring that calamity. The trumpet judgments are in part (a third of the earth, a third of the sea, a third of the springs of water, a third of the sun and the moon and the stars). The bowl judgments are emphatic in their intensification.

The seals and the trumpets and the bowls have been interpreted in a variety of different ways. Some have looked at these as pointing to a future seven year period of great tribulation, but the book of Revelation makes no mention of a seven year period and such an absence is striking in light of all the other times we see the number seven arise in this book. That does not mean it cannot be fulfilled in such a manner, but it does mean that such a view is notably lacking in evidence. This brings me to a fundamental observation regarding the interpretation of future prophecy. It is that prophecy is always easier to interpret after it has been fulfilled, and even then it is not always so simple.

These bowls are described as the bowls of the wrath of God. In the first chapter of Romans, the apostle Paul describes the wrath of God as a present and ongoing reality: *For the wrath of God is revealed from heaven against all ungodliness and unrighteousness of men who suppress the truth in unrighteousness (Romans 1:18).* He then proceeds to show the way in which God's wrath is revealed as God gives over unregenerate men to the lusts of their hearts as they exchange the truth of God for a lie and the natural function of their own bodies for that which is foreign to that design. What we are told specifically in Romans 1 is now going to be displayed in a terrible vision of bowls of wrath being poured out upon the earth.

THE FIRST BOWL

> *So the first angel went and poured out his bowl on the earth; and it became a loathsome and malignant sore on the people who had the mark of the beast and who worshiped his image. (Revelation 16:2).*

As the first bowl is poured out, it is manifested in "a loathsome and malignant sore." This affliction is not seen upon all men, but specifically upon those who had the mark of the beast and who worshiped his image. Both the affliction as well as the distinction upon whom it falls calls to mind the plague of boils that came upon the Egyptians and their cattle in the days of the Exodus. Indeed, the same Greek term that was used in the Septuagint to describe the plague of the boils in the days of Moses is used here. As it took place then, so also here it seems to be the case that this affliction is only described as being upon the enemies of God and His people.

Does this mean that God's people are never afflicted with physical ailments? It does not. Even Paul described how a "thorn in the flesh" was given to torment him (2 Corinthians 12:7). Yet that was not a sign of the wrath of God in his life, but was instead a helpful messenger of God that might assist him from falling into the sin of exalting himself. We dare not take the stance of Job's friends when we see someone afflicted with a physical ailment to assume that it is necessarily a sign of God's wrath upon that particular person. But we should not take the opposite stance to assume that such afflictions are never a sign of God's anger against sin, but we have the words of this vision that there are times when such ailments are indeed a sign of God's judgment upon men.

THE SECOND BOWL

> *The second angel poured out his bowl into the sea, and it became blood like that of a dead man; and every living thing in the sea died. (Revelation 16:3).*

The pouring of the second bowl is upon the sea and it turns to blood. That blood is described as being *like that of a dead man*, that is, it is of a decaying and putrefying nature. Both this bowl as well as the one to follow will be reminiscent of the first plague upon Egypt that resulted in the Nile River being turned to blood. But rather than being confined to the land of Egypt, this plague affects the sea and results in the death of every living thing in the sea. The point is that the same God whose judgment that was once directed toward the land of Egypt is the One who judges the whole world. When you read the story of the Israelites and the Egyptians

269

during the plagues, you are reading your own story. You are either among the number of God's people or you are numbered with those who suffer the wrath of God.

THE THIRD BOWL

> *Then the third angel poured out his bowl into the rivers and the springs of waters; and they became blood.*
>
> *5 And I heard the angel of the waters saying, "Righteous are You, who are and who were, O Holy One, because You judged these things; 6 for they poured out the blood of saints and prophets, and You have given them blood to drink. They deserve it."*
>
> *7 And I heard the altar saying, "Yes, O Lord God, the Almighty, true and righteous are Your judgments." (Revelation 16:3-7).*

If the second plague affects all of the bodies of salt water upon the earth, the third plague is poured out to turn all of the bodies of fresh water to blood. The reference to rivers and springs calls to mind the words of the Psalmist in a song of praise of the mighty hand of God.

> *Let them give thanks to the LORD for His lovingkindness,*
> *And for His wonders to the sons of men!*
> *32 Let them extol Him also in the congregation of the people,*
> *And praise Him at the seat of the elders.*
> *33 He changes **rivers** into a wilderness*
> *And **springs of water** into a thirsty ground;*
> *34 A fruitful land into a salt waste,*
> *Because of the wickedness of those who dwell in it. (Psalm 107:31-34).*

Notice that both in the Psalm as well as here in Revelation, the affliction of the rivers and the springs of water are accomplished *because of the wickedness of those who dwell in it.* We see echoes here of the words of Paul when he speaks of how *the whole creation groans and suffers the pains of childbirth together until now* (Romans 8:22). This brings us to an important principle. It is that sin not only infects and spreads, but it also inflicts its results, even upon that which did not partake of that sin. We see this all the time in life. A man might be abusive and his family and neighbors suffer the results of that sin through no fault of their own. At the same time, we should note that the rest of the Psalm goes on to show, not only the judgment of God, but also the lovingkindness of God toward His people.

> *He changes a wilderness into a pool of water*
> *And a dry land into springs of water;*

36 And there He makes the hungry to dwell,
So that they may establish an inhabited city (Psalm 107:35-36).

At this point, we have our focus upon the bowls of wrath and upon the righteous judgment of God against sin. But the Psalmist reminds us that the grace of God is such that it takes that which has been cursed and brings about a blessing. We will see the same thing taking place here in Revelation. Right now we are looking at the judgment of God, but when we get to the end of this book, we will see a picture of springs of water flowing from the throne of God to water his heavenly city. The point is that the judgment is given as a warning that we might turn from that which brings judgment in order to receive the grace and lovingkindness of God.

Verse 7 describes a voice coming from the altar: *"Yes, O Lord God, the Almighty, true and righteous are Your judgments."* Our problem is that our attitudes have been warped and distorted by sin. Included in this is our attitudes toward justice and fairness. We tend to be either too lenient or too vengeful in our judgments. But God's justice is perfect. On the one hand, it is patient. It waits for the sinner to repent. It is still waiting today. When the period of waiting is completed, it judges with perfect and holy justice.

THE FOURTH BOWL

> *The fourth angel poured out his bowl upon the sun, and it was given to it to scorch men with fire. 9 Men were scorched with fierce heat; and they blasphemed the name of God who has the power over these plagues, and they did not repent so as to give Him glory. (Revelation 16:8-9).*

In following the same pattern as the trumpet judgments, so the fourth bowl now makes reference to the sun. But instead of a portion of the sun being darkened, the result of this judgment is that the sun scorches men with fire and a fierce heat. This description finds its roots in the Old Testament. It was used by Moses to describe the cursings that God would send against Israel if they did not obey the voice of the Lord.

> *The LORD will smite you with consumption and with fever and with inflammation and with fiery heat and with the sword and with blight and with mildew, and they will pursue you until you perish. 23 The heaven which is over your head shall be bronze, and the earth which is under you, iron. (Deuteronomy 28:22-23).*

In the context of this passage, the "fiery heat" sounds very much like a natural phenomena. This should not surprise us as one of the things that we have seen through the book of Revelation is that nature bends to do the will of God.

Rather than causing them to repent and return to the Lord, we see them blaspheme the name of God. This is one of the differences between the believer and the unbeliever. The believer faces suffering with fortitude. He may not understand why it has come, but he knows that God is in control and that He has a purpose for it. The unbeliever's reaction is to blame God and to blaspheme the name of God. Just as the heat of the sun bakes the clay and hardens it, so these plagues have the effect of hardening his heart and increasing his rebellious words against his Creator. This same theme carries over into the next judgment.

THE FIFTH BOWL

> *Then the fifth angel poured out his bowl on the throne of the beast, and his kingdom became darkened; and they gnawed their tongues because of pain, 11 and they blasphemed the God of heaven because of their pains and their sores; and they did not repent of their deeds. (Revelation 16:10-11).*

Up to this point, there has been a direct correlation between the trumpet judgments of Revelation 8-11 with the bowl judgments of this chapter. The first trumpet saw a third of the earth being burned up while the first bowl was poured upon the earth. The second trumpet saw a third of the sea being turned to blood while the second bowl impacted all life in the sea. The third trumpet was upon waters and springs while the third bowl was a plague upon rivers and springs. The fourth trumpet darkened a portion of the sun while the fourth bowl also affected the sun.

But now there is a change. While the fifth trumpet saw a vision of the bottomless pit, there is no mention here in the fifth bowl of the bottomless pit. Instead the focus is upon the throne of the beast and upon his kingdom, though in later chapters we shall see the beast consigned to the lake of fire and that might be construed as an alternate term for the bottomless pit.

In contrast to the scorching from the sun that was seen in the fourth bowl, this fifth judgment brings darkness. Once again, we are reminded of the plague upon Egypt that resulted in the sun being darkened for three days. You will remember that the darkness that afflicted Egypt did not extend to the land of Goshen where the Israelites were living. It was a selective darkness. So also here, we read that it is the throne of the beast and his kingdom that becomes darkened. A darkness comes upon the enemies of God that is a counterpart to the spiritual darkness manifested in their hearts.

Just as the fourth bowl failed to bring men to repentance, so again the pattern of blasphemy and a failure to repent is repeated here with the fifth bowl. While one might think that the judgments that fall upon the earth might turn the hearts of unbelievers back to God, this does not take place. It is not that they do not believe God exists, for the Scriptures tell us that *His eternal power and divine nature, have been clearly seen, being understood through what has been made* (Romans 1:20). But even when they know of God, they refuse to honor Him and instead blaspheme Him.

THE SIXTH BOWL

> *The sixth angel poured out his bowl on the great river, the Euphrates; and its water was dried up, so that the way would be prepared for the kings from the east.*
>
> *13 And I saw coming out of the mouth of the dragon and out of the mouth of the beast and out of the mouth of the false prophet, three unclean spirits like frogs; 14 for they are spirits of demons, performing signs, which go out to the kings of the whole world, to gather them together for the war of the great day of God, the Almighty. 15 ("Behold, I am coming like a thief. Blessed is the one who stays awake and keeps his clothes, so that he will not walk about naked and men will not see his shame.") 16 And they gathered them together to the place which in Hebrew is called Har-Magedon. (Revelation 16:12-16).*

The sixth bowl directs our attention to a specific geographical location. It is poured out upon the Euphrates River. This is not the first time we have read about the Euphrates in the book of Revelation. It was seen in the sixth trumpet judgment of Revelation 9:13-14. We noted that the Euphrates served as the northernmost boundary of the lands over which David and Solomon exerted influence during the heights of their reigns. It was from across the Euphrates that the invading armies of the Assyrians, the Babylonians, and the Persians had come. Isaiah had told of the coming of a great king from the east.

> *Coastlands, listen to Me in silence,*
> *And let the peoples gain new strength;*
> *Let them come forward, then let them speak;*
> *Let us come together for judgment.*
> *2 Who has aroused one from the east*
> *Whom He calls in righteousness to His feet?*
> *He delivers up nations before him*
> *And subdues kings.*
> *He makes them like dust with his sword,*
> *As the wind-driven chaff with his bow. (Isaiah 41:1-2).*

A few chapters later, Isaiah picks up this same theme to talk of a king before whom the Lord would dry up the waters.

> It is I who says to the depth of the sea,
> "Be dried up!" And I will make your rivers dry.
> 28 It is I who says of Cyrus,
> "He is My shepherd! And he will perform all My desire."
> And he declares of Jerusalem, "She will be built,"
> And of the temple, "Your foundation will be laid." (Isaiah 44:27-28).

Isaiah's prophecy was fulfilled in the coming of Cyrus the Great, king of the Medes and the Persians who established the Persian Empire. There are ancient accounts that tell a story of Cyrus diverting the waters of the Euphrates which served as a defensive barrier around the city of Babylon so that he was able to capture the city without a fight. Once he had captured Babylon, he gave permission for the Jews to return to their homeland and rebuild their temple so that they could worship the Lord. Cyrus can be seen as something of a proto-type, for when we come to the New Testament, we again see officials from the east in the magi who come at the birth of Jesus to worship Him.

Here in Revelation, we see what looks like a parody of those former officials who came to worship Jesus and whose decrees were seen as a blessing upon the people of God. While the magi came to worship the Lord, the intent of these kings from the east is diametrically opposed to the Lord and to His people.

Calling these kings are *three unclean spirits*. They are said to be like frogs. This calls to mind the plague of frogs in Egypt, but this is not a plague of frogs. Rather, it is a spiritual attack that is characterized by frogs in that it is of an unclean nature. The sending of unclean spirits as a call to military action is a familiar theme in the Old Testament. 1 Kings 22 tells the story of how Ahab, king of Israel, entered into a joint military operation with Jehoshaphat, king of Judah to fight against Aram. One of Ahab's prophets of Baal was consulted and he prophesied that Israel and Judah would win a great victory, but Jehoshaphat insisted on consulting a prophet of the Lord. The prophet Micaiah was summoned and, at first, he told the kings what they wanted to hear. But when he was pressed to tell the truth of the matter, he gave this report:

> *Micaiah said, "Therefore, hear the word of the LORD. I saw the LORD sitting on His throne, and all the host of heaven standing by Him on His right and on His left. 20 The LORD said, 'Who will entice Ahab to go up and fall at Ramoth-gilead?' And one said this while another said that. 21 Then a spirit came forward and stood before the LORD and said, 'I will entice him.' 22 The LORD said to him, 'How?' And he said, 'I will go out and be a deceiving spirit in the mouth of all his prophets.' Then He said,*

'You are to entice him and also prevail. Go and do so.' 23 Now therefore, behold, the LORD has put a deceiving spirit in the mouth of all these your prophets; and the LORD has proclaimed disaster against you." (1Kings 22:19-23).

God had allowed a lying spirit to go forth in the mouth of these prophets. What took place in the past is again seen to be taking place in John's vision here in Revelation. Lying spirits are sent out to entice the kings of the world to gather them to what they think will be a great victory, but which turns out to be the judgment of God. When does this judgment take place? We are told that it takes place *the great day of God*. We are used to hearing the phrase, "the day of the Lord" to speak of God's judgment, both in time as well as the climactic day of judgment when the Lord Himself shall come. In the same way, Jude 1:6 speaks of fallen angels who are awaiting *the judgment of the great day* and John has already described the wrath of one who sits on the throne of heaven and of the lamb coming upon the kings of the earth on *the great day of their wrath* (Revelation 6:17). The language here would also seem to point to the final judgment that awaits all mankind. As if to underscore this point, John pauses to make mention of the coming of the Lord. Two specific areas are mentioned regarding His coming.

- The unexpectedness of His coming: *Behold, I am coming like a thief* (16:15).

  This is the second time in this book that the coming of Jesus has been characterized as being like a thief. The first time was in Revelation 3:3 and the warning to the church at Sardis for a spiritual awakening. Here again is the same warning and it comes juxtapositioned with a description of the gathering for judgment upon the nations. Some have taken this to be a silent and secret return of Jesus is a "rapture" that is to be followed at a later date by the Second Coming of the Lord, but there is no hint here that we are to understand the words of Jesus in such a way. Indeed, we would do well to remember that Peter also describes how *the day of the Lord will come like a thief, in which the heavens will pass away with a roar and the elements will be destroyed with intense heat, and the earth and its works will be burned up (2 Peter 3:10)*. The point is not that this coming takes place quietly or in secret, but that it comes unexpectedly. Just as a thief does not call and warn his victims that their home is going to be burglarized at a certain time, so also the Lord has not announced to us the time and date of His coming. We are therefore to be always ready. This brings us to the second point.

- The necessity of spiritual readiness: *Blessed is the one who stays awake and keeps his clothes, so that he will not walk about naked and men will not see his shame* (16:15).

275

The image of clothing as a part of spiritual readiness has already been seen in the message to the church at Laodicea. You will remember that Jesus told them, "Buy from Me gold refined by fire so that you may become rich, and white garments so that you may clothe yourself, and that the shame of your nakedness will not be revealed" (Revelation 3:18). The image calls to mind the actions of Adam and Eve in the garden of Eden and how, after they had sinned, they were both aware and ashamed of their nakedness.

There is a blessing here for the one who *stays awake and keeps his clothes*. When we come to Christ in faith, we find that we have been clothed with His righteousness. Paul says that *all of you who were baptized into Christ have clothed yourselves with Christ* (Galatians 3:27). But the blessing here is given to the one who keeps his clothes. The emphasis here is not merely in coming to Christ, but in continuing to hold to Christ. It is not merely in an initial act of faith, but in an enduring faith and an ongoing wakefulness.

Verse 16 returns to the previous theme of the gathering of the kings of the whole world and tells us that *they gathered them together to the place which in Hebrew is called Har-Magedon*. This phrase has been rendered in some translations with the much more familiar Armageddon, but we are told here that it is a Hebrew name. It is actually made up of two words:

Har is the Hebrew term for mountain or hill.
Megiddo is the name of an ancient city on the edge of the Valley of Jezreel.

Ruins of Megiddo with a Canaanite altar in the foreground and the Valley of Jezreel in the distance.

The name of Meggido is biblically significant. It was at here that Deborah and Barak fought the Canaanite armies and defeated them. In Judges 5:19 where we read the victory song of Deborah, we learn that the battle was fought *at Taanach*

276

near the waters of Megiddo. Many hundreds of years later, it was here that Ahaziah, king of Judah, fled and died after being shot be the men of Jehu (2 Kings 9:27). And it was here that King Josiah died at the hands of Pharaoh Necho (2 Kings 23:29; 2 Chronicles 35:22-23). When we examine the imagery of the Song of Deborah in Judges 5, we find that quite a number of those images are echoed in the book of Revelation.

Judges 5	Revelation
The kings came and fought; Then fought the kings of Canaan At Taanach near the waters of Megiddo (5:19)	...which go out to the kings of the whole world, to gather them together for the war of the great day of God, the Almighty (16:16).
	And they gathered them together to the place which in Hebrew is called Har-Magedon (16:16).
The stars fought from heaven, From their courses they fought against Sisera (5:20).	...the stars of the sky fell to the earth, as a fig tree casts its unripe figs when shaken by a great wind (6:13).
The torrent of Kishon swept them away, The ancient torrent, the torrent Kishon (5:21).	And the serpent poured water like a river out of his mouth after the woman, so that he might cause her to be swept away with the flood (12:15).
The mountains quaked at the presence of the LORD, This Sinai, at the presence of the LORD, the God of Israel (5:5).	...and there was a great earthquake, such as there had not been since man came to be upon the earth, so great an earthquake was it, and so mighty (16:18).

Strictly speaking, there is no "Mount Megiddo." It is a bit like describing Mount Miami; anyone who has been to that area knows that it is flat. On the other hand, there are hills in the area of Megiddo including Mount Carmel and this could be a reference to those hills.

Does that mean we must necessarily await some future battle to take place on this site? Perhaps it does. On the other hand, the imagery invoked by this language would be similar to speaking of a final Waterloo. Or for those who may not be so familiar with English and French history, we could invoke the image of a final Watergate. In either case, the language brings to mind a great event that had lasting repercussions upon the world stage. The point is that there is coming a day when the strength of this world will be brought to naught and when the enemies of God's people will be defeated.

Mounce correctly concludes that "wherever it takes place, Armageddon is symbolic of the final overthrow of all the forces of evil by the might and power of God. The great conflict between God and Satan, Christ and Antichrist, good and evil, that lies behind the perplexing course of history will in the end issue in a final struggle in which God will emerge victorious and take with him all who have placed their faith in him" (1997:302).

THE SEVENTH BOWL

> *Then the seventh angel poured out his bowl upon the air, and a loud voice came out of the temple from the throne, saying, "It is done."*
> *18 And there were flashes of lightning and sounds and peals of thunder; and there was a great earthquake, such as there had not been since man came to be upon the earth, so great an earthquake was it, and so mighty. 19 The great city was split into three parts, and the cities of the nations fell. Babylon the great was remembered before God, to give her the cup of the wine of His fierce wrath. 20 And every island fled away, and the mountains were not found. 21 And huge hailstones, about one hundred pounds each, came down from heaven upon men; and men blasphemed God because of the plague of the hail, because its plague was extremely severe. (Revelation 16:17-21).*

It is John who recorded the single word of Jesus as He gave up His life on the cross -- *Tetelestai!* -- "It is finished." Once again John records a single word that is proclaimed -- *Gegonen!* -- "It has become." In both cases, the Greek text consists of a single word. In both cases, it is given with a perfect tense, indicating an action that is meant to have continuing results.

On the cross, Jesus said, "It has been finished!" and the use of the tense indicates that what was accomplished there has results that continue even for today. Here in Revelation, the voice from the temple proclaims, "It is done!" and the use of the tense suggests that the statement will have a continuing effect upon the rest of eternity.

It is interesting to note that the first biblical use of this specific term with this particular tense is found in the Greek translation of Genesis 3:22 where God says, "The man **has become** as one of us..." If that first use marked the expulsion of mankind from the garden of Eden because of sin, this second use marks the completion of God's judgment with regard to these visions of wrath that have marked this central section of the book of Revelation.

We have already seen this same climactic scene played out in the pages of the book of Revelation.

Revelation 11	Revelation 16
The **seventh angel** sounded (11:15).	The **seventh angel** poured out his bowl (16:17).
There were **loud voices** in heaven, saying, "The kingdom of the world has become the kingdom of our Lord and of His Christ; and He will reign forever and ever." (11:15).	A **loud voice** came out of the temple from the throne, saying, "It is done" (16:17).
And the temple of God which is in heaven was opened; and the ark of His covenant appeared in His temple, and there were flashes of **lightning and sounds and peals of thunder** and an **earthquake** and a great hailstorm (11:19).	And there were flashes of **lightning and sounds and peals of thunder**; and there was a great earthquake, such as there had not been since man came to be upon the earth, so great an **earthquake** was it, and so mighty (16:18).
And the **nations** were enraged, and Your **wrath** came, and the time came for the dead to be judged (11:18).	The great city was split into three parts, and the cities of the **nations** fell. Babylon the great was remembered before God, to give her the cup of the wine of His fierce **wrath** (16:19).

Every part of creation is affected in these closing signs of judgment. The reader's attention is taken full circle from the heavens to the earth, from the cites to the islands and mountains before returning once again to the heavens.

1.   Earthly Upheaval: *And there were flashes of lightning and sounds and peals of thunder; and there was a great earthquake, such as there had not been since man came to be upon the earth, so great an earthquake was it, and so mighty (16:18).*

The reference to thunder and lightning calls to mind the presence of the

279

Lord at the giving of the Law on Mount Sinai. This is the fourth time here in the book of Revelation that we have seen this same phenomenon.

- Thunder and sounds and flashes of lightning were seen in John's initial vision of the throne of God in Revelation 4:5.

- At the breaking of the seventh seal and as the seven trumpets were about to be sounded, John experienced peals of thunder and sounds and flashes of lightning and an earthquake (8:5).

- With the sounding of the seventh trumpet, John described flashes of lightning and sounds and peals of thunder and an earthquake and a great hailstorm (11:19).

These references underscore the observation that we have already made; that these series of seven seals and seven trumpets and seven bowls are not to be understood and all taking place consecutively, but that they are in parallel, each ending in the same way with the coming of the Lord.

2.   Fall of Cities: *The great city was split into three parts, and the cities of the nations fell. Babylon the great was remembered before God, to give her the cup of the wine of His fierce wrath (16:19).*

John has already spoken of "the great city" back in Revelation 11:8 where he described how the bodies of the slain witnesses of God would *lie in the street of the great city which mystically is called Sodom and Egypt, where also their Lord was crucified.* Even though he refers to that city as Sodom and Egypt, this is merely symbolic language. John makes this clear when he describes the city as the place where the Lord was crucified. This is a reference to Jerusalem.

Now he again makes reference to the great city. This time he will not call it Sodom or Egypt. This time he will refer to it as Babylon. Some have suggested we ought to take this literally as a reference to the fall of the ancient city of Babylon, but that city had long since ceased to be a major world power. Others have seen it as a veiled reference to Rome, but John has already told us what is the "great city." That is not to say that either the cities of Babylon or Rome are exempt from the judgment of God, for we read that *the cities of the nations fell.* Perhaps the point is that we are to see Jerusalem as the forerunner of the world. What happens to Jerusalem eventually happens to the entire world.

When we read that the great city was split into three parts, it calls to mind a prophetic sign that was given to Ezekiel concerning the fall of Jerusalem. In Ezekiel 5:1-2, the prophet was told to take a razor to his hair and beard and to divide the hair into three parts.

- A third was to be burned with fire.
- A third was to be struck with a sword.
- A third was to be scattered to the wind.

This was a picture of the fate that was to befall Jerusalem in Ezekiel's day. He would see the city destroyed, its inhabitants slain, and the survivors scattered to the wind. Here in the book of Revelation, John says it is going to happen again.

3.   Islands and Mountains: *And every island fled away, and the mountains were not found (16:20).*

The Preterist view of this passage focuses upon Jerusalem as the fulfillment of this passage and sees only the events surrounding the fall of Jerusalem in A.D. 70. But the reference to every island fleeing suggests that this action extends far beyond the events that took place in and around Palestine in the first century. At the same time, we need not take these words with rigid literalism, for we will see similar language when we come to Revelation 20:11 where earth and heaven will be said to flee away from the presence of the Lord who comes in judgment. The language calls to mind the poetry of the Old Testament:

> You covered it with the deep as with a garment;
> The waters were standing above the mountains.
> 7 At Your rebuke they fled,
> At the sound of Your thunder they hurried away.
> 8 The mountains rose; the valleys sank down
> To the place which You established for them.
> 9 You set a boundary that they may not pass over,
> So that they will not return to cover the earth. (Psalm 104:6-9).

Whereas the Psalmist speaks of God's work in creating the earth and the seas, the vision of Revelation speaks of a dismantling of that work. Instead of the sea having boundaries, the islands flee. Instead of the mountains rising, they are not to be found.

4.   Judgment of Hail: *And huge hailstones, about one hundred pounds each, came down from heaven upon men; and men blasphemed God because of the plague of the hail, because its plague was extremely severe (16:21).*

We have already seen hail described by John as a sign of God's judgment (8:7 and 11:19). One of the plagues upon Egypt was a plague of hail.

281

When Joshua led the Israelites into the promised land, God caused great hailstones to fall from heaven upon the armies that had gathered against His people (Joshua 10:11).

One would think that all of these signs and wonders would be enough to turn the heart of the unrepentant, but this is not the case. Rather than changing hearts, these great plagues serve to harden their hearts and even to blaspheme God.

How are we to understand all of these events? Are they literal phenomenon which we are to expect to precede the coming of the Lord? Are they symbolic of God's present wrath against sin? Are both true? The claim is often made that we ought to take the book of Revelation literally. But the truth of the matter is that no one does this. Even those who argue for a literal interpretation are seldom consistent in such a literal handling of the book.

- The vision of Revelation 1 pictures Jesus with a sharp sword coming from His mouth.
- Jesus is said to have seven stars in His right hand (1:20).
- Revelation 5 pictures a lamb standing as though slain (5:6).
- The same chapter speaks of the Lion of the tribe of Judah (5:5).
- We read of a dragon and a beast and their rebellion against the Lord (12-13).
- Chapters 17-18 will speak of a prostitute sitting on the dragon.

No one takes these literally. In each and every case, interpreters of the Bible have understood these to be symbolic. It is in this light that Kraybill suggests "one way to understand these symbols is to read them like political cartoons. Neither Daniel nor John was trying to be funny. But political cartoons make a serious point by reducing nations or rulers or events to a few symbols or characters" (2010:42). The point is that those things that are the most solid in your life are going to be overturned. Those foundations upon which you have built your life are going to collapse. When your world comes crashing down, you can find yourself shaking your fist at God and uttering blasphemies or you can know that God is your rock, your fortress, and your sure foundation.

THE VISION OF THE HARLOT
Revelation 17:1-18

When God wanted to describe the most intimate relationship which He enters with those who follow Him, He used the illustration of marriage. Two people come together and pledge themselves to one another for life. They who were originally from two different families are bound together to form a new family of their own. They are no longer merely two individuals. They have now become one.

This is why unfaithfulness in marriage is so tragic. It is the polluting and the dirtying of that which was good and pure. It is the taking of that "one flesh" relationship and splitting it apart. By the same token, God describes unfaithfulness to Him in terms of spiritual adultery.

> *Now the word of the LORD came to me saying,*
> *2 "Go and proclaim in the ears of Jerusalem, saying,*
> *'Thus says the LORD,*
> *"I remember concerning you the devotion of your youth,*
> *The love of your betrothals,*
> *Your following after Me in the wilderness,*
> *Through a land not sown."'" (Jeremiah 2:1-2).*

The Lord goes on to recount the blessings that He offered to His bride and how He redeemed her from her bondage and set her free.

> *"For long ago I broke your yoke*
> *And tore off your bonds;*
> *But you said, 'I will not serve!'*
> *For on every high hill*
> *And under every green tree*
> *You have lain down as a harlot." (Jeremiah 2:20).*

This theme of the faithfulness of the Lord and the contrasting unfaithfulness of those whom He called to be His people is a prominent theme throughout the prophets. Prostitution was used throughout the Old Testament as a picture of Israel's unfaithfulness. That symbol took on a vivid incarnation when the prophet Hosea was told to take a wife of harlotry and to marry her and have children by her. His subsequent marriage became a living parable to the people of Israel as they were given this vivid picture of how God felt about their spiritual unfaithfulness. In this chapter we are going to see that same image vividly used to speak of the enemies of God's people.

17:1-2	17:3-5	17:6-15	17:16-18
The Harlot introduced	The Harlot described	The Vision explained	Destiny of the Harlot

When we come to verse 5, we will see this great harlot labeled as Babylon the Great, the mother of harlots. This is significant because we have already seen the announcement as early as Revelation 14:8 that Babylon the great is "fallen, fallen." Then again we were told in Revelation 16:19 that "the great city was split into three parts" and that "Babylon the great was remembered before God, to give her the cup of the wine of His fierce wrath." This indicates that we are not to take this chapter as a prophecy of what takes place after the previous seal judgments and trumpet judgments and bowl judgments, but that this is a picture of those same judgments examined from a different perspective and through the lens of different imagery.

INTRODUCTION TO THE GREAT HARLOT

> Then one of the seven angels who had the seven bowls came and spoke with me, saying, "Come here, I will show you the judgment of the great harlot who sits on many waters, 2 with whom the kings of the earth committed acts of immorality, and those who dwell on the earth were made drunk with the wine of her immorality." (Revelation 17:1-2).

John is called to be a witness of judgment. He has been seeing pictures of judgment throughout this book, but this next image will be particularly striking because it is characterized by the image of a woman. We were first introduced to the image of a woman in the message of Jesus to the church at Thyatira. They were warned that they had tolerated the woman Jezebel *who calls herself a prophetess, and she teaches and leads My bond-servants astray so that they commit acts of immorality and eat things sacrificed to idols (Revelation 2:20)*. When we came to Revelation 12, we saw another image of a woman. This time, she represented the nation of Israel which gave birth to the Messiah and was subsequently persecuted by the dragon and forced to flee into the wilderness.

The image of a harlot is a familiar one to the Old Testament. It goes all the way back to the book of Exodus where Israel was warned against entering into treaties or covenants with the people of Canaan, *otherwise you might make a covenant with the inhabitants of the land and they would play the harlot with their gods and sacrifice to their gods (Exodus 34:15; see also Leviticus 17:7; 20:5-6; Numbers 15:39; 25:1; Deuteronomy 31:16; Judges 2:17; 8:27; 1st Chronicles 5:25; 2nd Chronicles 21:11; Psalm 106:39).*

The Old Testament prophets regularly picked up on this theme. Jeremiah described Israel as *a harlot with many lovers* (Jeremiah 3:1) and then goes on to describe how her sister Judah followed in her footsteps and how *she polluted the land and committed adultery with stones and trees* (Jeremiah 3:9). In the same way, Ezekiel gives a graphic portrayal of how Jerusalem played the part of a harlot: *You built yourself a high place at the top of every street and made your beauty abominable, and you spread your legs to every passer-by to multiply your harlotry (Ezekiel 16:25).*

When John describes a harlot *with whom the kings of the earth committed acts of immorality*, he is drawing his description from the pages of Ezekiel who declares that Jerusalem has played the harlot with the Egyptians (Ezekiel 16:26), with the Assyrians (Ezekiel 16:28), and with the Chaldeans (Ezekiel 16:29).

DESCRIPTION OF THE GREAT HARLOT

> *And he carried me away in the Spirit into a wilderness; and I saw a woman sitting on a scarlet beast, full of blasphemous names, having seven heads and ten horns. 4 The woman was clothed in purple and scarlet, and adorned with gold and precious stones and pearls, having in her hand a gold cup full of abominations and of the unclean things of her immorality, 5 and on her forehead a name was written, a mystery, "Babylon the great, the mother of harlots and of the abominations of the earth." (Revelation 17:3-5).*

John is now carried in the Spirit into a wilderness. The last time he made mention of a wilderness was in Revelation 12:14 when the woman who represented Israel fled into the wilderness to escape the attacks of the serpent. In that chapter, the woman who represented Israel had been clothed with the sun and had worn a crown of twelve stars. This woman is presented in a very different way:

- She is clothed in purple and scarlet, the robes of royalty.
- She is adorned with *gold and precious stones and pearls*.
- She has in her hand a golden cup that is filled with abominations and wickedness.
- She has a name on her forehead which is declared to be a mystery. The fact that it is declared to be a mystery tells us that we are not meant to take it at face value. That is, we are not meant to understand this as a literal reference to the city of Babylon on the Euphrates River, but instead, that it has a more symbolic and figurative meaning.

The fact that she is sitting on the scarlet beast has caused many to identify the woman as the city of Rome. We shall see in verse 9 that the seven heads of the beast represent seven mountains or hills and we will note that the city of Rome sat upon seven hills. But we need to recognize that this passage will make a distinction between the woman versus the beast. When we get to verse 16, we will see that the beast hates the woman and seeks to destroy her. Therefore the picture is of a woman who attempts to ride the beast but who, in the end, finds that the beast turns upon her and seeks to devour her.

This is the story of Jerusalem and its destruction at the hands of the Romans in A.D. 70. The same city that once rejected her Messiah and joined forces with the Roman government to have Him put to death found itself, within forty years, surrounded by the legions of that same Roman Empire as they besieged her, tore down her walls, burned her temple, and carried her inhabitants off into captivity.

The coin commemorates the fall of Jerusalem which is pictured as a conquered woman seated before the victorious General Vespasian.

The woman has a name written on her forehead. This is not the first time we have seen writing on a forehead. There were 144,000 who carried the seal of God on their forehead. There was also a mark of the beast whose number was placed upon the foreheads of his people. The name this woman carries is *"Babylon the great, the mother of harlots and of the abominations of the earth."* We have seen Babylon mentioned several times already in this book. Each time it has been called "Babylon the great." It is reminiscent of "the great city which mystically is called Sodom and Egypt, where also their Lord was crucified" (Revelation 11:8).

The spirit of Babylon was being personified in the city of Jerusalem. The great blasphemy was that those people who had been given the word of God and the temple and the prophets did not believe. They rejected the Son of God and decided instead to hold to their religious system.

The Woman in Revelation 12	Woman in Revelation 17
Clothed with the sun, the moon under her feet, and on her head a crown of twelve stars	Clothed in purpose and scarlet and adorned with gold and precious stones and pearls

She was in labor as she was giving birth to the Child	She was drunk with the blood of the saints
She runs from the dragon	She sits on the beast
The dragon seeks to make war with the rest of her offspring	The beast hates the woman and makes her desolate and burns her up with fire

The woman is seen in the role of persecutor. The first persecutions of the early church began in Jerusalem as the religious Jews tried to stamp out the new faith. The world religious systems always persecute the truth. Do you want to know one of the ways to recognize the truth? Look to see who is persecuting whom.

Notice that the world religious system often resembles the truth. As people look at the world religious systems and then at Christianity, they often have trouble telling them apart. The world religious system looks just like the truth to the uninitiated. Only those who have been initiated into the plan of God comprehend the difference between the two women, even when one is persecuting the other.

Today the spirit of Babylon can be seen when the form of our worship becomes more important than the worship itself. It is seen when churches become influenced by liberal philosophy and stop teaching the Bible as the word of God. It is seen when prayer in the public schools is outlawed and when the killing of babies through abortion is justified and when Christian schools come under persecution. The message of this chapter is that Babylon is going to fall.

EXPLANATION OF THE VISION

> *And I saw the woman drunk with the blood of the saints, and with the blood of the witnesses of Jesus. When I saw her, I wondered greatly. 7 And the angel said to me, "Why do you wonder? I will tell you the mystery of the woman and of the beast that carries her, which has the seven heads and the ten horns." (Revelation 17:6-7).*

John is not left to guess what this vision means. An angel will explain it to him. We have seen this happen throughout the book of Revelation. The symbolism within the Bible is explained by the Bible. Many of these symbols have been obvious in their meaning. We saw a lamb standing as though slain and we heard about the Lion of the tribe of Judah and we knew who that was.

Other symbols were explained in the Old Testament. We saw the four horsemen and we saw the two witnesses and the beast and we recognized that these symbols came from the Old Testament and that they had been explained there. Finally, there have been symbols that are new to us. In the first chapter of Revelation, we saw seven golden lampstands and, while we recognized this as an image from the Temple, the context of the passage explained the significance of the image. That is what happens now in this chapter. John sees the vision and then, lest there be any misunderstanding, it is explained to him.

The Symbol	The Meaning of the Symbol
The woman	Babylon the great, the great city which reigns over the kings of the earth (a spiritual title for Jerusalem)
The waters where the woman sits	People and multitudes and nations and tongues
The beast	The world system (explained earlier)
The seven heads of the beast	They are seven mountains on which the woman sits. They are seven kings.
The ten horns of the beast	They are ten kings who have not yet received authority

1. Explanation of the Beast: *"The beast that you saw was, and is not, and is about to come up out of the abyss and go to destruction. And those who dwell on the earth, whose name has not been written in the book of life from the foundation of the world, will wonder when they see the beast, that he was and is not and will come" (Revelation 17:8).*

    This is the same beast we saw back in Revelation 13. The symbolism goes all the way back to the book of Daniel where it represents the world system.

    Notice the contrast between the beast and the Lamb. The Lamb was put to death and then came back to life and is now alive forevermore. The beast was alive and is not and is about to come up out of the abyss only to go to final destruction. What does this mean? It is a picture of Satan and his system. As goes Satan, so goes his world system.

    Someone wrote a book quite a long time ago that had the title, "Satan is Alive and Well on Planet Earth." It was a nice title, but it is wrong. The truth is that Satan is not alive and well. He used to be alive and well, but he was defeated at the cross. It was there that the head of the serpent was crushed. Satan has a new home. It is not planet earth; it is the abyss. The only problem is that he does not stay there. He keeps coming up out of the abyss.

He was seen in Antiochus Epiphanes who came into Jerusalem and erected a statue of himself in the temple. He was seen in Nero who burned Christians at the stake to light his garden parties. He was seen in Titus, the Roman general who burned the temple in 70 A.D. He was seen in Julian the Apostate who tried to turn the Roman Empire back to paganism. He is seen again and again through history, but his end is always the same. In the end, he goes to destruction.

2.   Explanation of the Seven Heads: *"Here is the mind which has wisdom. The seven heads are seven mountains on which the woman sits, 10 and they are seven kings; five have fallen, one is, the other has not yet come; and when he comes, he must remain a little while. 11 The beast which was and is not, is himself also an eighth and is one of the seven, and he goes to destruction" (Revelation 17:9-11).*

The reference to seven mountains or hills (the term is the same in the Greek) hearkens to something that was very familiar in the first century. It is that Rome was a city built upon seven hills.

> *Rome... the city of the seven hills.* Cicero, c. 76 BC, Letters to Atticus 6:5.

> *...glorious Rome shall bound her empire with earth, her pride by heaven, and with a single city's wall shall enclose her seven hills.* - Virgil, c. 40 B.C.; Aeneid IV.

> *...sing the hymn in honor of the gods who love the Seven Hills. ...ne're mayest thou be able to view aught greater than the city of Rome!* - Horace, c. 35 BC, A Secular Hymn, The Odes and Epodes, p. 351.

> *The city high-throned on the seven hills, the queen of all the world... Rome take thy triumph...* - Propertius, c. 20 BC, The Elegies 3:11.

> *...Rome, that gazes about from her seven hills upon the whole world - Rome, the place of empire and the gods.* - Ovid, c. 12 BC, Tristia 1:70.

> *...may you see the seven sovereign hills and take the measure of all Rome...* - Martial, 40-104 AD, Epigrams 4:64.

This designation of the "city on seven hills" was found, not only among Roman writers, but also among Jewish writers.

> *Among most men, and robbery of temples.*
> *And then shall, after these, appear of men*
> *The tenth race, when the earth-shaking Lightener*
> *Shall break the zeal for idols and shall shake*
> *The people of seven-hilled Rome, and riches great*
> *Shall perish, burned by Vulcan's fiery flame.* (Jewish Sibylline Oracles, Book II, lines 15-20, 150 BC - 300 AD).

If the seven hills are a designation of the city of Rome, does it follow that this city of Babylon is really a reference to Rome? Not necessarily. Remember that the image is of a woman who is riding upon a beast. This means the beast and the woman are one and the same. Indeed, when we get to verse 16 we shall see that both the beast and its horns will hate the harlot and will make her desolate and naked. This suggests there is a strong difference between the identity of the beast and its heads versus the harlot. The picture is of the harlot who attempts to ride the beast but instead find that it turns on her and seeks to devour her.

In addition to being a picture of the seven hills of Rome, these seven hills are said to refer to seven kings. From the vantage point of when John is writing, some of these kings are from his past, one is present, and one is still to come. Matching these kings with names from history would be easier if we knew exactly when John had his vision and exactly when the book of Revelation was written. The first six emperors of Rome were as follows:

(1)   Julius Caesar
(2)   Octavius Augustus
(3)   Tiberius
(4)   Caligula
(5)   Claudius
(6)   Nero

Under this scenario, the five which have fallen would be the first five of the Roman emperors. The one that "now is" would be Nero. The one that would come for a little while would be fulfilled in the three men who tried to take the title of emperor for themselves following the death of Nero in 69 A.D. They were Galba, Otho, and Vitellius and each reigned "for a little while." By the end of that year, it was the Roman general Vespasian who had taken the rule of Rome; this was the same Vespasian who had put down the Jewish revolt and who left his son, Titus, to complete the conquest of Jerusalem in 70 A.D.

The beast that is to come could be a reference to Vespasian and Titus, the father and son team who brought an end to the Jewish revolt and eventually destroyed Jerusalem and the temple. The only difficulty with this view is that it would mandate that the book of Revelation was written during the reign of Nero and we do not have conclusive evidence either way as to when the book was written.

3.   Explanation of the Ten Horns: *"The ten horns which you saw are ten kings who have not yet received a kingdom, but they receive authority as kings with the beast for one hour. 13 These have one purpose, and they give their power and authority to the beast. 14 These will wage war against the Lamb, and the Lamb will overcome them, because He is Lord of lords and King of kings, and those who are with Him are the called and chosen and faithful"* (Revelation 17:12-14).

We are now confronted with the riddle of the ten horns. They represent ten kings, though as John writes his book, they have not yet received a kingdom. When they do receive a kingdom, they will be made kings for a short time, but it will be the beast who gives them their authority. In the letter to the church at Smyrna, Jesus spoke of a tribulation that would involve ten days (Revelation 2:10). It is conceivable that these ten kings are leaders of that tribulation. Accordingly, it has been suggested that these ten kings point to the various Roman emperors who oversaw ten periods of persecution against the early church in the years before the coming of Constantine. We read that they *will wage war against the Lamb, and the Lamb will overcome them.* This is the message of Revelation, repeated once again. It is that Jesus is going to win. No matter what the opposition, no matter how dark things look, He will overcome.

4.   Explanation of the Waters: *And he said to me, "The waters which you saw where the harlot sits, are peoples and multitudes and nations and tongues"* (Revelation 17:15).

The final piece of the puzzle are the waters. They refer to people and multitudes and nations and tongues. They flow everywhere.

THE DESTINY OF THE WOMAN

"And the ten horns which you saw, and the beast, these will hate the harlot and will make her desolate and naked, and will eat her flesh and will burn her up with fire. 17 For God has put it in their hearts to execute His purpose by having a common purpose, and by giving their kingdom to the beast, until the words

of God will be fulfilled. 18 The woman whom you saw is the great city, which reigns over the kings of the earth." (Revelation 17:16-18).

Now the reader is given the explanation of the various parts of this vision. The woman who has been the focus of this vision is identified as "the great city." The description takes us back to the Old Testament where the city of Jerusalem was described as "this great city" in a context that speaks of many nations passing by and seeing its destruction (Jeremiah 22:8). Furthermore, Revelation 11:8 described the dead bodies of the two witnesses lying "in the street of the great city which mystically is called Sodom and Egypt, where also their Lord was crucified."

The problem with this identification is that this city is said to reign over the kings of the earth. That would seem to preclude the city of Jerusalem since Jerusalem was a relatively minor city in the eyes of the kings of other nations. The answer is seen in how this reference to the "kings of the earth" is used by the Old Testament writers. In particular, this phrase is used in Psalm 2:

Why are the nations in an uproar
And the peoples devising a vain thing?
*2 **The kings of the earth** take their stand*
And the rulers take counsel together
Against the LORD and against His Anointed, saying,
3 "Let us tear their fetters apart
And cast away their cords from us!" (Psalm 2:1-3).

What makes this passage so significant is that it was quoted by the early church to refer to those who had conspired with the Jewish authorities to have Jesus crucified and to refer to those same Jewish authorities who continued to persecute the church. After being arrested, John and Peter met with the church who cited this passage in their prayer and then went on to elaborate:

For truly in this city there were gathered together against Your holy servant Jesus, whom You anointed, both Herod and Pontius Pilate, along with the Gentiles and the peoples of Israel, 28 to do whatever Your hand and Your purpose predestined to occur. (Acts 4:27-28).

In the mind of those Christians, Herod and Pontius Pilate along with the leaders of Israel represented the kings of the earth and the rulers who had acted against Jesus, the Lord's Anointed. They had come together at the behest of the leaders of the Jews to nail Jesus to the cross and in this way, it could be said that the city had exercised its reign over them. Though they had acted out of their own individual motives, it was understood that their actions had been that which God's hand and God's purpose had predestined to occur. Here in Revelation 17, we find that same

292

factor of God's predestined plan coming to pass as He *has put it in their hearts to execute His purpose by having a common purpose.* That purpose involves their own judgment which is brought about at their own hands.

You would think that the Satanic world system and the world religious system would get along. They do, but only for a time. Eventually the day comes when they turn against each other. This was fulfilled in 70 A.D. when the Roman legions turned their banners against the center of religious Judaism. Prior to that time, the Jewish religious system had conspired together with the governor of Rome to put Jesus to death. They had worked together to persecute and to destroy the infant church. But when the woman had completed her task, the beast had no more use for her.

In conclusion, the woman represents the city of Jerusalem. She is the wife who has turned to prostitution. She is the beloved one who turned from the love of her Lord to run after other lovers. She is seen riding on the beast; she is trying to ride on the political strength of Rome. But the lady who rides on the tiger will soon end up inside her. This will take place in 70 A.D.

When the Roman soldiers slaughtered thousands of Jews before the doors of the temple, they were only a stone's throw away from the place when a Jewish crowd had cried out to Pilate, "His blood be upon our heads and upon the heads of our children" (Matthew 27:25). This was the nation to whom God had sent the prophets, the people who had been entrusted with the Scriptures, the city, and the temple of God.

> *"Jerusalem, Jerusalem, who kills the prophets and stones those who are sent to her! How often I wanted to gather your children together, the way a hen gathers her chicks under her wings, and you were unwilling. 38 Behold, your house is being left to you desolate!" (Matthew 23:37-38).*

There is a warning here for me. It is that I take care that I do not follow in the footsteps of the adulterous wife. It is a call for me to remain faithful to the Lord, or else my house might be left desolate to me, too.

THE JUDGMENT OF THE HARLOT
Revelation 18:1-24

In the last chapter, we were introduced to the figure of the harlot. She was described in graphic detail as a prostitute seated on a seven-headed dragon whom she is attempting to ride. As we come to this chapter, our focus will still be upon the harlot, but now it will be specifically upon her future destiny.

Revelation 17	Revelation 18
Babylon Described	Babylon Destroyed

We have already been introduced to another city in the book of Revelation that was given a mystical identity. It was in Revelation 11:8 that we saw "the great city which mystically is called Sodom and Egypt." That verse went on to identify this city as the place where the Lord was crucified. It is a reference to Jerusalem.

Does this chapter also speak of Jerusalem? We are not given such a clear indication that it is, but the Jerusalem motif has already been established within this book and it will continue on through to the end of the book where, in contrast to the earthly Jerusalem that is described as a spiritual Sodom and Egypt, we will see a heavenly Jerusalem where God Himself resides. The destruction of the city which is mystically and mysteriously described as Babylon will be described in three parts.

Revelation 18					
1-3	4-8	9-10	11-17	18-20	21-24
Warning of Babylon's Fall		Lament over Babylon			Sign of the Stone
Oracle against Babylon	Reason for the judgment	Kings	Merchants	Ship Masters	

In the Jewish mind, the center of the world was Jerusalem. It was here that the temple sacrifices were offered. It was here that the house of God stood. For over a thousand years, the Jews had seen the city of Jerusalem as the symbol of their identity. In the days of the Babylonian Captivity, the psalmist sang about Jerusalem:

> *If I forget you, O Jerusalem,*
> *May my right hand forget her skill.*
> *6 May my tongue cling to the roof of my mouth*

If I do not remember you,
If I do not exalt Jerusalem
Above my chief joy. (Psalm 137:5-6).

To this day, the city of Jerusalem is called "the holy city." Thus, it is with some wonderment that we suggested in the last chapter that it is Jerusalem that fills the image of the adulterous woman. That theme continues into this chapter as we see the fall of that city which bears the title of Babylon the Great.

ORACLE AGAINST BABYLON

After these things I saw another angel coming down from heaven, having great authority, and the earth was illumined with his glory. 2 And he cried out with a mighty voice, saying, "Fallen, fallen is Babylon the great! She has become a dwelling place of demons and a prison of every unclean spirit, and a prison of every unclean and hateful bird. 3 For all the nations have drunk of the wine of the passion of her immorality, and the kings of the earth have committed acts of immorality with her, and the merchants of the earth have become rich by the wealth of her sensuality." (Revelation 18:1-3).

The chapter opens with an angel. John has already seen seven angels with seven bowls of wrath bringing the judgment of God upon the earth. One of those seven angels had then introduced this new series of visions involving a prostitute. Now another angel is introduced.

Have you noticed how involved angels are in the affairs of men? We have seen this involvement all throughout John's vision. Even we who believe in the existence of angels seem to feel that they are long ago and far away. We believe that God used to do miracles and involve Himself in the works of men, but we often act as though He has put His cellphone on vibrate and isn't currently taking calls. This is reflected in our prayer life. We pray answering machine prayers. You know what I mean. You call someone to talk to them and you hear a recording telling you to leave a short message that you hope will be heard sometime in the future. All too often, we pray like that. We give these short little messages to God and we hope that His will get around to listening. But the truth is that God doesn't use messaging; He always hears. Indeed, He hears before we even pray.

An oracle is pronounced against the city that is represented by the name of Babylon. The city is declared to be fallen. This fallen state is repeated: Fallen, fallen! When you want to affirm the truthfulness of a statement in Hebrew, you say it twice. This is not Hebrew, but the point is still made that this is a firm oracle. The oracle goes on to state the reasons for Babylon's fall. It is because this city has become thoroughly polluted.

When a first century Christian looked at Jerusalem, it did not appear to be polluted. There were Scriptures that were being read and sacrifices that were being made and prayers that were being voiced. The problem was that they had the ritual without the reality. There is nothing wrong with rituals. The rituals that were practiced in the temple in Jerusalem had been ordained by God. They were good rituals, but they were only good because there was a reality behind them.

When the priest took an offering of incense into the temple and sprinkled it on the altar so that the sweet smelling smoke rose into the sky, it illustrated the reality that our prayers ascend to God. When a lamb was slaughtered on the altar, it illustrated that God would one day provide a substitute to give Himself for our sins. When the high priest took the blood of calves and goats into the Holy of Holies to sprinkle it on the Mercy Seat, it illustrated the reality that the Son of God would offer His own blood for our sins.

The Jews observed all of these rituals faithfully. But when the Son of God came to earth to present Himself as the reality behind the ritual, what did they do? They took Him and they crucified Him. They were more interested in preserving their rituals than they were in seeing the reality. As a result, Jerusalem was no longer the city of God. Rather, she was the spiritual equivalent of Sodom and Gomorrah and Babylon. Like those cities before her, she was destined to come under the judgment of God. Notice the parallelism:

> A _dwelling place_ of **demons**
> A _prison_ of every **unclean spirit**
> A _prison_ of every **unclean and hateful bird**

This threefold pattern continues into the next portion of the passage:

> _All the nations have drunk of the wine of the passion of her_ **immorality**
> _The kings of the earth have committed acts of_ **immorality** _with her_
> _The merchants of the earth have become rich by the wealth of her_ **sensuality**

The language of this oracle is borrowed from the book of Jeremiah where the prophet calls for judgment against the original Babylon. Now those same words are echoed against this new Babylon and her spiritual immorality. Though actual immorality might also be in view, we should remember that the Old Testament often utilizes the image of physical immorality as a picture of spiritual unfaithfulness. Indeed, it might be argued that one will not exist without the other.

THE REASON FOR JUDGMENT

> *I heard another voice from heaven, saying, "Come out of her, my people, so that you will not participate in her sins and receive of her plagues; 5 for her sins have piled up as high as heaven, and God has remembered her iniquities. 6 Pay her back even as she has paid, and give back to her double according to her deeds; in the cup which she has mixed, mix twice as much for her. 7 To the degree that she glorified herself and lived sensuously, to the same degree give her torment and mourning; for she says in her heart, 'I sit as a queen and I am not a widow, and will never see mourning.' 8 For this reason in one day her plagues will come, pestilence and mourning and famine, and she will be burned up with fire; for the Lord God who judges her is strong." (Revelation 18:4-8).*

The harlot wishes to picture herself as a queen rather than as a widow. This is obviously meant to be a wrong self-image, for the truth is that she is really a widow rather than a queen. To what does this refer? In what way is she a widow? Perhaps the idea is that she is a widow because she has murdered her husband. This is a reference to the way Jerusalem conspired to have Jesus put to death.

In Revelation 17-18 we have a graphic picture of the prostitute who is drunk on the blood of the saints. In Revelation 18:4, there is the warning, "Come out of her, my people, that you may not participate in her sins and that you may not receive of her plagues." Notice to whom the warning is given. It is given to *my people*. It is given to the people of God. They are warned to depart from the woman and what she represents before the coming of the judgment that is to befall here. Then we turn the page and, in chapter 19, we find ourselves invited to a wedding. Again there is a woman. But this time she is a bride.

The warning to "come out of her" is an echo of the same warning that was given by Jesus in His Olivet Discourse. It was the week before His crucifixion that He gathered His disciples to the slopes of the Mount of Olives overlooking the city of Jerusalem and gave this warning:

> *"But when you see Jerusalem surrounded by armies, then recognize that her desolation is near. 21 Then those who are in Judea must flee to the mountains, and those who are in the midst of the city must leave, and those who are in the country must not enter the city; 22 because these are days of vengeance, so that all things which are written will be fulfilled.*
> *23 "Woe to those who are pregnant and to those who are nursing babies in those days; for there will be great distress upon*

the land and wrath to this people; 24 and they will fall by the edge of the sword, and will be led captive into all the nations; and Jerusalem will be trampled under foot by the Gentiles until the times of the Gentiles are fulfilled." (Luke 21:20-24).

Christians in the early church took this prophecy very literally. To understand their reaction, you need to know a little about the events that led up to the fall of Jerusalem. When the Jewish revolt began in Jerusalem in 66 A.D., there was a large population of Christians living in the city. The revolt fanned into open flames of rebellion as the Roman garrison was slaughtered.

A Roman legion was sent down from Syria under the command of Certius Gallus. He surrounded Jerusalem and even managed to enter into the city. However, the Jews counterattacked before the walls of the temple and he was driven out. The Jews chased the Romans and attacked them in the pass of Beth-horon, inflicting terrible losses and capturing the Roman standards. In the face of this victory, the Jews returned to Jerusalem rejoicing over the way they had gained their independence.

When news of this revolt arrived in the courts of Nero, Rome's best general was ordered to Palestine. His name was Vespasian. From 67 to 68 A.D., he fought against the Jews, subjugating Galilee and Samaria in a series of bloody battles. Then, in late 68 A.D., the emperor Nero committed suicide. He had left no surviving heir and this immediately created a power struggle among those who would be emperor. After three different would-be emperors had come and gone, Vespasian pulled back his forces and set sail for Rome. The Jews were ecstatic, believing they had won their independence against Rome's finest general. However, the reaction of the Christian community living in Judea was quite different. Remembering the warnings of Jesus, they evacuated the area. Eusebius tells us the story:

> But the people of the church in Jerusalem had been commanded by a revelation, vouchsafed to approved men there before the war, to leave the city and to dwell in a certain town of Perea called Pella. And when those that believed in Christ had come thither from Jerusalem, then, as if the royal city of the Jews and the whole land of Judea were entirely destitute of holy men, the judgment of God at length overtook those who had committed such outrages against Christ and his apostles, and totally destroyed that generation of impious men (2005:1:5).

When Vespasian's son, Titus, surrounded Jerusalem in January of 70 A.D., effectively trapping the inhabitants within the city, the Christians had already "come out of her."

I want to suggest that there is a wonderful invitation here. It is an invitation to all who identify with the prostitute, with all who are of unbelief. It is an invitation to "come out of her," to come to faith in Christ so that they will find themselves transformed from a prostitute into a spotless bride. But with that invitation is a sober warning.

Pay her back even as she has paid (18:6): The judgment against Jerusalem was especially harsh. The reason it was so harsh was because she had been given so much light. Jesus Himself had spoken in her temple. She had heard the preaching of Peter and John. The testimony of Stephan was heard within her walls. She had witnessed the miraculous power of the Holy Spirit working in the church, yet she had rejected the truth.

For this reason in one day her plagues will come, pestilence and mourning and famine, and she will be burned up with fire (18:8): The destruction of Jerusalem in A.D. 70 was one of the most terrible events in history. The siege began in January and lasted for eight months. During that time, Titus built a wall around the city so that no one could come in or go out. Anyone caught trying to escape the city was crucified on this wall. Within a short time, the city was reduced to famine and there were even cases of cannibalism. Josephus tells the story of a woman who was reduced to eating the body of her infant son, only to be interrupted by a roving band of men who burst upon her in their search for food. In the end, the Romans broke through into the city and burnt the temple to the ground. The prophecy of Jesus regarding not one stone being left upon another was so completely fulfilled that scholars today argue about exactly where on the mountain the temple was located.

LAMENT OVER THE WOMAN

John now takes us into a series of lamentations. These laments are issued from various people of all sorts of society, whether kings or merchants or even passengers and sailors aboard ships. The lament is patterned after Ezekiel's lamentation over Tyre (Ezekiel 27). Just as that pagan city had once been judged by God, so also Jerusalem was judged.

1.   The Lament of the Kings of the Earth: *"And the kings of the earth, who committed acts of immorality and lived sensuously with her, will weep and lament over her when they see the smoke of her burning, 10 standing at a distance because of the fear of her torment, saying, 'Woe, woe, the great city, Babylon, the strong city! For in one hour your judgment has come.'"* (Revelation 18:9-10).

This is a reference back to Revelation 17:2 where we first read of how the kings of the earth had engaged in acts of immorality with the woman.

They now look at the destruction of the city and lament. This description echoes the words of the Book of Lamentations in describing the destruction of Jerusalem at the hands of Nebuchadnezzar.

> *The kings of the earth did not believe,*
> *Nor did any of the inhabitants of the world,*
> *That the adversary and the enemy*
> *Could enter the gates of Jerusalem (Lamentations 4:12).*

In both cases, we can see the unexpectedness of the judgment. The strong city became a weak city and it happened in a single hour. This will be a refrain echoed through this chapter.

- The kings of the earth cry: *In **one hour** your judgment has come. (18:10).*
- The lament is made by the merchants: *In **one hour** such great wealth has been laid waste! (18:17).*
- The sailors and the ship's captains mourn: *In **one hour** she has been laid waste! (18:19).*

This is a warning to us of the uncertainty of the future. Perhaps things are going good in your life. You have that promotion for which you were looking and your family is together and you are enjoying good health. It can all change. How do you handle change? How do you react to life detours? You are going in a certain direction in life and then suddenly you are forced to make a detour. Do you see such events with irritation or as God's redirection?

2.   The Lament of the Merchants of the Earth: *"And the merchants of the earth weep and mourn over her, because no one buys their cargoes any more-- 12 cargoes of gold and silver and precious stones and pearls and fine linen and purple and silk and scarlet, and every kind of citron wood and every article of ivory and every article made from very costly wood and bronze and iron and marble, 13 and cinnamon and spice and incense and perfume and frankincense and wine and olive oil and fine flour and wheat and cattle and sheep, and cargoes of horses and chariots and slaves and human lives. 14 The fruit you long for has gone from you, and all things that were luxurious and splendid have passed away from you and men will no longer find them. 15 The merchants of these things, who became rich from her, will stand at a distance because of the fear of her torment, weeping and mourning, 16 saying, 'Woe, woe, the great city, she who was clothed in fine linen and purple and scarlet, and adorned with gold and precious stones and pearls; 17 for in one hour such great wealth has been laid waste!'" (Revelation 18:11-17a).*

The emphasis in the section of the lament is upon material possessions. It is not that material possessions are bad in themselves, but they can easily become the source of coveting. There is an old saying that whatever you own owns you. Jesus had something to say about this.

> *Then He said to them, "Beware, and be on your guard against every form of greed; for not even when one has an abundance does his life consist of his possessions." (Luke 12:15).*

He then went on to tell a story about a man who was rich in material possessions. His problem was that he had so much that he had no place to store all of those possessions, so he set about building larger storage places. Great effort and great expense was put forth to achieve this goal and, when it was all done, the man died. The point is that he died without ever actually enjoying any of the fruit of his labor. He is like the man who worked all his life to build up a large retirement, only to die the day he actually retired. Henry Fielding once said that if you make money your god, it will plague you like the devil. God has a judgment prepared for those who place their trust in riches. It is to do away with them.

3.   The Lament of the Shipmaster, Passenger, and Sailor: *"And every shipmaster and every passenger and sailor, and as many as make their living by the sea, stood at a distance, 18 and were crying out as they saw the smoke of her burning, saying, 'What city is like the great city?' 19 And they threw dust on their heads and were crying out, weeping and mourning, saying, 'Woe, woe, the great city, in which all who had ships at sea became rich by her wealth, for in one hour she has been laid waste!'" (Revelation 18:17b-19).*

The reference to shipmasters and sailors is unexpected when we think of a lament on the fall of Jerusalem, for that city is located in the mountains and far from the sea. But the vision does not place the city near the sea and instead speaks of how the shipmasters, passengers, and sailors *stood at a distance*. Likewise, Ezekiel 27:18 speaks of how Judah and the land of Israel were trading partners with seagoing people like the Phoenicians.

THE JOY OF HEAVEN

> *"Rejoice over her, O heaven, and you saints and apostles and prophets, because God has pronounced judgment for you against her." (Revelation 18:20).*

In the midst of all these woes, there is also rejoicing. The rejoicing comes because God's righteous judgment has been accomplished. This is to be the attitude of the Christian. He is called to rejoice over the judgment of evil because that judgment is on our behalf.

Evil has no right to exist. That is not a popular concept. We have been saturated with a live and let live philosophy, but such a philosophy is in itself evil. It presents a world without absolutes; a world in which nothing is really right or wrong. Too often we have swallowed the world's thinking. That is why we often cringe when the Bible speaks of judgment.

THE SIGN OF THE STONE

> *Then a strong angel took up a stone like a great millstone and threw it into the sea, saying, "So will Babylon, the great city, be thrown down with violence, and will not be found any longer. 22 And the sound of harpists and musicians and flute-players and trumpeters will not be heard in you any longer; and no craftsman of any craft will be found in you any longer; and the sound of a mill will not be heard in you any longer; 23 and the light of a lamp will not shine in you any longer; and the voice of the bridegroom and bride will not be heard in you any longer; for your merchants were the great men of the earth, because all the nations were deceived by your sorcery. 24 And in her was found the blood of prophets and of saints and of all who have been slain on the earth." (Revelation 18:21-24).*

John sees another angel; he is described as a "strong angel." This angel has a great stone that resembles a millstone. A millstone was a heavy boulder with rounded edges, giving it the shape of a thick wheel. It was used by farmers to crush grain, grinding it into flour. But this millstone is not crushing grain; the angel takes this millstone and throws it into the sea.

What happens when you throw a millstone into the sea? It sinks and it sinks fast. You don't see too many millstones floating in the sea. In the same way, when the Lord's heavy hand of judgment comes against a city or a people or a nation, they go down and they go down quickly and completely.

There is an astonishing parallel in language between the language of Jeremiah 51 that tells of the fall of Babylon versus the language of Revelation 17-18 that speaks of the fall of spiritual Babylon.

Jeremiah 51	Revelation 17-18
O you who dwell by **many waters**, Abundant in treasures, Your end has come, The measure of your end (Jeremiah 51:13).	And one of the seven angels who had the seven bowls came and spoke with me, saying, "Come here, I shall show you the judgment of the great harlot who sits on **many waters**" (Revelation 17:1).
Babylon has been a golden cup in the hand of the LORD, Intoxicating all the earth. **The nations have drunk of her wine**; Therefore the nations are going mad. (Jeremiah 51:7).	...with whom the kings of the earth committed *acts of* immorality, and **those who dwell on the earth were made drunk with the wine** of her immorality (Revelation 17:2).
The mighty men of Babylon have ceased fighting, They stay in the strongholds; Their strength is exhausted, They are becoming *like* women; **Their dwelling places are set on fire**, The bars of her *gates* are broken (Jeremiah 51:30).	And the ten horns which you saw, and the beast, these will hate the harlot and will make her desolate and naked, and will eat her flesh and **will burn her up with fire** (Revelation 17:16)
Flee from the midst of Babylon, And each of you save his life! Do not be destroyed in her punishment, For this is the LORD's time of vengeance; He is going to render recompense to her (Jeremiah 51:6). **Come forth from her midst**, My people, And each of you save yourselves From the fierce anger of the LORD (Jeremiah 51:45).	And I heard another voice from heaven, saying, "**Come out of her**, my people, that you may not participate in her sins and that you may not receive of her plagues" (Revelation 18:4).
"Then **heaven** and earth and all that is in them will **shout for joy over Babylon**, For the destroyers will come to her from the north," Declares the LORD (Jeremiah 51:48).	**Rejoice over her, O heaven**, and you saints and apostles and prophets, because God has pronounced judgment for you against her (Revelation 18:20).

"And it will come about as soon as you finish reading this scroll, you will tie **a stone** to it and throw it into the middle of the Euphrates, 64 and say, 'Just so shall **Babylon sink down** and **not rise again**, because of the calamity that I am going to bring upon her; and they will become exhausted.'" Thus far are the words of Jeremiah (Jeremiah 51:63-64).	And a strong angel took up **a stone** like a great millstone and threw it into the sea, saying, "Thus will **Babylon, the great city, be thrown** down with violence, and will **not be found any longer**." (Revelation 18:21).

The city of Babylon was destroyed following the prophecy of Jeremiah and it has not since risen to the status of a world power. What then shall we make of the prophecy of Revelation 17-18 that speaks of the fall of a city that is designated as Babylon and which is couched in the same terms as Jeremiah's prediction of that city's fall?

I believe that what we have in Revelation 17-18 is the fall of a city that has taken on the spiritual characteristics of ancient Babylon. It is a city that has set herself up in rebellion against God, much as the first Babylon was built as a sign of rebellion.

- It is a city that prostituted herself with the kings of the earth (17:2).
- The city is pictured as a woman (17:3). We have already seen a picture of a symbolic woman back in chapter 12. She was a representation of the nation of Israel.
- This time, the woman is pictured as sitting on a scarlet beast with seven heads and ten horns. These are explained in verse 10 where we read that the seven horns are seven kings; *five have fallen, one is, the other has not yet come; and when he comes, he must remain a little while*. This tells us that these kings are not to be found at sometime in the future, but were kings who were contemporary with John.
- The woman is pictured as being *drunk with the blood of the saints, and with the blood of the witnesses of Jesus* (17:6).

To whom does this blasphemous city refer? I believe it has application to all of the kingdoms of this world who reject Jesus Christ as Lord and Savior. The most immediate application would have been first century Jerusalem, the city that prostituted herself and joined in league with her hated Roman oppressors in order to put her Messiah to death.

The picture of Jerusalem as a harlot should not surprise us, for it is a common theme in the Old Testament. We often read of the indictment that Israel has played the part of a harlot (Psalm 106:39; Jeremiah 2:20; 3:1-10; Ezekiel 16; the entire book of Hosea).

> *How the faithful city has become a harlot,*
> *She who was full of justice!*
> *Righteousness once lodged in her,*
> *But now murderers. (Isaiah 1:21).*

This chapter closes with the sober condemnation: *And in her was found the blood of prophets and of saints and of all who have been slain on the earth" (18:24).* This is what the Jews called for at the trial of Jesus. When Pilate offered to release Him, those who had gathered cried out, "His blood be upon us and on our children!" (Matthew 27:25). It was to be in that same place that the forces of Titus would break through to slaughter thousands of the Jewish people.

THE HALLELUJAH CHORUS
Revelation 19:1-10

Have you ever heard Handel's Messiah? There is something truly thrilling as the choir and the orchestra break into the Hallelujah Chorus. Your heart seems to swell up inside you as the music lifts you up and carries you along to its thunderous climax. This chapter is like that. Indeed, this chapter provides not only the inspiration for that musical score, but even the words of the famed chorus are taken from these verses.

The last three chapters of Revelation have been full of gloom and doom and death and despair. We have seen the wrath of God poured out again and again upon the unbelieving world. But now there is a change. The mood has suddenly changed. We have gone through the darkness and we have come to the light.

There is a principle here. Things are often going to get bad before they get good, but once they get good, you can look back at the bad times and say that it was worth it. Mothers know that instinctively. They go through the pain of childbirth, but then they come to the other side and they hold that precious little life in their arms and they see that the gain was worth the pain.

This is important for you to know because it will help you to make it through the bad times. We are living in bad times. We are living in the days when we are seeing the wrath of God at work. We are seeing disease and earthquakes and wars and rumors of wars and crime and all manner of unrighteousness. You need to know that there is coming a day when it will all change. You need to fix your eyes on those coming days.

> *...fixing our eyes on Jesus, the author and perfecter of faith, who for the joy set before Him endured the cross, despising the shame, and has sat down at the right hand of the throne of God. 3 For consider Him who has endured such hostility by sinners against Himself, so that you will not grow weary and lose heart. (Hebrews 12:2-3).*

Notice how Jesus made it through the bad times. He looked for the good time that was to follow. That is what gave Jesus the strength to endure the cross. That is what will give you the strength to endure your cross.

There will be four "Hallelujahs" in this passage. The word "Hallelujah" is actually not a Greek word. It is borrowed from the Hebrew language and means "praise the Lord" (*Hallel* is "praise" and *Jah* is the shortened form of "Yahweh"). Each one of these Hallelujahs will begin the stanza of a song.

19:1-2	19:3	19:4-5	19:6-8
Praises God for His judgment against Babylon	Praises God that His judgment is eternal	Calls for all of God's people to praise Him	Praises God for His marriage to His bride

For several chapters we have seen men blaspheming the name of the Lord. Now we are going to see men praising Him. As I was first studying this passage and writing the first draft for this book, I had to fly up to Jacksonville on business. It was a long time ago and it was the same day that United Airlines Flight 232 had crashed in Iowa.

I had my Bible open to this chapter and I was writing some of the thoughts that I have just shared about the bad times that Christians go through when the plane flew into a great cloud bank. I was seated next to the window, so I could see the dark storm clouds and the occasional flashes of lightning. The ride began to get a little bumpy to the point where I could no longer write legibly.

Suddenly, the plane burst from the clouds and into the clear. A golden sun was casting its molten rays off the shimmering lakes of northern Florida in a majestic display of color as the St. John's River snaked its lazy way across the breathtaking panorama. That is what heaven will be like. One of these days, we are going to break out of the storm clouds and we will catch our breath at the glorious scene. Instead of the sun, our attention will be riveted to the Son.

THE FIRST STANZA

> *After these things I heard something like a loud voice of a great multitude in heaven, saying, "Hallelujah! Salvation and glory and power belong to our God; 2 because His judgments are true and righteous; for He has judged the great harlot who was corrupting the earth with her immorality, and He has avenged the blood of His bond-servants on her." (Revelation 19:1-2).*

As John stands listening to the oracle of judgments against Babylon, the sound of a great crowd comes to his ears. Have you ever heard a great crowd? You cannot hear what a great crowd is saying because they are usually all saying something different. This crowd is different. It is unified. They are all saying the same thing. They are all praising the Lord. The church is seeing a lot of disunity these days. That is because they are talking about all sorts of side issues. But when the church gets together and praises the Lord, there will be unity.

307

The reason we are called to praise the Lord is *because His judgments are true and righteous (19:2)*. We usually like to praise the Lord because of His love and grace and kindness. But we should also praise Him because of His truth and righteousness and judgments. In Revelation 6:10, we saw the souls of those who had been slain for the word of God crying out for vengeance. Now we see that vengeance carried out on their behalf. How was this judgment carried out? We saw the answer back in Revelation 17:16-17 where the ten horns executed the purpose of God by bringing judgment against the harlot.

This is an important distinction. We often think of the Lord's judgment coming with a great, visible hand coming down out of the sky, but His judgment often takes the form of the actions of intermediaries. In this case, there are pagan leaders who act out of their own motives while, unbeknown to them, they are really fulfilling the judgment of God.

THE SECOND STANZA

> *And a second time they said, "Hallelujah! Her smoke rises up forever and ever." (Revelation 19:3)*.

The second stanza focuses on the eternal nature of the judgment of God. That initial judgment was seen in 70 A.D. when the Roman general Titus destroyed the city of Jerusalem and burned the temple to the ground. It was seen again in 135 A.D. when the Romans crushed the Bar-Kochba revolts and banished all Jews from the area of Jerusalem. I imagine that it is still seen today where there stands a Muslim mosque on the site of the original temple.

But that is only a pale reflection of the ultimate judgment that all men face. There is coming a day when God's final judgment will take place and the results of that judgment will be eternal in nature.

THE THIRD STANZA

> *And the twenty-four elders and the four living creatures fell down and worshiped God who sits on the throne saying, "Amen. Hallelujah!" 5 And a voice came from the throne, saying, "Give praise to our God, all you His bond-servants, you who fear Him, the small and the great." (Revelation 19:4-5)*.

The twenty-four elders and the four living creatures were first introduced to us in Revelation 4. Since then, we have seen them a number of times. This is the last time they will be mentioned. They began with songs of praise to the Lord and now they close out their part in this vision by calling all men to praise the Lord.

THE FOURTH STANZA

> *Then I heard something like the voice of a great multitude and like the sound of many waters and like the sound of mighty peals of thunder, saying, "Hallelujah! For the Lord our God, the Almighty, reigns. 7 Let us rejoice and be glad and give the glory to Him, for the marriage of the Lamb has come and His bride has made herself ready."*
>
> *8 It was given to her to clothe herself in fine linen, bright and clean; for the fine linen is the righteous acts of the saints. (Revelation 19:6-8).*

The words of this fourth stanza are the ones that were borrowed by George F. Handel for his famous Hallelujah Chorus. The theme of the chorus is that God reigns. He is in control. He is in control when the beast attacks the church and when Babylon spreads her lies and when Babylon falls.

Notice that God is called the Almighty. This title is found ten times in the New Testament; nine of those times are in the book of Revelation. This tells me something about the theme of this book. It is a book about the sovereignty of God. But it also tells me that it is a book that is rooted in the Old Testament, for this is a term used extensively there and especially in the book of Job. Think about that; the book that speaks the most of suffering is also the book that emphasizes God as the Almighty.

1. The Marriage of the Lamb: *The marriage of the Lamb has come and His bride has made herself ready (19:7).*

    We were introduced to a woman in Revelation 12. She wore a crown of twelve stars and we immediately recognized her as Israel. She gave birth to the Messiah and she was forced to flee into the wilderness as the Serpent tried to destroy her. When we came to Revelation 17-18, we were confronted with the image of another woman. This woman was a harlot and she wore that which pointed to her profession. She was seen drunk with the blood of the saints and trying to take the dragon out for a ride, only to be eaten alive by the beast and the dragon.

    Both women, the one in Revelation 12 as well as the one of Revelation 17-18, are a picture of Israel. The one shows Israel as she was meant to be; the other shows unbelieving Israel that had rejected her Messiah and as she sought to persecute her followers. The good news is that it does not end there. There is a call in Revelation 18:4 to *come out of her, my people, that you may not participate in her sins and that you may not receive of her plagues*. Those who heed this call to repentance are invited to a marriage ceremony in the next chapter where we see a picture, not of a prostitute, but of a spotless bride. This is the same message that was given to Hosea and it is the same message that was lived out in the person of Rahab – the prostitute turned bride who finds her sins forgiven and her robes made spotless in the blood of the lamb.

Now the scene changes. We are treated to a vision of a faithful and loving bride. This picture of the marriage of the Lord to His people is not a new concept. It has its roots in the Old Testament.

> *"Fear not, for you will not be put to shame;*
> *And do not feel humiliated, for you will not be disgraced;*
> *But you will forget the shame of your youth,*
> *And the reproach of your widowhood you will remember*
> *no more.*
> *5 For your husband is your Maker,*
> *Whose name is the LORD of hosts;*
> *And your Redeemer is the Holy One of Israel,*
> *Who is called the God of all the earth.*
> *6 For the LORD has called you,*
> *Like a wife forsaken and grieved in spirit,*
> *Even like a wife of one's youth when she is rejected,"*
> *Says your God. (Isaiah 54:4-6).*

> *I will betroth you to Me forever;*
> *Yes, I will betroth you to Me in righteousness and in*
> *justice,*
> *In lovingkindness and in compassion,*
> *20 And I will betroth you to Me in faithfulness.*
> *Then you will know the LORD. (Hosea 2:19-20).*

The closest possible union that can exist between two people is that of marriage. The concept of marriage is presented in the opening chapters of the Bible where it is described in terms of two people becoming "one flesh." When God desired to illustrate the intimacy of the relationship He sought with His people, He described it in terms of a marriage. The parallels between that original design for marriage and the relationship to which He calls His people today are pervasive.

The First Marriage	Our Spiritual Marriage
The purpose of the woman was to be a helper for the man	We have been created to serve the Son
The woman was made by God	We are His workmanship, created in Christ Jesus
The woman was taken from the body of the man	We are called Christians because we have been taken from Christ
The man was put to sleep so that the Lord could take a rib to form the woman	Jesus died upon the cross, suffering a "sleep" so that we might become the church
The woman was brought to the man	We have been brought to Jesus in faith
It was ordained that a man should leave his father and mother and cleave to his wife	Jesus left heaven to come for us and we are called to leave the world to be joined to Him

The marriage of the first man and woman was consummated in their "one flesh" relationship. Likewise, we have entered into a union with Jesus in which we have become one with Him. And yet, there is coming a day when we shall undergo a final consummation; when we shall be like He is as we see Him face to face.

2.   The Clothing of the Bride: *It was given to her to clothe herself in fine linen, bright and clean; for the fine linen is the righteous acts of the saints (19:8).*

This calls to mind the words of Jesus to the church at Laodicea in Revelation 3. He told them to buy white garments from Him. He was not talking about a yard sale. He was speaking of spiritual clothing. Imagine what it would look like if our Sunday morning clothes were all suddenly transformed into their spiritual counterparts. Would the church appear as a spiritual nudist colony? It is an unfortunate truth that people within the church have been far more concerned with physical clothing and appearances than with the spiritual reality within their lives.

When we read that the church is clothed with *the righteous acts of the saints*, that is not a denial of the truth of the imputation of Christ's righteousness through faith. Paul teaches us in Romans 4 that we have been credited with the righteousness of Christ when we believe in Him and

311

are declared to be righteous in the sight of God on that basis. But Paul's teaching about salvation does not stop there. He goes on to say in the subsequent chapters that we are also sanctified and that the Holy Spirit begins to produce new life within us, a life that results in good works.

This is important because there is a teaching that has made some inroads within modern Christianity that says a person can hear the gospel and believe and be saved without it ever having fruit in his life; that one can accept Jesus as savior without also recognizing and accepting Him as Lord; that it is possible to believe in Jesus without repenting of sin and yielding to His authority. In such teaching, faith becomes a mere intellectual exercise. Instead of people being called to repentance, they are called only to assent to certain historical facts about Jesus. Discipleship becomes optional. It simply is not true.

Faith involves more than just mere assent to certain historical facts. Even the devil has that kind of faith. *You believe that God is one. You do well; the demons also believe, and shudder. 20 But are you willing to recognize, you foolish fellow, that faith without works is useless?* (James 2:19-20). Faith that saves is a faith that works. If it doesn't work in your life, then it doesn't work in your salvation, either. It is a bit like breathing. Breathing does not give life to you. But breathing is one of the signs of life. If there is no breathing and no pulse and no brain activity, then we rightly conclude that there is no life, especially when we take such measurements over an extended period of time. Does that mean you work your way into God's good graces or that you someone earn or merit salvation? Not at all. It is God who saves.

> *For by grace you have been saved through faith; and that not of yourselves, it is the gift of God; 9 not as a result of works, that no one should boast. (Ephesians 2:8-9).*

Your salvation comes through faith. It does not come as a result of your works. No one will ever be able to boast about their contribution to the work of their salvation. But that verse goes on to point out that your salvation is not an end unto itself. You were not saved BY good works, but you were saved FOR good works.

> *For we are His workmanship, created in Christ Jesus for good works, which God prepared beforehand, that we should walk in them (Ephesians 2:10).*

You are God's workmanship. He has done the work of creating in you a new life. The result of being saved is that you will walk in those good works for which you were created.

THE TESTIMONY OF JESUS

Then he said to me, "Write, 'Blessed are those who are invited to the marriage supper of the Lamb.'" And he said to me, "These are true words of God." 10 Then I fell at his feet to worship him. But he said to me, "Do not do that; I am a fellow servant of yours and your brethren who hold the testimony of Jesus; worship God. For the testimony of Jesus is the spirit of prophecy." (Revelation 19:9-10).

As John listens to the concluding strains of the original Hallelujah Chorus, he becomes aware of the one who is standing next to him. We are not specifically told who this is. It is likely the same angel that has been talking with John since Revelation 17:1. Up to this point, John has been so caught up with the vision that he has been ignoring the angel standing next to him. But now the angel speaks.

1.   The Beatitude: *Blessed are those who are invited to the marriage supper of the Lamb (19:9).*

We have seen several beatitudes within this book. Each of them pronounce a blessing upon the people of God. This one is no different. It pronounces a blessing on those who are invited to the marriage supper of the Lamb. What is this marriage supper? It is the time of rejoicing when the Lamb comes to consummate His wedding with His bride.

This calls to mind the parable that Jesus told of the ten virgins. They had been invited to a marriage supper and they were awaiting the coming of the bride and the groom. Weddings in those days were a bit different than they are today. In those days, the friends of the groom would assemble at his house on the day of the wedding. The friends of the bride would gather outside, but they would not come in because the bride was not there yet.

At a certain time, the groom and his best man and a few select friends would leave and make their way to the home of the father of the bride. They would take the bride and, in a great procession, they would return to the house of the groom. When they arrived, they would be met by the friends of the bride who were still waiting outside the groom's house. Once they all came together, they would all enter inside for a time of rejoicing.

In the parable Jesus told, five of the friends of the bride left and went into town to buy oil for their lamps. By the time they got back, they had missed the wedding procession. When they knocked at the door, the groom looked at them as party-crashers and would not allow them entrance.

Here is the point of the parable. You have received an invitation to the wedding, but are you ready to enter? There are a lot of people who have received the invitation and think that is all there is to it. But there is also a time of waiting and a time where patience and endurance are needed.

2.   John's Response: *I fell at his feet to worship him (19:10).*

Why did John do this? It was not because he was in the presence of the angel. He has just gone through 19 chapters of angels. He was likely getting used to seeing angels by now. The reason John falls down to worship this angel is because of the words this angel has just spoken:

> *"These are the true words of God."*

John took the words of God very seriously. He only made one mistake. He confused the sanctity of the message with the sanctity of the messenger. We can be guilty of that, too. We are guilty of that when we take a preacher or an evangelist or a Bible teacher and put him up on a pedestal. We are guilty of that when we forget that such men are merely vessels whom God has chosen to use.

3.   The Spirit of Prophecy: *The testimony of Jesus is the spirit of prophecy (19:10).*

The book of Revelation is a book about prophecy. Prophecy has been described as "history written beforehand," but this is incorrect. If that is the purpose of prophecy, then the prophets did a miserable job. They should have written a much more concise and coherent history.

The purpose of prophecy is to uphold the testimony of Jesus. It is to turn your eyes to Jesus. This is what Jesus said to His disciples on the night before His crucifixion.

> *"From now on I am telling you before it comes to pass, so that when it does occur, you may believe that I am He." (John 13:19).*

Have you entered into the spirit of prophecy? Have you come to meet the One to whom all prophecy points? He is waiting. Come to Him in faith and then you will be able to join in that same Hallelujah Chorus.

THE RIDER ON THE WHITE HORSE
Revelation 19:11-21

Revelation is a book about Jesus. It is not primarily a book about prophecy, though it has prophecy within it. It is not a book about angels, although it is filled with angels. It is not a book about tribulation, although it does talk about difficult times. It is exactly what the title suggests. It is a revelation of Jesus. It reveals who and what Jesus really is. This chapter will be no different. It is going to tell us some exciting things about Jesus. We will see four names of Jesus:

- *Faithful and True* (19:11). When we speak of faith. We usually think in terms of our faith in Christ. But we should realize that faith in itself is not of much value unless it is placed in something or someone that is faithful and true. There are two ways in which we can say that Jesus is true. First, He is true in what He says. He cannot lie. If He says something to us, then we can believe that what He says is true. Secondly, He is the true One in contrast to the false ones. Many people claim to have the answers to life. Jesus said there would be many who would be self-proclaimed messiahs, but He is the only true One.

- *The Unknown Name* (19:12). It is interesting that Jesus is going to have a name that no one knows. We often get to thinking that, if we study the Bible hard enough, we will come to the point where we will know all there is to know about Jesus. We write books on Systematic Theology (and I have been guilty of doing this) that purport to tell us all about God. But God is bigger than my book. You cannot put a label on Him and catalog Him and think that you have fully come to know all about Him. He is the Unknown God and we would not know Him at all were it not that He has revealed a portion of Himself to us. The Scripture's revelation of God is accurate, but it is not exhaustive.

- *The Word of God* (19:13). Jesus is called the Word of God because He has communicated God to man, not merely in what He has said, but also by what He is. Do you want to know God? Come to Jesus. If you have seen Jesus, then you have also seen the Father.

- *King of kings and Lord of lords* (19:16). This has been the central theme of the book of Revelation. It is the theme of sovereignty. It is that Jesus is in control, even when beastly rulers rise up and do beastly things.

This section will be seen in four parts, each corresponding to the four names we have just mentioned.

19:11-13	19:14	19:15-18	19:19-21
The Rider	The Followers	The Victory	The Final Conflict

THE RIDER

> *And I saw heaven opened, and behold, a white horse, and He who sat on it is called Faithful and True, and in righteousness He judges and wages war. 12 His eyes are a flame of fire, and on His head are many diadems; and He has a name written on Him which no one knows except Himself. 13 He is clothed with a robe dipped in blood, and His name is called The Word of God. (Revelation 19:11-13).*

In Revelation 4, John saw a door opened in heaven. That opening introduced a series of visions. Now he sees all of heaven opened. In Revelation 4, he was caught up into heaven; now he will see the Son of Man coming down from heaven.

1.   His White Horse: *And I saw heaven opened, and behold, a white horse (19:11).*

When Roman generals enjoyed the honor of a triumph, their chariots would be led by white horses. The symbol of a white horse came to be that of a conqueror.

Image of Domitian on horseback

Jewish dreams were full of the warrior messiah who would ride in on a white horse, leading the armies of Israel against the Roman Empire. We have already seen a picture of a rider on a white horse. He was one of the four horsemen described in Revelation 6. Although some have taken that to be a description of Jesus, I suggested otherwise. In chapter 6, the rider on the white horse is merely one in a group of riders. When we come to this passage in Revelation 19, there is no mistaking the identity of the rider.

2.   His eyes: *His eyes are a flame of fire (19:12).*

We saw this same description of Jesus back in Revelation 1:14 and that description was repeated in Revelation 2:18. It pointed to His ability to see all things, but it also might point to the fire of judgment.

3.   The Diadems: *On His head are many diadems (19:12).*

The normal Greek word for "crown" is *stephanos*. This is a different word; it is the Greek word *diadema* from which we derive our English word "diadem." This word is only used three times in the New Testament, all of them here in the book of Revelation. It is also used in the Old Testament to describe the crown worn by the Persian queens in the book of Esther and which was given to Mordecai to honor him. The word literally means "to bind around" and described the royal band that went around the head of nobility to bind his turban in place. We have already read of the dragon wearing diadems on each of his seven heads and the beast with diadems on each of his ten horns. They are contrasted with the Son of God who wears many diadems.

Julian the Apostate with a diadem

Egyptian pharaoh with diadem

We tend to think of a king as wearing only one crown. But in the ancient world, a king might wear a separate crown for each of the kingdoms over which he ruled. For example, the pharaohs of Egypt regularly wore two crowns, one for Upper Egypt and another for Lower Egypt. In the same way, when Ptolemy made his triumphal entry into Antioch, he wore both the crown of Egypt and the crown of Asia.

Jesus is the Lord of many crowns. He is not just the Lord of the church. He is not just the Lord of a certain geographical area. He is the Lord of all men.

317

4.   His Clothing: *He is clothed with a robe dipped in blood (19:13).*

In the next verse, we are going to see the saints clothed in fine linen, white and clean. By contrast, Jesus wears a robe that has been dipped in blood. One is clean and pure, the other has been soiled by the signs of death. At first glance, this seems to be a reference to His sacrifice on our behalf. On the other hand, it could be a reference to a vision of the Lord from the Old Testament.

> *Who is this who comes from Edom,*
> *With garments of glowing colors from Bozrah,*
> *This One who is majestic in His apparel,*
> *Marching in the greatness of His strength?*
> *"It is I who speak in righteousness, mighty to save."*
> *2 Why is Your apparel red,*
> *And Your garments like the one who treads in the wine press?*
> *3 "I have trodden the wine trough alone,*
> *And from the peoples there was no man with Me.*
> *I also trod them in My anger*
> *And trampled them in My wrath;*
> *And their lifeblood is sprinkled on My garments,*
> *And I stained all My raiment.*
> *4 For the day of vengeance was in My heart,*
> *And My year of redemption has come." (Isaiah 63:1-4).*

The blood which stains the garments of the Lord is not His own blood. It is the blood of His enemies. It signifies the fierceness of His judgment. The One who shed His own blood for us will one day shed the blood of His enemies.

THE FOLLOWERS

> *And the armies which are in heaven, clothed in fine linen,*
> *white and clean, were following Him on white horses. (Revelation*
> *19:14).*

Who are these armies that accompany Jesus? They are clothed in fine linen, white and clean. This description sounds very much like the bride in verse 6 who was clothed in fine linen. We saw in that verse that this clothing was a reference to the righteous acts of the saints. Are these the same people? I believe they are. That means we are described in terms of an army. That means we are in a spiritual battle. The armies of the King of light are pitted against the forces of the prince of darkness.

This brings up another important point. It is that we are not fighting a defensive war. We are not hiding behind the barred doors of the church, holding on by our fingertips against the siege of the enemy. We are on the offensive. We are attacking. We are the ones who are riding out against the enemy and battering against his defenses. This is what Jesus said to Peter.

> *"I also say to you that you are Peter, and upon this rock I will build My church; and the gates of Hades will not overpower it." (Matthew 16:18).*

The picture that Jesus presents is not of the church defending herself against the forces of hell, barely holding on in the face of repeated attacks. The picture is of the church smashing a great battering ram against the gates of hell and those gates are weakening and they are about to spring asunder. Jesus is going to win the battle and we are going to win with Him.

THE VICTORY

> *From His mouth comes a sharp sword, so that with it He may strike down the nations, and He will rule them with a rod of iron; and He treads the wine press of the fierce wrath of God, the Almighty. 16 And on His robe and on His thigh He has a name written, "King of kings, and Lord of lords."*
> *17 Then I saw an angel standing in the sun, and he cried out with a loud voice, saying to all the birds which fly in midheaven, "Come, assemble for the great supper of God, 18 so that you may eat the flesh of kings and the flesh of commanders and the flesh of mighty men and the flesh of horses and of those who sit on them and the flesh of all men, both free men and slaves, and small and great." (Revelation 19:15-18).*

Now we come to the culmination of the battle. The end was never in doubt. Jesus said from the beginning that He was going to win.

1.   The Source of the Victory: *From His mouth comes a sharp sword, so that with it He may strike down the nations (19:15).*

We are obviously not meant to take this literally. This is not describing a case of cosmic bad breath. There is some obvious symbolism here. It is taken from the Old Testament.

Then a shoot will spring from the stem of Jesse,
And a branch from his roots will bear fruit.
2 The Spirit of the LORD will rest on Him,
The spirit of wisdom and understanding,
The spirit of counsel and strength,
The spirit of knowledge and the fear of the LORD.
3 And He will delight in the fear of the LORD,
And He will not judge by what His eyes see,
Nor make a decision by what His ears hear;
4 But with righteousness He will judge the poor,
And decide with fairness for the afflicted of the earth;
*And He will strike the earth with **the rod of His mouth**,*
*And with **the breath of His lips** He will slay the wicked.*
(Isaiah 11:1-4).

Jesus has already been called the Word of God here in Revelation. Now we see pictured the power of that word. It reaches down to touch all men. Either it touches them with the gospel or else it touches them with the righteous judgment of God and condemns them.

This vision of the judgment of God is not limited to the final day of judgment. It includes that day, but its implications are much broader than that. In John's initial vision of Jesus, he described a "sharp two-edged sword" coming from His mouth (Revelation 1:16). Jesus went on to warn that He was going to wage war against the Nicolatitans with the sword of His mouth (Revelation 2:16).

When you share the gospel with someone, you are wielding the sword of God. It will not be in vain. It will produce an effect. Either it will draw that person to Christ, or else it will judge him.

2.   The Strength of the Victory: *He will rule them with a rod of iron (19:15).*

Once again we have an Old Testament symbol. This one finds its source in one of the Messianic Psalms.

I will surely tell of the decree of the LORD:
He said to Me, "You are My Son,
Today I have begotten You.
8 Ask of Me, and I will surely give the nations as Your
inheritance,
And the very ends of the earth as Your possession.
9 You shall break them with a rod of iron,
You shall shatter them like earthenware." (Psalm 2:7-9).

Iron was the hardest substance in the ancient world. To be ruled by a rod of iron was more than merely a harsh rule. It was a reference to destruction. This is seen in the parallelism of the psalm. To break people with a rod of iron is the same thing as shattering them like earthenware. This is clearly seen in the next clause.

3.   The Image of Victory: *He treads the wine press of the fierce wrath of God, the Almighty (19:15).*

We have already referenced the prophecy of Isaiah 63:1-3 with reference to bloodstained garments. Now we see the source of their staining. What happens to grapes in a wine press when the worker steps on them? They are crushed. This is the image of judgment. The unrighteous are crushed beneath the feet of the Lord.

4.   The Title of Victory: *On His robe and on His thigh He has a name written, "King of kings, and Lord of lords" (19:16).*

The significance of this title is seen from its first usage in the Old Testament. It is the title that Moses attributed to the God of Israel.

> *For the LORD your God is the God of gods and the Lord of lords, the great, the mighty, and the awesome God who does not show partiality nor take a bribe. (Deuteronomy 10:17).*

This is a title for God. The implications for this are striking. John takes a title that belongs to God and gives it to Jesus. He is saying that Jesus is Lord.

5.   The Declaration of Victory: *I saw an angel standing in the sun, and he cried out with a loud voice, saying to all the birds which fly in midheaven (19:17).*

This picture is reminiscent of Ezekiel's vision of the destruction of Gog and Magog, an event that will be referenced again when we come to Revelation 20. Just as was done in Ezekiel, there is a call to the birds to come and feast on the corpses of the dead.

> *As for you, son of man, thus says the Lord GOD, "Speak to every kind of bird and to every beast of the field, 'Assemble and come, gather from every side to My sacrifice which I am going to sacrifice for you, as a great sacrifice on the mountains of Israel, that you may eat flesh and drink blood. 18 You will eat the flesh of mighty men*

and drink the blood of the princes of the earth, as though they were rams, lambs, goats and bulls, all of them fatlings of Bashan.'" (Ezekiel 39:17-18).

For a corpse to lie unburied so that it was eaten by scavengers was considered to be a great dishonor in the ancient world. For that matter, it is not very well thought of today, either.

Ezekiel's prophecy was fulfilled, at least in part, when the Seleucid forces of Antiochus Epiphanes were defeated in the days of the Maccabees. In the same way, we read here that the forces of God are going to win the spiritual battle we are fighting.

This "supper of God" stands in violent contrast to the marriage supper of the Lamb that was described in verse 9. You have been invited to the first, but if you do not accept the invitation, then you will find yourself in attendance at the second.

THE FINAL CONFLICT

> *And I saw the beast and the kings of the earth and their armies assembled to make war against Him who sat on the horse and against His army. 20 And the beast was seized, and with him the false prophet who performed the signs in his presence, by which he deceived those who had received the mark of the beast and those who worshiped his image; these two were thrown alive into the lake of fire which burns with brimstone. 21 And the rest were killed with the sword which came from the mouth of Him who sat on the horse, and all the birds were filled with their flesh. (Revelation 19:19-21).*

We have seen the beast representing Satan's world system. In John's day, it was embodied in the Roman Empire. We have seen the false prophet representing Satan's religious system. In John's day, it was embodied in the Jewish religious system centered in Jerusalem. Both of these were at enmity with Jesus and with His church. Both of them brought persecution against the church. For a time, they were united in that persecution. You will remember how the Jews cried out at the trial of Jesus, "We have no king but Caesar!" (John 19:15). It is interesting to see how often the world and religion team up to attack the truth.

The actual battle is not described. Instead, we read that the beast and the false prophet are seized and thrown into the lake of fire. What does it mean? When do these events take place? Are they all in the future or have aspects of them already come to pass? There are several schools of thought.

1.   The Preterist View.

        We have already made several passing references to Preterism. This is the
        view that all of the prophecies of the book of Revelation were fulfilled in
        the fall of Jerusalem in 70 A.D. Accordingly, the view sees the beast and
        the false prophet fulfilled in Vespasian and Titus who destroyed the
        Temple in order to do away with the religion of the Jews and the Christians.

        When we read that the beast and false prophet are cast alive into the Lake
        of Fire, this view interprets that as the suicide of Nero and the political
        chaos that ensued in the following years. Another preterist view sees the
        Lake of Fire as symbolic of the destruction of Israel and Jerusalem in 70
        A.D. and the way Vespasian and Titus were "thrust alive" into that burning
        land. Neither of these seem to have a satisfactory treatment of this passage
        in its entirety since neither led to the defeat of Rome.[1]

2.   The Futurist View.

        This view sees these events in chapter 19 as describing the second coming
        of Jesus to the earth. This final conflict is often equated with the Battle of
        Armageddon mentioned earlier in this book. However, there is a problem.
        The passage does not actually say that Jesus comes to the earth. He is seen
        judging the beast and the false prophet, but we have seen visions of similar
        judgment all through the book of Revelation.

        We have noted that the second coming of Jesus is depicted repeatedly
        within the book of Revelation. It is mentioned in each of the seven letters
        to the seven churches and it was seen at each grouping of seven seals, seven
        trumpets, and seven vials of wrath. It is seen in the Battle of Armageddon
        and this passage can be seen as still another relating of that climactic event.

3.   The Continuous Historical View.

        This third view sees these events in Revelation 19 as taking place again and
        again throughout the last 2000 years, but finally culminating in the future
        second coming of Christ. In this, it is not entirely divorced from either of
        the two previous views. On the one hand, it agrees with the preterist in
        seeing a first century application to the vision. On the other hand, it also
        agrees with the futurist view that the culmination of the prophecy is to be
        seen in the future second coming of Christ.

_____

[1] For more on Preterism, See Appendix 1.

Whenever the world system rises up against God's people, then Christ and His armies move to judge that system. They do so, not with physical weapons of warfare, but with the Word of God. This judgment was seen in the destruction of Jerusalem in 70 A.D. It was also seen in the subsequent fall of Rome many hundreds of years later. It has been seen in the fall of any power that pits itself against the forces of righteousness. If this seems a strange interpretation to you, then call to mind the words of the old Christian song:

> Onward, Christian soldiers, marching as to war,
> With the cross of Jesus going on before!
> Christ, the royal Master, leads again the foe;
> Forward into battle, see his banner go!
>
> At the sign of triumph Satan's host doth flee;
> On, then, Christian soldiers, on to victory!
> Hell's foundations quiver at the shout of praise;
> Brothers, lift your voices, loud your anthems raise!
>
> Onward, Christian soldiers, marching as to war,
> With the cross of Jesus going on before!

THE THOUSAND YEAR REIGN
Revelation 20:1-15

There is perhaps no more controversial chapter in all of the book of Revelation than the one to which we now come. Interpretations of this passage have divided the church. There are four primary views.

1.   The Premillennial View.

In keeping with the futurist view of the previous chapter, this view sees the rider on the white horse of Revelation 19 as the second coming of Jesus. It then postulates that Jesus will set up an earthly kingdom over which he will rule for a thousand years during which time Satan will be bound. At the end of that time, Satan is released and permitted to stir up a rebellion against God. There is a final battle followed by a final judgment and then the heavens and the earth are destroyed. After this, God creates a new heaven and a new earth. In defense of this view, the following points must be noted:

a.   It involves a literal interpretation of Revelation 20. It simply takes the chapter at face value. As such, this is one of the oldest interpretations espoused by the early church fathers. It is in this vein that Justin Martyr speaks of *"a thousand years in which Jerusalem will be built up, adorned and enlarged, as the prophets Ezekiel and Isaiah and others declare"* (Dialogue with Trypho the Jew).

While holding to Premillennialism himself, Justin observed that not all Christians in his day shared the same views of future prophecy when it came to the millennium: *I admitted to you formerly, that I and many others are of this opinion, and [believe] that such will take place, as you assuredly are aware; but, on the other hand, I signified to you that many who belong to the pure and pious faith, and are true Christians, think otherwise* (Dialogue with Trypho 80).

b.   It can be easily reconciled with the Old Testament prophecies that depict a physical kingdom on earth with Israel at its center. The millennium is seen as the time when the nation of Israel is given the land of Palestine for an everlasting possession, or at least a possession for a thousand years.

c.   The promise of David's throne can be fulfilled. God promised David an eternal kingdom, saying, "Your house and your kingdom shall endure before Me forever; your throne shall be established forever" (2 Samuel 7:16). The Premillennialist argues that this prophecy can only be fulfilled in the context of the thousand year reign of Jesus on an earthly throne in Palestine. Of course, the issue here is that David is promised an eternal kingdom, not one of only a thousand years.

d.   Satan does not appear to be bound today. As we look at the progress of sin and the problems of the world around us, it does not appear as though Satan is limited. Rather, it looks more like he is going about *like a roaring lion, seeking someone to devour* (1 Peter 5:8).

One particular form of Premillennialism is known as Dispensationalism. This view teaches that there are two future comings of Jesus, the first in a secret "rapture" which is to be followed at a later date by the Second Coming of Christ. Dispensationalism is a recent innovation in Christianity, first being proposed in the early 1800's, but it has gained a large audience since that time. By contrast, Historic Premillennialism is a very old teaching and was held by such church fathers as Justin Martyr and Irenaeus.

The Premillennial scheme has the following events at the Second Coming of Christ:

> (1) Resurrection.
> (2) Judgment of wicked.
> (3) Judgment of Satan.
> (4) Entrance into 1000 year Kingdom.

All four of these events are described in Revelation 20.

- Resurrection: *They came to life* (Revelation 20:4).
- Judgment of wicked: *The beast was seized, and with him the false prophet... and the rest were killed with the sword which came from the mouth of Him who sat on the horse* (Revelation 19:20-21).
- Judgment of Satan: *He laid hold of the dragon, the serpent of old, who is the devil and Satan, and bound him for a thousand years* (Revelation 20:2).
- Entrance into 1000 year Kingdom: *They came to life and reigned with Christ for a thousand years* (Revelation 20:4).

As the chart below will demonstrate, the Premillennial scheme has these events taking place both at the beginning and at the end of their Millennium.

Premillennial Scheme	
At the Second Coming of Christ	**At the End of the Millennium**
(1) Resurrection.	(1) Resurrection.
(2) Judgment of wicked.	(2) Judgment of wicked.
(3) Judgment of Satan.	(3) Judgment of Satan.
(4) Entrance into 1000 year Kingdom.	(4) Entrance into the eternal kingdom.

The Premillennial sees the events of the future happening twice. While this is certainly a possibility, this brings us to a second view; one that teaches these two series of events are to be understood as one and the same.

2.   The Amillennial View.

The term Amillennial means "no millennium." However that is not entirely accurate as a designation. Those who hold to this position do not deny the words of Revelation 20, they merely see John's vision as a symbol for the present reality of this age. This view sees the reference in Revelation 20 to a thousand year reign of Christ to speak of His spiritual reign upon the earth today and the reference to a thousand years being symbolic of a long period of time.

a.   When we read of Satan being bound, that is not a new concept. Jesus spoke of the binding of Satan in Matthew 12. It was in the context of His having cast out a demon. There were those present who suggested that He was able to do this because He was secretly in league with Satan. But He pointed out that Satan does not work at cross purposes with himself and the fact that he was being bound by Jesus made it evident that they were not allies: *But if I cast out demons by the Spirit of God, then the kingdom of God has come upon you. 29 Or how can anyone enter the strong man's house and carry off his property, unless he first binds the strong man? And then he will plunder his house." (Matthew 12:28-29).*

The characters of whom Jesus speaks are obvious. When he speaks of binding "the strong man," it is evident that He is speaking of the manner in which He has bound Satan by the casting out of demons. The very fact that Satan was being cast out and the strong man was being bound was in itself evidence that the kingdom of God had come.

b. The specific manner in which Satan is said to be bound in the Millennium is with regard to his ability to deceive the nations (20:3). Prior to the first advent of Christ, the nations were completely deceived by Satan to the point that very few outside of the confines of the tiny nation of Israel ever heard the truth of the gospel. But with the coming of Christ and the advent of the church, the gospel exploded throughout the world. The very fact that the gospel has gone to the nations and that gospel has been received by people in those nations is a sign of Satan's having been bound in his ability to deceive those nations.

OLD TESTAMENT PERIOD	CHURCH PERIOD	END TIME PERIOD
SATAN LOOSE	SATAN BOUND	SATAN LOOSE
Nations deceived by satanic rulers	Nations no longer deceived by Satan	Nations again deceived by Satan
People of God oppressed	Nations of world reached by Gospel	Saints attacked

When Jesus gave His disciples their great commission, He told them to go and make disciples of the nations. This presupposed that Satan would not be able to continue his same level of deception against those nations. The result is that you can go everywhere in the world today and find Christians.

The Bible says that during the kingdom, *"the earth will be flooded with the knowledge of the glory of the Lord as the waters cover the sea"* (Isaiah 11:9; Habakkuk 2:14). At the same time, Revelation 20 makes it clear that evil is also present in the Millennium as it ends in revolt against the reign of Christ.

c. This brings up an objection from 2 Corinthians 4:3-4. *And even if our gospel is veiled, it is veiled to those who are perishing, in whose case the god of this world has blinded the minds of the unbelieving, that they might not see the light of the gospel of the glory of Christ, who is the image of God.*

Paul says that people and nations have been blinded to the gospel. Does Paul mean that no one believes or that only a very few will necessarily believe because everyone else has been blinded? It would seem to me that this is the case and would continue to be the case were it not for the binding of the god of this world as per Revelation 20. If Satan had not been bound, then we would not see the growth of the gospel in the world today. At the same time, Paul indicates that there is still a blinding. Thus the Amillennial view states that both of these phenomenon are taking place today. There has been a blinding that has taken place since the beginning. Yet despite this ongoing blindness, Satan is being bound with respect to his blinding abilities and therefore the gospel has and continues to be preached in and believed by many of those who are in the nations.

d. The Amillennial view sees the reference to a thousand years as symbolic of a long, undesignated period of time. This has precedence in the Bible such as when the Psalmist tells us that the Lord owns the cattle on a thousand hills (Psalm 50:10) and we do not thereby conclude that the Lord does not own the cattle on hill number 1001. Likewise, when we read that a thousand years with the Lord are as a single day (Psalm 90:4), we do not press this in an overly literal manner (see also Deuteronomy 7:9, Psalm 105:8; 1st Chronicles 16:15-16, and 2nd Peter 3:8).

The number 10 is presented in the Bible as a complete number. There were ten commandments and we read of a beast with ten horns. The kingdom is said to be of a duration of ten cubed: 10x10x10=1000. It is a number of fulness.

e. We read in Peter's second epistle that *the day of the Lord will come like a thief, in which the heavens will pass away with a roar and the elements will be destroyed with intense heat, and the earth and its works will be burned up. (2 Peter 3:10).* If we are to understand that Revelation 20 is outlining the specific time of this judgment as a literal thousand years, then how can that judgment be said to come unexpectedly like a thief?

f. This present age as culminates when *"death is swallowed up in victory"* (1 Corinthians 15:54). This takes place when Christ returns *"at the last trumpet; for the trumpet will sound, and the dead will be raised imperishable, and we shall be changed"* (1 Corinthians 15:52). If death will be defeated at Christ's return, then we can understand that Christ is reigning now and will continue to reign until death has been defeated: *For He must reign until he has put all His enemies under His feet. The last enemy that will be abolished is death. (1 Corinthians 15:25-26).* If death is defeated at the return of Christ and if this is the last enemy to be defeated, then this does not allow room for a further enemy to arise a thousand years later.

g.   A comparison of what takes place in this chapter with what the Bible says about the church today is used to support this position.

The Church	The Millennial Reign
Begins with the victory of Jesus on the cross	Begins with the victory of Jesus
Satan's head was crushed at the cross and he was defeated	Satan is bound and cast into the bottomless pit
Jesus said that all authority had been given to Him on heaven and on earth (Mat 28:18)	Believers reign with Christ for a thousand years
Judgment has been given to the church	Judgment is given to those who reign with Christ
There are believers and unbelievers living side by side in the world	There are believers and unbelievers living side by side in the world
He who restrains will be taken out of the way and then the lawless one will be revealed (2 Thess 2:7-8)	At the end of the thousand years, Satan will be released from his prison
Satan will be permitted to deceive with all power and signs and false wonders (2nd Thess 2:9-12)	Satan will come out to deceive the nations which are in the four corners of the earth
The Lord Jesus will be revealed with flaming fire dealing out retribution (2 Thess 1:7-10)	Fire comes down from heaven and devours them
There is a resurrection from the dead	The dead rise and stand before the throne
The judgment seat of Christ	The great white throne judgment

This view sees the similarities are a sign that they are referring to one and the same thing.

3.   The Post millennial View.

This view also sees the rider on the white horse of Revelation 19 as the victory of Jesus and His church in bringing the gospel to the earth. The gospel succeeds in filling the earth and beginning a new era of a thousand years during which the church will reign over the earth. At the end of that time, Jesus will return in triumph and the heavens and the earth are destroyed by fire in the last judgment after which God creates a new heaven and a new earth.

This is a view that looks for the church to be victorious; in the words of the book of Revelation, it believes that the church will overcome. It takes on a special significance when we look at the progress of the gospel through the ages. Beginning with a small band of eleven disciples, the gospel has spread from one end of the earth to the other. In a very real sense, the church has been victorious so that today there is no place on the face of the earth where the gospel has not been proclaimed.

4.   The Preterist View.

The word "Preterist" is taken from the Latin word meaning "past." This view denies any future fulfillment of the book of Revelation and sees the events it describes as already having been fulfilled within the first century after Christ. There are several different forms of Preterism. Full Preterism views all of the prophecies of the Bible as having already been fulfilled in their entirety since the fall of Jerusalem in A.D. 70. Full Preterism is a very recent innovation that has no adherents in any of the writings of the early church. Partial Preterism maintains a future return of Christ, but views His "coming in the clouds" as described in Matthew 24:29-31 as having been fulfilled in A.D. 70 with the fall of Jerusalem. Let me say for the record that I do not endorse any of the different sorts of Preterism, but my comments henceforth are directed primarily to Full Preterism.

Fundamental to full Preterism is the idea that there is no future physical resurrection of the dead. But the pattern for our resurrection is that of Jesus. The big idea presented in 1 Corinthians 15 is that Jesus arose from the dead. This was not merely some sort of spiritual resurrection. The point is made throughout this chapter that His resurrection was bodily and physical. Furthermore we are told that His resurrection serves as the paradigm for our own resurrection. *But now Christ has been raised from the dead, the first fruits of those who are asleep* (1 Corinthians 15:20). He is the first fruits and we are the "later fruits."

When Paul came to Athens, he was mocked by the Greeks for believing in a physical resurrection. Such mockery would not have been forthcoming had he held that the resurrection was only going to be of a spiritual or mystical nature. But he went out of his way to side himself with the Pharisees who believed in a physical resurrection of the dead (Acts 23:6-8).

In denying any future resurrection at the coming of Christ, the preterist also finds himself out of accord with the words of Paul when he says, "We shall not all sleep, but we shall all be changed" (1 Corinthians 15:51). The reference to sleep is used throughout this epistle as a euphemism for death (11:30; 15:6; 15:18; 15:20). While Paul says of the coming of the Lord that it will be a time when all do not die, the preterist is left with the rather obvious historic truth that everyone who lived in the first century did indeed die.

When it comes to the resurrection, the Bible teaches that Jesus is our prototype. His resurrection is the forerunner and the pattern for our own resurrection. This point is made in 1 Corinthians 15 where Paul says that if there is no resurrection then even Jesus has not risen.

The resurrection of Jesus was a physical resurrection. He was able to stand before His disciples in His resurrection body and say, *"See My hands and My feet, that it is I Myself; touch Me and see, for a spirit does not have flesh and bones as you see that I have."* (Luke 24:39). 1 John 3:2 says that *when He appears, we shall be like Him, because we shall see Him just as He is*. Therefore we can conclude that our future resurrection will be of both a physical and spiritual nature. Romans 8:11 confirms that it is not merely the soul or the spirit that will be raised, but our mortal bodies: *But if the Spirit of Him who raised Jesus from the dead dwells in you, He who raised Christ Jesus from the dead will also give life to your mortal bodies through His Spirit who dwells in you.*

When Paul preaches to the Athenians on the Areopagus, he declares to them that God *has fixed a day in which He will judge the world in righteousness through a Man whom He has appointed* (Acts 17:31). The Preterist interpretation of this verse is that it points to the A.D. 70 fall of Jerusalem, yet that fall would have absolutely no impact upon the Athenians who had gathered to listen to Paul. He says that they ought to repent because of this coming judgment and such a warning is nonsensical if it only refers to a local judgment in a far away land.

Preterists do not believe that there will be an end to this heaven and earth. They typically seek to avoid biblical references to the contrary by redefining any references to the end of the world as referring to the end of the Jewish world system. However, a survey of the Bible's use of the phrase "heaven and earth" quickly shows this to be an exercise in futility.

The phrase "heaven and earth" goes back all the way to Genesis 1:1 where God is seen as the creator of heaven and earth. That is further defined throughout the first chapter of Genesis in a way that makes it very obvious that more than a mere "Jewish world" is in view. Such a usage continues unabated throughout the Old Testament. While it is true that there are times when the term "earth" can be used in a localized sense, this is by no means always to be the case. For example, we read in Psalm 135:6 of how the Lord does as He pleases "in heaven and in earth, in the seas and in all deeps." Isaiah cites the words of the Lord Himself as he says: "I, the LORD, am the maker of all things, stretching out the heavens by Myself and spreading out the earth all alone" (Isaiah 44:24). The prophet goes on to speak of a day of judgment when "the Lord will punish the host of heaven on high, and the kings of the earth on earth" (Isaiah 24:21).

2 Peter 3:3-4 warns that *in the last days mockers will come with their mocking, following after their own lusts, and saying, "Where is the promise of His coming? For ever since the fathers fell asleep, all continues just as it was from the beginning of creation."* Bearing a remarkable resemblance to these last days mockers, preterists similarly deny any future coming of the Lord or any judgment of heaven and earth as they seek to make any such references to be limited to the events of A.D. 70. By contrast, Peter goes on to liken the future judgment of heaven and earth to the judgment of the flood that removed all human life in the days of Noah. Just as the world at that time was destroyed, being flooded with water, Peter goes on to say that *the present heavens and earth are being reserved for fire, kept for the day of judgment and destruction of ungodly men (2 Peter 3:7).*

Peter goes on to describe how *the day of the Lord will come like a thief, in which the heavens will pass away with a roar and the elements will be destroyed with intense heat, and the earth and its works will be burned up (2 Peter 3:10).* Peter's earlier reference to the heavens and earth in 1 Peter 3:5 can hardly be said to refer to the nation of Israel since it cites the creation of both heaven and earth and turns our attention back to the first chapter of Genesis. Therefore to attempt to re-interpret Peter's description of the passing of the heaven and earth only to the destruction of the city of Jerusalem in A.D. 70 is to do violence to the text of Scripture and to completely ignore the context of the passage. Contrary to the false teaching of the preterist, we must echo the words of Jesus when He promises that *heaven and earth will pass away* (Matthew 24:35 and Luke 21:33).

It is no surprise to find that Preterists hold the prophecy in Revelation 20 of a thousand year reign to be symbolic. The idea of a symbolic fulfillment of this passage has been argued back and forth since the early days of the church. What is particularly problematic for the Preterist treatment of this passage is the view that this thousand year reign is to be understood as having been fulfilled in the 40 years between the resurrection of Jesus and the A.D. 70 destruction of Jerusalem. One cannot help but wonder what is to be meant by the use of an obviously long period of time as suggested by a thousand years.

There are some eschatological differences that exist between Christians that I consider to be relatively benign and within the realm of Christian orthodoxy. Full Preterism is not one of them. To the contrary, the teaching of Preterism comes uncomfortably close to the spiritual gangrene that is described by Paul in 2 Timothy 2:18 when he speaks of those *who have gone astray from the truth saying that the resurrection has already taken place, and thus they upset the faith of some*. The teachings of preterism have not resulted in stronger and more loving Christians. Though I am happy to report that there are some exceptions, this teaching for the most part has been divisive and destructive. I cannot help but to be reminded of the litmus test suggested by Jesus: *You will know them by their fruits. Grapes are not gathered from thorn bushes, nor figs from thistles, are they? 17 Even so, every good tree bears good fruit; but the bad tree bears bad fruit* (Matthew 7:16-17).

THE BINDING OF THE DRAGON

Then I saw an angel coming down from heaven, holding the key of the abyss and a great chain in his hand. 2 And he laid hold of the dragon, the serpent of old, who is the devil and Satan, and bound him for a thousand years; 3 and he threw him into the abyss, and shut it and sealed it over him, so that he would not deceive the nations any longer, until the thousand years were completed; after these things he must be released for a short time. (Revelation 20:1-3).

This chapter begins with an angel. This angel sounds very much like the same angel that was seen in Revelation 9:1-2. That angel had been introduced by the fifth trumpet and he had opened the bottomless pit. It had resulted in the releasing of smoke that darkened the earth and brought forth a strange type of locusts. The king of these locusts had been Satan himself. The abyss was also mentioned in Revelation 9. It is the place from which the beast was said to have come (11:7) and now it is the place where the dragon in thrown.

John has just seen the end of the beast and the false prophet in the previous chapter. Now his vision focuses on the third member of that unholy trinity, the dragon. The dragon was first introduced in chapter 12.

Revelation 12	**Revelation 20**
"And the great dragon was thrown down, the serpent of old who is called the devil and Satan" (12:9).	"And he laid hold of the dragon, the serpent of old, who is the devil and Satan" (20:2).
"...who deceives the whole world; he was thrown down to the earth, and his angels were thrown down with him" (12:9).	"...he threw him into the abyss, and shut it and sealed it over him, so that he would not deceive the nations any longer, until the thousand years were completed" (20:3).
"Woe to the earth and the sea, because the devil has come down to you, having great wrath, knowing that he has only a short time" (12:12).	"...after these things he must be released for a short time" (20:3).

We read in verse 2 that Satan is bound for a thousand years. The Premillennial view sees this binding and its subsequent reign of Jesus as a literal and political kingdom in which He rules over the kingdoms of the world, thus fulfilling the Old Testament promises of the rule of Israel over the nations. The problem is that those prophecies promised an eternal reign, not one of merely a thousand years. This means it is important for the Premillennialist to see this reign only as "phase one" of that eternal kingdom and that the later "phase" which runs through all eternity will necessarily be of a different nature since it takes place on a new heaven and a new earth.

By contrast, the Amillennial view sees this reign of Christ as taking place today in His church and in His administration of the gospel throughout the world today. We have already noted that Jesus spoke to His disciples about binding Satan. It was at a time when He had just healed a demon possessed man.

> "But if I cast out demons by the Spirit of God, then the kingdom of God has come upon you. 29 Or how can anyone enter the strong man's house and carry off his property, unless he first binds the strong man? And then he will plunder his house." (Matthew 12:28-29).

When you want to rob a strong man, you do not go into his house and ask him to help you. He will throw you out on your ear. You must first tie him up. Jesus came to bind Satan. But this is not an end to itself. The binding of Satan was only the prelude to the plundering of Satan's house. When a man turns to Christ, Satan's house is plundered. When a sinner turns to the Lord and is rescued from his sin,

Satan's house is plundered. When a child hears the gospel and is saved, Satan's house in plundered. John described that process in terms of Satan being driven out and it is interesting to note that he made use of the same wording that we find here.

"Now judgment is upon this world; now the ruler of this world will be **cast out** [Greek: *ekballo*]. And I, if I am lifted up from the earth, will draw all men to Myself" (John 12:31-32).	"...he laid hold of the dragon, the serpent of old, who is the devil and Satan, and bound him for a thousand years; and he **threw** [Greek: *ballo*] him into the abyss" (Revelation 20:2-3).

Verse 3 tells us the manner of Satan's binding. It is with regard to his ability to deceive the nations. This is made clear in verse 8 when Satan is released at the end of the thousand years and we are told that he "will come out to deceive the nations." Satan was unrestricted in his deception of the nations in the days before the first coming of Christ. Polytheism and paganism were the rule and not the exception. But then Jesus came and the gospel went out and something changed with regard to the deceiving of the nations. Today you can go to every nation in the world and you can find Christians there. This is a sign that Satan's deceiving power has been severely limited. Paul alluded to this in his epistle to the Thessalonians when he spoke of how the man of sin was being restrained.

> *And you know what restrains him now, so that in his time he will be revealed. 7 For the mystery of lawlessness is already at work; only he who now restrains will do so until he is taken out of the way. 8 Then that lawless one will be revealed whom the Lord will slay with the breath of His mouth and bring to an end by the appearance of His coming; (2 Thessalonians 2:6-8).*

Satan is being restrained today. But there comes a time when he is not restrained. There is a mystery of lawlessness at work today, but when the restraints are taken off, the lawless one will no longer be a mystery, but will be openly revealed.

In Paul's day, the loosening of the restrains led to a "lawless one" who destroyed the temple and who endorsed the worship of other gods. Is there a different mystery of lawlessness at work in the world today? Perhaps there is, but I suspect it has not yet been revealed. In any case, we still await the coming of the Lord who will overcome every enemy.

THE FIRST RESURRECTION

> *Then I saw thrones, and they sat on them, and judgment was given to them. And I saw the souls of those who had been beheaded because of their testimony of Jesus and because of the*

word of God, and those who had not worshiped the beast or his
image, and had not received the mark on their forehead and on
their hand; and they came to life and reigned with Christ for a
thousand years. 5 The rest of the dead did not come to life until the
thousand years were completed. This is the first resurrection. 6
Blessed and holy is the one who has a part in the first resurrection;
over these the second death has no power, but they will be priests
of God and of Christ and will reign with Him for a thousand years.
(Revelation 20:4-6).

A surface reading of this passage would seem to point to an obvious premillennial view, describing the coming of Christ that is accompanied by the first resurrection of those souls who had been faithful to the cause of Christ. They come to life and they reign with him for a thousand years as priests of God and of Christ. It is understandable how many of the early church fathers saw this in terms of a future physical kingdom on the earth.

The description of this as the "first resurrection" is a particular problem for the Dispensational segment of premillennialism. Those who try to distinguish between a future "rapture of the church" versus a separate Second Coming event would be forced to explain how that Second Coming can be described as a first resurrection if we are to understand that there is an earlier resurrection prior to the first resurrection.

Historical Premillennialism also sees this passage as an evidence that the amillennial view is to be rejected. The two positions can be contrasted in the following chart:

Premillennialism	Amillennialism
The first resurrection takes place at the Second Coming of Christ	The first resurrection refers to the new life that we have in Christ today
This first resurrection is a physical resurrection	This first resurrection is a spiritual resurrection
Those who partake in the first resurrection are saved from the second death	
The rest of the dead are not raised until the second resurrection	The unsaved do not share in this spiritual resurrection

The amillennial regularly points to the fact that the rest of the Scriptures prophesy a general physical resurrection, not two different resurrections separated by a thousand years. For example, Daniel 12:2 speaks about how many who sleep in the dust of the ground will awake, some to everlasting life and others to everlasting contempt. In the same way, Paul speaks of a resurrection of both the righteous and the wicked (Acts 24:15) and John speaks elsewhere of the resurrection that is to take place in an hour:

> *Do not marvel at this; for an hour is coming, in which all who are in the tombs will hear His voice, 29 and will come forth; those who did the good deeds to a resurrection of life, those who committed the evil deeds to a resurrection of judgment. (John 5:28-29).*

On the other hand, Waymeyer points out that these passages "neither state nor require that the two resurrections happen simultaneously" (2016:9). He goes on to say that

> ...sometimes a given prophecy will predict two or more future events and present them in such a way that it appears they will occur simultaneously, and yet later revelation indicates a significant gap of time separating them. Commonly referred to as "telescoping," "prophetic perspective," or "prophetic foreshortening," this phenomenon is often compared to seeing two mountain peaks off in the distance—initially they appear to be right next to each other, but a closer look reveals that they are separated by a valley (2016:10).

A separate issue is how John speaks in a number of passages about the resurrection that is to take place "on the last day." If we are meant to understand these as being separated by a thousand year millennium, it is difficult to see how the resurrection of believers can be described as taking place "on the last day" (John 6:39-40; 6:44; 6:54) when the judgment of unbelievers also take place "on the last day" (John 12:48).

Here in Revelation 20, the contrast we are meant to see is between the first resurrection versus the second resurrection.

First Resurrection	**Second Resurrection**
If you have partaken in the first resurrection, then you will not be harmed by the second death	If you missed the first resurrection, then you are in danger of the judgment of the second death
Premillennial: "Physical resurrection" Amillennial: "Spiritual resurrection"	Premillennial: "Physical resurrection" Amillennial: "Physical resurrection"
Leads to the new birth	Leads to the second death

THE FINAL BATTLE

> *When the thousand years are completed, Satan will be released from his prison, 8 and will come out to deceive the nations which are in the four corners of the earth, Gog and Magog, to gather them together for the war; the number of them is like the sand of the seashore. 9 And they came up on the broad plain of the earth and surrounded the camp of the saints and the beloved city, and fire came down from heaven and devoured them. 10 And the devil who deceived them was thrown into the lake of fire and brimstone, where the beast and the false prophet are also; and they will be tormented day and night forever and ever. (Revelation 20:7-10).*

John returns to the closing of the career of Satan. He described Satan in chapter 12 as he was going to war against the woman. Now we see the final battle of that war. It begins with Satan being released from his prison. As he is released, he goes out to deceive the nations. His role in this conflict is the same role that he played in the Garden of Eden; it is the role of the deceiver. This time, the result of the deception is that those nations are gathered for war.

The nations that Satan goes out to deceive are identified by a peculiar designation. They are called "Gog and Magog." This designation is obscure to us today, but it was not so obscure to John's Jewish readers of the first century. The land of Magog had been referenced in the listing of nations found in Genesis 10 and 1 Chronicles 1 while the paired reference to "Gog and Magog" is seen in a prophetic oracle in Ezekiel 38-39. This oracle pictures a great horde coming down against the land of Israel. It describes this invading force falling upon the mountains of Israel in defeat. In the same way that Revelation 20 has given rise to a number of different interpretations, so also Ezekiel 38-39 has been the occasion for considerable speculation as to how this might be fulfilled.

Josephus equates Magog with the Scythians (Antiquities 1:123) and Ezekiel's prophecy calls to mind the Scythian invasion of Israel as described by Herodotus. Book 1 of his Histories tells how the Scythians pushed all the way to Israel, holding sway over the entire Levant for a period of 28 years and even threatening Egypt before finally returning to their homeland north of the Caucasus Mountains. This took place several decades before Ezekiel and his prophecy, and it may have established the paradigm for the prophecy as the prophet made use of language from his own past to predict an event in his future.

Have the prophecies of Ezekiel 38-39 been fulfilled of do they await a future fulfillment? Several possibilities have been suggested:

The Maccabean Revolt	In 168 B.C. the Jews revolted against their Seleucid oppressors and saw wave after wave of expeditionary forces come against them. The Jews were ultimately victorious and won their independence.	This interpretation has the advantage in seeing the conquest of the invaders; something that is promised in Ezekiel's prophecy.
The Roman Conquest of Jerusalem	In 66 A.D. the Jews rebelled against Rome and the response was a Roman invasion of Israel and the destruction of Jerusalem and the Temple.	The problem is that Ezekiel describes the destruction of the invaders and this did not take place in the Roman War.
Futurist	This view sees this prophecy as still yet to be fulfilled at some time in the future, but even here, there is no uniformity as some have equated this with the Battle of Armageddon while others have placed it at the end of the Millennium.	
Symbolic	This view sees the prophecy as using the image of a past invasion to describe God's eventual victory over evil.	A number of minor details are given that would be meaningless or ambiguous.

Notice that these views are not necessarily mutually exclusive to one another. It is entirely possible that there was a historic fulfillment in the days of the Maccabees or the Romans, a symbolic application that can be appropriately taken for all time, and also a future fulfillment. As such, it would be the same as if we spoke of the rise of another Hitler and another Nazi movement today. We would not be understood as saying that a historical figure was about to be raised from the dead. We might not even be specifically talking about the geographical region of Germany. Instead, we would be describing a movement that had a similar character to the one which the world saw in the 1940's.

Most Premillinialists take the view that the Gog and Magog battle described in Ezekiel 38-39 will take place during a future tribulation prior to the Second Coming of Christ. Some equate it with the Battle of Armageddon while others see it as a different conflict taking place a few years earlier, but most see it as taking place during that period of tribulation. The reason for this is because Ezekiel 39 goes on to speak of the cleansing of the land following the battle and how it takes place over a seven month period (Ezekiel 39:14) followed by a return of Israelites to the land..

If this is the case, then they are looking at our passage here in Revelation as referring to a different battle involving Gog and Magog nearly a thousand years later that merely happens to have the same names associated with it.

Second Coming
of Christ

Final
Judgment

Ezekiel's
Battle of Gog
& Magog

2nd Battle
of Gog &
Magog

Tribulation

1000 Year Millennium

Premillennial View of two Battles of Gog & Magog

On the other hand, an Amillennial approach is able to see both the Ezekiel reference and the description here in Revelation 20 as one and the same event, both taking place prior to the Second Coming. A comparison of Ezekiel and Revelation as it pertains to this Battle of Gog and Magog is striking.

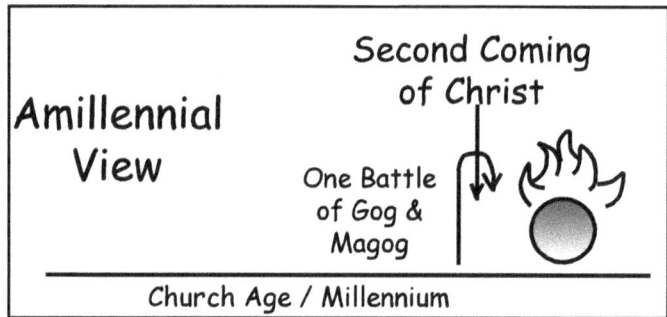

Amillennial
View

Second Coming
of Christ

One Battle
of Gog &
Magog

Church Age / Millennium

Ezekiel 38-39	Revelation
Addressed to Gog of the land of Magog (38:2).	Describes Gog and Magog being gathered for war (20:8).
They come against the land of Israel (38:18).	Described as gathering at Armageddon (16:16).
Birds and beasts are called to assemble to eat the flesh of the fallen army (39:17-19).	Birds are called to assemble to eat the flesh of the fallen army (19:17-18).

The battle here takes place *on the broad plain of the earth*, but it is also said to involve surrounding *the camp of the saints and the beloved city*. The problem here is that the city of Jerusalem is not located on a broad plain; it is in the mountains. But the problem vanishes when we note that the phrase "broad plain of the earth" is taken from the Greek πλατος της γης (*platos tes ges*) and can be rendered "breadth of the earth." The same phrasing is used in the Septuagint of Habakkuk 1:6 where the Chaldeans are seen marching throughout the breadth of the earth.

The point of our passage here in Revelation is that God wins the battle. The language is taken from the days of Moses and Joshua when the people of Israel lived in a military camp that surrounded the tabernacle of the Lord. Later, the tabernacle was replaced by the temple that stood in the midst of the city of Jerusalem. Like those Old Testament believers, we also live in a community of saints with the Lord in our midst. Like them, we live in the midst of a hostile world, surrounded by enemies on every side. It is in such a situation that we are given a vision of victory. There is coming a day when that victory will be seen by all.

THE LAST JUDGMENT

> *Then I saw a great white throne and Him who sat upon it, from whose presence earth and heaven fled away, and no place was found for them. 12 And I saw the dead, the great and the small, standing before the throne, and books were opened; and another book was opened, which is the book of life; and the dead were judged from the things which were written in the books, according to their deeds. 13 And the sea gave up the dead which were in it, and death and Hades gave up the dead which were in them; and they were judged, every one of them according to their deeds. 14 Then death and Hades were thrown into the lake of fire. This is the second death, the lake of fire. 15 And if anyone's name was not found written in the book of life, he was thrown into the lake of fire. (Revelation 20:11-15).*

Now we come to the final judgment. It is introduced by *a great white throne*. We have seen thrones depicted throughout the book of Revelation, but this is the first time that the throne of God has been depicted as being white. This is a symbol of its purity and indicates the pure judgments of God. But greater than the throne is the One who sits upon it. Nothing can withstand Him; even earth and heaven retreat from His presence.

One of the questions that I am frequently asked is about the man who never heard the gospel. How can he be judged? The answer is given here. He will be judged according to his works. He will be responsible for what he has done in life. Twice in this passage it is stated that these are judged *according to their deeds* (verses 12 and 13). This is not a new teaching. It is found throughout the Bible.

> *And lovingkindness is Yours, O Lord,*
> *For You recompense a man according to his work. (Psalm 62:12).*

> *I, the LORD, search the heart, I test the mind,*
> *Even to give to each man according to his ways,*

According to the results of his deeds. (Jeremiah 17:10).

> *"For the Son of Man is going to come in the glory of His Father with His angels, and will then repay every man according to his deeds." (Matthew 16:27).*

> *But because of your stubbornness and unrepentant heart you are storing up wrath for yourself in the day of wrath and revelation of the righteous judgment of God, 6 who will render to each person according to his deeds: 7 to those who by perseverance in doing good seek for glory and honor and immortality, eternal life; 8 but to those who are selfishly ambitious and do not obey the truth, but obey unrighteousness, wrath and indignation. (Romans 2:5-8).*

Each of these passages teach the same truth that all men are judged on the same basis. There is no partiality. God does not judge one man on a different basis than another man. The rich is judged the same as the poor. The good is judged the same as the bad. The religious is judged the same as the non-religious. This brings up the question, what about the Christian? Is the Christian also judged according to his deeds? Although we are promised in Scripture that there is no condemnation for those who are in Christ, it is nevertheless also true that the Christian's deeds will be judged.

> *For we must all appear before the judgment seat of Christ, so that each one may be recompensed for his deeds in the body, according to what he has done, whether good or bad. (2 Corinthians 5:10).*

Is this the same judgment that is being depicted here in Revelation 20? The premillennial stance is to see these as very different, separated by a thousand years. The amillennial and post millennial views these as being different aspects of the same judgment. It is helpful to compare what the Bible has to say about these judgments.

Judgment Seat of Christ	Sheep & Goats	Great White Throne
2 Corinthians 5:10	Matthew 25:31-46	Revelation 20:11-15
Focus upon believers	Divides between believers & unbelievers	Focus on unbelievers
Recompensed for their deeds	Focus on their deeds	Judged according to their deeds

Dispensationalism sees these as three separate judgments taking place at three different times. Historical Premillennialism sees the first two as taking place at the same time while Amillennialism sees all three as being different aspects of the same judgment.

Verse 12 speaks of books being opened along with the Book of Life. The reference to books being opened comes from the Old Testament vision of Daniel where he has a vision of the Ancient of Days.

> *I kept looking Until thrones were set up,*
> *And the Ancient of Days took His seat;*
> *His vesture was like white snow*
> *And the hair of His head like pure wool.*
> *His throne was ablaze with flames,*
> *Its wheels were a burning fire.*
> *10 A river of fire was flowing*
> *And coming out from before Him;*
> *Thousands upon thousands were attending Him,*
> *And myriads upon myriads were standing before Him;*
> *The court sat,*
> *And **the books were opened**. (Daniel 7:9-10).*

The reference to the books being opened seems to be connected to the idea of judgment. Jeremiah 17:1 describes how "the sin of Judah is written down with an iron stylus." The picture is of all our deeds having been recorded so that they might be judged. The Scriptures consistently teach that we will be judged according to our works. But there is another book that will be opened in addition to those books. It is the Book of Life. Though we have seen a number of references to the Book of Life in Revelation, we ought to remember that it is an Old Testament reference.

> *May they be blotted out of the book of life*
> *And may they not be recorded with the righteous. (Psalm 69:28).*

This is a case of Hebrew parallelism where the second line repeats the idea of the first line while putting it into different words. This mean that having your name in the book of life is synonymous with having your name recorded with the righteous. Who are the righteous? They are those who have come to Christ in faith, who have been credited with the righteousness of Christ, and who have been cleansed from the inside out by His sanctifying work in their lives.

Is your name written in the book of life? It is if you are one of God's people. It is if you have come in faith to the Keeper of the Book.

A NEW CREATION
Revelation 21:1-8

With this chapter we come full circle. The book of Genesis began with God creating the heavens and the earth. Now John sees a new heaven and a new earth, replacing that which has passed away. The Genesis account went on to tell of the coming of sin and death and the curse upon creation. In this chapter, we shall get a glimpse of the day when there will be no more death or curse.

NEW HEAVEN AND NEW EARTH

> *Then I saw a new heaven and a new earth; for the first heaven and the first earth passed away, and there is no longer any sea. (Rev 21:1).*

The last chapter ended with heaven and earth fleeing from the presence of the One who sat on the great white throne. Now we are told that this is not a temporary situation. There is coming a day when things are going to change and they will stay changed.

Have you ever tried to make a new beginning? Perhaps you decided that you were going to have family devotions. You planned it all out and you set an appointed time and you sat down with your family and an open Bible. You did it again on the second day. But on the third day, something came up and you could not get to it. It is like the man who said, "It's easy to stop smoking; I've done it hundreds of times." It is hard to change because change usually doesn't stay changed. But there is coming a day when things are going to change and they will stay changed.

The description of a new heaven and a new earth comes to us from the pages of the Old Testament. The prophet Isaiah makes mention of the new heavens and a new earth twice at the close of his book.

> *For behold, I create new heavens and a new earth;*
> *And the former things will not be remembered or come to mind.*
> *(Isaiah 65:17).*

> *"For just as the new heavens and the new earth*
> *Which I make will endure before Me," declares the LORD,*
> *"So your offspring and your name will endure.*
> *23 And it shall be from new moon to new moon*
> *And from sabbath to sabbath,*
> *All mankind will come to bow down before Me," says the LORD.*

(Isaiah 66:22-23).

Isaiah began his book with a call for the heaven and earth to take witness against the sinfulness of the people of Judah. The first half of the book of Isaiah is filled with judgment, just as much of the book of Revelation is filled with judgment. But toward the end of the book of Isaiah, there is a change and there is hope for the future in the same way that we have seen a change here in the closing chapters of Revelation.

In describing his vision of the new heavens and the new earth, John adds that *"there is no longer any sea."* The Genesis account went from the creation of the heavens and the earth to the darkness that lay over the face of the deep. But here in Revelation, there will be no darkness and there is no sea.

To the ancient Jew, the sea was the object of fear. There are no natural harbors along the coast of Canaan and the Jews were therefore not primarily a seagoing people. When he thought of the sea, the Jewish reader thought of the flood in the days of Noah, passing through the Red Sea which came together to destroy the armies of the Pharaoh, or the experiences of Jonah and his adventures in the sea.

In the Old Testament, Daniel's vision of beasts coming out of the sea represented nations that would arise. In the same way, we saw in Revelation 13:1 the blasphemous beast coming out of the sea and Revelation 17:1 had the harlot sitting on many waters. This pictures the sea as a place of chaos, darkness, and danger. Now that is gone, for there is no longer any sea.

THE HOLY CITY

> *And I saw the holy city, new Jerusalem, coming down out of heaven from God, made ready as a bride adorned for her husband. (Rev 21:2)*.

The next thing John sees is the holy city. It is also described as "new Jerusalem." We have already seen a reference to the new Jerusalem in Revelation 3:12 where it is called "the city of God." Jesus had promised that overcomers would receive the name of God and the name of the city of Jerusalem. That is to say, they would be citizens of that city.

The new Jerusalem is seen coming from heaven *made ready as a bride adorned for her husband*. We have already seen a reference to a bride in Revelation 19 and we saw how that stood in contrast to the harlot of the previous chapters. We suggested that the harlot sounded very much like the old Jerusalem. Now we see the new Jerusalem. The description of Jerusalem as a bride is an Old Testament concept.

Isaiah 62:1-7 presents this theme in which Jerusalem is pictured shining forth in righteousness. Addressing the city of Jerusalem, he says:

> *For as a young man marries a virgin,*
> *So your sons will marry you;*
> *And as the bridegroom rejoices over the bride,*
> *So your God will rejoice over you. (Isaiah 62:5).*

When we come to the New Testament, we see that same image used of the church. This should not surprise us. The Bible regularly speaks of the church in the same terms that the Old Testament used to describe Israel. The term "church" is not used here in Revelation 21-22, but that does not mean it is absent. When you see the bride of the Lord, you are seeing the church, whether it is here in the New Testament or back in the Old Testament.

In Revelation 19:7 we read that "His bride has made herself ready." We were told about the bride, but we did not see the bride. Now we see the bride who has made herself ready. This is the language of a wedding. This is significant to the millennial question since the Premillennial view sees the wedding to have taken place a thousand years earlier. The Amillennial can view this as the next event following the return of Christ that was pictured in Revelation 19.

THE VOICE FROM THE THRONE

> *And I heard a loud voice from the throne, saying, "Behold, the tabernacle of God is among men, and He will dwell among them, and they shall be His people, and God Himself will be among them, 4 and He will wipe away every tear from their eyes; and there will no longer be any death; there will no longer be any mourning, or crying, or pain; the first things have passed away." (Revelation 21:3-4).*

We will return to the vision of Jerusalem, but first, John's attention is drawn to a voice coming from the throne. An announcement is about to be made. It is an announcement pertaining to God and His relationship with His people.

The children of Israel were God's special people. While they were camping before Mount Sinai, the tabernacle of God was set up in their very midst. Each morning when they awakened, they would see the column of smoke and they would know that the Lord was in their midst. Each evening when they went to bed, they would look at the tabernacle and see a pillar of fire rising up into the desert sky and they would know that the Lord was with them. In his gospel account, John uses this same idea of the tabernacle to refer to the first coming of Jesus.

> *And the Word became flesh, and **dwelt** among us, and we saw His glory, glory as of the only begotten from the Father, full of grace and truth. (John 1:14).*

When John says that the Word "dwelt" among us, the term that he uses is the Greek word σκηνοω (*skenoo*). This verbal form is related to the Greek word σκηνη (skene), meaning "tent." The birth of Jesus was when God put on flesh and "tabernacled" with His people. Paul uses this same analogy when he speaks about the earthly tent in which we live.

> *For we know that if the earthly tent which is our house is torn down, we have a building from God, a house not made with hands, eternal in the heavens. 2 For indeed in this house we groan, longing to be clothed with our dwelling from heaven, 3 inasmuch as we, having put it on, will not be found naked. 4 For indeed while we are in this tent, we groan, being burdened, because we do not want to be unclothed but to be clothed, so that what is mortal will be swallowed up by life. (2 Corinthians 5:1-4).*

Paul speaks of our earthly bodies as a tent, a tabernacle. Elsewhere, he describes our bodies as the temple of God (1 Corinthians 6:19). The tabernacle and the temple were the places where God dwelled. We have entered into that same relationship with the God of the universe. He has pitched His tent with us. It is not a literal tent. He has pitched His tent in our hearts.

This brings us to a question. Is this something that is going to take place in the future, or is it something that is taking place today? It is both. God is with us today and He is also going to continue to be with us in the future.

He will wipe away every tear from their eyes. There is something very tender here. I cannot read this without thinking of the times that my daughter came to me as a little girl with a skinned knee or a hurt finger, wanting to be comforted. God is in the tear-wiping business. He does not say that there are no hurts in this life. He does say that He is able to heal those hurts. One day they will be banished for good.

What does He do in the meantime? Where do we find comfort today? We find it in His Spirit; that is why He is called the Comforter. We also find it in one another. If we are children of God, then we need to be in the tear-wiping business, too. The former things have not completely passed away. The world in which we live still has tears and death and mourning and pain.

Steve Brown tells the story of two little girls who were playing when one of them stepped on the other's foot. There were some tears and then one girl asked the other, "Will you forgive me?" The other replied through her tears, "I can forgive you for stepping on my foot, but I can't forgive the pain because it still hurts."

Why does God allow the pain to linger? I don't have an easy answer, but I know that sometimes we can serve the Lord better through our wound than through our wellness. In the meantime, we wait for the day when these things will have passed away.

THE ANNOUNCEMENT OF THE KING

> *And He who sits on the throne said, "Behold, I am making all things new." And He said, "Write, for these words are faithful and true." 6 Then He said to me, "It is done. I am the Alpha and the Omega, the beginning and the end. I will give to the one who thirsts from the spring of the water of life without cost. 7 He who overcomes will inherit these things, and I will be his God and he will be My son. 8 But for the cowardly and unbelieving and abominable and murderers and immoral persons and sorcerers and idolaters and all liars, their part will be in the lake that burns with fire and brimstone, which is the second death." (Revelation 21:5-8).*

The One who sits upon the throne is the same one who was sitting upon the Great White Throne in the previous chapter. He is the same one who was sitting upon the throne in Revelation 4:2 and 5:7. He is the Lord.

Earlier in the book of Revelation, we have seen God speaking through intermediaries. He has spoken through angels, through prophets, and through apostles. Now He makes His own pronouncement. He instructs John to write down His words. He begins with the announcement: *"It is done."* You will remember that it was in the Gospel of John that we read of the dying words of Jesus: "It is finished." Although the expressions are similar, they are not the same, but they are related in a cause and effect relationship. Because the first cry took place, the second will also take place.

I am the Alpha and the Omega, the beginning and the end. This is the same title of which we read at the beginning of the book in Revelation 1:8. But it also calls to mind the words of Jesus in that same chapter:

> *When I saw Him, I fell at His feet like a dead man. And He placed His right hand on me, saying, "Do not be afraid; I am the first and the last, 18 and the living One; and I was dead, and behold, I am alive forevermore, and I have the keys of death and of Hades." (Revelation 1:17-18).*

349

Jesus was able to take for Himself the same title that is used here for God. He is the first and the last. This is an Old Testament reference. (Isaiah 44:6; 48:12).

His promise of provision is given in the words, *"I will give to the one who thirsts from the spring of the water of life without cost."* This calls to mind the conversation that Jesus had with the Samaritan woman. That conversation was recorded in the Gospel of John. Jesus asked the woman for a drink and they had begun talking about the well at which they were sitting. We tend to take water for granted in our western culture. But in the ancient world, water was considered to be precious. A stream of flowing water would be in great demand. That is why the words of Jesus were so striking.

> *Jesus answered and said to her, "Everyone who drinks of this water will thirst again; 14 but whoever drinks of the water that I will give him shall never thirst; but the water that I will give him will become in him a well of water springing up to eternal life." (John 4:13-14).*

What is this water? What does it symbolize? We are not left in any doubt as Jesus Himself later explained His words.

> *"He who believes in Me, as the Scripture said, 'From his innermost being will flow rivers of living water.'" 39 But this He spoke of the Spirit, whom those who believed in Him were to receive; for the Spirit was not yet given, because Jesus was not yet glorified. (John 7:38-39).*

Water is used for a number of purposes. It is used for cleansing. This symbolizes the cleansing ministry of the Holy Spirit in our lives. Water is also used to quench thirst. When you are hot and dry, there is nothing like a cool glass of water. When we hunger and thirst for righteousness, it is the Holy Spirit that satisfies. Sometimes we make the mistake of trying to give water to people who are not thirsty. There are a lot of people who are not interested in God. They don't really want to know God. They have never stood in the shoes of the Psalmist as he cried out:

> *As the deer pants for the water brooks,*
> *So my soul pants for You, O God.*
> *2 My soul thirsts for God, for the living God;*
> *When shall I come and appear before God? (Psalm 42:1-2).*

Have you ever come to the point in your life where you have thirsted for God? If you have, then there is good news here. There is a source of His Spirit available for you.

He who overcomes will inherit these things. This is the twelfth and final time that the book of Revelation speaks of overcoming. In each of these instances, the Greek word used has been the Greek word νικαω (*"nikao"*). The same word has been adopted by a company today making sports shoes; they are called "Nike Shoes." This is the Greek word for "victory." This idea of victory has been seen throughout the Book of Revelation. We have seen repeatedly this promise that Jesus wins. He is the overcomer and we are given a promise that we overcome with Him when we believe.

In verse 8, we are told of a different group of people. In contrast to those who overcome, these are the vanquished. They are described in a series of short, terse attributes:

- Cowardly
- Unbelieving
- Abominable (detestable)
- Murderers
- Immoral persons
- Sorcerers
- Idolaters
- All liars

These are also given an inheritance: *their part will be in the lake that burns with fire and brimstone, which is the second death*. We have already seen the spring of water of life. By contrast, we are told of a lake that burns with fire and brimstone.

An inheritance awaits every man. Either it will be an inheritance of life or else it will be an inheritance of death. This is not a scare tactic. It is the Word of God. It is a solemn warning to all who would take God's message lightly.

When we read that the cowardly and unbelieving and abominable and murderers and immoral persons and sorcerers and idolaters and all liars are excluded from heaven, our natural question is to ask, "Who does enter in?" We would expect to read that only those who are nice are able to enter. This passage does not say that. Instead, we read several verses earlier that there is only one requirement. You must be thirsty. Jesus says in verse 6, "I will give to the one who thirsts from the spring of the water of life without cost." No cost, just need. All you need is need. All you need is nothing. Most of us do not have it.

This is why Christ came as the perfect sacrifice. He is the Savior who saves. He paid our penalty, suffering the punishment that we deserved in order to give us His inheritance. He came to us when we were likened to the spiritual prostitute of Revelation 17-18 and He changes us into the virgin bride that is presented in this chapter.

Steve Gregg points out that, following the introductory statement of verse 1, this section serves as an outline of the rest of the book of Revelation (1997:492):

Content	21:1-8	Rev 21-22
New Jerusalem	21:2	21:9-21
God dwells among men	21:3	21:22-27
Renewal of the world	21:5a	22:1-5
"These words are true and faithful"	21:5b	22:6-10
Work complete: "I am Alpha & Omega"	21:6a	22:11-15
Final blessing: Water of life to all who thirst	21:6b-7	22:16-17
Final curse upon the rebellious	21:8	22:18-19

THE CITY OF GOD
Revelation 21:9 - 22:5

The last six chapters of the book of Revelation could be described as the tale of two cities. We saw one of those cities in Revelation 17-18. It was seen in the form of a prostitute who had the name of Babylon engraved on her forehead. Now as we come to Revelation 21, we shall see another city. It will also be represented as a woman, but this woman shall be a virgin bride.

In a beautiful song which praises God as our refuge and our strength, the Psalmist pictures a place that he calls the city of God. It is not merely a city that God owns, for He owns all there is. Rather, this describes the place where God resides. It is His dwelling place.

> *There is a river whose streams make glad the city of God,*
> *The holy dwelling places of the Most High.*
> *5 God is in the midst of her, she will not be moved;*
> *God will help her when morning dawns.*
> *6 The nations made an uproar, the kingdoms tottered;*
> *He raised His voice, the earth melted.*
> *7 The LORD of hosts is with us;*
> *The God of Jacob is our stronghold. Selah. (Psalms 46:4-7).*

In the midst of all the stress and strife of this world, there is a place of rest. We have a refuge. It is the city of God, the place where God lives. The nations might be in an uproar, the economy might be as turbulent as storm-tossed waves, everything else might be in a state of upheaval, but there is a place of calm and security in that place where God is.

THE ADVENT OF THE CITY

> *Then one of the seven angels who had the seven bowls full of the seven last plagues came and spoke with me, saying, "Come here, I will show you the bride, the wife of the Lamb." 10 And he carried me away in the Spirit to a great and high mountain, and showed me the holy city, Jerusalem, coming down out of heaven from God, 11 having the glory of God. Her brilliance was like a very costly stone, as a stone of crystal-clear jasper. (Revelation 21:9-11).*

John receives an angelic invitation to come and see the bride. It comes from one of the seven angels who had previously held one of the seven bowls of wrath. One of these angels had already served as a guide with an invitation to come and to see the harlot. That had been a picture of shame and of judgment. Now John is treated to a picture of honor and delight. It is a movement from prostitute to princess, from a vanquished harlot to a virgin bride.

Revelation 17:1-3	Revelation 21:9
Then one of the seven angels who had the seven bowls came and spoke with me, saying...	*Then one of the seven angels who had the seven bowls full of the seven last plagues came and spoke with me, saying...*
"Come here, I will show you the judgment of the great harlot who sits on many waters"	*"Come here, I will show you the bride, the wife of the Lamb."*
And he carried me away in the Spirit into a wilderness...	*And he carried me away in the Spirit to a great and high mountain...*

The angel tells John that he is going to show him the bride, the one who is the wife of the lamb. This is the title of the church. Only here she is called the holy city, Jerusalem. This is the city for which Abraham was looking.

> *By faith Abraham, when he was called, obeyed by going out to a place which he was to receive for an inheritance; and he went out, not knowing where he was going. 9 By faith he lived as an alien in the land of promise, as in a foreign land, dwelling in tents with Isaac and Jacob, fellow heirs of the same promise; 10 for he was looking for the city which has foundations, whose architect and builder is God. (Hebrews 11:8-10).*

Abraham was looking for a city. It was not a city that had been built by human hands. It was a city that had been built by God. There is such a city. It is made up of the citizens of the kingdom of God. It is made up of those who are the sons of Abraham through faith (Galatians 3:7).

The thing that characterizes the city in John's vision is that it has the glory of God. This has been a familiar theme throughout the Old Testament. The presence of God as he led the children of Israel through the wilderness was seen in a cloud by day and a pillar of fire by night, marking the glory of God. When the tabernacle was first constructed, the radiant cloud of the glory of God came and moved into it.

> *Then the cloud covered the tent of meeting, and the glory of the LORD filled the tabernacle. 35 Moses was not able to enter the tent of meeting because the cloud had settled on it, and the*

glory of the LORD filled the tabernacle. (Exodus 40:34-35).

Years later, when Solomon built the temple to the Lord, the glory of the Lord moved into the temple, indicating that God had come to dwell among His people.

> *It happened that when the priests came from the holy place, the cloud filled the house of the LORD, 11 so that the priests could not stand to minister because of the cloud, for the glory of the LORD filled the house of the LORD. (1 Kings 8:10-11).*

This theme of the glory of the Lord filling the house of the Lord continued into the period of the prophets. Isaiah tells of a vision in which he saw the temple and it was filled with the glory of the Lord (Isaiah 6:1-4). When the temple was destroyed by the Babylonians, that destruction was announced by Ezekiel's vision of the Lord leaving His temple (Ezekiel 8-11). Even after the Jewish return from captivity and the rebuilding of the temple in the days of Haggai and Zechariah, the people waited in vain for a return of God's glory. It did not come.

John has already described the coming of Jesus as the One who became flesh to manifest God in our presence. The glory of God was demonstrated in Him.

> *And the Word became flesh, and dwelt among us, and we saw His glory, glory as of the only begotten from the Father, full of grace and truth. (John 1:14).*

This brings us to a question. Where is the glory of God today? Where is His presence manifested? It is in the church. It is in the hearts of His people. This is why Paul says that your body in the temple of the Holy Spirit (1 Corinthians 6:19). He says that there is a sense in which, as we mirror the person of Christ in our lives, we *are being transformed into the same image from glory to glory* (2 Corinthians 3:18).

When I was writing the first draft of this chapter, I found myself getting excited about the truth of how God's people are called to reflect His glory today. That ought to make the church a spectacular place to be. Everyone who comes to church ought to be enthralled by our love and our unity. As I was thinking such lofty thoughts, I heard the washing machine start banging in our laundry room. Paula had put in a load of laundry and it had become imbalanced as it entered the spin cycle. It thunked its way to a halt and then started an awful buzzing. As I went out to rearrange the laundry and restart the machine, I could not help but to note that this is what happens to the church. We are filled with the glory of the Lord, but we have become imbalanced by this issue or by that sin and the result is an awful buzzing.

What is the answer. It isn't only to press a button and make the buzzing go away. It is also to readjust the laundry. Some of us have laundry that needs readjusting.

The good news is that we worship a God who provides clean laundry, fine linen white and clean. We can come to Him in repentance, looking for forgiveness and we will find it.

WALLS, GATES, AND FOUNDATIONS

> *It had a great and high wall, with twelve gates, and at the gates twelve angels; and names were written on them, which are the names of the twelve tribes of the sons of Israel. 13 There were three gates on the east and three gates on the north and three gates on the south and three gates on the west. 14 And the wall of the city had twelve foundation stones, and on them were the twelve names of the twelve apostles of the Lamb. (Revelation 21:12-14).*

The city of John's vision is surrounded by a great, high wall. It is a secure city. Cities in the ancient world were only as strong as the walls that surrounded them. The greater the walls, the greater the city was considered to be.

There are twelve gates and twelve foundation stones. It is a significant number in the Scriptures. There were twelve tribes of Israel and there were twelve apostles. It is a number that indicates the people of God.

John sees twelve angels standing before twelve gates. These angels bear the names of the twelve tribes of Israel. They represent the Old Testament people of God. There are also twelve foundation stones. These stones bear the names of the twelve apostles. They represent the New Testament people of God.

The point is that God's church is made up of both Old Testament saints and New Testament saints. God does not have one church for Old Testament Israel and another for the New Testament church. He has made both groups into one. There is only one church and one New Jerusalem and one bride.

THE MEASURING OF THE CITY

> *The one who spoke with me had a gold measuring rod to measure the city, and its gates and its wall. 16 The city is laid out as a square, and its length is as great as the width; and he measured the city with the rod, fifteen hundred miles; its length and width and height are equal. 17 And he measured its wall, seventy-two yards, according to human measurements, which are also angelic measurements. (Revelation 21:15-17).*

In Revelation 11:1, we saw that John was given a measuring rod and told to measure the temple. This time it is the angel who measures the city. This symbolism of measuring a holy area is drawn from the Old Testament book of Ezekiel. In Ezekiel 40, the prophet is taken "in the visions of God" to a high mountain in the land of Israel where measurements are taken of each wall and each gate. This is more than a lesson in ancient architectural trivia. It is connected to a spiritual principle.

> *Then I heard one speaking to me from the house, while a man was standing beside me. 7 He said to me, "Son of man, this is the place of My throne and the place of the soles of My feet, where I will dwell among the sons of Israel forever. And the house of Israel will not again defile My holy name, neither they nor their kings, by their harlotry and by the corpses of their kings when they die, 8 by setting their threshold by My threshold and their door post beside My door post, with only the wall between Me and them. And they have defiled My holy name by their abominations which they have committed. So I have consumed them in My anger. 9 Now let them put away their harlotry and the corpses of their kings far from Me; and I will dwell among them forever." (Ezekiel 43:6-9).*

The first part of the book of Ezekiel was a series of visions of judgment in which the temple and the city of Jerusalem were destroyed and the Jewish people carried off into captivity to Babylon. But the last portion of the book contains a vision of a rebuilt temple. The purpose of this vision of the temple is that Israel might recognize the results of her former sins and be encouraged to return and walk in obedience to the Lord. If this took place, then God would grant them a part in His new temple.

In the same way, the first part of the book of Revelation has contained judgments and seals and trumpets and vials of wrath. But we have come now to the end of the book containing the vision of a new Jerusalem. As John watches the angel measure the city of God, that is a picture of what God is doing with His people today. God has measured us. He has set us apart and made us different. We are His select people. We are His city.

Now we come to the measurement of the city.

Our English translation puts these measurements in English equivalents. On the surface, this seems to be a good thing since we do not normally speak in terms of stadia and cubits. But this may be a case where the old King James Version is a more helpful translation as it gives an exact numerical translation rather than equivalent distances. Why would this make a difference? It makes a difference because numbers throughout the book of Revelation have symbolic significance. Think of the significance of the following numbers:

357

666	The number of the Antichrist
7	A number signifying perfection
12	God's people (12 tribes of Israel, 12 apostles)
144,000	12 x 12,000 - a lot of God's people

Now we have some new numbers. The first is the length of the walls. Our translation says that *he measured the city with the rod, fifteen hundred miles*. Though this is technically an accurate rendition of the distance being described, it misses the importance of the symbolism. The Greek text says, *"He measured the city with the rod, twelve thousand stadia."* A stadia is approximately 600 feet and it is true that this comes out to around fifteen hundred miles, but it is not the distance that is important but the symbolism behind the numbers, twelve thousand. We have seen that the symbolic ideal behind the number twelve. That is a number that represents the people of God with twelve tribes of Israel and twelve apostles of the New Testament church. We also saw the number of a thousand in Revelation 20. The reign of Jesus with His saints was said to last for a thousand years. It is a great number. We also saw the number of people sealed out of each tribe in Revelation 7 as being 12,000.

This brings us to the point of the measurement of the city. It implies that the church of God is going to be very big. Its citizens will be more in number than any other city on earth. This did not appear to be the case in John's day. The church had started with a handful of disciples in an upper room. It had grown since then, but it was still a minority religion and under increasing persecution. People could only wonder whether it would survive at all. The church has grown a lot since that time. It will continue to grow until the Master Architect declares it to be completed.

Notice also that the length and width and height of the city are equal. It has been suggested by at least one commentator that this is a pyramid, but there is no indication from the text that this is the case. Instead we naturally visualize a perfect cube. What is so special about this shape? This was the same shape of the Holy of Holies in the Tabernacle. It was also the same shape of the Holy of Holies in Solomon's Temple (1 Kings 6:16; 2 Chronicles 3:8). The Holy of Holies was the place of the presence of God. The New Jerusalem is also the place of the presence of God.. In verse 22 we shall read that there was no temple in this city. It is all temple. The Father and the Son are temple enough.

Next, the angel measures the wall. Again, our English translation is accurate while obscuring the symbolism of the measurement. *Seventy-two yards* is actually one hundred forty four cubits. You will remember that the symbolic number of the redeemed in Revelation 7 numbered 144,000. They carried the representative names of the twelve sons of Israel, but we noted that the passage went on to describe them as being from every tribe and tongue and nation.

MATERIALS OF THE CITY

> *The material of the wall was jasper; and the city was pure gold, like clear glass. 19 The foundation stones of the city wall were adorned with every kind of precious stone. The first foundation stone was jasper; the second, sapphire; the third, chalcedony; the fourth, emerald; 20 the fifth, sardonyx; the sixth, sardius; the seventh, chrysolite; the eighth, beryl; the ninth, topaz; the tenth, chrysoprase; the eleventh, jacinth; the twelfth, amethyst. 21 And the twelve gates were twelve pearls; each one of the gates was a single pearl. And the street of the city was pure gold, like transparent glass. (Revelation 21:18-21).*

Remember that the city is being described in terms of a bride. As we come to the materials of the city, we are seeing the jewelry of the bride. These are her ornamentations. The wall is jasper and the city is pure gold like clear glass. The city has a translucent veil of the most costly kind.

The twelve foundation stones are adorned with the most precious stones known to man at that time. These stones had a special significance to one schooled in the Jewish religion. A number of these stones are parallel to the stones that were on the breastplate of the high priest, especially when we consult the Septuagint reading and note that the names of some of the stones seem to have changed over time (Exodus 28:17-20).

Stones in Revelation		Stones in High Priest's Breastplate	
1	*Jasper*	First Row	Sardius (LXX), topaz and emerald
2	*Sapphire*		
3	*Chalcedony*		
4	*Emerald*	Second Row	A turquoise, a sapphire and a jasper (LXX)
5	*Sardonyx*		
6	*Sardius*		
7	*Chrysolite*	Third Row	A jacinth, an agate and an amethyst
8	*Beryl*		
9	*Topaz*		
10	*Chrysoprase*	Fourth Row	a beryl and an onyx and a jasper
11	*Jacinth*		
12	*Amethyst*		

The high priest had these stones upon his breastplate. Engraved upon each of the stones was one of the names of one of the tribes of Israel, a stone for each tribe. That means the stones represented the twelve tribes of Israel. They represented the people of God. As was the case with the breastplate of the high priest, so it is with the foundation stones of the city.

> *...you also, as living stones, are being built up as a spiritual house for a holy priesthood, to offer up spiritual sacrifices acceptable to God through Jesus Christ. (1 Peter 2:5).*

You are part of God's spiritual house and his spiritual city. These precious stones represent you and make it clear that you are greatly valued by the Lord. It also shows that you are part of something that goes back to the Old Testament. You have been grafted into the family of Israel.

The twelve gates are made up of twelve pearls. Does this represent the twelve tribes of Israel or the twelve apostles of the church? The answer is yes. There is an interesting parallel to be made between John's vision of the New Jerusalem in Revelation 21-22 with Ezekiel's vision of a new temple.

Ezekiel's Vision	John's Revelation
A Temple within the city (40-48)	The New Jerusalem (21-22)
Ezekiel is taken in this vision to a very high mountain (40:2)	John is carried in the Spirit to a great and high mountain (21:10)
A man uses a rod to measure the dimensions of the temple (40:5-ff)	An angel measures the city with a rod (21:15-17)
The entire temple area is measured as a perfect square (42:15-20)	The entire city is measured as a perfect cube (21:16)
The presence of the glory of the Lord enters the temple (43:3-4)	There is no need of sun or moon because the Lord illumines His city (22:5)
No foreigner is admitted into the temple (44:9)	Nothing unclean and no unbeliever is allowed into the city (21:8, 27)
A river of water flows out of the temple (47:1)	A river of the water of life comes from the throne of God (22:1)
There are a total of 12 gates around the city (48:30-34)	There are 12 gates to the city (21:21)

The name of the city shall be: "The Lord is there" (48:35).	The throne of God shall be there (22:3)

THE TEMPLE OF THE CITY

> *I saw no temple in it, for the Lord God the Almighty and the Lamb are its temple. (Revelation 21:22).*

A city without a temple would be highly unusual in the ancient world. Most cities were filled with temples. The temple would traditionally be placed at the highest point of the city. Even the temple of Jerusalem stands at the highest part of the old city.

To the Jewish mind, a city without a temple would be a city to be avoided. But John does not see a temple in this city because the Lord and the Lamb are its temple. It does not have a temple built with brick and stone; this temple is God Himself. Jesus stood in Jerusalem and said, "Destroy this temple and in three days I will raise it up," but He was speaking of the temple of His body. This also reminds us of another conversation that is recorded in the Gospel of John. It was the discussion with the Samaritan woman.

> *Jesus said to her, "Woman, believe Me, an hour is coming when neither in this mountain nor in Jerusalem will you worship the Father. 22 You worship what you do not know; we worship what we know, for salvation is from the Jews. 23 But an hour is coming, and now is, when the true worshipers will worship the Father in spirit and truth; for such people the Father seeks to be His worshipers." (John 4:21-23).*

Jesus did not say this day was going to come far in the future. He did not even say that it was drawing near. He said that an hour is coming and now is when men shall enter into a spiritual worship. This means His words are describing a present reality.

Our worship is to consist of more than mere rote liturgy. It is not to be limited to a building or even to a specific day of the week. When John says there is no temple, he means that it is all temple. That is to be our present reality today. Our worship is not to be confined to what we do on Sunday morning. Our church experience is to be "all church." You are the Lord's house and that house is to be open for prayer and for worship throughout the week.

THE LIGHT OF THE CITY

> *And the city has no need of the sun or of the moon to shine on it, for the glory of God has illumined it, and its lamp is the Lamb. 24 The nations will walk by its light, and the kings of the earth will bring their glory into it. 25 In the daytime (for there will be no night there) its gates will never be closed; 26 and they will bring the glory and the honor of the nations into it; 27 and nothing unclean, and no one who practices abomination and lying, shall ever come into it, but only those whose names are written in the Lamb's book of life. (Revelation 21:23-27).*

The references to the absence of sun and moon are echoes of a prophecy found in the book of Isaiah where that prophet describes the conditions of the renewal of the land following its captivity.

Revelation 21	Isaiah 60
And the city has no need of the sun or of the moon to shine on it, for the glory of God has illumined it, and its lamp is the Lamb (21:23).	*No longer will you have the sun for light by day, Nor for brightness will the moon give you light; But you will have the LORD for an everlasting light, And your God for your glory (60:19).*
The nations will walk by its light (21:24).	*Nations will come to your light, And kings to the brightness of your rising (60:3).*
And the kings of the earth will bring their glory into it (21:24).	*Foreigners will build up your walls, And their kings will minister to you (60:10).*
Its gates will never be closed (21:25).	*Your gates will be open continually; They will not be closed day or night (60:11).*
And they will bring the glory and the honor of the nations into it (21:26).	*So that men may bring to you the wealth of the nations, With their kings led in procession. (60:11).*
And nothing unclean, and no one who practices abomination and lying, shall ever come into it (21:27).	*Then all your people will be righteous (60:21).*

There used to be a popular saying that the sun never set on the British Empire. It meant that there were British colonies all around the world and the sun was always shining upon one of them. That image is described as a reality here. The theme of light and darkness is a common one in John's writings.

> *This is the message we have heard from Him and announce to you, that God is Light, and in Him there is no darkness at all. 6 If we say that we have fellowship with Him and yet walk in the darkness, we lie and do not practice the truth; 7 but if we walk in the Light as He Himself is in the Light, we have fellowship with one another, and the blood of Jesus His Son cleanses us from all sin. (1 John 1:5-7).*

> *Then Jesus again spoke to them, saying, "I am the Light of the world; he who follows Me will not walk in the darkness, but will have the Light of life." (John 8:12).*

> *"While I am in the world, I am the Light of the world." (John 9:5).*

> *So Jesus said to them, "For a little while longer the Light is among you. Walk while you have the Light, so that darkness will not overtake you; he who walks in the darkness does not know where he goes. 36 While you have the Light, believe in the Light, so that you may become sons of Light." (John 12:35-36a).*

God is light. Jesus is also the light and His people are sons of light. The thing about light is that it lets you see things the way they are. When it is dark, you have to be careful not to bump into things. There is always a danger of falling when you walk in the dark. But light lets you see.

City gates were usually closed at night. The purpose of the gates of a city were to keep people out. They were closed whenever there was a danger from hostile forces and, because you never knew when an invader might come, they were closed at night. But the gates of this city will never be closed because the enemies of this city have all been defeated.

The open gate reminds us of the way that entry to the Garden of Eden was closed and guarded after the fall. Adam and Eve were excluded from the garden and their reentry was barred by an angelic guard. Here in the New Jerusalem, an open gate is an invitation to enter. There is such an invitation to all who stand without. But there is also a warning. The warning comes in the qualification which must be met in order to enter.

Those Forbidden to Enter	Those Permitted to Enter
Nothing unclean, and no one who practices abomination and lying, shall ever come into it... (21:27).	*But only those whose names are written in the Lamb's book of life (21:27).*

Sin is prohibited from entering into the city. That is what makes it a holy city. It is a city where people are welcome, but where sin is not. This is why Christ came, to deal with the sin issue. It is our sins that separate us from God. Jesus died to take the penalty of our sin upon Himself. It has been said that the only manmade things that will ever be permitted into the holy city will be the scars in his hands, feet, and wounded side. They shall serve as eternal testimonies of God's love for His people.

THE RIVER AND THE TREE OF LIFE

> *Then he showed me a river of the water of life, clear as crystal, coming from the throne of God and of the Lamb, 2 in the middle of its street. On either side of the river was the tree of life, bearing twelve kinds of fruit, yielding its fruit every month; and the leaves of the tree were for the healing of the nations. (Revelation 22:1-2).*

The river that John sees is mirrored in the book of Ezekiel where that prophet described a river flowing out from the Temple and down to the Dead Sea (Ezekiel 47:1-12). Ezekiel goes on to relate how the river would heal the Dead Sea of its saltiness so that fish would again live in it.

Here we see that the river flows from the throne of God and of the Lamb. This is not describing two thrones. It is only one throne; the throne of God (Revelation 7:15; 12:5). But there are two people on the one throne. God shares His throne with His Son. The river flows from the throne the way water flowed from the rock to give water to the Israelites in the wilderness.

On either side of the river is the tree of life. The tree of life had been in the Garden of Eden. Adam and Eve had enjoyed free access to every tree of the garden until they had sinned and that included the tree of life. When they were banished from the garden, it was so that they would not eat from the tree of life and thereby continue to live forever.

What we have described here is not just one tree, but a number of trees. They grow on both sides of the river. There is no shortage of this precious fruit. There is plenty for all to partake. Furthermore, we read that these trees bore twelve different kinds of fruit, yielding fruit every month. There are twelve months in a year and there were twelve kinds of fruit and it sounds as though there was a different kind each month. There is a wonderful variety presented in this description. It reminds us that we worship a God of variety. Sometimes we get stuck doing the same old thing in the same old way. We forget that God brings variety. He makes people and churches and ministries in all different shapes and sizes.

The leaves of the tree were for the healing of the nations (22:2). The nations today are in need of healing. They have sought to find it in many ways. They have tried philosophy, learning, and treaty after treaty. Nothing has worked. There is only one cure for the ailment that afflicts the nations. It is the tree of life. Only then will the nations be able to be healed.

IN THE PRESENCE OF THE LORD

> *There will no longer be any curse; and the throne of God and of the Lamb will be in it, and His bond-servants will serve Him; 4 they will see His face, and His name will be on their foreheads. 5 And there will no longer be any night; and they will not have need of the light of a lamp nor the light of the sun, because the Lord God will illumine them; and they will reign forever and ever. (Revelation 22:3-5).*

Jerusalem was a blessed city. It was blessed because this is where the temple of God was located. The New Jerusalem is the place where God's presence is manifested. It does not need to have a temple because the entire city is the temple.

There will no longer be any curse (22:5). The removal of the curse is especially significant. The curse goes all the way back to the Garden of Eden. It was there that God brought a threefold curse against the man, the woman, and the earth.

- The curse against the man was that he had now entered into a war with the earth and he would have to fight the earth in order to force it to yield its produce. This would come through great effort and the earth would produce thorns and thistles to hinder that effort. In the end, the earth would win and he would return to the ground to be buried in it.

- The curse against the woman was that childbirth would now be accompanied by pain. Man would rule over woman and that rule would not necessarily be pleasant.

- The curse would extend to all the earth so that life on earth would be a struggle for survival of the fittest.

We are still under the curse today. The curse is heard in the cry of pain coming from a maternity ward. It is seen in a man's tiresome toil. It is seen when weeds choke out a failing crop and in the coming of a natural disaster. It is seen in a graveyard filled with tombstones. Because of the curse, there is crying, pain, and death. Because of the curse, there is the need of a temple where man can approach God. Because of the curse, men find themselves in spiritual darkness. But one day there will be no more curse. When that happens, all these things that accompany the curse will also come to an end.

They will see His face (22:4). Moses once asked if he might be permitted to see the face of God. He was denied as God replied, "No man can see Me and live" (Exodus 33:20). Instead, Moses was hidden by God in a cleft of the rock and God laid a covering hand of protection over him as he was permitted to glimpse just an afterglow of the glory of God. John picked up this same theme in the prologue of his gospel account.

> *No one has seen God at any time; the only begotten God who is in the bosom of the Father, He has explained Him. (John 1:18)*.

In the ancient world, criminals were sometimes banished and not allowed to see the face of their king. You will remember the story of Absalom who was banished from the presence of his own father. It is sin that has separated us from the face of our God. But that is going to change. There is coming a day when we will see the face of God. We will be able to do this because we will be different.

> *Beloved, now we are children of God, and it has not appeared as yet what we will be. We know that when He appears, we will be like Him, because we will see Him just as He is. (1 John 3:2)*.

We have been declared to be righteous through the atoning work of Jesus, but one day we shall be righteous. When that day comes, we will be able to see God face to face.

His name will be on their foreheads (22:4). We have already seen 144,000 of the people of God with the seal of God on their forehead. Then we saw the mark of the beast upon the foreheads and hands of his people. Now we see the name of God upon the foreheads of all His people.

366

THE FINAL CHAPTER
Revelation 22:6-21

In the last chapter, we saw the city of God coming down from the sky. It was a new beginning. Old things were passed away. There was no more sea. There was no more mourning or crying or pain. The was no temple or sun or moon or night. There was no more unclean thing or curse.

Now the pagent is over. The complete panorama of the plan of God has been unfolded before John and recorded for us. The triumph of God's people is certain. The only thing that needs to be done now is to impress upon the readers the importance of this message. This takes place in this epilogue. The book is actually finished, but the epilogue remains. The book of Revelation began with a prologue and it ends with an epilogue.

Prologue	Epilogue
Revelation 1:1-8	Revelation 22:6-21
He sent and communicated it by His angel to His bond-servant John (1:1)	*Lord, the God of the spirits of the prophets, sent His angel (22:6).*
To show to His bond-servants, the things which must soon take place (1:1).	*To show to His bond-servants the things which must soon take place. (22:6).*
His bond-servant John (1:1)	*I, John, am the one who heard and saw these things (22:8)*
For the time is near (1:3).	*Do not seal up the words of the prophecy of this book, for the time is near (22:10).*
"I am the Alpha and the Omega," says the Lord God, "who is and who was and who is to come, the Almighty" (1:8).	*"I am the Alpha and the Omega, the first and the last, the beginning and the end" (22:13)*
Blessed is he who reads and those who hear the words of the prophecy, and heed the things which are written in it (1:3).	*Blessed are those who wash their robes, so that they may have the right to the tree of life, and may enter by the gates into the city (22:14).*

John to the seven churches that are in Asia (1:4).	"I, Jesus, have sent My angel to testify to you these things for the churches" (22:16).
Behold, He is coming with the clouds (1:7).	"Yes, I am coming quickly" (22:20)
So it is to be. Amen (1:7).	The grace of the Lord Jesus be with all. Amen. (22:21).

THE WITNESS OF THE ANGEL

> *And he said to me, "These words are faithful and true";*
> *and the Lord, the God of the spirits of the prophets, sent His angel*
> *to show to His bond-servants the things which must soon take*
> *place. 7 And behold, I am coming quickly. Blessed is he who heeds*
> *the words of the prophecy of this book." (Revelation 22:6-7).*

John is assured that the message of the book of Revelation bears the authority of God. Jesus had called Himself the "faithful and true Witness" back in Revelation 3:14. The words that John had been given have that same authority. This is not something that John had merely imagined to pass the time on Patmos. Neither is this the mere meditations of a good man. It is the word of God.

The messenger says in verse 5 that these things must take place "soon" and it verse 6 he says that he is coming "quickly." Though the translators have rendered this with two different words, they are both taken from the same Greek word. It does not necessarily mean that everything in this prophecy will happen immediately, but it does mean that those things would begin to take place very soon. Throughout this study, we have noted the implications of the way these visions would have appeared in John's day. Without taking a Preterist interpretation, we have seen throughout the book of Revelation quite a number of first century applications of the prophecies within this book.

THE WITNESS OF JOHN

> *I, John, am the one who heard and saw these things. And*
> *when I heard and saw, I fell down to worship at the feet of the*
> *angel who showed me these things. 9 But he said to me, "Do not do*
> *that. I am a fellow servant of yours and of your brethren the*
> *prophets and of those who heed the words of this book. Worship*

God." (Revelation 22:8-9).

John identifies himself as the writer and witness to these things. This is in contrast to his gospel account where he does not give his name. For this reason, some have puzzled over the authorship of the book of Revelation.

Gospel of John	Book of Revelation
This is the disciple who is testifying to these things and wrote these things, and we know that his testimony is true (21:24)	*I, John, am the one who heard and saw these things (22:8)*

And when I heard and saw, I fell down to worship at the feet of the angel who showed me these things (22:8). This is the second time John has done this. We saw it happen in chapter 19.

Revelation 19:10	**Revelation 22:8-9**
Then I fell at his feet to worship him.	*And when I heard and saw, I fell down to worship at the feet of the angel who showed me these things.*
But he said to me, "Do not do that; I am a fellow servant of yours and your brethren who hold the testimony of Jesus; worship God."	*But he said to me, "Do not do that. I am a fellow servant of yours and of your brethren the prophets and of those who heed the words of this book. Worship God."*

God is to be the only object of our worship. Even angels, glorious though they might be, are only created beings and therefore not adequate for our worship.

THE TESTIMONY OF THE BOOK

> *And he said to me, "Do not seal up the words of the prophecy of this book, for the time is near. 11 Let the one who does wrong, still do wrong; and the one who is filthy, still be filthy; and let the one who is righteous, still practice righteousness; and the one who is holy, still keep himself holy." (Revelation 22:10-11).*

The instructions given to John are meant to be seen in contrast to that which was said to Daniel at the close of his prophecy: *But as for you, Daniel, conceal these words and seal up the book until the end of time (Daniel 12:4).*

Daniel 12:4	Revelation 22:10
Seal up the book.	Do not seal up the words of the prophecy of this book.
Conceal these words.	This entire book is described as a "revelation."
Concealing is to take place "until the end of time."	The time is near.

When Daniel came to the end of his book, he was told to conceal the words and seal up the book until the time of the end (Daniel 12:4). The implication is that the details of his prophecy would not be understood in his day. But John is told not to seal up the words of this prophecy of his book. The implication is that he book was relevant to the people who lived in John's day. These events were not reserved for some time in the future. They had application to his day.

Throughout our study of the book of Revelation, we have seen again and again that this book is describing the work of God in the world today. I don't mean that it is only relevant to the 21st Century. I mean that it was relevant in the day in which it was written and that it is still relevant for today. We are not meant to take all of the events of this book and to try to push them into some future time of tribulation. These things were happening in the day in which they were written and they are still happening today. That means this book has something to say about how we live today.

Let the one who does wrong, still do wrong (22:11). The man who wants to ignore the testimony of this book is told that he will be allowed to do so. God isn't going to write His message on the clouds. He isn't going to do anything else to convince you. He says, "Here is My message. You can either believe it or you can ignore it." There are a lot of people who have chosen to ignore God. He has allowed them to do so. One day, they will pay the price for their actions. This was a familiar theme among the Old Testament prophets. When God commissioned Ezekiel to the ministry of prophecy, He had this to say about the effect that his preaching would have upon the people:

> *But when I speak to you, I will open your mouth and you will say to them, "Thus says the Lord GOD." He who hears, let him hear; and he who refuses, let him refuse; for they are a rebellious house. (Ezekiel 3:27).*

Your decisions are eternally significant. When you decide to ignore God or to disobey Him, you are setting a path for your future. It is like the sign on the old country road that proclaimed, "Choose your rut carefully, you will be in it for a long time."

THE TESTIMONY OF THE LORD

"Behold, I am coming quickly, and My reward is with Me, to render to every man according to what he has done. 13 I am the Alpha and the Omega, the first and the last, the beginning and the end. 14 Blessed are those who wash their robes, so that they may have the right to the tree of life, and may enter by the gates into the city. 15 Outside are the dogs and the sorcerers and the immoral persons and the murderers and the idolaters, and everyone who loves and practices lying. 16 I, Jesus, have sent My angel to testify to you these things for the churches. I am the root and the descendant of David, the bright morning star." (Revelation 22:12-16).

We have seen the testimony of the angel, or John and of the book. Now we come to the most important testimony of all. It is the testimony of Jesus. This section completes a chiastic pattern that was begun in the first chapter. It was introduced by the proclamation by God that He is the first and the last.

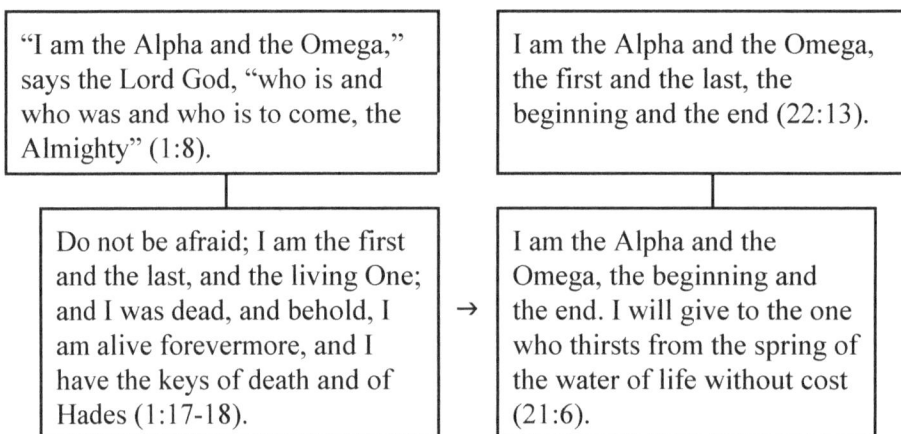

"I am the Alpha and the Omega," says the Lord God, "who is and who was and who is to come, the Almighty" (1:8).	I am the Alpha and the Omega, the first and the last, the beginning and the end (22:13).
Do not be afraid; I am the first and the last, and the living One; and I was dead, and behold, I am alive forevermore, and I have the keys of death and of Hades (1:17-18).	I am the Alpha and the Omega, the beginning and the end. I will give to the one who thirsts from the spring of the water of life without cost (21:6).

I am coming quickly (22:12). This is the fifth time in the Book of Revelation that Jesus has said that He will come quickly (2:5; 2:16; 3:11; 22:7). He will say it twice more in Revelation 22:20. Does this mean that the Second Coming was to take place soon? If that is the case, we need to redefine either the Second Coming or "soon." The answer of Preterism has been to redefine the Second Coming. We have looked at that view that defines the Second Coming as the fall of Jerusalem in A.D. 70. But such a redefinition is not necessary. The term translated "quickly" can have one of two meaning:

- It can mean shortly, in just a little while.
- It can mean suddenly, without warning.

There are several places in the Septuagint which this same Greek phrase is used to describe something that was coming, but which did not actually arrive for hundreds of years (Isaiah 13:22; 51:4; 58:8). The point here is that the Second Coming is going to be sudden. It will take everyone by surprise. Elsewhere it has been described like a thief.

My reward is with Me, to render to every man according to what he has done (22:12). The reason it is important to know that the coming of Jesus will be unexpected is because He is bringing a reward. That reward is based upon what you ar doing now. Paul describes this principle in his letter to the Corinthians.

> *...each man's work will become evident; for the day will show it because it is to be revealed with fire, and the fire itself will test the quality of each man's work. 14 If any man's work which he has built on it remains, he will receive a reward. (1 Corinthians 3:13-14).*

A new building usually must pass an official inspection before a certificate of occupancy can be issued. Government officials come out to the site of the building and test its structure to make sure it is built to proper codes. This is to insure the building is sound. God also has a set of standard by which He will judge the quality of our labors. There is coming a day of judgment.

> *For we must all appear before the judgment seat of Christ, so that each one may be recompensed for his deeds in the body, according to what he has done, whether good or bad. (2 Corinthians 5:10).*

No one is exempt from this judgment. Paul says that we must all appear before the judgment seat of Christ. He also says that the purpose of this judgment is to recompense each one for his deeds in the body. This judgment is action-oriented. It is a judgment of deeds, involving actions that you took while you were in the body. You might object that God judges the heart. He does, but your actions come forth as the fruit of what is in your heart. The way you live is a direct result of what you believe.

This judgment will include everything that we have done, whether good or bad. Nothing is to be hidden. It will all be brought out into the open. Your work is not evident today. People can look at the things you do today and they cannot be certain whether they are of the Spirit or of the flesh. But there is coming a day when such uncertainty will vanish away and when the true character of your work will be known.

Blessed are those who wash their robes, so that they may have the right to the tree of life, and may enter by the gates into the city (22:14). Even though men are judged according to their works, it is the one who has washed his robe in the cleansing work of Christ who has admittance into the holy city of God. Though we are judged by our works, we are not saved by those works. Our salvation is through the work of Christ on our behalf.

> There is a textual difference in this verse between the Sinaiticus, Vaticanus, and a number of minuscules over against the Textus Receptus. The critical text, mirrored in the NAS, reads μακαριοι οἱ πλυνοντες τας στολας αυτου, "Blessed are those who wash their robes." The Textus Receptus reads, μακαριοι οἱ ποιουντες τας ἐντολας αυτων, Blessed are those who keep His commands."

The word "blessed" in this verse is the Greek μακαριος (*makarios*). It can also be translated "happy." It is the same word that was used by Jesus in the Beatitudes. We have seen it used six times in the Book of Revelation (1:3; 14:13; 16:15; 19:9; 20:6; 22:7). This is the seventh and last time. This is the final blessing of the book.

"I, Jesus, have sent My angel to testify to you these things for the churches" (22:16).

Jesus is not addressing these things to people living during a future seven year tribulation. He is not addressing this to people of another dispensation. He is addressing this to the churches. Which churches? They are the churches of Asia Minor. They are the church at Ephesus and Smyrna and Laodecia and all of the other churches that existed in that day. In a wider sense, this is addressed to all of the spiritual offspring of those churches. Therefore we can say that it is also addressed to us.

"I am the root and the descendant of David" (22:16). There is an interesting metaphor here. Jesus is both the root as well as the fruit of the vine of David. He is the Creator of David, but He is also the Son of David.

This was contrary to the popular Jewish teaching of that day. The Jews taught that the Messiah would be the son of David, but they never realized that He would be the Creator of David. They did not realize that He would be the Son of God. That is why Jesus pointed out to them the prophecy of Psalm 110:1 where David himself expressed his own hearing of a heavenly conversation:

> *The LORD says to my Lord:*
> *"Sit at My right hand*
> *Until I make Your enemies a footstool for Your feet." (Psalm 110:1).*

The Jews understood that the Messiah was to be the Son of David. But this passage refers to the Messiah also as David's Lord. It was a puzzle over which they stumbled. He is both the root and the descendant of David. He is both David's Creator and David's Son.

THE INVITATION

The Spirit and the bride say, "Come." And let the one who hears say, "Come." And let the one who is thirsty come; let the one who wishes take the water of life without cost. (Revelation 22:17).

The book of Revelation closes with an invitation. It is an invitation to a wedding; that is why it comes from both the Spirit and the bride. The picture of Jesus as the coming bridegroom who takes and marries the bride is meant to remind us of the creation of Adam and his bride, Eve.

The First Adam	The Second Adam
Creation of heaven and earth	A new heaven and a new earth
Adam put into a garden out of which flowed a river that divided into four parts	There is a river flowing out of the new Jerusalem
The tree of life in the midst of the garden	The tree of life in the new Jerusalem
Death comes	No more death
Adam names his wife Eve as the mother of all living	The bride is made up of those whose names are written in the book of life
Eve led Adam to sin by giving him of the forbidden fruit of the tree	Jesus took the bride's sin upon Himself by going to death on the tree
Adam was placed into a deep sleep and then Eve was taken from his side and God closed up the flesh	Jesus died and his side opened and the blood served as the purchase price for his bride; God then awakened Him from death to claim His bride

It was stated in Genesis 2 that it was not good that Adam be alone. In the same way, we come to see here in the book of Revelation that it is not good for the Son to be alone and so a bride has been prepared for him.

You have been invited to a wedding. It is an invitation, not only to attend the wedding, but to take part in the wedding. You have been invited to partake of all of the blessings that have been revealed in this book. As such, it is a twofold invitation.

- The invitation comes from the Spirit and the bride.
- The invitation is to all who are thirsty.

THE WARNING

> *I testify to everyone who hears the words of the prophecy of this book: if anyone adds to them, God will add to him the plagues which are written in this book; 19 and if anyone takes away from the words of the book of this prophecy, God will take away his part from the tree of life and from the holy city, which are written in this book. (Revelation 22:18-19).*

This is a serious warning, but it is not without precedent. You will remember that the Apostle Paul gave a similar warning in his epistle to the Galatians over the possibility that someone might come preaching a different gospel.

> *But even if we, or an angel from heaven, should preach to you a gospel contrary to what we have preached to you, he is to be accursed! 9 As we have said before, so I say again now, if any man is preaching to you a gospel contrary to what you received, he is to be accursed! (Galatians 1:8-9).*

The same principle was stated back in the Old Testament, both in the Torah as well as in the Proverbs:

> *You shall not add to the word which I am commanding you, nor take away from it, that you may keep the commandments of the LORD your God which I command you. (Deuteronomy 4:2).*

> *Whatever I command you, you shall be careful to do; you shall not add to nor take away from it. (Deuteronomy 12:32).*

> *Every word of God is tested;*
> *He is a shield to those who take refuge in Him.*
> *6 Do not add to His words*
> *Or He will reprove you, and you will be proved a liar (Proverbs 30:5-6).*

There is a principle here and it is an important one. Don't mess with God's message. This is not saying don't try to understand the book. It calls for understanding, but don't try to exclude it or add to it.

CONCLUSION

> *He who testifies to these things says, "Yes, I am coming quickly." Amen. Come, Lord Jesus.* 21 *The grace of the Lord Jesus be with all. Amen. (Revelation 22:20-21).*

Come, Lord Jesus! This is the unifying cry of the church. It is a cry that crosses all denominational lines. It does not matter if you are Baptist, Presbyterian, Methodist, Charismatic, Roman Catholic, or Eastern Orthodox. In this one desire, we are united.

The closing benediction suggests to us that the book of Revelation is a book of worship. It contains epistles, it contains prophecy, it contains warnings and invitations, but it is wrapped in the language of worship.

APPENDIX

THE PROBLEM WITH PRETERISM

The word "Preterist" is taken from the Latin word meaning "past." This view denies any future fulfillment of the book of Revelation and sees the events it describes as already having been fulfilled within the first century after Christ.

There are several different forms of Preterism. Full Preterism views all of the prophecies of the Bible as having already been fulfilled in their entirety since the fall of Jerusalem in A.D. 70. Full Preterism is a very recent innovation that has no adherents in any of the writings of the early church.

Partial Preterism maintains a future return of Christ, but views His "coming in the clouds" as described in Matthew 24:29-31 as having been fulfilled in A.D. 70 with the fall of Jerusalem. Let me say for the record that I do not endorse any of the different sorts of Preterism, but my comments henceforth are directed primarily to Full Preterism.

1.   Jesus and Preterism.

        With regards to Preterism, I am reminded of the words of Jesus when He said to the disciples, *"The days will come when you will long to see one of the days of the Son of Man, and you will not see it. And they will say to you, 'Look there! Look here!' Do not go away, and do not run after them. For just as the lightning, when it flashes out of one part of the sky, shines to the other part of the sky, so will the Son of Man be in His day."* (Luke 17:22-24).

        It seems to me that the Preterist is one who is pointing to the A.D. 70 event and saying, "Look there! Look here!" But there is going to be no mistaking the coming of the Son of Man when He finally returns. By contrast, none of the believers of the early church viewed the 70 A.D. fall of Jerusalem as fulfilling the promise of the return of Christ. This brings us to our next point.

2.   The Church Fathers and Preterism.

        It is clear from a reading of the apostolic and church fathers that all of them expected a future return of Jesus Christ. It would be strange indeed if the entire church failed to understand the fulfillment of so many of the New Testament prophecies on such a major point. This is especially striking when we remember the promise of Revelation 1:7 that tells us, *He is coming with the clouds, and every eye will see Him, even those who pierced Him; and all the tribes of the earth will mourn over Him.* A preterist interpretation calls for this to be a reference to the "tribes of the land" of

Israel, even though Israel was never described in such a way elsewhere in the Bible. But such an interpretation would demand that the Jews who suffered through the A.D. 70 event would have recognized that their sufferings were a punishment for their treatment of Jesus since the prophecy is not merely that they would mourn, but that they would mourn "over Him." Just as there is no evidence that anyone in the church ever recognized the fall of Jerusalem as the return of Jesus, so also there is a complete absence of evidence that the Jews ever recognized the coming of Jesus in those events.

3.   The Resurrection and Preterism.

Fundamental to full Preterism is the idea that there is no future physical resurrection of the dead. But the pattern for our resurrection is that of Jesus. The big idea presented in 1 Corinthians 15 is that Jesus arose from the dead. This was not merely some sort of spiritual resurrection. The point is made throughout this chapter that His resurrection was bodily and physical. Furthermore we are told that His resurrection serves as the paradigm for our own resurrection. *But now Christ has been raised from the dead, the first fruits of those who are asleep* (1 Corinthians 15:20). He is the first fruits and we are the "later fruits."

When Paul came to Athens, he was mocked by the Greeks for believing in a physical resurrection. Such mockery would not have been forthcoming had he held that the resurrection was only going to be of a spiritual or mystical nature. But he went out of his way to side himself with the Pharisees who believed in a physical resurrection of the dead (Acts 23:6-8).

In denying any future resurrection at the coming of Christ, the preterist also finds himself out of accord with the words of Paul when he says, "We shall not all sleep, but we shall all be changed" (1 Corinthians 15:51). The reference to sleep is used throughout this epistle as a euphemism for death (11:30; 15:6; 15:18; 15:20). While Paul says of the coming of the Lord that it will be a time when all do not die, the preterist is left with the rather obvious historic truth that everyone who lived in the first century did indeed die.

When it comes to the resurrection, the Bible teaches that Jesus is our prototype. His resurrection is the forerunner and the pattern for our own resurrection. This point is made in 1 Corinthians 15 where Paul says that if there is no resurrection then even Jesus has not risen.

The resurrection of Jesus was a physical resurrection. He was able to stand before His disciples in His resurrection body and say, *"See My hands and My feet, that it is I Myself; touch Me and see, for a spirit does not have flesh and bones as you see that I have."* (Luke 24:39). 1 John 3:2 says that *when He appears, we shall be like Him, because we shall see Him just as He is.* Therefore we can conclude that our future resurrection will be of both a physical and spiritual nature.

Romans 8:11 confirms that it is not merely the soul or the spirit that will be raised, but our mortal bodies: *But if the Spirit of Him who raised Jesus from the dead dwells in you, He who raised Christ Jesus from the dead will also give life to your mortal bodies through His Spirit who dwells in you.*

4.   Preterism and the Lord's Supper.

One wonders whether the Full Preterist is completely consistent in his views. After all, most Full Preterists continue to partake of the Lord's Supper in spite of the fact that Paul said that the eating and drinking serves to *"proclaim the Lord's death **until He comes"*** (1 Corinthians 11:26).

5.   Preterism and the Promise of a Soon Coming.

Preterists like to point out that Jesus and the disciples stated that the kingdom was near and at hand. What they often ignore is that this same formula was used in the Old Testament in instances where the eventual fulfillment was a long way off.

An example of this is seen in Isaiah 13:6 where, speaking of a coming judgment against the city of Babylon, the prophet says, *"Wail, for the day of the LORD is near! It will come as destruction from the Almighty."* Isaiah writes these words in the 8th century B.C. but it is not until 539 B.C. that Babylon fell to the Persians.

The preterist attempts to make a similar case via the words of Jesus in Matthew 24:34 where Jesus says, *"Truly I say to you, this generation will not pass away until all these things take place."* What is conveniently ignored is the earlier context of Jesus' words in the previous chapter.

> *"Therefore, behold, I am sending you prophets and wise men and scribes; some of them you will kill and crucify, and some of them you will scourge in your synagogues, and persecute from city to city, 35 that upon you may fall the guilt of all the righteous blood shed on earth, from the blood of righteous Abel to the blood of Zechariah, the son of Berechiah, whom you murdered between the temple and the altar. 36 Truly I say to you, all these things shall come upon this generation." (Matthew 23:34-36).*

Notice that it was "this generation" that murdered Zechariah, the son of Berechiah." The problem is that this murder took place 400 years earlier as recorded in 2 Chronicles 24:20-21. This tells us that Matthew's use of the term "generation" is able to mean something different than a mere life span of the people who were living at that time.

Another common argument by preterists is the use of the second person such as when Jesus says, "You shall see the Son of Man sitting with power" (Mark 14:62). It is maintained that such a prophecy must necessitate a fulfillment within the lifetime of those to whom it is addressed. But such a claim ignores the multitude of prophecies in the Bible that addressed people as representing a future generation. Several examples will suffice.

- As he is about to die, Joseph tells his brothers, "You shall carry my bones up from here" (Genesis 50:25), yet the fulfillment of this prophetic command would not be seen for many generations.

- Jeremiah addresses the elders who were taken into the Babylonian Captivity (Jeremiah 29:1) and says to them, "When seventy years have been completed for Babylon, I will visit you and fulfill My good word to you, to bring you back to this place" (29:10). Because he is addressing the elders, we do not need to assume that they must all have lived another 70 years to see the fulfillment of this prophecy.

- In Malachi 4:5, the prophet says, "Behold, I am going to send **to you** Elijah the prophet before the coming of the great and terrible day of the LORD." This prophecy was not fulfilled for at least 400 years, yet it utilizes the same 2nd person in addressing those to whom Malachi addresses his prophecy.

6.   Preterism and the Angels at the Ascension.

Another problem facing the Preterist is seen in the promise that was given to the disciples at the ascension of Jesus. The event took place on the Mount of Olives.

> *And after He had said these things, He was lifted up while they were looking on, and a cloud received Him out of their sight. 10 And as they were gazing intently into the sky while He was departing, behold, two men in white clothing stood beside them; 11 and they also said, "Men of Galilee, why do you stand looking into the sky? This Jesus, who has been taken up from you into heaven, will come in just the same way as you have watched Him go into*

heaven." (Acts 1:9-11).

The promise that was given by the angels is that Jesus would come again in exactly the same way as they had watched Him go into heaven. This had not been a spiritual ascension, but a physical and visible one. It is for this reason that Christians throughout the ages fully expect a future physical and visible return of Christ.

7.   Preterism and the Judgment of the World.

When Paul preaches to the Athenians on the Areopagus, he declares to them that God *has fixed a day in which He will judge the world in righteousness through a Man whom He has appointed* (Acts 17:31). The Preterist interpretation of this verse is that it points to the A.D. 70 fall of Jerusalem, yet that fall would have absolutely no impact upon the Athenians who had gathered to listen to Paul. He says that they ought to repent because of this coming judgment and such a warning is nonsensical if it only refers to a local judgment in a far away land.

Preterists do not believe that there will be an end to this heaven and earth. They typically seek to avoid biblical references to the contrary by redefining any references to the end of the world as referring to the end of the Jewish world system. However, a survey of the Bible's use of the phrase "heaven and earth" quickly shows this to be an exercise in futility.

The phrase "heaven and earth" goes back all the way to Genesis 1:1 where God is seen as the creator of heaven and earth. That is further defined throughout the first chapter of Genesis in a way that makes it very obvious that more than a mere "Jewish world" is in view. Such a usage continues unabated throughout the Old Testament. While it is true that there are times when the term "earth" can be used in a localized sense, this is by no means always to be the case. For example, we read in Psalm 135:6 of how the Lord does as He pleases "in heaven and in earth, in the seas and in all deeps." Isaiah cites the words of the Lord Himself as he says: "I, the LORD, am the maker of all things, stretching out the heavens by Myself and spreading out the earth all alone" (Isaiah 44:24). The prophet goes on to speak of a day of judgment when "the Lord will punish the host of heaven on high, and the kings of the earth on earth" (Isaiah 24:21).

2 Peter 3:3-4 warns that *in the last days mockers will come with their mocking, following after their own lusts, and saying, "Where is the promise of His coming? For ever since the fathers fell asleep, all continues just as it was from the beginning of creation."* Bearing a remarkable resemblance to these last days mockers, preterists similarly deny any future coming of the Lord or any judgment of heaven and earth as they seek to make any

such references to be limited to the events of A.D. 70. By contrast, Peter goes on to liken the future judgment of heaven and earth to the judgment of the flood that removed all human life in the days of Noah. Just as the world at that time was destroyed, being flooded with water, Peter goes on to say that *the present heavens and earth are being reserved for fire, kept for the day of judgment and destruction of ungodly men (2 Peter 3:7).*

Peter goes on to describe how *the day of the Lord will come like a thief, in which the heavens will pass away with a roar and the elements will be destroyed with intense heat, and the earth and its works will be burned up (2 Peter 3:10).* Peter's earlier reference to the heavens and earth in 1 Peter 3:5 can hardly be said to refer to the nation of Israel since it cites the creation of both heaven and earth and turns our attention back to the first chapter of Genesis. Therefore to attempt to re-interpret Peter's description of the passing of the heaven and earth only to the destruction of the city of Jerusalem in A.D. 70 is to do violence to the text of Scripture and to completely ignore the context of the passage. Contrary to the false teaching of the preterist, we must echo the words of Jesus when He promises that *heaven and earth will pass away* (Matthew 24:35 and Luke 21:33).

8.   Preterism and the Redemption of Creation.

In Romans 8, Paul teaches that the creation has fallen as a result of sin and that *the creation itself also will be set free from its slavery to corruption into the freedom of the glory of the children of God* (8:21). He goes on in verse 22 to describe how the *whole creation groans and suffers the pains of childbirth together until now* as it looks to its final redemption.

The Preterist foresees no physical redemption of creation. According to his scheme, the world is fallen and will always be fallen. In this way, Preterism embraces the tenants of Gnosticism with its lack of regard for the redemption of the physical world.

Jesus said that the meek would inherit the earth (Matthew 5:5) and Abraham was promised that he and his descendants would be the heirs of the world (Romans 4:13). The preterists deny that Abraham or his spiritual descendants will ever have anything to do with the earth.

9.   Preterism and a Brief Millennium.

It is no surprise to find that Preterists hold the prophecy in Revelation 20 of a thousand year reign to be symbolic. The idea of a symbolic fulfillment of this passage has been argued back and forth since the early days of the church. What is particularly problematic for the Preterist treatment of this passage is the view that this thousand year reign is to be understood as having been fulfilled in the 40 years between the resurrection of Jesus and the A.D. 70 destruction of Jerusalem. One cannot help but wonder what is to be meant by the use of an obviously long period of time as suggested by a thousand years.

10.   A View of Perpetual Sin and Death.

Because there is no future Second Coming or final judgment, Preterists believe that sin will continue indefinitely. 1 Corinthians 15:26 tells us that *the last enemy that will be abolished is death* and Revelation 21:4 tells us of a time when *there will no longer be any death; there will no longer be any mourning, or crying, or pain*, but the Preterist would have us believe that death will never be abolished and that it will always be with us.

There are some eschatological differences that exist between Christians that I consider to be relatively benign and within the realm of Christian orthodoxy. This is not one of them. To the contrary, the teaching of Preterism comes uncomfortably close to the spiritual gangrene that is described by Paul in 2 Timothy 2:18 when he speaks of those *who have gone astray from the truth saying that the resurrection has already taken place, and thus they upset the faith of some.* The teachings of preterism have not resulted in stronger and more loving Christians. Though I am happy to report that there are some exceptions, this teaching for the most part has been divisive and destructive. I cannot help but to be reminded of the litmus test suggested by Jesus: *You will know them by their fruits. Grapes are not gathered from thorn bushes, nor figs from thistles, are they? 17 Even so, every good tree bears good fruit; but the bad tree bears bad fruit* (Matthew 7:16-17).

THE RAPTURE QUESTION

It has become increasingly popular in the last hundred years for Christians to speak of the "Pre-Tribulational Rapture of the Church." To add to that popularity, we saw around the turn of the century the publication of a set of Christian fiction called "The Left Behind" Series. While one's taste in fictional literature is a matter of personal taste, it is my feeling that the Biblical accuracy that is espoused by this position leaves much to be desired.

The Pre-Tribulational Rapture position follows this general outline:

1.   In a sudden and unannounced instant, all those who have died will rise from the dead and will be gathered along with all living believers to meet the Lord in the air. At this time, their bodies shall be changed as they receive new glorified bodies (1 Thessalonians 4; I Corinthians 15:51-52).

2.   All of these believers will then be taken to heaven (John 14:3).

3.   In heaven there will be a judgment of all the believers who are there (1 Corinthians 3:11-15; 1 Corinthians 5:10-11).

4.   With all Christians suddenly disappeared from the earth, the world will be plunged into a terribly destructive seven years of tribulation (Daniel 9:27; Revelation 6-18). During this time, Russia will invade Palestine (Ezekiel 38-39) and a world-wide dictator will arise - the Anti-christ who will mandate that all must receive his mark on the forehead or on the hand (Revelation 13).

5.   Toward the end of this period, all of the nations of the world will be gathered together to the northern plains of Israel known as Armageddon.

6.   Jesus will return with His saints and will divide between the just and the unjust in a judgment of "sheep and goats" (Matthew 24-25). The "sheep" will be ushered into His kingdom while the "goats" will be cast into hell. The basis of this judgment will be the treatment that people accorded the Jews since only Christians will befriend the Jews during the tribulation (Matthew 25).

7.   Jesus will begin a 1000 year reign from His throne in Jerusalem (Revelation 20:4-6).

8.   At the end of that time, there will be another rebellion against God's rule as Satan is loosed upon the earth. Fire will come from heaven and devour them and a final judgment shall take place in which all heaven and earth is

385

destroyed (Revelation 20:11-15).

9.   A new heaven and a new earth will be instituted which shall exist forever (Revelation 21-22).

We can chart out these events like this:

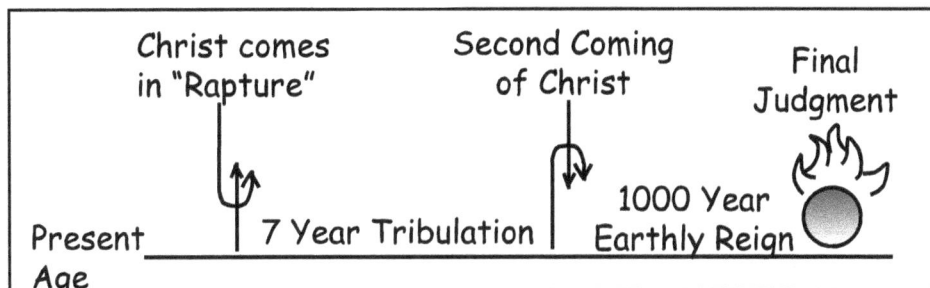

There are several presuppositions that are proposed by Pre-Tribulationalists:

*   There are two future comings of Christ.
    The first is to return for His saints.
    The second is to return with His saints.

*   God has two distinct plans and programs in history.
    One is for the church.
    The second is for the nation of Israel.

*   There will be a distinct 7 year period in the future called the "tribulation" or "Jacob's trouble."

*   The church will not go through this period of future tribulation, but will instead be "raptured out.".

Let me say for the record that I do not believe that the Bible teaches any of these presuppositions. For the remainder of this chapter, I propose to go through each presupposition and discuss it at length.

TWO FUTURE COMINGS OF CHRIST?

One of the initial problems that the Pretribulationalist runs into is that of terminology. How shall he differentiate between these two future comings of Christ? The verses that he uses to teach of these events simply refer to "His coming." This itself is a clue that the writers of the Bible believed that there was only one future coming of Christ and simply referred to it as "His coming."

Therefore, the term "rapture" of the church has been coined to describe the initial coming - the "secret" one. Note - it does not bother me that a theological term is coined; we coin terms all the time. It does bother me that there is no Scriptural term or statement for what is claimed by this teaching.

But enough of what bothers me - let's look at the Scriptures and see how they describe the second coming of Christ.

Rapture	Second Coming
For the Lord Himself will descend from heaven... (1 Thessalonians 4:16).	*They will see the Son of man coming... (Matthew 24:30).*
With the trumpet of God...(1 Thessalonians 4:16).	*He will send forth His angels with a great trumpet (Matthew 24:31).*
We who are alive shall be caught up together... (1 Thessalonians 4:16).	*And they will gather together His elect from the four winds... (Matthew 24:31).*
*We... shall be caught up together with them in **clouds** (1 Thessalonians 4:17).*	*They will see the Son of Man coming on the **clouds** of the sky... (Matthew 24:30).*
...if you will not wake up, I will come like a thief (Revelations 3:3).	*The Son of Man is coming at an hour when you do not think He will (Matthew 24:44; see also 1 Thessalonians 5:2-6 and 2 Peter 3:10).*
*...the coming of our Lord Jesus **with** all His saints (1 Thessalonians 3:13).*	*...the Lord came **with** many thousands of His holy ones (Jude 14).*

As you look at the way Christ's coming is described in each of these verses, they appear to be speaking of the same thing. That is because they are the same event. There is not a single passage of Scripture that makes a clear distinction between two future separate comings of Christ.

TWO DISTINCT PLANS & PROGRAMS?

The theory that there are two distinct plans and programs which God has for people (one for the nation of Israel, the other for the church) is called Dispensationalism. Although the word "dispensation" is found in the Bible, it is not used in the same way that the Dispensationalist uses it. Fore example, Paul speaks of a "stewardship" or a "dispensation" that was entrusted to him. He is speaking of the gospel in I Corinthians 9:17; Ephesians 3:2; and Colossians 1:25.

As to the theory that God has two plans and programs which are separate and distinct, Paul says that Jesus *made both groups into **one**, and broke down the barrier of the dividing wall* (Ephesians 2:14). He goes on to say that Jesus did this to *make the two into **one** new man, thus establishing peace, and might reconcile them both into **one** body to God through the cross* (Ephesians 2:15-16).

In the Old Testament, the Lord revealed Himself to Abraham and promised him a great nation. In the New Testament, we read that *if you belong to Christ, then you are Abraham's seed, heirs according to promise* (Galatians 3:29). Can you claim the promises of all the Bible? Yes, you can because *you brethren, like Isaac, are children of promise* (Galatians 4:28).

A FUTURE 7-YEAR TRIBULATION?

One of the things that we must do when looking at prophecy is ask ourselves if the prophecy in question has already been fulfilled. In this case, I want to suggest that it has been fulfilled quite literally. Furthermore, it has been fulfilled twice. The first time took place in the year 168 B.C. During that time, an invading king named Antiochus Epiphanes came down from the north and committed great atrocities against the Jews, forbidding them to read the Scriptures or to circumcise their children or to observe the Sabbath day. He even went so far as to have a statue of himself erected inside the Temple with orders that it be worshiped by all on pain of death. This was the "abomination of desolation" which Daniel prophesied of in Daniel 11:31.

However, Jesus told His disciples that it would happen again (Matthew 24:15; Mark 13:19). Sure enough, in 66 A.D. the Jews in Jerusalem rebelled against the Roman empire. The following war lasted 7 years. In 70 A.D. Jerusalem was taken and the Temple was again trodden underfoot by Gentile soldiers. This time, the Temple was destroyed and a great carnage ensued. However, the last resistance did not fall until 73 A.D. when the Romans took Masada, only to find that the last remnant of 930 Jews had committed suicide rather than be taken captive.

Is there still a future time of tribulation? I do not know. But I do know that Jesus said to His disciples that "in the world you have tribulation" (John 16:33 - notice the present tense). Indeed, the history of the church has been a history of tribulation. The promise that we have in Scripture is not that we will escape such tribulation, but that the Lord will see us through it.

THE CHURCH IN TRIBULATION?

Do the Scriptures teach that the church will avoid tribulation? I have already noted that it will not. The world will always hate the church and seek to destroy it (John 15:18-20). The good news is that we have a promise of relief *when the Lord Jesus shall be revealed from heaven with His mighty angels in flaming fire* (2nd Thessalonians 1:7).

Will there be a future Antichrist who will persecute the church? Once again, I must answer that it is already happening and that it was happening in John's day. *Children, it is the last hour, and just as you heard that Antichrist is coming, even now many antichrists have arisen; from this we know that it is the last hour* (1 John 2:18).

THE LAST DAY

You will recall that the Pre-Tribulational Rapture position holds to a "rapture" in which all believers are either taken or resurrected followed by a number of years prior to the Second Coming. But the Scriptures describe how our resurrection is to take place "on the last day."

> *And this is the will of him who sent me, that I shall lose none of all that he has given me, but raise them up at the last day. For my Father's will is that everyone who looks to the Son and believes in him shall have eternal life, and I will raise him up **at the last day**. (John 6:39-40).*

> *Whoever eats my flesh and drinks my blood has eternal life, and I will raise him up **at the last day**. (John 6:54).*

If we who believe in Christ are to be raised up on the last day, then how can there possibly be a subsequent period of tribulation that take place after the last day? It is at this point that the Pretribulational claim to a literal interpretation falls flat on its face.

Furthermore, John writes elsewhere in his gospel, not only about those who are raised on the last day, but also those who are to be judged on the last day. *He who rejects Me, and does not receive My sayings, has one who judges him; the word I spoke is what will judge him **at the last day** (John 12:48).*

Note that both the resurrection of the righteous and also the judgment of the wicked take place *at the last day*. If the judgment of which Jesus speaks is to take place at the last day, then it seems obvious that there cannot come another judgment that will take place at a later time.

THE LAST TRUMPET

There are a number of Scriptures that speak of the sounding of a trumpet at the return of our Lord.

Matthew 24:30-31	1 Corinthians 15:51-52	1 Thessalonians 4:16-17
A Great Trumpet	**The Last Trumpet**	**The Trumpet of God**
*The sign of the Son of Man will appear in the sky, and then all the tribes of the earth will mourn, and they will see the Son of Man coming on the clouds of the sky with power and great glory. 31 And He will send forth His angels with **a great trumpet** and they will gather together His elect from the four winds, from one end of the sky to the other.*	*Behold, I tell you a mystery; we shall not all sleep, but we shall all be changed, 52 in a moment, in the twinkling of an eye, at **the last trumpet**; for the trumpet will sound, and the dead will be raised imperishable, and we shall be changed.*	*For the Lord Himself will descend from heaven with a shout, with the voice of the archangel, and with **the trumpet of God**; and the dead in Christ shall rise first. 17 Then we who are alive and remain shall be caught up together with them in the clouds to meet the Lord in the air, and thus we shall always be with the Lord.*
• The Son comes • No mention of rising • The elect of God gathered (no mention of them being changed)	• No mention of the Son • The dead raised • The living are changed (no mention of them being caught up)	• The Lord descends • The dead raised • The living gathered (no mention of them being changed)

When we come to the book of Revelation, we are introduced to seven angels with seven trumpets. It is the last of these trumpets that draws our attention.

> *5 And the angel whom I saw standing on the sea and on the land lifted up his right hand to heaven, 6 and swore by Him who lives forever and ever, who created heaven and the things in it, and the earth and the things in it, and the sea and the things in it, that there shall be delay no longer, 7 but in the days of the voice of **the seventh angel**, when he is about to sound, then the*

390

mystery of God is finished, as He preached to His servants the prophets. (Revelation 10:5-7).

The sound of the seventh trumpet of Revelation is said to signify...

- There is no more delay (10:6).
- The mystery of God is finished (10:7).

The angel does not sound until the following chapter. When he does sound this last trumpet, there is a great proclamation:

> *And the seventh angel sounded; and there arose loud voices in heaven, saying, "The kingdom of the world has become the kingdom of our Lord, and of His Christ; and He will reign forever and ever." (Revelation 11:15).*

This verse is even more specific. The sounding of the seventh trumpet signifies that the kingdom of the world has come completely under the kingdom of the Lord. This can be nothing less than the Second Coming of Christ.

Paul has already stated in 1 Corinthians 15:51-52 that we are to expect the resurrection of the dead and the changing of those who are still alive at the LAST trumpet. If the "rapture" takes place at the last trumpet, then how can there be another trumpet to sound the return of Christ at some later period? Our conclusion is inescapable. It is that the "rapture" and the Second Coming of Christ are one and the same event.

CONCLUSION

I believe that Christ is coming. I make no claim as to knowing the day or the hour. There are already too many who have made this mistake. It could be today. Or it could be a thousand years from now. But I join with all Christians in *looking for the blessed hope and appearing of our Great God and Savior, Jesus Christ* (Titus 2:13).

I furthermore believe that these different views of future prophecy should not divide the church. They are not given to divide. They are not given so that we might draw charts and outlines. They are given so that we might live in a way that shows we are looking for His return.

EVIDENCES FOR A PRETRIBULATIONAL RAPTURE

Having already given some reasons why I do not believe the Pretribulational Rapture View to be taught in the Scriptures, I will now move to deal with those supposed evidences that are used in support of that view.

On a personal note, I should point out that this is the interpretation that I was first taught in my early days of Christianity and the one which I initially accepted. My gradual shift away from this position was not initially prompted by evidences which were presented for any alternate view, but rather because of the general lack of real evidence that I noted in a study of my own view that I held at that time.

ARGUMENT #1: THE JEWISH NATURE OF THE FUTURE TRIBULATION

The passages which are used to teach of a future "Great Tribulation" always describe a time of judgment when God is dealing specifically with the nation of Israel. As such, it is called "the time of Jacob's distress" in Jeremiah 30:7. Accordingly, it is argued that the Church cannot be present on earth while God is dealing with Israel. Therefore, the Church must first be removed from the earth before this future period of tribulation can begin.

I have stated elsewhere that I am not convinced that there must necessarily be such a future period of tribulation. There have already been, not merely one, but two such periods when nations moved against the nation or Israel so that the temple was desecrated by an invading "anti-Christ."

The objection raised under this point is really an objection based upon the theological system known as Dispensationalism. It is a system which holds that God has two different plans and programs and people through whom He works and that He shall always keep them separate and distinct. It is supposed that He cannot be working with Israel while He is also working with the church.

This objection is removed when we examine the book of Acts. All of the events and the growth of the Church which are recorded in the books of Acts took place while the nation of Israel was still in existence. In fact, certain passages in Acts seem to show that the Kingdom was still being offered to the Jews during the first years of the Church (Acts 3:19-26; 28:20-31). Thus, we have an excellent example of God dealing with the Church and Israel at the same time.

ARGUMENT #2: THE NATURE OF THE CHURCH

The Church is the Body and the Bride of Jesus Christ (Ephesians 5:23; Colossians 1:18). It is the object of His infinite love and the recipient of every spiritual blessing. The believer finds himself in union with Christ.

If the Church is to go into or through such a time of future tribulation, she will be subjected to the wrath and judgments which will characterize that period. Thus, the Church cannot go into the Tribulation, since she has been delivered from judgment (Romans 8:1; John 5:24).

The problem with this argument is that there have been many instances in history when the Church has gone through terrible persecutions and tribulations. To say that Christ would not permit His Bride to go through this time of trouble is inconsistent with history.

At the same time, I would submit that just because the Church goes through tribulation, it would not necessarily follow that the judgments and indignations of such tribulation would be directed at her, any more than the plagues against Egypt meant that God was judging the Israelites in the days of the Exodus.

ARGUMENT #3: DELIVERED FROM THE WRATH TO COME

Twice during the Epistle to the Thessalonians Paul states that believers are to be delivered from wrath. This fact is used by Pretribulationalists to teach that the church must be "raptured away" before that wrath can take place.

> For they themselves report about us what kind of a reception it had with you, and how you turned to God from idols to serve a living and true God, and to wait for His Son from heaven, whom He raised from the dead, that is Jesus, who **delivers us from the wrath to come**. (1 Thessalonians 1:9-10).

> For God has not destined us for wrath, but for obtaining salvation through our Lord Jesus Christ. (1 Thessalonians 5:9).

We need to make several observations from these two passages. First of all, notice that neither of these passages tell us specifically to what this "wrath" refers. Neither one makes reference to a period of seven years and neither one speaks of something that must necessarily take place prior to the Second Coming of Christ.

The word "wrath" is translated from the Greek word *orge* which is found 35 other times in the New Testament. When describing the anger of God, it is often seen as describing the judgment of Hell (Matthew 3:7; Luke 3:7), the wrath which is seen on the unbeliever in general (John 3:36; Romans 1:18), as well as the day of coming judgment which takes place when Christ returns (Revelation 6:16-17; 11:18; 19:15).

An unbiased reading of this passage in its context would lead most people to think that this was a reference to the deliverance from the eternal condemnation that shall take place when Christ returns in the judgment of His Second Coming.

Finally we should note that this deliverance does not look to the future but to the present. 1 Thessalonians 1:9 states that Jesus delivers us from the wrath to come. Notice the tense that is utilized. The wrath is in the future (it is to come), but the deliverance is present. The believer is delivered today from God's wrath at the very moment when he places his faith in Jesus Christ.

ARGUMENT #4: KEPT FROM THE HOUR OF TESTING

In Revelation 3:10, the church in Philadelphia is given a special promise — that they would be kept from the hour of testing which was about to come upon the whole world. The Pretribulationist sees this as a promise to take the church out of the earth before the coming of the Tribulation.

> *Because you have kept the word of My perseverance, I also will keep you from the hour of testing, that hour which is about to come upon the whole world, to test those who dwell upon the earth. (Revelation 3:10).*

The phrase "I also will keep you from the hour" is translated from a Greek phrase which carries the idea of safely guarding one so that he can escape. It is therefore maintained that God will safely guard the Church out of a future period of tribulation rather than allowing her to go through it.

Now I want to ask you a question. If this verse is a reference to this future tribulation, then what is it actually saying? That only the church at Philadelphia is going to be taken off the earth in the Rapture before the coming of the Tribulation? Or does it mean that only those believers who have kept the word of His perseverance will take part in the Rapture — that there will only be a partial Rapture of believers?

I do not think so. In fact, I do not think that this is a reference to a future period of tribulation at all. Instead, I would suggest that this is a promise to that specific church in Asia Minor that would be delivered from the great persecutions which were soon to come upon the whole world and which did come during the early years of the church. Indeed, the promise was fulfilled, for church history relates that the church in Philadelphia not only survived that hour of testing, but also that it remained a constant in that city for over a thousand years.

Furthermore, this specific Greek phrase that is used to describe how Jesus *will* **keep you from** (the Greek phrase is τηρησω εκ) *the hour of temptation* is also found in John 17:15 where Jesus prays, *I do not ask Thee to take them out of the world, but to* **keep** *them from* (τηρησω εκ) *the evil one.* This phrase very obviously does not necessitate a removal of believers from the earth or even from the ability of Satan to tempt them, but rather is described by Jesus as a "protecting in place."

ARGUMENT #5: STRUCTURE OF THE BOOK OF REVELATION

This is an argument from silence. It takes note of the fact that the Church is not mentioned in Revelation 6-19 which is said to deal with the a time of future tribulation. What is usually overlooked is the fact that the Church is also not mentioned in Revelation 20-22 (aside from the final farewell at the end of chapter 22), an area in which all agree that the Church is present.

If one wishes to argue that the primary focus of Revelation 6-19 is upon the nation of Israel, I am inclined to agree. But this in no way necessitates the removal of the church. The message of Revelation is addressed to the church; there are seven specific churches addressed. This message is for them.

ARGUMENT #6: CHURCH IN HEAVEN DURING TRIBULATION

Revelation 4-5 begins with John being caught up in the Spirit into Heaven. This is seen by some Dispensationalists to be a type of the Rapture of the Church. While in Heaven, he sees 24 elders (4:4) around the throne of God, accompanied by a host of angels (5:11). These 24 elders are said to represent the Church which is Raptured and taken to Heaven before the beginning of the Tribulation which is then related in Revelation 6-19.

However, John was not "Raptured." He was given no resurrection body as will be the case in the Rapture (1 Corinthians 15:51-53). Instead, we are told that he was *"in the spirit"* (Revelation 4:2).

Furthermore, the presence of 24 elders around the throne would point to a Jewish presence as opposed to a presence that was exclusively the church and apart from Israel. The 24 elders correspond to the 24 courses in which the priests were organized. The language of Revelation 4-5 is temple language. It points to a gathering of all of God's people from every age.

ARGUMENT #7: CHURCH AS A MYSTERY

It is maintained by Dispensationalists that the New Testament presents the Church as a mystery that was never before revealed in the Old Testament. On the other hand, the Tribulation is said to be described in great detail in the Old Testament. This line of reasoning is sometimes used to indicate that the Church could not enter the Tribulation.

This type of logic is invalid. Just because the Church is not mentioned in the Old Testament does not mean that the Church cannot exist within a period or in a place which is described therein. If this were the case, then by the same line of reasoning, we would have to say that the Church cannot exist during the Kingdom, since this is also described in great detail in the Old Testament.

ARGUMENT #8: THE REMOVAL OF THE RESTRAINER

2 Thessalonians 2:7-8 describes the work of the Holy Spirit in restraining the purposes of Satan. At the proper time, this restrainer will be taken out of the way.

> *For the mystery of lawlessness is already at work; only he who now restrains will do so until he is taken out of the way.*
> *And then that lawless one will be revealed whom the Lord will slay with the breath of His mouth and bring to an end by the appearance of His coming. (2 Thessalonians 2:7-8).*

The Pretribulationalist sees this as an evidence of all of the believers being taken of the earth before the revealing of a future anti-Christ. Since the Holy Spirit indwells all believers and since the Holy Spirit will be removed, then it logically follows that all believers must also be removed.

The problem with this line of reasoning is that it reads into the passage something that is not there. The passage is not saying that the Holy Spirit will ever cease to be omnipresent. It is merely saying that there comes a time when the Spirit's work of restraining lawlessness ceases and when God allows men to go their own way.

ARGUMENT #9: IMMINENT RETURN OF JESUS

The Pretribulationist contends that the Scriptures teach that Christ could return at any moment and that no sign or promise remains to be fulfilled before He returns to gather His saints.

In this particular case, I tend to agree with the Pretribulationalist. I affirm that Christ could indeed return at any moment in His Second Coming. It could be today. Or it could be a thousand years from now. A number of passages are normally presented to support this teaching of an imminent return of Christ.

> *When Christ, who is our life, is revealed, then you also will be revealed with Him in glory. (Colossians 3:4).*

> *So that you are not lacking in any gift, awaiting eagerly the revelation of our Lord Jesus Christ, 8 who shall also confirm you to the end, blameless in the day of our Lord Jesus Christ. (1 Corinthians 1:7-8).*

> *Looking for the blessed hope and the appearing of the glory of our great God and Savior, Christ Jesus. (Titus 2:13).*

> *You too be patient, strengthen your hearts, for the coming of the Lord is at hand. (James 5:8).*

Do these passages specifically state that Christ could come back at any moment? Perhaps not. What they do teach is that we are looking forward to the coming of the Lord. This is true for all believers, whether they think that the Rapture will take place before, in the middle of, or after some future tribulation.

However, this same sort of language is seen in 2 Peter 3:13 which declares that we look for new heavens and a new earth. If these passages do teach of an imminent return of Christ, then we must of necessity also hold that 2 Peter 3:13 teaches of an imminent destruction of heaven and earth and entry into the eternal state. I personally concur, but that must remain the subject of a different discussion.

ARGUMENT #10: FOR HIS SAINTS / WITH HIS SAINTS

It is maintained by the Pretribulationalist that Christ is going to come back twice; the first time as He comes FOR His saints and the second time as He returns with His saints. But do the Scriptures actually keep such a distinction?

Remember that the "Rapture" is to be descriptive of Jesus coming back only FOR His saints. Yet we read the following in a Passage that the Pretribulationalist regards as testifying to this separate "Rapture":

> *For if we believe that Jesus died and rose again, even so God will bring **with** Him those who have fallen asleep in Jesus. (1*

Thessalonians 4:14).

By the same token, how can it be denied that a passage that describes the Lord coming and gathering together *His elect from the four winds, from one end of the sky to the other* is a coming for those very elected ones? The language of Matthew 24:30-31 is admitted by the Pretribulationalist to describe the Second Coming of Christ and yet obviously pictures Him coming for those who are alive and remain upon the earth.

The truth is that the return of Christ involves both a coming for His saints as well as a coming with His saints. These are not two separate comings, but it does involve two kinds of believers; those who are still alive and those who have already died. Those who have already died in the Lord shall come **with** Him while those who are alive and remain shall find that Jesus comes **for** them.

ARGUMENT #12: IN THE AIR OR TO THE EARTH

Pretribulationalism points to 1 Thessalonians 4 and insists that it is a separate coming of Christ that only involves His coming in the air as opposed to coming all the way to planet earth.

> *For the Lord Himself **will descend from heaven** with a shout, with the voice of the archangel, and with the trumpet of God; and the dead in Christ shall rise first. 17 Then we who are alive and remain shall be caught up together with them in the clouds to meet the Lord **in the air**, and thus we shall always be with the Lord. (1 Thessalonians 4:16-17).*

However we read this and ask, if Christ "descends from heaven," then where exactly could he be expected to "descend" to - other than the physical realm of the earth?

Yet Pretribulationalism insists that this does not amount to a return of Christ. It is claimed, "He does not come to the earth, but this is a meeting in the air. From there He takes the church to the Father's house where He has been and He does not come to earth at this time."

The problem with such a statement is that many of the passages used by the Pretribulationalist to describe the Second Coming also speak of Christ coming in the clouds.

> *But immediately after the tribulation of those days the sun will be darkened, and the moon will not give its light, and the stars will fall from the sky, and the powers of the heavens will be*

> *shaken, 30 and then the sign of the Son of Man will appear **in the*** > ***sky**, and then all the tribes of the earth will mourn, and they will* > *see the Son of Man coming **on the clouds of the sky** with power* > *and great glory. 31 And He will send forth His angels with a great* > *trumpet and they will gather together His elect from the four* > *winds, from one end of the sky to the other. (Matthew 24:29-31).*

Although the Pretribulationalist accepts this passage as the Second Coming, it makes no mention of Christ coming to the earth or setting foot upon the earth. To the contrary, it states only that Christ is coming on the clouds of the sky even though the Pretribulationalist admits that this coming culminates with a landing on planet earth.

Neither is this an isolated instance. In Revelation 19 we read of a glorious vision of Christ returning on a white horse with the armies of heaven following, but nowhere do we read that he actually sets foot upon the earth.

We must therefore conclude that the Scriptures do not make a distinction between a coming in which there is a landing on planet earth as opposed to a separate and distinct coming that only has the clouds of the sky as its arena.

ARGUMENT #12: EPISTLES AS REPRESENTATIVE

Some scholars, clearly embarrassed by the lack or clear teaching in the Bible of a Pretribulational Rapture, have suggested that perhaps the epistles are not representative of the normal preaching and teaching of the apostles. They would contend that the reason that none of the writers of the New Testament set forth a Pretribulational Rapture is because everyone had already been taught this and there was no need to further explain it.

This is just too much of an assumption on which to base a doctrine. The teaching of the Second Coming / Rapture is found all throughout the New Testament again and again. The idea of a Pretribulational Rapture stands out by nature of its total lack of Scriptural support.

Thus, an in-depth examination of the evidences used to support the Pre-tribulation Rapture position shows us that these essential arguments will not stand up to a literal interpretation of the Scriptures. We are forced to the conclusion that the Bible does not promise a Pretribulational Rapture.

BIBLIOGRAPHY

Aharoni, Yohanan & Avi-Yonah, Michael,
1978   *The MacMillan Bible Atlas Revised Edition*, New York, NY: MacMillan

Alnor, William N.
1989   *Soothsayers of the Second Advent*. Old Tappan, MJ: Flemmig H. Revell

Chafer, Lewis Sperry
1936   *Dispensationalism*. Dallas, TX: Seminary Press

Chilton, David
1987   *Paradise Restored: A Biblical Theology of Dominion*. Fort Worth, TX: Dominion Press

Engelsma, David J.
2001   *Christ's Spiritual Kingdom: A Defense of Reformed Amillennialism*. Redlands, CA: Reformed Witness

Eusebius Pamphilius
2005   *Church History*. Grand Rapids, MI: Eerdmans / ccel.og

2005   *The Fathers of the Church: Ecclesiastical History*, Translated by Roy Deferrari. Washington, D.C.: Catholic University of America Press

Friesen, Steven J.
2001   *Imperial Cults and the Apocalypse of John: Reading Revelation in the Ruins*. Oxford, NY: Oxford University Press

Gage, Warren Austin and White, Fowler
2002   *The John-Revelation Project*. Fort Lauderdale, FL: Knox Theological Seminary

Gregg, Steve
1997   *Revelation: Four Views, A Parallel Commentary*. Nashville, TN: Thomas Nelson Publishers

Gundrey, Robert H.
1974   *The Church and the Tribulation*. Grand Rapids, MI: Zondervan

Hendriksen, William
1987   *The Bible on the Life Hereafter*. Grand Rapids, MI: Baker

2001   *More Than Conquerors: An Interpretation of the Book of Revelation.* Grand Rapids, MI: Baker

Hoekema, Anthony A.
1991   *The Bible and the Future.* Grand Rapids, MI, Eerdmans

Josephus, Flavius
2011   *Wars of the Jews.* Translated by William Whiston. Amazon Digital Services

Kistemaker, Simon J.
2007   *Exposition of the Book of Revelation.* Grand Rapids, MI: Baker Academic

Kostenberger, Andreas J.
2006   "The Use of Scripture in the Pastoral and General Epistles and the Book of Revelation," *Hearing the Old Testament in the New Testament*, Stanley Porter, Editor, Grand Rapids, MI: Eerdmans

Kraybill, J. Nelson
2010   *Apocalypse and Allegiance: Worship, Politics, and Devotion in the Book of Revelation.* Grand Rapids, MI: Brazos

Ladd, George Eldon
1985   *A Commentary on the Revelation of John.* Grand Rapids, MI: Eerdmans

Lahaye, Tim
1972   *The Beginning of the End.* Wheaton, IL: Tyndale

Lenski, Richard C. H.
1961   *The Interpretation of St. John's Revelation.* Minneapolis, MN: Augsburg

Lindsey, Hal
1974   *There's A New World Coming: A Prophetic Odyssey.* Santa Anna, CA: Vision House

Lupieri, Edmondo F.
2006   *A Commentary on the Apocalypse of John.* Translated by Maria Poggi Johnson and Adam Kamesar. Grand Rapids, MI: Eerdmans

MacArthur, John
1999   *Revelation 1-11.* Chicago. IL: Moody
2000   *Revelation 12-22.* Chicago. IL: Moody

Mangina, Joseph L.
2010   *Revelation*. Grand Rapids, MI: Brazos Press

Matthewson, Dave
2001   "A Re-examination of the Millennium in Revelation 20:1-6:
        Consummation and Recapitulation." *JETS 44:2*, Pg 237-51.

Morris, S. L.
1982   *The Drama of Christianity: And Interpretation of the Book of
        Revelation*. Grand Rapids, MI: Baker

Papandrea, James L.
2011   *The Wedding of the Lamb: A Historical Approach to the Book of
        Revelation*. Eugene, OR: Pickwick

Pentecost, J. Dwight
1973   *Things to Come: A Study in Biblical Eschatology*. Grand Rapids, MI:
        Zondervan

Plumber, Christopher
2006   Contributing editor, *Pulpit Commentaries*. Rio, WI: AGES Digital
        Library

Philo of Alexandria
1962   *On the Embassy to Gaius*. Translated by F. H. Colson. Cambridge, MA:
        Loeb Classical Library

Ryrie, Charles
1965   *Dispensationalism Today*. Chicago, IL: Moody

Shaff, Philip
1996   *History of the Christian Church*. Peabody, MS: Hendrickson Publishers

Skofield, Ellis H.
1991   *Hidden Beast 2*. Fort Myers, FL: Fish House

The Sibylline Oracles
1899   Translated by Milton S. Terry. New York, NY: Eaton & Mains

The Syriac New Testament
2001   Translated by James Murdock. Piscataway, NJ: Georgia Press

Suetonius, Gaius Tranquillus
1979   *The Twelve Caesars*. Translated by Robert Graves. New York, NY:
        Penguin Books

Taylor, R. A.
2005   *Revelation: A Reference Commentary*. R. A. Taylor

Waymeayer, Matt
2016   "The First Resurrection in Revelation 20." *Masters Seminary Journal*
        27:1; Sun Valley, CAL: MSJ

www.ingramcontent.com/pod-product-compliance
Lightning Source LLC
Chambersburg PA
CBHW080453110426
42742CB00017B/2880